KEY CONCEPTS IN PHILOSOPHY

D0076539

Palgrave Key Concepts

Palgrave Key Concepts provide an accessible and comprehensive range of subject glossaries at undergraduate level. They are the ideal companion to a standard textbook making them invaluable reading to students throughout their course of study and especially useful as a revision aid.

Key Concepts in Accounting and Finance
Key Concepts in Business Practice
Key Concepts in Criminal Justice and Criminology
Key Concepts in Cultural Studies
Key Concepts in Drama and Performance (second edition)
Key Concepts in e-Commerce
Key Concepts in Human Resource Management
Key Concepts in Information and Communication Technology
Key Concepts in International Business
Key Concepts in Innovation
Key Concepts in Language and Linguistics (second edition)
Key Concepts in Law (second edition)
Key Concepts in Leisure
Key Concepts in Management
Key Concepts in Marketing
Key Concepts in Operations Management
Key Concepts in Philosophy
Key Concepts in Politics
Key Concepts in Public Relations
Key Concepts in Psychology
Key Concepts in Social Research Methods
Key Concepts in Sociology
Key Concepts in Strategic Management
Key Concepts in Tourism

Palgrave Key Concepts: Literature
General Editors: John Peck and Martin Coyle

Key Concepts in Contemporary Literature
Key Concepts in Creative Writing
Key Concepts in Crime Fiction
Key Concepts in Medieval Literature
Key Concepts in Modernist Literature
Key Concepts in Postcolonial Literature
Key Concepts in Renaissance Literature
Key Concepts in Romantic Literature
Key Concepts in Victorian Literature
Literary Terms and Criticism (third edition)

Further titles are in preparation
www.palgravekeyconcepts.com

Palgrave Key Concepts
Series Standing Order
ISBN 1–4039–3210–7
(outside North America only)

You can receive future titles in this series as they are published by placing a standing order. Please contact your bookseller or, in the case of difficulty, write to us at the address below with your name and address, the title of the series and the ISBN quoted above.

Customer Services Department, Macmillan Distribution Ltd
Houndmills, Basingstoke, Hampshire RG21 6XS, England

Key Concepts in Philosophy

Paddy McQueen and Hilary McQueen

palgrave
macmillan

WITHDRAWN

PROPERTY OF
SENECA COLLEGE
LIBRARIES
KING CAMPUS

JAN 13 2011

© Paddy McQueen and Hilary McQueen 2010

All rights reserved. No reproduction, copy or transmission of this
publication may be made without written permission.

No portion of this publication may be reproduced, copied or transmitted
save with written permission or in accordance with the provisions of the
Copyright, Designs and Patents Act 1988, or under the terms of any licence
permitting limited copying issued by the Copyright Licensing Agency,
Saffron House, 6-10 Kirby Street, London EC1N 8TS.

Any person who does any unauthorized act in relation to this publication
may be liable to criminal prosecution and civil claims for damages.

The authors have asserted their rights to be identified
as the authors of this work in accordance with the Copyright, Designs
and Patents Act 1988.

First published 2010 by
PALGRAVE MACMILLAN

Palgrave Macmillan in the UK is an imprint of Macmillan Publishers Limited,
registered in England, company number 785998, of Houndmills, Basingstoke,
Hampshire RG21 6XS.

Palgrave Macmillan in the US is a division of St Martin's Press LLC,
175 Fifth Avenue, New York, NY 10010.

Palgrave Macmillan is the global academic imprint of the above companies
and has companies and representatives throughout the world.

Palgrave® and Macmillan® are registered trademarks in the United States,
the United Kingdom, Europe and other countries

ISBN 978-0-230-23158-0

This book is printed on paper suitable for recycling and made from fully
managed and sustained forest sources. Logging, pulping and manufacturing
processes are expected to conform to the environmental regulations of the
country of origin.

A catalogue record for this book is available from the British Library.

A catalog record for this book is available from the Library of Congress.

10   9   8   7   6   5   4   3   2   1
19 18 17 16 15 14 13 12 11 10

Printed in China

Contents

Acknowledgements

We would like to express our gratitude to Palgrave Macmillan for commissioning this volume. In particular we would like to thank Suzannah Burywood and Jenni Burnell for their encouragement and support throughout the process. Our sincere thanks also go to our copy editor, Ann Edmondson.

We are both grateful to those people in our academic studies and in our lives who have contributed in different ways to the production of this book. Specific thanks go to Alex Carruth, Philip O'Hanlon, David Hill, Gareth Jones and, in particular, Tom Bates for their insightful comments. Paddy would like to thank all members of Durham University's Department of Philosophy for their support, enthusiasm and inspiration during his time there. Thanks must also go to the School of Politics, International Studies and Philosophy at Queen's University Belfast for granting the time needed to complete this book. Special thanks, as always, to AF.

Finally, this book represents the reading, thinking and discussion of three generations of one family. Posthumous thanks are therefore due to James O'Hare for his philosophical and linguistic contributions.

Introduction

The question 'what is philosophy?' is notoriously difficult to answer. Indeed, there does not seem to be a universally accepted definition of philosophy. Part of the problem is that it does not have a specific subject matter because, in its broadest sense, philosophy is the attempt to make sense of ourselves, our place in the world and the universe itself. Therefore, *any* aspect of human life or the world may be subjected to philosophical analysis. It is better to think of philosophy as an activity, as something we *do*. Philosophy is a 'search' for understanding. This is why philosophers are often more interested in asking questions than in getting specific answers. Unless the right questions are asked in the right way, we will not get satisfactory answers. To think 'philosophically' is to examine everything we believe and experience. It is a refusal to take anything for granted.

A key aspect of philosophy, then, is the importance of justifying our beliefs. What makes a 'philosophical' belief different from an 'everyday' belief is that the former has been arrived at after a process of intellectual reflection, discussion and investigation. Philosophers are concerned with giving persuasive reasons for their conclusions, often presented in the form of a logical argument. Importantly, this does not simply mean sitting in an armchair and 'having a think' (although this may well form part of the process). The early Greek philosophers, for example, were fascinated with the natural world and the methods of investigating it. Nowadays they would be considered biologists, astronomers and mathematicians as much as 'philosophers'.

This raises an important point for understanding what philosophy is. It is only fairly recently that such a wide variety of academic disciplines has developed. In the UK one can study many different subjects, such as law, music, English, biology and so on. The fact that we also have the subject 'philosophy' implies that it is somehow separate from these other subjects. However, philosophers may be concerned with any aspect of human life and the world around us. The concept of being either a 'scientist', a 'poet' or a 'philosopher' would have appeared nonsensical to Plato or Aristotle. This is reflected in current philosophical sub-disciplines such as the philosophy of biology, the philosophy of religion and the philosophy of language. One can even attend lectures on the philosophy of food, the philosophy of wine, or the philosophy of football. The point is that almost anything can be approached 'philosophically'.

How, then, do we learn to approach something 'philosophically'? The simple answer is, 'by doing philosophy'. We learn through experience, and this experience comes from reading philosophical texts, understanding philosophical ideas and engaging in philosophical discussions. However, this is easier said than done. Philosophy can be frustratingly difficult. There are many reasons for this. One is the type of language used. Philosophers tend to employ unusual terms, sometimes even inventing new ones. Furthermore, they may write in an unfamiliar style or assume a level of knowledge which is unrealistic for, say, an undergraduate student or an interested amateur. Even a professor of philosophy may struggle if confronting the writings of Heidegger or Derrida for the very first time. Part of the problem is historical. When Kant was writing, he was communicating with a fairly small community of highly educated aristocrats with plenty of spare time for philosophising. Thus, he could afford to assume that they would be familiar with the context in which his work was produced and the philosophical ideas he discussed. In addition, the style in which he wrote would be easily understood by his contemporaries, whereas it can appear strange by modern standards. This problem is not limited to philosophy, as most students faced with Shakespeare's works will testify.

Another reason why philosophy can be difficult is that it is concerned with very fundamental questions: 'who am I?', 'what am I?', 'what is the meaning of life?', 'what is the nature of time?', 'does God exist?', 'does the world exist independently of how I think about it?', 'is it possible to know anything at all?', 'did the universe have a beginning?'. Curious children often ask questions like these, and they are indeed difficult, or perhaps impossible, to answer satisfactorily. We may continue to ponder these issues throughout our whole lives. Although such questions are problematic, it is our job, as philosophers, to make sure we explore them as fully as possible. We must leave no stone unturned. This is a demanding task that requires a lot of concentration and careful reflection. If we want to be philosophers, we must be willing to make this commitment.

The final reason is that philosophy cannot just give us an answer. As noted, philosophy is about examining what we are told and analysing what we already believe. Therefore, reading a philosopher's work is not like reading a science textbook. We do not just have to remember what the philosopher said and then be able to repeat it. We must decide whether we agree or not, assess the strengths and weaknesses of the argument, consider what assumptions are made, and the consequences of the conclusions drawn. Reading a philosophical text is a dialogue. We must debate with it and see if it can answer our questions. Indeed, sometimes we must read it two or three times before we discover whether it can offer an answer to our questions.

None of these reasons should put us off doing and studying philosophy. Despite, or even because of, its difficulty, philosophy is hugely rewarding and immensely enjoyable. Given that you are reading this book – or perhaps just because you are a thinking human – it is a fair bet that you have asked at least one of the big 'philosophical questions'. There is great pleasure in exploring possible answers to such questions, whether they concern the nature of reality or just what the 'mind' is. Philosophy can offer insights into the world and our place in it. It can also have great benefits for how we live our everyday lives. This might be through formulating a consistent set of moral principles, which we feel justified in holding. It might be in finding ourselves able to challenge those we disagree with in a constructive, thorough and detached way (possibly even managing to change their minds). Or else it might offer the possibility of helping people around us who are also struggling to confront questions about the world and their experiences within it.

If philosophy is a vast, complicated and difficult subject, then we will certainly need some help in studying and practising it. Herein lies the value of this book. Whilst we do not pretend to provide comprehensive accounts of every major philosophical concept and philosopher, our aim has been to guide the reader through the maze of philosophy and its history, including ideas that have been formulated in other cultures. In particular, the book presents important concepts and theories that are necessary for making sense of philosophical writings and debates, without relying on the specialist and confusing language that can be characteristic of much philosophy. Furthermore, it assumes no prior philosophical knowledge on the part of the reader nor does it rely on 'dumbing down' the ideas presented and discussed. The entries are designed to be both accessible and accurate.

It should be noted that the precise interpretation of many philosophical ideas has been hotly disputed. No doubt people will question some of this book's descriptions of both the philosophers and their ideas. It would be impossible to give an exhaustive account of all the interpretations of all the concepts included in this book. We have strived to be as precise as possible, whilst ensuring the description is clear and accessible to all readers. The guiding principle was to present the 'standard' or 'textbook' interpretation of a philosopher or concept.

Every effort has been made to ensure that each entry can be read as a stand-alone entry. However, as noted, philosophy is a subject rich with complicated and unusual terms, some of which are rarely (if ever) encountered outside of philosophical texts. Furthermore, certain terms are used differently by different philosophers, and occasionally two different terms are used to refer to the same idea. For these reasons, and given restrictions on the size of each entry, the reader is encouraged to make full use of the *See also* section at the end of each entry. Many concepts which are mentioned within a particular entry will also have their own entry, which will provide a much more comprehensive description.

Each entry contains a number of suggestions for further reading. For entries on specific philosophers, this will always include their major works and at least two secondary sources. Frequently, one of the secondary sources will be an introductory text and the other a collection of essays offering more detailed and technical discussions of the philosopher. For entries on concepts, the further reading will contain both introductory and advanced texts representing a wide spectrum of views and interpretations. The aim of the further reading is, thus, to direct the reader to the kind of comprehensive account of an idea or thinker which cannot be provided in a book of this size.

Finally, a number of entries contain a set of key questions. These are designed to encourage critical reflection upon the philosophical ideas raised in the respective entries. As we have already highlighted, philosophy is a dialogue, and the key questions are intended to reveal the kinds of questions we must ask of a text or person when discussing philosophical concepts. Naturally, there are many more 'key questions' which must also be asked but have not been included here. We hope that the ones provided in the text will help you, the reader, to generate your own, and to make links between the wealth of ideas covered.

Pulling all these aspects together we sincerely hope that, armed with this book, you will be able to battle your way through the rich and wonderful world of philosophy.

Notes on the text

We have used the abbreviations BCE (Before Common Era) and CE (Common Era) in preference to the abbreviations BC (Before Christ) and AD (*Anno Domini*) throughout the text.

Certain terms, particularly those relating to Indian and Chinese philosophy, have numerous English translations. For example, *karma* is also translated as *kamma*, depending on the system of translation being used. We do not intend to show preference for one system of translation over another. Our criterion was whichever translation appeared to be the most frequent in the literature, as this would likely be the most commonly encountered, and thus searched for, form of the word.

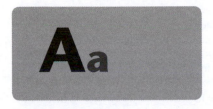

Ad hominem

Ad hominem (against the person) is a type of fallacy (error in reasoning) which occurs when someone directs a personal criticism at an opponent, rather than attacking their argument. For example, we might refer to a person's appearance, hobbies or reputation as a reason to doubt their argument even though how a person looks or behaves has no bearing on the strength (validity) of their argument. Political debates often contain many examples of the *ad hominem* fallacy, such as when politicians are criticised for their personal tastes, hair-cut or dress sense. Implicit within such criticisms is the false assumption that these characteristics somehow affect the force of political arguments.

> *See also:* **begging the question; fallacy; impartiality; logic; slippery slope argument; straw man; validity; vicious circle**
>
> *Key question:* Can there be any justification for judging the strength of an argument according to a person's appearance or lifestyle?
>
> *Further reading:* Engel (1994); Hansen and Pinto (1995); Walton (1989)

Adorno, Theodor W. (1903–1969)

Adorno was an influential figure in the Frankfurt School that was set up to discuss Marxist philosophy. His ideas were influenced by his experiences of the Holocaust, and his studies in philosophy and music. Having left Germany because of the Nazi regime, he and Horkheimer wrote a critique of modernity called the *Dialectic of Enlightenment* (1947). They argued that, rather than simply serving to free people from fear of the unknown through scientific endeavour and rational thinking, enlightenment also produces irrationality. Within modernity, rationality and irrationality co-exist. Rational progress occurs at the expense of whatever needs to be dominated. For example, the fear of illness has led to attempts to dominate the causes of illness, both in the environment and in people. Sanitation and genetic engineering are examples of such attempts. According to Adorno and Horkheimer, domination requires destruction of whatever is causing fear, and this is promoted by capitalism and technological advances. However, we should not make the straightforward assumption that pre-enlightenment times were bad and post-enlightenment will be radically different and greatly improved. For example, whilst modern science might bring about positive change such as improved health or better forms of communication, it can also deprive the world of meaning.

Adorno is well known in psychology for his work on the authoritarian personality, and in cultural studies for writing about aesthetics. For Adorno, art works are historical and socio-cultural productions that cannot be judged in terms of natural beauty. Art is produced by a dialectic process in which a person's desire to express their subjectivity (experiences, feelings, desires, and so on) confronts a social reality which represses this subjectivity. Art, then, can be seen as the demand for freedom from repression, as well as an important form of social criticism.

Another important contribution was Adorno's idea of *Negative Dialectics* (1966). He criticised 'identity-thinking', which is an individual's attempt to incorporate an object into their conceptual scheme. Rather than making an object conform to our expectations or assumptions about what it is, we should try to see it in its distinctness. This requires us to appreciate it as a genuine 'other', something unique and independent of us. This is achieved in part by considering what an object is not. Adorno also expanded on Marx's idea of alienation by emphasising the control of the masses through the media and popular culture.

See also: **alienation; aesthetics; dialectic; enlightenment; Frankfurt school; identity; Marxism; modernism; rationalism**

Further reading: Adorno (1966, 1970); Horkheimer and Adorno (1947); Jarvis (1998); Jay (1984); O'Connor (2000); http://www.marxists.org/subject/frankfurt-school/index.htm

Aesthetics

The term 'aesthetics' originates from the Greek word *aisthanomai*, which means 'perception through the senses'. Aesthetics is primarily concerned with the philosophy of art, and the exploration of issues such as our experience and judgement of beauty. Interest in aesthetics dates back to Greek philosophers such as Plato, whose theory of forms led him to claim that art is an imitation of an imitation of reality. However, the development of the term is chiefly associated with Kant's *Critique of Judgement* (1790). Kant started by asking what kind of a judgement we make when we say something is beautiful. According to Kant, there are four vital features of our aesthetic judgements. Firstly, the judgements are 'disinterested', meaning that we find something pleasurable because we judge it to be beautiful, rather than judging something to be beautiful because we find it pleasurable. Secondly, they are 'universal' because, in saying that a thing is beautiful, we demand that others find it beautiful too. When someone disagrees over the beauty of a thing, we try and convince them that they are mistaken. Thirdly, they are 'necessary', meaning that we are compelled to make the judgement and to try and compel others to make the same judgement. Fourthly, aesthetic judgements make an object appear 'purposive without purpose'. This means that a beautiful object appears to us as if it were designed, as if it had some purpose, although no such purpose can be found. According to Kant, aesthetic qualities such as beauty are not properties possessed by an object. Instead, they are a product of the mind, something that we impose upon the object in making an aesthetic judgement.

Aesthetic theories which deny that qualities such as beauty are genuine properties of an object are anti-realist, meaning that those qualities do not exist independently of the mind. The anti-realist, or subjectivist, view of aesthetics is summed up by the phrase 'beauty is in the eye of the beholder'. The relativist conception of aesthetics is often justified by the variation between different cultures' judgements of what is considered beautiful, musical, artistic, and so on. By contrast, if one argues that aesthetic qualities are inherent in an object and that we passively perceive them, then one is an aesthetic realist. Plato's theory is an example of realist aesthetics. He argues that something is made beautiful by possessing the form of beauty. Therefore all beautiful things share the one property – beauty – and we see something as beautiful when we recognise the presence of this form.

Aesthetics is also concerned with establishing what, if anything, makes something a work of art. Many modern artists have explored the boundaries of what constitutes an object of 'art' by using everyday 'non-artistic' objects in their works or by presenting intentionally unpleasant and unattractive images. Such works include Turner Prize winner Damien Hirst's cow chopped in half and John Cage's silent orchestral composition. Musical genres, such as jazz and classical, are often seen as 'truer' forms of music than modern pop and 'muzak', perhaps because they represent more established ideas of what musical works should be like.

See also: **Adorno; anti-realism; beauty; constructionism; cultural relativism; Hume; Kant; modernism; Plato; postmodernism; realism; relativism; value**

Key questions: Are aesthetic judgements subjective? What is it, if anything, that makes something a work of art?

Further reading: Adorno (1970); Cooper (1992); Hanfling (1992); Kant (1790); Townsend (1997)

Agency

Agency refers to autonomous action. You demonstrate agency by choosing to read this sentence. However, the sense that we are in control of, and make choices about, what we do does not necessarily give us free choice. Therefore agency is not equivalent to free will. Agency includes the idea that we agree with what we are doing or at least agree to do it. A drug addict could be said to be agreeing to take a drug under circumstances of reduced autonomy. The extent to which we are acting autonomously has implications for responsibility, both morally and legally. If our agency is destroyed by addiction, are we legally and morally responsible for taking illegal drugs? Agency might be seen as illusory. For example, Hegel and Marx would view agency as inseparable from social structures because they conceived individuals as being shaped by these structures. Choosing to study, for instance, is a result of a social structure that places value on and rewards educational attainment. Therefore agency is dependent on pre-existing historical and cultural beliefs about what choices are possible and desirable. Yet structures depend on individually acting people. Attempts to reconcile the dilemma of an agentic individual and a determining structure have led to critical realism and the idea that both aspects are components of social reality.

See also: **critical realism; determinism; freedom; free will; Hegel; individual, the; Marx; moral agents; responsibility**

Key questions: To what extent do you feel in control of your actions? Are our lives controlled by our education, family, economic circumstances and/or geographical location?

Further reading: Archer et al. (1998); Dilman (1999); Reath (2006); Roessler and Eilan (2003); Skinner (1971)

A

Alienation

Alienation refers to the process by which a person is distanced from (made foreign to) their environment. It is an important term within Marxist philosophy and was developed by Marx in his early work *Economic and Philosophical Manuscripts* (1844). According to Marx, workers within a capitalist system are alienated in four ways: (1) by the product of their labour being instantly removed from them; (2) by their work being close to unbearable; (3) by producing goods which are not of their choosing and which do not correspond to their human needs and abilities; and (4) by no longer working with others for their mutual benefit but to satisfy the needs of the bourgeoisie (ruling class). All four forms of alienation equate to a loss of control, namely the loss of control over labour. Marx viewed humans as beings whose nature it is to produce goods from their environment to satisfy their human needs. Therefore, those labouring within capitalism are essentially severed from themselves, each other and society. Only by overthrowing the capitalist system, which is achieved by a worker-led revolution, can alienation be escaped.

See also: **Adorno; communism; dialectical materialism; Marx; Marxism**

Further reading: Marx (1844); Ollman (1976)

Analytic philosophy

Analytic philosophy, although difficult to define precisely, refers to those developments in thinking since the turn of the twentieth century which were greatly influenced by the logic and method of science, as well as the systematic analysis of language. Such developments are most strongly connected with philosophers in the UK and USA. In particular, the cultivation of analytic philosophy is associated with the philosophies of Frege, Russell, Moore and the early work of Wittgenstein. They collectively initiated a rejection of the dominant philosophical tradition of their time, which had been based upon Kantian and Hegelian idealism. Russell and Wittgenstein believed that concepts and propositions, properly analysed, could reveal the logical form of reality. Wittgenstein's key idea in his early and influential *Tractatus* (1921) was that the structure of language reveals the structure of reality. As suggested by its vague definition, analytic philosophy is not based on a unified set of beliefs, methods and topics.

Analytic philosophy stresses the importance of analysing and clarifying our linguistic concepts in order to solve philosophical problems and clarify our views on the nature of the world. These ideas were central to logical positivism which claimed that the only meaningful statements were those which could be empirically (scientifically) verified. Those which could not, such as claims about God, were regarded as meaningless. Although logical positivism died a quick death, many philosophers today continue to stress the need for logical analysis of philosophical problems. This is demonstrated best by contemporary metaphysics.

Analytic philosophy is traditionally contrasted with 'continental philosophy' because the two approaches are seen as (a) representing two very different ways of conducting philosophy; and (b) concerned with very different areas of philosophical investigation. However, many philosophers deny the distinction is a valid one, pointing out that there are numerous similarities between them which the distinction ignores.

A

See also: **Ayer; continental philosophy; empiricism; Frege; Hegel; Kant; Kripke; logical positivism; Moore; Quine; reason; Russell; scientific method; Vienna Circle; Wittgenstein**

Further reading: Ayer (1936, 1940); Baldwin (1993); Moore (1903); Quine (1953); Russell (1905, 1910, 1921, 1927a); Wittgenstein (1921)

Analytic/Synthetic distinction

The analytic/synthetic distinction refers to the way in which we know things to be true. An analytic sentence, such as 'all husbands are married', is one which we know to be true simply by understanding the meaning of the words in the sentence. Providing we are competent English speakers, it seems we cannot doubt the truth of analytic statements. Synthetic sentences, such as 'some husbands are bald', are ones which we know to be true by both understanding the meaning of the words and certain features of the world. In order to know that some husbands are bald we must know something about the kind of things that are husbands.

The distinction was first introduced by Kant (1781), who described an analytic state-ment as one in which the concept of the predicate (something which completes a sentence) is 'contained' within the concept of the subject. This means, for example, that the predicate 'is married' is contained within the concept 'husband'. Kant be-lieved that analytic truths were necessary truths, knowable *a priori*. The distinction was a popular one until the middle of the twentieth century when philosophers started to challenge it. The most influential attack was produced by Quine (1953) who argued that even analytic truths could be made false by experience and con-sequently all truths are synthetic. Here Quine follows the strongly empiricist claim made by Mill that there is no *a priori* knowledge. Analytic truths merely express convention rather than necessity and thus any sentence supposed to be true by virtue of its meaning is susceptible to that meaning being revised.

See also: **a priori** and **a posteriori; Kant; knowledge; Mill; Quine; truth**

Further reading: Grice and Strawson (1956); Kant (1781); Quine (1953)

Anarchism

Derived from the Greek word *anarchos* meaning 'without authority', anarchy de-fends the concept of a society without any authoritative power. Although often seen as simply advocating a society without government, anarchy can also ex-tend to questioning the coercive power of religion, the family, business, or educa-tion. Common to anarchist theories is an affirmation of the fundamental value of freedom and the belief that government is detrimental to the promotion of this freedom. Consequently anarchist writings portray government as oppressive and present alternative images of a society existing without any state authority. Some anarchists argue for violent revolution as the only means by which to overthrow the state, whereas others call for change through education and debate. Impor-tantly, anarchism does not simply mean the removal of all moral and social laws, or the abolition of society. Rather, anyone in society with power must use it for the good of all, and must be accountable to those they have power over. In this sense, anarchism is closely related to communism and strongly opposed to conserva-tism and capitalism. Social contract theories (also called 'contractarianism'), which

A

start from the premise that life without government would be intolerable, are also strongly opposed to anarchism.

See also: **communism; conservatism; contractarianism; freedom; liberalism; libertarianism; liberty; Marxism; nationalism; political philosophy; socialism; state of nature; utopianism**

Key questions: Would society be better if there were no government? How would such a society function?

Further reading: Miller (1984); Woodcock (1977)

Angst/Anxiety

Angst, also referred to as 'anxiety', is a highly complex term employed by existentialists. It is both a process and an experience; angst is a kind of psychological 'breakdown' that reveals the nature of the world and our own existence. According to Heidegger, when in a state of angst we are confronted with our own individual being (our Dasein), which is ultimately free. Angst also reveals the world and our lives as ultimately lacking any intrinsic or essential meaning. However, because we are normally immersed in the 'they' or 'herd', merely 'following the crowd', most of us fail to ever realise this emptiness. Angst drags us out of the world, making us feel 'uncanny', or 'not at home'. As a result of this, 'everyday familiarity collapses' (Heidegger, 1927: 232) and we are struck by the fact that because nothing is necessary, everything is possible. Similar ideas are found in Kierkegaard's *The Concept of Anxiety* (1844), in which he describes anxiety as 'the dizziness of freedom' (1844: 55), and in the work of Sartre, who argues that the experience of angst forces us to confront the freedom which is a fundamental part of human existence (Sartre 1943).

See also: **authenticity; Dasein; existentialism; freedom; Heidegger; Kierkegaard; Sartre**

Key questions: Are we all just 'part of the herd'? Is the experience of angst desirable? If so, how would we go about entering such a state?

Further reading: Grøn (2008); Heidegger (1927); Kierkegaard (1844); Sartre (1943)

Animal ethics

Interest in animal ethics can be traced back nearly 2000 years to Plutarch's *Eating Flesh*, in which he defends vegetarianism on the grounds of animal welfare and the fact that it is not necessary to eat animals in order to survive. However, during the Middle Ages and Renaissance periods there was little concern for animals, mainly because they were not thought to have souls. Descartes declared them incapable of suffering and was impressed by how well these 'machines' imitated being in pain. A common view at that time, held by Kant, was that animals lacked the rationality required to be a moral being. Kant suggested it can be good to avoid harming animals, for the reason that if we become accustomed to harming animals, then we may find it easier to harm humans. Consequently, animals do not have 'intrinsic value', meaning they do not have moral worth in their own right. Bentham (1789) was the first major figure in modern philosophy to propose that we must consider the interests of animals, arguing that the ability to suffer is the sole criterion for being given moral consideration. However, it was not until the 1970s that animal ethics became an important part of moral theory.

One major contemporary debate is the moral status of animals. Should animals be subject to the same moral considerations as humans? If humans have a different moral status to animals, on what grounds can this difference be justified? Certain characteristics such as intelligence, rationality or self-awareness are often offered, but the problem with these is that they also seem to exclude very young humans and those with certain mental disabilities and illnesses. Singer (1975) argued that excluding animals from the moral sphere (the group of things worthy of moral consideration) is 'speciesism', comparable to racism and sexism. He also argued that all sentient beings – those capable of experiencing pain and pleasure – must be included in the moral sphere because they can be treated well or badly.

It is useful to distinguish between moral subjects and moral agents. Moral subjects are beings which can be treated in a moral (good or bad) way. Moral agents are beings which are expected to act in moral ways. Animals may be considered to be moral subjects without being deemed moral agents. Tom Regan has strongly defended the idea that animals have moral rights. He says that animals, like humans, are 'subject-of-a-life', meaning that what happens matters to them. All beings that are subject-of-a-life have intrinsic value and their rights cannot be ignored in moral discussions. Other important issues in animal ethics include: the use of animals in scientific experiments; the use of animals as meat; the use of animal products such as fur, leather and ivory; whether animals should be kept as pets; and whether all or only some animals have moral worth. Animal ethics has close connections with environmental ethics, particularly because of the effect the environment has on a creature's well-being.

See also: **Bentham; environmental ethics; moral agents; Singer; vegetarianism**

Key questions: Which animals have rights or moral value? Is this value intrinsic? If only humans have moral value, then what is it about humans that separates them from animals?

Further reading: Armstrong and Botzler (2003); Bentham (1789); Clark (1977); Hurst-house (2000); Regan (1983, 2001); Singer (1975, 1979); Sunstein and Nussbaum (2004)

Anselm, Saint (1033–1109)

A

One of the great philosophers and theologians of the medieval period, Anselm is best known for his version of the 'ontological argument' for the existence of God. According to Anselm, God is 'something than which nothing greater can be thought' (*aliquid quo nihil maius cogitari potest*). Although there is debate over the precise interpretation of this statement (which in the medieval period was simply known as 'Anselm's argument'), a common interpretation runs as follows:

we cannot conceive of a greater being than God ⇨
given that God is the greatest being, God must exist because a being which exists in reality is greater than a being which exists solely in the mind ⇨
given that God is the greatest of all possible beings, God must, necessarily, exist in reality.

Anselm's argument was famously attacked by a contemporary of his, a monk called Gaunilo. Gaunilo asserted that Anselm's argument gives us no reason to assume that God exists in reality. He asks us to imagine the greatest possible island. According to Anselm's argument, this island must exist because otherwise it is not the greatest conceivable island, but clearly we do not think the most perfect island actually does exist in reality. Therefore Anselm's argument fails and gives us no reason to suppose God must exist in reality. Many philosophers have been persuaded by Gaunilo's argument, though many others have offered their own version of the ontological argument (see Descartes, for example).

Anselm also formulated an early version of the correspondence theory of truth, arguing that statements are true when they 'correspond' or 'map onto' reality. He believed that the ability to correspond is part of a statement's 'function' and so statements are true when they perform their function in the right way.

See also: **Augustine; correspondence theory; Descartes; God; God, arguments for the existence of; reality**

Further reading: Davies and Leftow (2004); Evans (1989); Williams (2007)

Anti-realism

Anti-realists deny the realist claim that (a) there exists a mind-independent world, and (b) our beliefs about this world are true if they correctly correspond to it. An anti-realist claims that the world, or some part of it, is at least partly constituted by human thought. The way the world appears to us is determined to some extent by the concepts and theories we have to describe it. There are many versions of anti-realism, each denying different realist positions.

Berkeley, a strict idealist, famously claimed that the only things which exist are ideas and minds capable of perceiving these ideas. He reasoned that we only ever experience ideas of objects, rather than the objects themselves, and therefore we are only ever justified in claiming that ideas exist. Despite the coherence and strength of Berkeley's work, very few philosophers have taken it seriously. Unlike Berkeley, most anti-realists limit their claims to specific features of the world. For example, the statement 'beauty is in the eye of the beholder' is an expression of anti-realist aesthetics because it denies that there is such a thing as 'beauty' existing outside of the mind. Similarly, an ethical anti-realist would deny that there are objective moral truths existing independently of human thoughts and feelings. There is an important contemporary debate between realists and anti-realists within the philosophy of science. Those who defend anti-realism in science deny that science gives us an objective picture of how the world really is and question the existence of theoretical (unobservable) entities, such as quantum particles, which cannot be directly observed.

Postmodernists have targeted realist conceptions of truth, arguing that all ideas of truth are constructions (narratives/discourses) which serve to create, rather than represent, reality. This is not to deny that there is a physical world existing outside of our minds. Instead, it is the claim that there is no direct, true access to reality. One argument for this is that we can only understand the world through language and language imposes a particular 'conceptual scheme' onto the world. In

A

other words, we are 'trapped' in our language which determines our understanding of reality.

See also: **aesthetics; Berkeley; constructionism; idealism; instrumentalism; Kuhn; moral subjectivism; objectivism; perspectivism; postmodernism; pragmatism; realism; Rorty; relativism; scientific realism; truth**

Key questions: What things, if any, are mind-dependent? How could we ever know whether they are mind-dependent or not? What difference does it make to say that something's existence is mind-dependent, rather than existing independently of the mind?

Further reading: Alston (2002); Berkeley (1710, 1713); Mackie (1977); Psillos (1999); Putnam (1983); van Fraassen (1980); Wittgenstein (1953)

A priori and *a posteriori*

The terms *a priori* (literally 'what comes before') and *a posteriori* (literally 'what comes after') typically refer to the basis on which a proposition is known to be true. If something is said to be known *a priori* then the reason we have for thinking it is true does not depend on experience. For instance, the statement 'a square has four sides' is true regardless of our experiences of squares. We do not need to check each time that the sentence is still true; simply understanding the words in the sentence is sufficient for knowing it is true. *A priori* truths are seen as necessary truths, or propositions which are true by virtue of their meaning, and include mathematical and logical truths. Truths attained through intuition would also represent *a priori* justification for our beliefs.

A posteriori truths are those which depend upon experience, such as the statement 'the grass is green'. The vast majority of knowledge appears to be *a posteriori*, including the natural and social sciences. The *a priori/a posteriori* distinction raises important questions about the nature of experience, the justification of beliefs and the concept of truth. For instance, if all knowledge is *a posteriori* and thus known to be true empirically (through the senses), we must establish whether our senses are reliable in order to avoid the sceptical thought that we cannot know anything.

See also: **analytic/synthetic distinction; experience; intuition; justification; knowledge; truth**

Further reading: Boghossian and Peacocke (2000); Casullo (2003); Greco and Sosa (1999)

Aquinas, Thomas (1225–1274)

An important medieval philosopher and theologian, Aquinas was greatly influenced by Aristotle and is best known for his *Summa Theologica* in which he presents the 'five ways' of proving God's existence. Aquinas believed that we discover the divine wisdom and power of God through rational examination of nature. This stood in contrast to the established religious view, which saw the newly discovered natural laws of science as replacing God as the causal force in the world. According to Aquinas, God created each thing's nature. The ordered structure of the world was ultimately the work of God rather than natural forces. The reason and freedom of man did not challenge God's omnipotence, but actually reflected the power of

God because man was made in God's image. To limit the freedom and rational/ scientific investigation of man was to blaspheme against God's work. These ideas are reflected in Aquinas's claim that God's existence is a matter of proof (natural reason) rather than faith. Aquinas formulated five ways in which God's existence can be proved. The first four ways relate to the cosmological argument (also known as the prime-mover argument), which states that there cannot be an infinite chain of causes in the world and thus God must be the thing which first began this chain. The fifth way is a version of the teleological argument (the argument from design). Here Aquinas reflects that, given how structured and coherent the universe appears to be, there must be some intelligent designer of it (God).

See also: **Aristotle; creationism; enlightenment; evolution; faith; God; God, arguments for the existence of; religious belief**

Further reading: Martin (1988); McInerny (1998, 2004); Stump (2003)

Arendt, Hannah (1906–1975)

A philosopher and political theorist, Hannah Arendt was a student of Heidegger and used a phenomenological approach to analyse politics and political life. She was strongly affected by the rise of Nazism and much of her work is directed towards analysing and understanding it (see, for example, Arendt, 1951). Rather than focusing on political concepts such as 'the state', 'international relations', 'authority' and 'globalisation', Arendt attempts to discover the structures of political experience. This requires an examination of us as 'political-beings', the way of life we experience as people embedded within a political culture. Arendt argues that the focus of politics should not be abstract political theories and concepts, a preoccupation which has been generated by the Western tradition of reflecting upon 'essences' and 'transcendental' truths. Instead the concern should be about human action that engages with real (concrete) situations, which she calls the *vita activa*. Within this analysis, human political activity such as labour and work is understood in relation to the inescapable biological needs and necessities of human existence that bind us. This definition of labour as enslavement and 'unfreedom' is strongly opposed to Marx's vision of communist society in which labour is essential to the best form of social living and the inevitable end-point of human existence. Arendt also argues that freedom must be understood within the concrete world of action rather than as part of some 'inner' conscious state. We come to understand freedom through our interaction with other people in the world, not through internal reflection. Arendt's work has influenced many political philosophers including Habermas and Lyotard.

A

See also: **agency; alienation; communism; freedom; Habermas; Heidegger; intersubjectivity; Lyotard; Marx; Marxism; phenomenology; political philosophy; socialism**

Further reading: Arendt (1951, 1958, 1962, 1970); Hansen (1993); McGowan (1997); Villa (2000)

Areté

See **virtue**

Aristotle (384–422 BCE)

Aristotle is undeniably one of the most influential figures in Western philosophy. At the age of 17 he entered Plato's academy, and later taught Alexander the Great. It is possible that Aristotle produced as many as two hundred texts, but only around thirty have survived. Aristotle's views differed strongly from the philosophy of Plato. In particular, Aristotle rejected the transcendental realm of the forms (a heavenly realm in which the true 'forms' or versions of all material things reside) arguing instead that the material world is the true reality and our senses reliably reveal this to us. Knowledge is gained through experience of the natural world, not by mental reflection of a non-material, transcendental reality. The primary substance of reality is ordinary 'things': a horse, a tree, a kettle. Secondary substances, which are less real, are the groups of individual things: horses, trees, kettles. Aristotle therefore turned Plato's philosophy on its head, for Plato thought true reality was the abstract form of things (such as the true form of a horse, residing in a heavenly realm).

Aristotle has been criticised for speaking of 'degrees' of existence as it seems strange to speak of something being 'less real' than another. Beside these metaphysical considerations, Aristotle made significant contributions to logic and ethics. His virtue ethics, which is currently receiving renewed interest, focuses on judgements of character rather than moral rights, duties or the consequences of actions. For Aristotle the highest good, the end towards which all our actions are directed, is *eudaimonia* (happiness/flourishing/fulfilling our potential) and the way to realise *eudaimonia* is by cultivating the appropriate set of virtues, such as courage, truthfulness and modesty. Consequently the moral person is the one who has correctly developed his virtuous character. Aristotle's emphasis on character differs from the approaches of consequentialism and deontology.

Aristotle conducted incredibly detailed studies of the natural world. He produced a comprehensive classificatory system of biological organisms, dividing them into 'genera' (types) and then sub-dividing these genera into species. His biological work remained the authoritative account for many centuries. Aristotle also believed that every object is composed of 'matter' and 'form'. Matter is the 'potential' a thing possesses. For example, the matter of a seed is to become a tree; the matter of a candle is to become a pool of wax. Form is the reality of a thing, what we might call the expression of matter (what a thing actually is). Aristotle argued that every object has a 'goal' (*telos*), meaning a 'right' way of developing. In living things, this *telos* was determined by their soul, which is the perfect way for a living thing to develop. Humans, Aristotle tells us, are unique in being both feeling and rational things. Therefore, the *telos* for humans is to develop into fully rational and virtuous beings, as this would bring their form into accordance with their soul.

See also: **consequentialism; deontology; Greek philosophy, ancient; Plato; Socrates; substance;** *summum bonum;* **virtue; virtue ethics**

Further reading: Anagnostopoulos (2009); Barnes (1984, 1995); Shields (2007)

A

Artificial Intelligence (AI)

Despite its futuristic connotations, the concept of artificial intelligence was first brought to prominence by the work of Alan Turing in 1950. Turing explored whether a machine could be designed to perform certain tasks in a way that was indistinguishable from humans. Subsequent work in AI has aimed to pass this Turing test; one particularly famous example being the chess-playing robot. AI has particular relevance to the philosophy of mind because, in order to replicate intelligence or human thought (cognition) in a computer, we must have some notion of what intelligence and cognition are. Dominant theories in the philosophy of mind, such as functionalism, have described the human mind as an incredibly complex machine, akin to a super-computer. These theories argue that the mind is entirely physical in nature and suggest that researchers in AI could, one day, build a machine that is entirely indistinguishable from a human. Although images abound in science fiction, it is far from clear that such a *Terminator* vision is ever achievable. Important objections to the limits of AI include Searle's famous Chinese Room Argument, which asserts that a computer could never understand its own processes, and the argument that computers cannot be said to possess mental states/consciousness. Briefly stated, the Chinese Room Argument runs as follows. Imagine an English speaker in a room with a comprehensive set of instructions on how to manipulate Chinese characters. Chinese characters are passed through a slot into the room, and the English speaker uses the instructions to produce another set of characters, which are posted back out. To the Chinese people feeding Chinese characters into the room, it looks like the English speaker understands Chinese. However, we would not want to say that the English speaker has any 'understanding' of Chinese. Since computers essentially function in the same way as the English speaker (that is, run on programs which manipulate symbols), there is no reason to assume that they are capable of ever understanding what they do. Another issue is the 'frame problem', which refers to the fact that the mind constantly filters huge amounts of information and selects just a tiny amount which is presented to our conscious awareness. It would be a major challenge to program a computer so that is was capable of performing this filtering. A similar problem relates to decision-making. At any moment we could perform a near-infinite number of actions, but we limit ourselves to a few options. Again, it is not clear how we could program this ability into a computer.

A final issue is whether we would want to create a machine capable of replicating, or improving upon, human cognition. Many works of science fiction portray a dystopian/apocalyptic world in which machines have become autonomous and compete with, rather than serve, humans. However, such developments in AI currently appear to be a long way off – that is, assuming they are even achievable.

See also: **cognition; consciousness; dualism; functionalism; mind, the; physicalism**

Key questions: Could human thought ever be replicated by a computer? Would such a computer be conscious? If we cannot create computers that think like humans, then what is the reason for this?

Further reading: Dreyfus (1992); Russell and Norvig (2003); Searle (1980, 1984); Turing (1950)

Augustine, Saint (354–430)

Augustine was a Christian philosopher who, following a religious conversion in Milan, preached that all activity must be directed towards the supreme will of God. All human activity was secondary; man's sole priority was serving God in the hope of attaining salvation. He was heavily influenced by Plato's philosophy, which he saw as leading people towards Christianity. Indeed, Augustine represents the major bridge between medieval Christian and classical Greek philosophy. Augustine draws a parallel between Plato's 'form of the good', which is both the source and illumination of all knowledge, and God. For Augustine, all knowledge is supplied by God. Furthermore, God creates what is good. Bad arises when things stray from their original nature. Augustine explains the presence of evil in humans by God having given them free will. Humans must necessarily have free will because, otherwise, God would be seen as tolerating wrong-doing and inflicting suffering on people. This identification of free will with moral responsibility has become the classic response to the problem of evil. By the end of his life Augustine was painting a bleak moral landscape in which the majority of the population were condemned to eternal punishment, whilst only a lucky few have been predestined to be saved. Augustine heavily influenced many medieval philosophers including Anselm and Aquinas, as well as more recent thinkers such as Descartes.

See also: **Anselm; Descartes; evil, the problem of; free will; Plato**

Further reading: Augustine (c. 386–7; c. 391–401); Chadwick (1986); Clark (1994); Fitzgerald (1999); Wills (1999)

Austin, John L. (1911–1960)

J.L. Austin was an English philosopher whose major contribution was his analysis of ordinary language. Traditionally, the main feature of language was considered to be its ability to state facts about the world which could be either true or false. However, Austin argued that truth-evaluative statements form a small part of everyday language and how we use it. Much of our language consists of 'performative utterances', statements which aim to accomplish something rather than represent reality. These 'illocutionary acts' include such things as promising, asking and accepting. They can never be true or false, only successful or unsuccessful. Rather than passively describing realities, illocutionary acts work to change and create reality. Austin believed that intentional mental states such as 'I believe' or 'I hope' are illocutionary and should be understood in terms of our behaving as if we believed or hoped such and such. Austin's work gave rise to the theory of 'speech acts', which has exerted a strong influence on linguistics, the philosophy of language and post-structuralist accounts of linguistic constructivism.

See also: **analytic philosophy; Butler; constructivism; post-structuralism; reality; Russell; speech-acts; Wittgenstein**

Further reading: Austin (1961, 1962a, 1962b); Warnock (1989)

A

Authenticity

Authenticity is a term used by existentialists, notably Sartre and Heidegger, to denote the type of life lived by someone who has become fully aware of their individual responsibility and freedom, and acts accordingly. To live authentically is to knowingly choose one's actions and projects. According to Heidegger, most of us are stuck in a herd-like, inauthentic state in which we merely follow the crowd, refusing to acknowledge our radical freedom. By tearing ourselves out of this comfortable acceptance we confront our existence as radically free beings. Heidegger described this confrontation as the experience of angst/anxiety, a state in which we are confronted by our freedom and thus realise the possibility of authenticity. Sartre discusses inauthenticity as 'bad faith', a mode of being in which we hide from our freedom. He describes a waiter whose actions are carefully tailored to what we expect a waiter to be like. The waiter has renounced his individuality and chosen instead to hide behind a mask.

Other examples of bad faith include psychological and sociological explanations of human behaviour in which the individual is 'determined' by such things as childhood experiences or political forces. For Sartre, nothing but our own will is able to determine who we are and what we do. To say 'that's just the way I am' is to live in bad faith, thus denying the fact that we are ultimately authentic beings. To live authentically is to take full responsibility for our actions by embracing our individual freedom and realising that no one else can determine the course of our lives. We should try to mould ourselves, rather than let ourselves be moulded by external circumstances and pressures. Authenticity forms the basis of Sartre's moral philosophy, in which the basic principle is never to harm the authenticity of another being.

See also: **angst; Dasein; determinism; existentialism; freedom; Heidegger; Kierkegaard; responsibility; Sartre**

Key questions: Do we spend most of our lives living in 'bad faith'? What are the advantages and disadvantages of living an 'authentic' life?

Further reading: Guignon (2004); Heidegger (1927); Macquarrie (1972); Sartre (1943, 1946)

Ayer, Alfred J. (1910–1989)

A precocious talent, Ayer's influential *Language, Truth and Logic* (1936) was published two years after he wrote it at the age of just 24. It became the definitive exposition of logical positivism, of which Ayer is often cited as a chief proponent. Heavily influenced by the empiricism of Locke and Hume, Ayer argued that the only meaningful statements are (a) those which can, in principle, be empirically tested, and (b) those which are true by virtue of their meanings. Statements such as 'God exists' and 'God does not exist' do not meet either of these criteria and are therefore rejected as meaningless. Regarding moral statements, Ayer argued that they merely express certain tastes or preferences rather than abstract laws. Consequently, in saying murder is wrong, we are simply expressing negative feelings about murder rather than appealing to moral principles. Ayer later decided that moral claims contain a prescriptive element, so when we say 'murder is wrong' we are asking others to also find murder emotionally unpleasant and to avoid such an action.

See also: **analytic philosophy; emotivism; empiricism; Hume; knowledge; Locke; logical positivism; moral subjectivism; Vienna Circle; truth**

Further reading: Ayer (1936, 1940, 1969, 1984); Hahn (1992); Hanfling (1999)

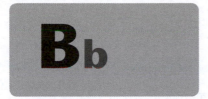

Bad faith

See **authenticity**

Beauty

The concept of beauty is central to aesthetics. Specifically, philosophers have been interested in understanding our experiences of beauty. Is beauty a property which objects possess or is it a feature of our minds which we impose upon certain things in the world? Similarly, are experiences of beauty universal or will people see beauty in different things? Plato argued that there is a single 'form' or 'idea' of beauty and something is made beautiful by our recognising this 'form' within it. This is an example of a realist conception of beauty. An anti-realist or relativist theory of beauty would argue that beauty is in the eye of the beholder. When we express an experience of beauty (for example, that sunset or that person is beautiful) it seems we attach 'normativity' to it. This means that our statement implies that others should find this thing beautiful and those that do not are somehow incorrect in their judgement.

We often defer to 'experts' who have trained their judgements, such as wine-tasters, art-critics and architects, to tell us what is beautiful in any given area. However, it is not necessarily true that such people have privileged access to knowing what is beautiful. Although it may seem that what is aesthetically pleasing is simply what is beautiful, it may not be so straightforward. Paintings which are considered to possess high aesthetic value may depict scenes of violence or suffering, or celebrated pieces of music may be discordant. These works may be called beautiful because they are highly aesthetic even if they are not immediately pleasing to the eye/ear. Therefore it appears that beauty must be something more than simply attractiveness or pleasantness.

See also: **aesthetics; anti-realism; Plato; realism; relativism**

Key questions: What makes something beautiful? Should all people agree on what is beautiful? How could we persuade someone who disagrees with our idea of beauty that they are wrong?

Further reading: Mothersill (1984); Zangwill (2001)

Begging the question

Begging the question (*petitio principia*) is a fallacy (flaw in one's reasoning) which is generated when the conclusion is used, either explicitly or implicitly, as one of the premises of an argument, so that one assumes what one is trying to prove. For instance, if asked why the law should be viewed as morally right, we cannot use the fact that moral wrongs are illegal as evidence for this conclusion. Religious arguments for God often commit this fallacy by using the Bible as evidence for God's existence, but the reliability of the Bible can only be guaranteed by assuming God exists.

See also: ad hominem; **fallacy; impartiality; logic; slippery slope argument; straw man; validity; vicious circle**

Further reading: Engel (1994); Hamblin (1970); Hansen and Pinto (1995)

Behaviourism

In psychology, behaviourism refers to a reductionist, scientific method of studying behaviour in preference to mental processes and also to an empiricist theory of learning. In terms of method, behaviourism means that all processes are simplified to the level of behaviour that can be publicly observed and measured. Any other method, such as introspection (thinking about one's own thoughts) or measuring people's descriptions of themselves, is seen as unnecessarily complicated, as well as too subjective to be classed as scientific. Humans are referred to as 'organisms', indicating that behaviourists do not distinguish between the qualities of humans and those of animals. The behaviourist theory of learning is that humans and animals are born as blank slates (*tabula rasa*) and that everything they are and do is learnt by experience in the environment (empirically).

Similarly, analytical or logical behaviourists in philosophy, such as Ryle, reject a dualistic approach to the mind–body problem, that is, the view that there is a mind or spirit separate from the physical body. They propose that behaviour represents mental processes, and can be described in that way. Mind is equivalent to behaviour and therefore this is a monist theory of mind; there is no 'ghost in the machine'. (Note, however, that Ryle did not consider himself to be a behaviourist.) There are several objections to logical behaviourism, including the possibility of abstract thought that does not relate to doing something (for example, imagining the end of the universe) or experiencing emotions such as pain or love that have personal meaning beyond their expression in behaviour, including speech. Behaviourism also seems to imply that a completely motionless person cannot be experiencing any mental states as they are not displaying any behaviour.

See also: **dualism; empiricism; mind, the; mind–body problem, the; monism; Wittgenstein**

Key questions: To what extent is the mind explained by reference to behaviour? What are the causes of our behaviour?

Further reading: Block (1981); Ryle (1949); Wittgenstein (1953); Zuriff (1985)

Being

To be, or not to be, is indeed one of the most important philosophical questions. Much of philosophy is concerned with what does or does not exist as well as what could/could not and might/might not exist. Common topics include the possible existence of God, moral principles and souls. Philosophers have also been concerned about the possible existence of such things as numbers, parallel universes, the past, future, present, and other people's minds. A further issue is establishing the nature of a thing's being, such as whether it exists necessarily or contingently and what elements of its being it could lose before it becomes a different thing. Some things, such as unicorns and Father Christmas, have been the subject of interest because they do not exist and yet we can talk meaningfully about them. Just how this is possible has puzzled philosophers who assumed that language must refer to things in the world in order to be meaningful. Alex Meinong suggested that such objects had an existence without having 'being'. They are 'non-being objects'. Bertrand Russell dismissed this view as incoherent and argued that statements about unicorns or Father Christmas do not denote (refer) to any existing thing. Being has held a distinctive meaning for existentialists such as Heidegger (who used the term 'Dasein' to describe this special kind of being) and Sartre. They employed 'being' to describe both an individual's reality, and that which allows there to be a reality for individuals.

See also: **anti-realism; change; constructionism; Dasein; definite descriptions; essentialism; existence; identity; metaphysics; modality; ontology; realism; reference**

Further reading: Butchvarov (1979); Heidegger (1927); Meinong (1904); Russell (1905); Sartre (1943); Williams, C.J.F. (1992)

Belief

Along with such things as thoughts, desires, perceptions and feelings, beliefs are key mental states which constitute what we may term 'the mind'. To believe something is to think it is true. If I believe that cats have four legs or that God exists, I am asserting that these statements are true. The mental phenomenon of knowledge would appear to be a belief coupled with justification or truth; to possess knowledge that cats have four legs would entail having the relevant belief and that belief being true. Because beliefs are about propositions such as 'cats are furry', they are often referred to as propositional attitudes. What is not clear, however, is just what a belief is. One theory, known as representationalism, states that beliefs are mental representations, stored within one's mind, of the propositions about which we have beliefs. Dispositionalism denies that beliefs should be understood as mental representations. It argues that belief should be understood more in terms of behaviour. To believe the proposition P is to exhibit certain behavioural dispositions towards P. For example, to believe that there is an elephant in the room is to display certain behaviours consistent with there being an elephant in the room, such as running away. However we choose to understand beliefs, it is clear that they are a key element in explaining behaviour. If someone reaches for a cold drink it is typical to explain this through reference to their belief that they are thirsty and the belief that a cold drink will quench their thirst. An interesting issue is whether some animals can be said to have beliefs. Although we often assume this to be the case, for example the cat believes there is a mouse under the piano, Davidson has argued that animals (and very young or mentally-handicapped humans) cannot have beliefs because they do not have language. However, others have argued that, language apart, the biological and behavioural similarities between humans and non-humans justify the claim that non-humans have beliefs.

B

See also: **cognition; concept; justification; mind, the; truth**

Key questions: What exactly is a belief? What things are capable of having beliefs?

Further reading: Davidson (1982); Price (1969); Stich (1983)

Bentham, Jeremy (1748–1832)

A philosopher and radical politician, Bentham is best known as one of the founders of utilitarianism. Although similar utilitarian theories had already been formulated in Ancient Chinese and Greek times, Bentham's version is the paradigmatic theory in Western philosophy. According to Bentham, an action is right if it promotes general happiness. This led to his 'utility calculus', a formula for working out which actions would produce the greatest amount of happiness for the greatest number of people. Although many criticised the attempt to quantify happiness, his theory is one of the most important and influential within moral philosophy. Bentham's utilitarianism theory was developed by J.S. Mill, who was tutored by Bentham.

Bentham was strongly opposed to the idea of 'natural' rights, which he famously dismissed as 'nonsense on stilts', arguing that all rights are derived from socially-constructed laws. There are no rights out there in the world for us to discover, only those we create. The radical nature of Bentham's views can be seen in his championing of animal welfare on the grounds that animals can suffer and thus must be given moral consideration. According to Bentham, the traditional criterion of rationality is unacceptable because some animals are clearly more rational than young babies. In addition, he campaigned for equality between the sexes and the decriminalisation of homosexuality.

Bentham also produced designs for the 'panopticon', a prison in which all the prisoners can be monitored by a single guard at any time. Crucially, however, the prisoners cannot see the guard which leads to them having to behave because at any point they could be being watched by the guard. This idea of self-regulation has, according to Foucault, been a central feature of the development of the state's control of its citizens and can be seen in modern forms of surveillance such as CCTV, which is somewhat ironic given Bentham's strong belief in individual freedom.

See also: **animal ethics; consequentialism; equality; Foucault; freedom; happiness; liberty; Mill; rights; Singer; utilitarianism**
Further reading: Bentham (1859); Harrison (1983)

Berkeley, George (1685–1753)

B

An Irish philosopher and theologian, Berkeley is arguably one of the most misunderstood and under-read philosophers of modern times. Berkeley was a brilliant critic of Descartes and Locke and is best known for his defence of idealism, the view that the world is made up of only minds and ideas. According to Berkeley all that we can know to exist are ideas and the minds that perceive them, summed up in his phrase '*esse est percipi*' (to be is to be perceived). However, if all that exists are ideas and minds, then why cannot we simply think things into being? Furthermore, why do many things happen that we do not think of? For instance, why do I return home to find my cat is very hungry, despite not having thought about my cat all day? The reason, Berkeley states, is that the world we perceive has been placed in our minds by God, who ensures that it is neatly ordered, clear and understandable. This shows that God must be wise and benevolent, as well as all-powerful. One of the major motivations for Berkeley was to provide proof to non-believers of

God's necessary existence. Many philosophers have dismissed Berkeley as patently false, often relying on the intuitive response that the external world simply must exist. Samuel Johnson, a contemporary of Berkeley, thought he had refuted his idealism by kicking a stone, thus demonstrating that the world is material. However it is increasingly being acknowledged that Berkeley's arguments are much stronger than that. Berkeley would probably have responded to Johnson that he had all the mental impressions (ideas) of kicking a stone, and this is entirely consistent with idealism. What Johnson does not demonstrate, according to Berkeley's theory, is the mind-independent existence of the stone. Nonetheless, despite failing to find serious faults in his work, few philosophers are willing to accept Berkeley's extreme conclusions.

See also: **Descartes; empiricism; experience; Hume; idealism; knowledge; Locke**

Further reading: Berkeley (1709, 1710, 1713); Dancy (1987); Grayling (1986); Turbayne (1982)

Bioethics

Recent developments in technology and medicine have given rise to a number of pressing ethical issues, which have been grouped under the term 'bioethics'. These include whether and when to (a) prolong and end lives (such as in the case of those in a coma and very premature babies); (b) safely conduct abortions; (c) alter the genetic make-up of foetuses; (d) offer blood and organ transplants; and (e) radically alter a person's body. Let us take the example of abortion. Should we conduct abortions? If so, at what point in the pregnancy should this be allowed? Who has the right to have an abortion? Should the father have a say in the matter? Answers to these questions are constantly being revised in the light of new scientific evidence and philosophical argument.

There are also the practical issues of what is legally permissible and what is achievable given economic constraints. It is not currently possible to meet every person's medical needs and wishes, and so decisions must be made regarding what resources to distribute and where. Alternatively, doctors may find their ethical views clashing with what is prescribed by law. A major source of conflict lies in the differences between certain medical practices (including abortion and euthanasia) and particular religious beliefs. For instance, there has been a vehement anti-abortion movement in the USA, led by certain Christian groups, which resulted in the murder of Dr George Tiller for conducting abortions. With more and more of us living longer, and thus requiring greater medical care, as well as the increasing availability and number of medical treatments, it is likely that all of us will some day face the questions being debated within bioethics.

See also: **death; existence; moral agents; morality; responsibility; rights**

Key questions: Does each person have the right to choose what to do with their body? What should we do if a person is unable to make a decision regarding their body? What principles should be applied when deciding who should benefit from medical procedures?

Further reading: Baron (2006); Harris (2001); Singer and Viens (2008)

B

Body, the

Because philosophers have tended to focus on the mind, they have often had little to say about the body. Indeed, the body was often treated as part of that which must be transcended by the mind as the philosopher moved beyond feelings, emotions and personal tastes in search of objective truths. However, more recently, philosophers such as Merleau-Ponty have drawn attention to the importance of the body. These theories of embodiment describe how the world is revealed *through* our bodies and how our thinking is conditioned by the body. For instance, we see the ground as something which is walked upon, rather than flown above; trees as things which can be climbed; pens as objects which can be held. The meanings of things in the world are determined by our physical relationship to them.

Other philosophers, such as Foucault and Butler, have been interested in ways in which the body is socially constructed. These theories of 'biopolitics' explore the often damaging effects of discourse upon the body. For instance, society expects that men and women cultivate a certain physical appearance. To be a man one should have a strong, muscular body. Anorexia is often used as an example of the negative effects that social expectations of beauty can have on individuals. Transsexuals and homosexuals often challenge our expectations of what a woman's or man's body should be like, frequently at the risk of severe verbal and physical abuse.

See also: **bioethics; Butler; constructionism; discourse; embodiment; Foucault; gender; Merleau-Ponty; phenomenology**

Key questions: To what extent does our body determine how we perceive the world? Do we have full control over our body, or does society influence its development?

Further reading: Butler (1993); Foucault (1984); Merleau-Ponty (1945); Schiebinger (2000)

Brain-in-a-vat

Descartes' sceptical notion that what you think to be reality could be the result of the evil-doings of a demon is the early equivalent of the brain-in-a-vat argument. How do you know that the world which you perceive to be real is not in fact a computer simulation that has been fed into your brain, which is floating in a jar? The science-fiction film *The Matrix* is based on this idea. Putnam (1981) challenges the logic of the thought experiment, a simple version of his argument being that if I am a brain-in-a-vat, then the word 'brain' (or 'vat') does not refer to the actual object, therefore I am not a brain (and there is no vat).

See also: **Descartes; doubt; idealism; knowledge; reality; scepticism; solipsism**

Further reading: Brueckner (1986); Putnam (1981)

Buddhism

Described as both a religion and a philosophy, Buddhism was founded during the fifth or sixth century BC. The founder, Siddhatta Gotama, became known as 'the Buddha' after his enlightenment. Although he is called *the* Buddha, Buddhists believe there to have been *many* Buddhas spanning the entire history of the universe.

B

The two dominant forms of Buddhism are Theravada Buddhism, popular in South-East Asia, and Mahayana Buddhism, popular in China, Japan and Tibet. Despite consisting of a great deal of schools, there is a shared core of beliefs. This essence of Buddhism is captured in the Four Noble Truths, taught by the Buddha in his first sermon. They are:

1. Life is *dukkha* (suffering; dissatisfaction; dis-ease; impermanence)
2. *Dukkha* is caused by *tanhā* (thirst; attachment; craving; greed; desire)
3. We can be free of *dukkha* by extinguishing *tanhā*
4. The way to eliminate *tanhā* is the 'Middle Way', consisting of the Eightfold Path

These truths tell us that all life is characterised by suffering, and that the way to eliminate this suffering is to remove all traces of craving and attachment from our minds. By eliminating our cravings we experience enlightenment and gain insight into the true nature of both ourselves and the world. On achieving this one is said to attain the state of *nirvana*. Until we achieve *nirvana* we are bound to the endless cycle of rebirths, referred to as *samsara* (literally 'wandering on'). Each of us has had countless past lives, which are governed by the law of *karma*. *Karma* is the universal law of cause and effect; all actions generate positive or negative *karma*, which determine future events. Losing my job is the consequence of *karma* accumulated at some point in this or a past life. *Karma* can be summed up by the phrase 'you reap what you sow'.

One of the most difficult, but well known, aspects of Buddhist teaching is the concept of 'not-self'. This is the idea that none of us possesses a 'self', a persisting and unchanging entity we call 'I'. A famous Buddhist analogy is that of a chariot. If we dismantle the chariot we find each part of the chariot – the wheel, the spokes, and so on – but we do not find the 'chariot' itself. The chariot is a term referring to a collection of parts, not a 'thing' in itself. Similarly, each person is simply a collection of physical and mental 'parts' and our mistake is to assume there is something over and above that. One implication of the not-self teaching is that, strictly speaking, 'I' do not enter *nirvana*, and nor do 'I' not enter *nirvana*, for there is no 'I' which could or could not do such a thing.

See also: **enlightenment; 'I'; Indian philosophy; karma; person; Schopenhauer; self, the; teleology; Zen**

Further reading: Batchelor (1997); Harvey (1990); Rahula (1959); Siderits (2007)

B

Butler, Judith (1956–)

Arguably the most influential feminist philosopher of the 1990s, Butler is often described as a post-structuralist and queer theorist and is best known for her idea of performativity. She is strongly influenced by Foucault, Hegel and Nietzsche. In her major work, *Gender Trouble*, Butler argued that gender is neither natural nor inevitable, but rather is 'performatively' constructed through social institutions and discourses. Influenced by Simone de Beauvoir's famous statement that 'one is not born, but rather becomes, a woman' (1949: 267), Butler believes a person's gender must be constantly re-created through performing certain social norms and values, such as walking in a 'feminine' way. Because society demands that we comply with these social norms and values, gender is always oppressive and exclusionary. In particular, Butler believes that definitions of gender are always based upon a heterosexual model of gender identity, which denies the legitimacy of homosexuality. Adopting Nietzsche's claim that there is no 'doer behind the deed', Butler argues that there is no ontological subject, no substantial 'I', behind the performative acts that create each individual. The 'self' which is conventionally described as the source of our actions (Nietzsche's 'doer' and Butler's 'ontological subject') is actually a product, not the cause, of performative actions. Controversially, Butler has claimed that the body itself is a product of discourse and that it is shaped by power rather than nature.

Some feminists, such as Benhabib (1992), have criticised Butler for removing the possibility of agency by denying there is a subject that performs their gender. In reducing people to the mere limited repertoire of actions they perform, it does not seem to leave much room for positive choice, freedom, identity and change. Consequently, her strongly anti-foundationalist position is seen as a threat to the coherency of a women's movement based upon a common identity. Others have criticised Butler's over-attention to language, arguing that she neglects the material and political situations and problems that people face every day.

See also: **agency; discourse; feminism; Foucault; foundationalism; Hegel; gender; identity; Nietzsche; post-structuralism; queer theory**

Further reading: Butler (1990, 1993, 2004); Benhabib (1992); Foucault (1976); Salih (2002)

B

Categorical imperative

The categorical imperative was formulated by Immanuel Kant and is the central component of his moral theory. It is a fundamental law of reason and as such it must be obeyed by all rational agents. Humans, as rational beings, are therefore required to act upon the demands of the categorical imperative. Kant's best-known formulation of the categorical imperative states: 'Act only in accordance with that maxim [principle] through which you can at the same time will that it become a universal law' (1785, 4: 421). What this means is that we can only perform actions which it would be acceptable for all other rational beings to adopt.

Let us use the example of lying. If we tell a lie we are implying that all other rational agents can/should also lie. However, if lying is universally adopted then the very concept of lying would break down because lying is dependent upon a general assumption of truth-telling. If everyone lies then there is no such assumption of truth-telling, and therefore the idea of lying would be meaningless. It would not even be conceivable to tell a lie in such a world, because the concept of truth-telling, upon which lying depends, would be similarly meaningless. So, in saying that it is acceptable to lie, I am trying to conceive of a world in which (a) there is no assumption of truth-telling (as everyone adopts the principle that it is acceptable to lie); and (b) there is an assumption of truth-telling (because I require it in order to be able to lie). This is clearly inconceivable; the effects of my principle are self-contradictory and absurd. Therefore the act of lying is irrational and, according to the categorical imperative, cannot be morally justified. In effect, the categorical imperative is a way of testing what is, and is not, morally acceptable. We input a principle, such as 'do not lie', and see whether it passes the test. The term 'categorical' means that it applies unconditionally to all rational beings, and the term 'imperative' is used because it tells us what we must do (for example, 'do not lie'). Kant contrasted categorical imperatives with hypothetical imperatives, which tell you what to do if you wish/desire a certain outcome. For instance, 'you must leave home very early in the morning if you wish to avoid the rush-hour traffic'.

Slightly confusingly, Kant produced other formulations of the categorical imperative. The humanity formulation states that we should never treat humans as a means to an end, but rather as ends-in-themselves. Kant writes: 'Act in such a way that you treat humanity, whether in your own person or in any other person, always at the same time as an end, never merely as a means' (1785, 4: 429). This promotes a respect for people since we always acknowledge that they are rational autonomous agents and must consider their own interests, desires and feelings in our dealings with them. Finally, Kant formulated the categorical imperative in terms of autonomy and the 'Kingdom of Ends'. According to this version of the imperative we must always act in accordance with 'the Idea of the will of every rational being as a will that legislates universal law' (1785: 431). The idea behind this formulation is that all rational beings are autonomous and must be respected as such. This concept of autonomy is described through reference to a 'Kingdom of Ends', which is an ideal community composed of rational, autonomous beings that collectively generate and obey moral laws. Kant saw these formulations as equivalent but failed to specify in what way, thus leaving the door open for a great deal of debate and interpretation by subsequent Kantian philosophers.

See also: **consequentialism; deontology; duty; egoism; Kant; morality; moral objectivism; moral subjectivism; prescriptivism; universability**

Key questions: Is the categorical imperative a suitable way to assess our moral principles? Is it right to assume that all people are, and should be, rational? Should our emotions play a role in deciding what a good act is?

Further reading: Kant (1785); Hill (1992, 2009); Paton (1947)

Causation

Causation, called the 'cement of the universe' by Hume (1739–1740), defines the relationship between cause and effect. Every single event that happens is said to have been caused to happen. To explain something is often to give the cause of that thing: the glass broke because you dropped it; I am not hungry because I have just eaten; turning the light on will illuminate the room. These sentences all describe causal relationships. It seems causation is essential to knowledge because we explain and understand things in terms of causal connections – the reason X happened is because of Y. Despite the seemingly obvious and unproblematic nature of causation, philosophers have dedicated a great deal of time and thought to trying to make sense of it. The most famous discussion of causation is David Hume's sceptical analysis.

Hume begins with the observation that we understand causation through experience. The first time an object is ever encountered there is no way of knowing what it will do. For example, the first person to ever see water could never know that it will cause them to drown if they submerge their head in it. This means that causal connections cannot be proved by *a priori* reasoning. We establish causal connections between things by repeated observations, which lead to a general conclusion. For instance, by watching what happens each time a moving foot connects with a football, we conclude that kicking a football causes it to move. What we do not experience, however, is the causal connection itself. We never see a little causal 'spark' each time there is a causal connection. In other words, we never directly experience causation. According to Hume, our justification for believing in causal connections is based upon our belief that the future will be like the past. However, what justification is there for our belief that the future will resemble the past? It is justified by appealing to causation. We are caught in a circle, and therefore we cannot reasonably establish a satisfactory justification for believing in causation.

Refuting Hume's sceptical analysis of causation has been a preoccupation for many philosophers, though there is little consent upon a satisfactory solution. Kant's response was to ground the principle of causation in the structure of reason.

His *a priori* conception of causation claimed that it was a necessary condition of possible experience. What this means is that our judgement that '*A* caused *B*' is a fundamental aspect of human rationality, without which we could not experience the world in a meaningful way. Causation is not an empirical aspect of the world, rather it is an essential component of the mind's ability to order the world so that it appears to us in a structured, coherent way. A separate issue relating to causation is how something mental, such as a belief or a desire, can cause a physical occurrence. How does my belief that I am thirsty 'cause' my arm to reach out for a glass of water? This problem is particularly relevant to dualism, which states that the mind and body are two different substances. How can an immaterial (non-physical) mind causally interact with a material (physical) body?

See also: **conditionals; empiricism; Hume; justification; Kant; mind–body problem, the; scepticism**

Key questions: How persuasive is Hume's analysis of causation? Is reasoning about cause and effect always dependent on assuming that the future will be like the past? Does Hume's analysis affect our everyday understanding of causation?

Further reading: Beauchamp and Rosenberg (1981); Hume (1739–1740, 1748); Mackie (1974); Strawson (1989)

Certainty

If philosophy aims at truth or knowledge, then being certain of something is very useful indeed. There are several notions of certainty under discussion by philosophers. A belief that is *psychologically* certain is one which a person is absolutely confident of being true. For instance, I am psychologically certain that the sun is currently shining. Psychological certainty is similar, but not identical, to the concept of incorrigibility. An incorrigible belief is one that a person cannot give up. It is possible to have a psychologically certain belief that is not incorrigible; for instance if a piece of new and totally unexpected information arose. History is littered with examples of this, including the beliefs that the earth is flat or is at the centre of the universe. Another form of certainty is *epistemic* certainty. A proposition is epistemically certain if there is no other proposition which is more justified. On this account, a belief could be said to be certain even if one has doubts about it, providing one has more doubts about every other belief. For instance, although I may have some doubt that it is definitely sunny outside, I am still certain it is sunny because I have far more doubts about believing it is raining or that my window has been replaced by a huge computer screen showing a picture of my garden on a sunny day.

In his *Meditations* (1641), Descartes argued that something is certain if there is no reason whatsoever to doubt it. On this account he could not be certain that the world or his body existed, for an evil demon could be tricking him into this belief, but he could not doubt that he was a thinking being, for he had to be able to think in order to doubt. Thus he could be certain that he existed as a mind (I am thinking, therefore I exist), and from there Descartes argued that he was certain about the existence of his body, the world and God. Other philosophers, however, have claimed that we can never be certain, for we can always entertain doubts about the truth of our beliefs. For instance, how can we be certain we are not simply a brain in a vat, with our entire world generated by a computer? Scepticism is the view that we cannot be certain about a particular piece of information. Extreme scepticism denies we can have *any* certain knowledge, and therefore we cannot be said to know anything at all (or at least we cannot justify our believing anything). Perhaps the only thing we can be certain of is that we cannot be certain of anything else.

See also: **belief; brain-in-a-vat; doubt; Descartes; foundationalism; justification; justified true belief; knowledge; relativism; reliabilism; scepticism; truth**

Key questions: What, if anything, can we be certain about? What do we mean when we say we are certain? Does giving up the notion of certainty mean giving up the idea of possessing knowledge?

Further reading: Descartes (1641); Klein (1981); Pollock (1986); Russell (1948)

Change

It seems obvious and uninteresting to say that objects change. A leaf can be green in summer and brown in autumn. Just because it changes colour we would not say it is a different leaf. However, this presents a puzzle, which David Lewis has called the 'problem of temporary intrinsics' (1986a: 203). It is clear that an object cannot be both green and brown, so how can we say that the same leaf possesses the property 'being green' and 'being brown'? There are two main responses to this puzzle. Endurance theory states that an object is entirely present at each point it exists, but the object's properties are relative to a certain time. Therefore when we say the leaf is both green and brown, we actually mean the leaf has a 'being-green' relation to the summer and a 'being-brown' relation to the autumn. Although this sounds strange, it is the same as saying that a cat has a 'being-bigger' relation to a mouse and a 'being-smaller' relation to an elephant. The point is that properties such as colour or height are not intrinsic to the object, but exist in relation to something else. According to the endurance theory, all properties of an object exist in relation to time. Therefore the leaf does not possess the property 'being green', but shares it with a certain time (namely summer).

The alternative view, known as perdurance theory, is that an object consists of many 'temporal parts', one of which is present at each moment the object exists. The leaf in summer and the leaf in autumn are actually two different temporal parts of the one leaf. Therefore the leaf is neither entirely present in summer, nor entirely present in autumn, but instead a part of itself exists in summer and another part in autumn. Although this sounds bizarre, it is based on an analogy with space. Just as a person has different physical parts spread throughout space, which explains how they can be both on the floor and typing on a keyboard at the same time (their feet are on the floor, their hands are on the keyboard), so they have different temporal parts existing at different times. To understand this, imagine watching a film. The film is made up of many individual frames which, when played together, give the impression of a single continuous image. According to perdurance theory, this is what is happening to all objects. There would have to be a near-infinite number of temporal parts for each object, for even the very smallest change in an object would mean a new temporal part has come into existence and replaced the previous one. There is little agreement amongst philosophers over which theory best explains change, and there are a number of problems with both positions. What is clear is that if either were entirely true (and the other entirely false), we would have to radically change our everyday understanding of change.

See also: **difference; identity; metaphysics; personal identity; Ship of Theseus, the; time**

Key questions: How is it possible for an object to undergo change and remain the 'same' thing? Could an object be composed of many temporal parts? When has something changed so much that it is no longer the 'same' thing?

Further reading: Hawley (2001); Lewis (1986a); Lowe (2002); Oderberg (1993); Sider (2001)

Chinese philosophy

Major philosophical works in China can be traced back to the 6th century BCE, during which time it is likely that both Confucianism and Taoism developed. These two schools of thought dominate the history of Chinese philosophy, although other influential schools include Legalism, Buddhism and Monism. Unlike many Western philosophers, who focused on theoretical issues such as what we can know, how we can know and the nature of the world, Chinese philosophy has been more occupied with political and practical problems. The major concern for Chinese philosophers is the question 'how should we live?' This existential and moral question is addressed by the two classics of Chinese philosophy: Lao Tzu's *Tao Te Ching* and Confucius's *Analects*. *Tao Te Ching* explores the idea of '*tao*' as the basis for all action and understanding. Roughly speaking, *tao* is the way or path which guides the development of the universe. To live well is to live in accord with *tao*. This naturalistic, perhaps mystical, philosophy stands in contrast to that of Confucius who argued that the key to a harmonious society, and a good life, lies in obeying traditional norms and values. Confucianism also speaks of the importance of learning about and obeying *tao*, the difference with Taoism being in how to achieve this. Indeed, the idea of *tao* is common to the majority of Chinese philosophies, as are the concepts of *yin* and *yang*.

Chinese philosophy was radically altered by the emergence of communist/Marxist philosophy in China during the 20th century. Chiefly associated with Mao Zedong and his followers, Chinese communist philosophy has shaped the face of contemporary Chinese thought. The political and social revolution which Mao oversaw led to the rejection of many established ideas, the banning of traditional philosophical and cultural works, and the outlawing of religious and social practices associated with these philosophies. It is only recently that Chinese philosophers have been able to explore openly their philosophical heritage and engage with Western philosophies. There has been an increasing interest amongst Western philosophers in Chinese philosophy, particularly early Taoism and Confucianism, with explorations of the parallels that can be drawn between the two traditions and how they can benefit and enrich each other.

See also: **communism; Confucianism; Greek philosophy, ancient; *tao*; Taoism; yin-yang; Zen**

Further reading: Carr and Mahalingam (1997); Chan (1973); Cheng and Bunnin (2002); Cooper (1996b); Kupperman (2001); Mou (2003); Yu-Lan (1948)

Cognition

Broadly speaking, the term cognition can be understood as referring to all intelligent activity. This incorporates animal and artificial intelligence as well as human. The understanding of cognition is quite limited. Many workings of the human mind – how we recognise an animal as a horse, or remember that today is an old friend's birthday – remain somewhat of a mystery. This could be because many cognitive processes are hidden from consciousness. If asked how I knew it was a horse in the field, I could not say how my brain processed the visual image and produced the word 'horse' along with a set of meanings associated with it, such as 'can run fast' or 'is used for pulling carts'. This is a major reason for the limited success in producing systems which replicate human cognition.

Many philosophers exploring cognition are physicalists, meaning they believe that the mind is purely physical in nature. If this belief is true, then it suggests that our cognitive capacities can be explained as something like the firing of neurons which produce (or simply are) the mental states, such as belief and understanding, that we associate with cognition. It would appear that with greater technological and physiological knowledge, the complex nature of cognition will eventually be fully understood and replicated. One key feature of cognition is that it seems to be 'intentional', that is, our thoughts are about aspects of the world. Our beliefs, desires, hopes and such like are directed towards phenomena in the world, and any satisfactory account of cognition must explain this intentionality. The precise workings of animal minds appear equally mysterious and it is far from clear whether such creatures as rabbits, jellyfish or pigs could be said to exhibit cognition.

See also: **artificial intelligence; belief; concept; consciousness; extended cognition; mind, the; monism; physicalism; rationalism; unconscious, the**

Key questions: How much of our cognition is conscious to the mind? Could cognition be fully replicated by a machine? Do any animals demonstrate cognition?

Further reading: Ashcraft (2002); Braddon-Mitchell and Jackson (1996); Fodor (2001); Lycan (1989)

Coherence theory

According to various versions of the coherence theory of truth, the truth of a statement depends upon the relationship between propositions. We treat a statement as true if it 'coheres' with other related statements. For example, if a person says 'There is a green flying pig outside the window' we compare it with other relevant statements to see if it coheres with them. Such statements might include: 'Pigs do not have wings'; 'They cannot fly'; 'They are not green in colour'; 'No one else in the room is seeing a green flying pig'. Because the person's statement does not cohere with other relevant propositions, we can dismiss his statement as false. In effect, coherence theories treat truth as a web of interconnecting beliefs. Each version of the coherence theory must establish the 'relevant' propositions with which beliefs must cohere. These might be 'my beliefs' or 'scientific statements' or 'the Bible'.

An important feature of a coherence theory is that the truth of a proposition does not depend upon its relation to the world. Traditionally, truth was assumed to be a correspondence between beliefs and reality. A true belief was one that correctly corresponded to reality. Coherence theory rejects this belief. Furthermore, because truth is treated as a matter of coherence between propositions, there need not be any fundamental or basic belief upon which all other beliefs are justified. We do not need to follow Descartes in his search for the foundation of all knowledge. Just like a web, there is no single supporting strand upon which all else rests. Instead, all the strands/beliefs are self-supporting. Therefore coherence theories of truth have proved attractive to philosophers who are suspicious of the idea of a 'single' and 'basic' truth, grounded in an objective reality. The coherence theory of truth allows for a plurality of truths across different societies.

One criticism of the coherence theory is that is difficult to see how radical shifts in beliefs can occur. For instance, the statement 'the world is round' would not have cohered with many, if any, propositions at the time it was made. Therefore those who initially held the belief should have dismissed it as false. The coherence theory seems essentially conservative as beliefs should only be accepted as true if they cohere with existing beliefs. A second criticism is that coherence theory can lead to a violation of the principles of non-contradiction and bivalence. According to these principles, statements can either be true *or* false, but not both true *and* false. However, imagine one person believes the world is round, and this coheres with their other beliefs, whist another believes the world is flat, and this coheres with their other beliefs. According to the coherence theory both beliefs are true and the world both is and is not flat at the same time. Many philosophers would prefer simply to say that each person believes the world is round/flat and that both views are coherent given their respective backgrounds of belief (although one happens to be true and the other happens to be false).

See also: **correspondence theory; deflationary theory of truth; foundationalism; justification; Kuhn; paradigm; pragmatism; reality; truth; truthmaker**

Further reading: Johnson (1992); Rescher (1973); Walker (1989)

Communism

Communism is chiefly associated with Karl Marx, who argued that communist society is the goal or end point of social history. All societies will eventually tend towards communism, and the stages they go through (such as feudalism and capitalism) are logical progressions in this inevitable social evolution. The basic communist vision is that of a society without private property, in which production contributes towards the common good. All members of the society have an equal standing in relation to this common good, so that no one person benefits any more or any less from the work of the community as a whole. This co-operative structure is intended to replace the competitive market of capitalist economies, which are seen as promoting inequality and serving individual, rather than common, interests. The former USSR, China and Cuba have all supposedly been communist societies, though the reality has been far from the idealistic vision described here. Communism was famously critiqued in George Orwell's *Animal Farm* (1945).

See also: **alienation; anarchism; conservatism; dialectical materialism; liberalism; libertarianism; Marx; Marxism; nationalism; utopianism**

Further reading: Lansford (2007); Marx and Engels (1848); Orwell (1945); Pipes (2001)

Concept

Concepts are central features of thought. Indeed, without concepts it is difficult to imagine having any conscious thoughts. For example, the statement 'I need to walk my dog' employs a number of concepts, including what a 'dog' is, what a 'walk' is and what it means to 'need'. An early discussion of concepts can be found in Locke (1690) who refers to them as 'general ideas'. According to Locke, general ideas are created by identifying the common characteristic among several particular things. So, for instance, by looking at a blade of grass, a leaf and an apple, we are able to form the general idea of 'green'. A similar discussion can be found in Hume (1739–1740) and Mill (1843), who spoke of general concepts being formed through 'abstraction'. Both Locke and Hume took these 'ideas' to be mental images. This belief can be found in the modern 'representational theory of mind', which treats concepts as mental (psychological) entities. An opposing, and less popular, theory of concepts is the view that concepts are abstract objects. According to this view, concepts are 'real' in the sense that they are not dependent on being thought about. There are concepts existing 'in the world' which have not yet been thought, and may never be. Deleuze and Guattari (1972) have argued that philosophy can be understood as the generation of concepts. This shifts philosophical activity from the discovering of truths or rational reflection to a creative process of concept-construction.

See also: **belief; cognition; Deleuze; epistemology; experience; Frege; Hume; Kant; knowledge; Locke; Mill; Plato; sign**

Further reading: Fodor (1998); Margolis and Laurence (1999)

Conditionals

Conditionals are an important feature of logical and metaphysical analysis. A conditional is a statement expressed in the form 'If A, then B'. For instance, 'If I drop this glass on the concrete floor, then it will break'. A is called the antecedent and B is called the consequent. Conditionals can be used to express logical truths or causal connections. In the above sentence, the conditional reveals that one thinks there is a causal connection between dropping a glass on a concrete floor and the glass breaking. Often we need to clarify the situation, such as by saying 'If I drop this glass on the concrete floor from a sufficient height, and nothing stops it falling, then it will break'. Conditionals can be very useful for analysing scientific experiments for which we want to isolate a single cause-and-effect relationship.

One distinctive type of conditional is a counterfactual conditional. As the name suggests, a counterfactual conditional is a statement that goes against (counters) the facts. For instance, 'If I had revised harder, then I would have passed my exam'. There is much debate about how we are to understand the truth of counterfactuals, given that they refer to possible (or impossible) rather than actual events. Counterfactuals are useful in understanding talk of possible worlds (modality) for they deal with how things might have been. In some possible world I did indeed pass my exam because I revised harder. One way of assessing the truth of a counterfactual is to say that it is true if, in the possible worlds most resembling this world in which I revised harder, I passed my exam.

See also: **causation; event; modality; logic, philosophical; truth**

Further reading: Adams (1975); Bennett (2003); McLaughlin (1990); Woods (1997)

Confucianism

Confucianism refers to a school of thought popular in East-Asian countries, particularly China, Japan and Korea. It is founded upon the work of Confucius (551–479 BCE), one of the great Chinese philosophers. Like his famous contemporary Lao Tzu, Confucius never wrote any texts himself. His famous book, *The Analects*, is a collection of his sayings written down by his students after his death. Confucius was concerned with explaining the ideal way to live in order to remedy the social and political unrest of his time. Confucianism is thus primarily a moral and political theory. The 'good life' (*jen*) is achieved through observing particular traditional norms and values. The term *li* refers to the observance of these rites. Particularly important values for Confucianists are *chung* (loyalty, commitment) and *shu* (consideration, reciprocity).

Confucianism does not prescribe a complete list of relevant norms and values. Rather, in each situation, one must work out whether one's actions accord with *yi* (rightness, duty), the ultimate ethical principle and motive. One must always act because it is right, rather than for any desired outcome. The person who has generated this ethical mindset is described as a *chun tzu*. Although this is often translated as 'gentleman', it is more appropriate to think of such a person as a 'superior' or 'higher' being. According to Confucius, each of us has this *chun tzu* nature within us, and the cultivation of our nature through *li* will lead us to become 'at one' with ourselves.

Other great Confucianists include Mencius (4th century BCE), who created an idealistic version of Confucianism based upon the belief that human nature is essentially good, and Hsun Tzu (3rd century BCE), who paints a far starker picture of humanity as greedy, self-interested and easily led into violence. An important critic of early Confucianism was Mo Tzu (5th century BCE). Mo Tzu objected that Confucianists ignore the Gods and spirits, and also that the observance of complicated and often time-consuming rites and rituals wastes the energy and resources of the people. Owing to its emphasis on respect for tradition, Confucianism is seen as an essentially conservative philosophy. It is often placed in direct opposition to the other dominant Chinese philosophy, Taoism. In many respects they are deeply divided, but there are also similarities. Both philosophies insist upon the importance of *tao* (translated as 'the way') and the necessity for living in accordance with it. Their major difference is in how one goes about discovering and obeying *tao*.

See also: **Chinese philosophy; tao; Taoism**

Further reading: Chan (1973); Goldin (2005); Waley (1945); Yao (2000)

Consciousness

Consciousness is one of the most familiar, and yet peculiar, features of the world. To explain consciousness satisfactorily remains one of the great philosophical challenges. There are several different definitions of what is meant by consciousness. Some philosophers argue that to be conscious is to be sentient: to be aware of the world, to be able to sense and feel, and to be able to respond to these sensations. Yet sentience is a very tricky issue; are ants or fish or trees sentient? Furthermore, it might be possible to have degrees of sentience, such as a tree being less sentient than a human, but would we then want to say that something is more or less conscious? It would appear that consciousness is 'all or nothing', that one either is or is not conscious. Another definition of consciousness is offered by Nagel, who argues that something is conscious if there is 'something it is like' to be that creature. In other words, something is conscious if it has a subjective experience of the world. Nagel uses the example of a bat as a conscious being with a unique way of experiencing the world. No being, except the bat itself, can understand how the bat experiences the world. Therefore consciousness is a subjective viewpoint on the world. A third definition of consciousness is the experience of mental states. Just what constitutes a mental state is another difficult philosophical question. However, states such as 'being hungry' or 'happiness' seem obvious examples. One could also include qualia, a term which refers to 'raw sensory experience' such as the redness of a rose, or the coldness of ice. To be conscious may be to experience qualia. Whatever definition one takes, it is clear that there will be great difficulty in deciding what is and is not conscious. Could a robot or zombie (if hypothetically existing) be conscious? Are animals or plants conscious? Is one conscious when asleep or in a coma? Such questions remain far from settled.

As well as defining consciousness, philosophers are also eager to explain it. To begin with, one may either be a dualist or monist. A dualist will argue that consciousness is a non-physical property. Famously, Descartes described consciousness as a non-physical substance, like a soul or spirit, which inhabits the body. There are less strong versions of dualism, which argue that consciousness cannot be reduced to a purely physical explanation. This is to say that a description of just the physical features of the brain, the body and the world will fail to account for every aspect of consciousness. Jackson's Knowledge Argument (1982, 1986) is a powerful attempt to secure this conclusion (see **qualia**). Monist theories of consciousness are most often physicalist and argue that, whatever consciousness is, it is entirely physical in nature. An extreme form of physicalism is Paul and Patricia Churchland's eliminativist materialism; they argue that talk of mental states is merely 'folk psychology', an outdated description of the mind which must be discarded. We should replace our notions of beliefs and emotions with neurophysiological descriptions of the mind. Thus, instead of saying 'I believe I am happy', we should say something like 'I am in brain state 142'. A less extreme, and more popular, version of physicalism is functionalism. Rather than trying to eliminate consciousness or conscious states, functionalism explains consciousness by its function (the role it plays) in the system we call consciousness.

See also: **artificial intelligence; belief; cognition; Descartes; dualism; eliminative materialism; embodiment; epiphenomenalism; folk psychology; functionalism; intentionality; mind, the; mind–body problem, the; phenomenology; physicalism; qualia**

Key questions: What things can possess consciousness? What makes something conscious? Is it possible to fully explain consciousness?

Further reading: Blackmore (2003); Block et al. (1997); Dennett (1986, 1987); Jackson (1982, 1986); Leopold (1998); Lycan (1995); Metzinger (1999); Nagel (1979)

Consequentialism

According to consequentialism, the rightness or wrongness of an act is judged solely in terms of its consequences. The classic example of consequentialism is utilitarianism, and the two terms are often used interchangeably. Classic utilitarians, such as Bentham and Mill, argued that the only morally relevant consequences

were those which affected a person's welfare (happiness). Non-utilitarian consequentialists may argue that an act must aim to promote justice or equality. Consequentialism can be contrasted with deontological moral theories, which argue
that the rightness of an act is intrinsic to it. For example, a consequentialist may
allow that lying can be the right act if it produces a greater overall amount of 'good'
(such as happiness or well-being). A deontologist, on the other hand, would argue
that lying is wrong in itself and therefore we can never tell a lie, regardless of the
effects of telling the truth.

There are many versions of consequentialism. Maximising consequentialism argues that an act is morally good or right if it produces the best consequences of all
available actions. Satisficing consequentialism argues that an act is morally good
or right if it has sufficiently good consequences. By this account many acts may be
allowable in a single situation, whereas maximising consequentialism would only
allow one. A common criticism of consequentialism is that in many situations it
is hard, or even impossible, to accurately predict the consequences of an action.
Furthermore it ignores people's intentions. One may accidentally produce good
consequences through an evil action, which would make the action a good one.
Deontologists argue that some actions are wrong in themselves, regardless of the
positive effects they may have. For example, consequentialists and deontologists
would tend to strongly disagree over whether it is right or wrong to kill a soldier
if it ends a war. Finally, there seems no room for giving special considerations to
our friends or family, for all people must be considered equally. For some, this is an
advantage rather than a disadvantage of consequentialism.

See also: **Bentham; deontology; egoism; happiness; good, the; impartiality; Mill;
morality; virtue ethics; Singer; supererogation; utilitarianism; Williams**

Key questions: Should the rightness of an act be judged purely in terms of its consequences? How can we work out what all the consequences of an act will be?

Further reading: Bentham (1789); Darwall (2003a); Mill (1861b); Scarre (1996); Scheffler
(1982)

Conservatism

Conservatism is a political philosophy that emphasises the importance of traditional values and argues for gradual rather than revolutionary or radical change.
The term 'conservative' arose following the French Revolution (1789–1799) and the
subsequent restoration of the French monarchy in 1815. It was used by John Croker
to describe the British Tory Party in 1830. In all cases, conservatism reflects the belief that government should maintain the *status quo* and seek to serve, rather than
change, society. Conservatism is inspired by a particular view of human nature as
imperfect and incapable of perfection. Traditional political and social institutions
are needed to curb the inherently selfish and violent nature of human beings. Con-
servatives highlight the importance of the family, traditional education and disci-
plinary methods of control both for passing on established norms and values, and
for maintaining social stability.

See also: **anarchism; contractarianism; communism; dialectical materialism; Marxism; political philosophy; socialism; utopianism**

Further reading: Honderich (1991); Kirk (1954); Layton-Henry (1982)

Constructionism (Constructivism)

To take a constructionist (also called constructivist) approach to some particular thing (an idea, a concept, an object, etc) is to argue that it is constructed or made rather than discovered. For example, the concept of football is a human construct; there did not exist something called 'football' until humans created it. One can take a constructionist stance towards a particular area of philosophy without committing oneself to an all-encompassing constructionism.

Moral constructionism is the view that moral properties (being 'good', 'bad', 'valued' and so on) are mind-dependent. Often these properties are generally agreed upon or are such that all rational people would agree with them (hence the idea of 'psychopaths' whose deviation from moral norms is explained in terms of mental disorder). This consensus prevents moral constructionism becoming pure subjectivism as it does not mean that something is right simply because I think it is right. Rather, it is right if we have agreed it is right or if it is rational to think it is right. Nonetheless, moral constructionism is committed to an anti-realist view of morality; moral facts and properties are dependent upon, and generated by, the mind. Scientific constructionism is the claim that scientific theories do not describe an objective theory-independent world. Instead, the scientific picture of the world is constructed out of existing theories. Constructionism is thus an anti-realist position for it denies the possibility of a neutral, objective account of the world. Two particularly influential constructivist theories can be found in van Fraassen's *The Scientific Image* (1980) and Kuhn's *The Structure of Scientific Revolutions* (1962). Both argue, albeit in different ways, that science cannot give us a literally true image or story of what the world is like.

Many social scientists (often called 'social constructionists' not 'social constructivists') have been influenced by constructionism, arguing that such things as gender, race, homosexuality/heterosexuality, rationality, emotions and mental illnesses are socially constructed. There are numerous justifications for this argument. Often cross-cultural and historical analyses are used to show how much the definitions of gender, sexuality or mental health have changed over time, suggesting that our notions of such phenomena are shifting and open to change rather than being fixed and static. Foucault's famous studies of sexuality and madness attempted to trace the history of these concepts to show both how they have changed and how these changes can be linked to social power relations, social control, knowledge and authority. In effect, he concluded, constructions of sexuality and madness manipulate the way people think, act and experience themselves and the world. Much feminist philosophy has been dedicated to revealing the way in which men have constructed the image of women in order to maintain superiority over them.

All forms of constructionism are strongly opposed to realism (the claim that there is a single, objective reality existing entirely independently of the mind) and essentialism (the claim that a thing must possess certain properties in order to be that thing). For example, a constructivist analysis of gender would deny that (a) there is a single, true and objective definition of what gender is; and that (b) there is a single set of characteristics, existing independently of the mind, which make a person a woman or man. This does not necessarily mean there are no women or men. Rather, what we define as being typical gender characteristics are socially constructed, and therefore open to change.

See also: anti-realism; Butler; concept; critical realism; cultural relativism; discourse; essentialism; feminism; Foucault; gender; kind, natural; moral subjectivism; performativity; race; realism; scientific realism; subjectivity

Key questions: To what extent is the world we experience constructed by human thought? If something is a social construction, how is it constructed and how can it be changed?

Further reading: Burr (1995); Butler (1990); Foucault (1961, 1978); Holstein and Miller (1993); Kuhn (1962); van Fraassen (1980)

Context

The idea of context plays an important role in many different philosophical areas. Morally speaking, it is often useful to acknowledge the effect of context on one's moral actions or judgement. Moral relativism asserts that what is right or wrong can vary across both time and culture. Furthermore, we might condone telling a lie in one context (such as avoiding hurting a friend's feelings) whilst condemning it in another (such as lying on our CV in order to get a job).

Context is also relevant to claims about knowledge and truth. Epistemological contextualism is the idea that knowledge and its justification vary from context to context. For instance, we may normally say we know what time it is simply by looking at our watch. However, if we have a very important meeting to go we may check the time on our watch against a friend's watch to make sure they are the same. Owing to the changed context, our justification for thinking we know the time has also changed. Postmodern philosophy also makes use of context to argue that truth, knowledge and meaning are relative to a specific time and place. Consequently, rather than searching for absolute truths, philosophy should seek to understand how a person's context leads them to believe what they do, and the effect this has on constructing their reality. The importance of context in relation to truth and meaning can be traced back to Wittgenstein's idea of language games, which demonstrated that meaning and truth cannot be generalised beyond a specific context.

See also: cultural relativism; Gadamer; hermeneutics; historicism; incommensurability; justification; language game; linguistic relativism; paradigm; postmodernism; relativism; truth

Further reading: Blaauw (2005); Streiffer (2003); Wittgenstein (1953)

Continental philosophy

Western philosophy is often divided into two separate spheres: analytic and continental philosophy. As the name suggests, continental philosophy covers the development of philosophical ideas in continental Europe, ideas that were seen as fundamentally different from those of Anglo-American analytic philosophy. Continental philosophy can be loosely characterised as existential and phenomenological in approach. It aims to explore and characterise such issues as one's subjective experience of the world, and how one should live in response to this. Key thinkers from this 'first generation' of continental philosophers include Husserl, Heidegger, Sartre, de Beauvoir and Merleau-Ponty. From the 1950s onwards, structuralism grew in popularity in continental Europe, particularly in France. This, in turn, developed into post-structural, postmodern and deconstructive modes of thinking, driven by theorists such as Foucault, Derrida, Barthes, Althusser, Lyotard, Kristeva and Deleuze.

Several features can be used to distinguish between continental and analytic philosophy. The methods of analytic philosophy tend to be scientific and logical in nature, whilst continental philosophers are concerned with exploring the experience of being and existence, which consequently affects the style of writing. Whereas analytic philosophers seek to explain their ideas clearly and succinctly using logical premises and conclusions, continental philosophers tend to be far more rhetorical, poetical and lengthy in style. Readers accustomed to one style often find it very difficult to switch to reading the other. Continental philosophers have been closely tied to political movements, particularly socialism and Marxism, as well as artistic and social developments. Finally, art is often seen as conveying philosophical ideas as successfully as any piece of academic text. The 'postmodern' movement, typically associated with continental philosophy, was as much an artistic and cultural phenomenon as it was a philosophical doctrine. Despite the common usage of the terms, many philosophers do not like the distinction and argue that it is an unjustifiable generalisation.

See also: **analytic philosophy; de Beauvoir; deconstruction; Deleuze; Derrida; existentialism; Foucault; Gadamer; Habermas; Heidegger; Merleau-Ponty; modernism; Nietzsche; phenomenology; postmodernism; post-structuralism; Sartre; Wittgenstein**

Further reading: Critchley and Schroeder (1998); Cutrofello (2005); Solomon and Sherman (2003)

Contractarianism

Contractarianism refers to political and moral theories which are based upon the idea of a social contract. Morally speaking, contractarianism is the theory that moral norms come into existence and are subsequently justified through a mutual agreement (a social contract). This contract is often assumed rather than made explicit, but in effect one treats others morally on the basis that one is treated morally in return. When someone breaks this moral contract, such as by attacking another individual, an individual or society is justified in punishing that person. There is a clear analogy with the legal system in that punishment of people is only justified when they break the law, which is in effect a legal contract between the state and its citizens.

Political contractarianism holds that a government derives legitimacy or what is allowable from the consent of those being governed. Individuals who accept being ruled thus enter into a contract with the government, which has the right to punish them when they break that contract. For instance, by choosing to live in the United Kingdom, a person enters into a contract with the UK government to obey UK law. In return, the UK government will keep its side of the bargain by looking after that individual's interests.

Contractarianism employs the idea of a 'state of nature', an imagined situation in which humans exist without any form of established society. The state of nature is portrayed as an undesirable situation characterised by competition between individuals for goods (of which there are not enough to go round) leading to confrontation and conflict. The way to resolve this situation is the installation of a government, the details of which must be agreed upon by those trapped in the state of nature. If no agreement is arrived at, then the individuals return to the state of nature. According to contractarianists, the individuals would agree to a fair and just government because that is the only situation to which all rational people would agree; there would be no agreement if one person benefitted more from the social contract than another.

Contractarianism has received a good deal of criticism for its use of the state of nature as a starting point, particularly regarding whether such a situation could ever exist and whether we could ever genuinely imagine being in that situation in the first place. Important historical social contract theorists include Thomas Hobbes, John Locke and Jean-Jacques Rousseau. Modern interest in contractarianism has largely been generated by the work of John Rawls.

See also: **anarchism; communism; conservatism; democracy; freedom; Hobbes; impartiality; Locke; morality; political philosophy; Rawls; Rousseau; state of nature**

Key questions: Should our moral and political obligations and values be understood in terms of a 'contract'? What should happen when this contract is broken? Is the concept of the 'state of nature' useful, or even meaningful?

Further reading: Chriss (2007); Hobbes (1651); Locke (1689a); Morris (1999); Rawls (1971); Rousseau (1762b)

Correspondence theory

According to correspondence theories of truth, something is true when it has a certain correspondence to, or 'match' with, reality. The idea that truth must be understood in terms of a correspondence between a proposition or belief and reality can be traced back to Plato and Aristotle. More recently, Russell and Wittgenstein have argued that a proposition is true when it corresponds to a fact about reality. Consider the proposition 'cats are animals'. According to their versions of the correspondence theory, this proposition is true if (a) some fact exists which demonstrates that cats are animals; and (b) the proposition 'cats are animals' correctly corresponds to this fact.

Correspondence theory is often seen as having an intuitive appeal, for it seems that truth, if it is anything, is determined by the nature of reality. However, major tasks to be faced by correspondence theorists include how to explain just what these 'facts' are, how propositions successfully correspond to them, and how we know when a proposition has successfully corresponded to a fact. Since the 18th century when Berkeley expressed his scepticism about our knowledge of a mind-dependent world, there has been a good deal of hostility towards the idea that our minds can have direct, objective access to the external world. It is argued that we cannot get outside of our minds to check whether our thoughts have correctly corresponded to reality. Consequently, the 'match' between thought and reality required by correspondence theory can never be established.

Whereas correspondence theories assume a realist conception of truth, coherence and pragmatic theories of truth argue that truth is dependent in some way upon the human mind. Many contemporary philosophers, motivated by a suspicion of realist theories of truth, have been sceptical towards correspondence theories of truth. However, Armstrong (1997) has defended a version of the correspondence theory according to which 'facts' (which he terms 'states of affairs') are what make things true.

See also: **Aquinas; Berkeley; certainty; coherence theory; deflationary theory of truth; facts; idealism; objectivism; Plato; realism; reality; Russell; truth; truthmaker; Wittgenstein**

Further reading: Armstrong (1973, 1997); Englebretsen (2006); Newman (2002); Russell (1912); Wittgenstein (1921)

Counterfactuals

See **conditionals**

Creationism

Creationism is the idea that the universe was created by a god, or a number of gods. Most cultures and religions throughout history have some form of creation story which explains how the universe was brought into existence. Common to all of them is the idea that the universe did not happen by chance or by natural means, but rather was created by the will of a god or set of gods. This gives meaning to life and the universe. If, however, the universe is simply a random construction, then there seems to be no inherent meaning to life. Nor, arguably, can there be any objective moral laws. Creationism also often asserts that a god can intervene with its creation at any point. In the West, creationism is challenged by the Big Bang theory, and there is much debate as to whether the two theories are compatible. Is it possible that God instigated the Big Bang in order to produce the universe? Creationism in the Christian sense is also challenged by Darwin's theory of evolution, which describes how the development of life can be explained through natural, rather than supernatural, processes. However, one still might argue that God created evolution to allow life to develop. If God created the universe, then it suggests God is transcendent (outside) rather than immanent (inside) of the universe, for in order to create something one must presumably be independent of that thing.

See also: **Darwinism; evil, the problem of; God; God, arguments for the existence of; religious belief**

Further reading: Eugenie (2005); Numbers (2006)

Critical realism

This term is a combination of 'transcendental realism' and 'critical naturalism'. Transcendental realism offers a view of science as 'a fallible social process' (Lawson, 1997: 26) rather than a rational, objective, deductive process. Critical naturalists apply scientific study to humans but the outcome is not so much prediction of what people will do as explanation of their actions. For critical realists such as Bhaskar the following apply: firstly, reality is not equivalent to what we know (the epistemic fallacy) and the social world is both structured by humans and structuring of them; secondly, scientific knowledge is a social production and can be wrong; thirdly, rational judgements can be made about different theories although those judgements will knowingly be dependent on, and therefore restricted by, existing knowledge. For example, in relation to the desire to have children, a critical realist would be interested in explaining the phenomenon in terms of both the meaning it has for individuals, for example femininity or status, and the social structures that influence the desire for children, such as media portrayals of the joys of parenthood. The critical realist would also accept that the explanation might not be true or could vary across time and cultures. The method applied is therefore one of 'analytical dualism' (Archer, 1995), exploring both agency (what people choose to do) and structure (what encourages people to make particular choices) as distinct but interconnected elements.

See also: **agency; hypothetic-deductive method; Popper; realism; naturalism; ontology; science, philosophy of; scientific method**

Further reading: Archer (1995, 2000); Archer et al. (1998); Bhaskar (1997); Collier (1994)

Cultural relativism

An important political and moral idea, cultural relativists argue that standards of right and wrong are relative to a particular time and place. Cultural relativism is thus strongly opposed to any form of moral objectivism, the idea that there is a universal moral standard. Cultural relativism is adopted by anthropologists when studying other cultures, where it is important not to judge or explain the actions and beliefs of another society in our own terms. A common argument for relativism is that if there were universal moral truths or laws, then there would be close agreement between cultures over what is right and wrong. However, because cultures apparently differ radically over what is and is not morally good, we should accept relativism. One response to this argument is that, although morals do differ culturally, the ultimate principles are the same but have simply been applied differently. For instance, in many cannibalistic tribes only fallen heroes or warriors may be eaten as a mark of respect. Here the ultimate principle is respect for persons, which is shared by Western cultures albeit expressed differently. The moral principle of respect is the same in each case. Similarly, the Inuit practice of sending the elderly out into the wilderness, in effect killing them because they cannot survive, has been highlighted as a strong moral difference between Western and Inuit societies. However, in such a harsh climate with limited resources, old people who can no longer contribute to Inuit society cannot be supported. Therefore they choose to walk into the wilderness to die. Here the ultimate principle is that one must work for the good of society rather than one's individual interests. Although cultural circumstances result in the same moral principle being expressed differently by different societies, this does not necessarily mean that they have radically different moral values.

A major appeal of cultural relativism is its respect for and tolerance of different people and cultures. In the multicultural societies of today, this is seen as very important. One need not be a cultural relativist in order to advocate tolerance, however being tolerant is necessary if one is a cultural relativist. Yet philosophers have pointed out that to demand respect for all cultures seems to be a universal principle which all people must obey. If so, then cultural relativism appears to contradict itself. If someone refuses to respect differences, must the cultural relativist therefore respect that person's decision? Many philosophers also do not want to give up the right to criticise both their own culture and other cultures. For instance, inflicting unnecessary suffering might be seen as always wrong and any culture which allows this to happen (such as stoning people to death) must be challenged. Importantly, one need not challenge the society as a whole in questioning one specific practice. Finally, how could we ever make moral decisions if we genuinely believed that one action was ultimately no better or worse than another? We seem to select our moral principles based on a conviction that they are better than other principles. How could we weigh up different options without some basic moral standard that goes beyond our cultural upbringing?

See also: **constructionism; context; difference; good, the; Hare; historicism; moral intuitionism; morality; moral objectivism; moral subjectivism; objectivism; prescriptivism; relativism; social constructivism; tolerance; Williams**

Key questions: To what extent are moral, political and social values determined by one's culture? Is it possible to criticise another culture, and if so, how?

Further reading: Cook (1999); Herskovits (1972); Williams (1972)

C

Dao

See *tao*

Daoism

See **Taoism**

Darwinism

Darwin's theory of evolution by natural selection (1859) has a number of philosophical implications. The theory that all species have developed as a result of small differences in what is now referred to as genetic material reduces or removes the need for supernatural explanations of the existence of animals (including humans), and offers an explanation for human characteristics in terms of their survival advantage. The publication of Darwin's theory thus marked a radical shift in Western philosophy's understanding of humans and their place in the universe. It should be noted, however, that Darwin's idea was not entirely original. In the 8th century, an Islamist philosopher called al-Jahiz (c. 776–869) had reflected on the effect of the environment on animals and their survival, discussing the 'struggle for existence' and the ability of the better adapted animals to survive and reproduce.

Darwinism is a naturalist explanation for human existence and, in the forms of social Darwinism and evolutionary psychology, human society and behaviour. In accepting that humans have evolved from what are classed as other species, Darwinism is non-essentialist, meaning that humans do not possess any particular traits such as compassion or courage that mark them out from other living things. It could be seen as challenging the humanist belief that humans possess a special place within the world, for Darwinism puts us on a 'level' with other animals. The theory can also be seen as fitting with a realist rather than an extreme idealist perspective of the world because, if the brain has evolved to become conscious, then there must be a world prior to our awareness of it (that is, prior to that point when consciousness developed). Debate continues as to whether Darwinism is compatible with religious beliefs and whether evolutionary principles undermine morality if competition and survival of the fittest (Spencer, 1864) are 'natural'. Pragmatists, such as Dewey, James and Rorty, have been heavily influenced by the idea that humans, consciousness and knowledge must be understood within the context of practical engagement with and development within an environment.

See also: **creationism; Dewey; God, arguments for the existence of; humanism; idealism; James; kind, natural; naturalism; pragmatism; reductionism; Rorty; social constructivism**

Further reading: Darwin (1859); Gould (2002); Ridley (1997); Ruse (2006); Spencer (1864)

Dasein

Dasein was used by Martin Heidegger (1927) to refer to a specific conception of 'being' (existing). The term in German means 'life' or 'existence', but for Heidegger Dasein is a special type of being which is possessed by those things for which being (existing) is an issue. We, as beings who have Dasein, are aware of our own being. Furthermore, it is what allows there to be a world for beings such as ourselves. It is a pre-subjective engagement in the world – how we find ourselves in the world (what Heidegger calls 'thrownness') – and the condition for there being a world in the first place. This is what separates Dasein from the everyday being of stones, beds, books, and so on. There is no world for a stone; its own existence is not an issue for it. Part of Heidegger's aim in introducing Dasein was to move away from the Cartesian picture of people as 'things' composed of material and possibly immaterial 'stuff', existing within a world of other 'things'.

The issue is not how to make sense of the objects in the world and our place in it. Rather, we must ask the more fundamental question of how we come to have a 'world' in the first place. This leads us to the concept of Dasein. Heidegger believed that in order to give an account of Dasein we must perform a 'fundamental ontology' which will reveal the structure of Dasein. This is achieved by the experience of a certain state of mind or 'perspective' on the world, which Heidegger called 'angst' or 'anxiety'. In such a state our familiarity with the world is stripped away and we are brought face-to-face with our own Dasein. This experience reveals that we are fundamentally free, devoid of any intrinsic meaning or purpose, and exist as pure possibility. However, whilst immersed in 'the crowd', following what we are taught to do and believe, we are unaware of our Dasein and exist simply as a member of the herd rather than an authentic, free being.

See also: **angst; authenticity; being; existentialism; freedom; Heidegger; nihilism; nothingness**

Further reading: Cooper (1996a); Dreyfus (1991); Heidegger (1927); Mulhall (2005)

Davidson, Donald (1913–2003)

An influential American philosopher, Davidson is particularly well-known for his work on the philosophy of mind. Davidson defended what he called the 'anomalism of the mental' (2001), the claim that mental events cannot be explained by physical laws alone. In other words, we cannot explain desires, beliefs and intentions, for example, just through reference to the physical world (such as neurons firing, or the sun shining). Nor can we explain physical events solely through reference to the mental. For instance, there is no strict law linking my desire to watch TV and the TV being switched on. However, Davidson rejected dualistic accounts of the mind, and so his position is one of non-reductive physicalism. He does not think that the mind is something separate from the physical world. Nonetheless, he denies that we can explain the mind purely in terms of physical laws operating on the world. His solution is to describe a person as a rational being and therefore their mind (mental states) is subject to, and explainable using, the rules of logic and reason.

See also: **belief; dualism; logic; mind, the; monism; physicalism; rationalism; semantic holism**

Further reading: Davidson (2001, 2005); Hahn (1999); Joseph (2004)

D

Death

The concept of death, although not often discussed, raises many important philosophical issues. A fundamental question concerns what it means to die. According to many religions, death means the separation of the soul from the body. In this sense we do not cease to exist, but rather enter a new state of existence, such as in a heaven. Atheists, on the other hand, argue that this life is the only one we have and upon dying we cease to exist altogether. One need not believe in a soul or spirit to argue that we have more than one life. Buddhists deny that there is any such thing as a spirit, yet still believe in rebirth. Furthermore, given that it takes seven years for all the cells in our body to have been replaced by new ones, it could be argued that, if we are nothing more than physical beings, then we have died and been reborn every seven years. A further issue is whether someone can be harmed after their death. We often talk of having respect for the dead, shown by elaborate funerals and well-kept graveyards, yet can something which no longer exists be disrespected? Some philosophers argue that one carries on existing in the memories of others, and so to harm the deceased is to harm those who carry that memory. Others may simply say that it is wrong to harm the dead because it upsets the living and in this sense it is only indirectly wrong to disrespect the dead.

Another debate over death is whether it is intrinsically wrong. Thomas Nagel (1979) claimed that death is always an evil, since there is always the possibility of experiencing happiness and doing some good whilst alive. Others might reject this view, arguing that when we reach old age life becomes uncomfortable and even painful. Furthermore, we may feel we have achieved all we want in life and thus embrace death. This raises the additional question of whether we should have the right to end our lives, and at what point that should be allowable. Sartre, the classic existentialist, described death as the one certainty in life and that which can motivate us to take full responsibility for our lives. The major problem for all debates surrounding death is that, necessarily, none of us has experienced it. Therefore we have no idea what it is actually like to die. By the time we have discovered this, it is quite likely to be too late.

See also: **Buddhism; dualism; existence; 'I'; life; physicalism; unexplainable, the**

Key questions: Is death the end of our life? Is death always an evil? Does each of us have the right to decide when we die?

Further reading: Fischer (1993); Nagel (1979); Scarre (2007); Shneidman (1976)

D

de Beauvoir, Simone (1908–1986)

Simone de Beauvoir is arguably the most important and influential thinker within feminist theory as well as a celebrated novelist. Her famous insight that 'one is not born, but rather becomes a woman' (1949: 249) has inspired feminists to explore the ways in which gender is an enforced social construct. According to de Beauvoir, any society's idea of what a woman is, and should be, is not a product of biology or psychology but a historically determined construction. This laid the way for feminists to challenge the supposedly inevitable state of woman as inferior and subordinate to men. De Beauvoir insisted that woman has been cast as man's 'Other', forever living in his shadow, defined as a 'lack' or 'absence', and treated as a mere object rather than a subject. In such a state, women can never realise their potential as individual, free beings. This provides a powerful critique of previous existentialist notions of freedom (for example, Sartre, 1943), which had ignored the effects that a society, built upon gender division, has on one's ability to choose and act. De Beauvoir also explored the ethics of existentialism, in particular the nature of individual responsibility and our relations to others (1944, 1947). She believed that through ethical action we can forge bonds with other people and encourage each other to realise our respective freedom. Her view on relationships is far more positive and ethically-orientated than the negative and conflictual description offered by Sartre, to whom she was married. De Beauvoir's writings, which show a consistent emphasis on freedom, oppression and responsibility, were strongly influenced by the social and political events of her time, particularly the Second World War.

See also: **Butler; constructionism; equality; existentialism; feminism; freedom; gender; negation; Sartre**

Further reading: de Beauvoir (1944, 1947, 1949); Moi (1990); Simons (1995)

Deconstruction

Deconstruction is a term used in post-structural and postmodern philosophy. It is particularly associated with the work of Jacques Derrida. However, Derrida always refused to be labelled a 'deconstructionist' and denied one could give any clear definition of deconstruction. Indeed, one could see deconstruction as, in part, the rejection of authoritative definitions and unambiguous meanings. It is neither a form of critique, nor a general theory, nor a particular method. It is a suspicion of the concept of 'is': a refusal of authority and the determining power of stating that something 'is' something. As Derrida says, deconstruction consists of 'deconstructing, dislocating, displacing, disarticulating, disjoining, putting "out of joint" the authority of the "is"' (1995: 25). It would be a mistake, therefore, to think that we could give an account of what deconstruction definitively is or is not. One reason for this is Derrida's belief that meaning is constantly deferred. Words depend upon other words for their meaning and only have meaning by being situated within an endless chain of 'substitutions' (related words). So deconstruction gets its meaning from, and can be substituted for, words such as 'difference'. To grasp this, we could think of referring to a dictionary for a definition of 'deconstruction'. However, in order to understand the word 'deconstruction' we would have to understand all the words used in the definition, which would require us to look up these words (which, in turn, would require further words to be looked up).

To realise this is to realise that all things are already in 'deconstruction'. Therefore, it is not simply a way of reading texts or challenging accepted ideas. Deconstruction is more like an 'event' or a 'happening' that is already going on. It is not a philosophical tool that we can pick up and apply to a text, for it is not something 'outside' of the text. Deconstruction is thus an awareness of the instability of binary oppositions, such as 'inside/outside', 'true/false' or 'male/female'. Such binary oppositions are 'violent' in that one 'rules' the other. They form a hierarchy in which one (inside, truth, male) defines the other as inferior, a lack, an 'absence'. To deconstruct 'truth' or 'gender' is to see that it is already in deconstruction; it is to see the cracks in the term, to see that it is not a 'given' out there in the world but rather it

D

is a construct that cannot sustain itself. In a sense, deconstruction amplifies the internal tensions within oppositions. It 'encourages' them to break them apart, if only by recognising their inherent instability. Deconstruction is a dismantling of texts and truths. It does not aim to destroy theories or texts; the purpose is to re-read them and, in doing so, change the interpretations of their meanings. It highlights the contradictions, hidden assumptions and ambiguities within a text. This 'reading between the lines' and 'against the grain' generates a plurality of meanings or, as noted above, reveals the endless chain of meanings within which texts are situated. Consequently there is always a gap between what the author of a text intended and the actual meanings of the text. The text is 'beyond' the author's intentions. Thus we should not think that we have ever discovered the 'fact of the matter' within a text. In shaking the foundations upon which traditional ideas of truth have been based, deconstruction is akin to an earthquake amplifying the cracks within all philosophical theory (including deconstruction itself).

See also: **anti-realism; Deleuze; Derrida; Descartes; Foucault; hermeneutics; post-modernism; post-structuralism; Rorty**

Further reading: Derrida (1967a, 1967b, 1972a, 1972b); Royle (2000); Sallis (1987)

Deduction

Deduction is a form of argument in which one is logically compelled to accept the conclusion if one accepts each premise. A deductive argument is valid when it conforms to the rules of deduction. A basic deductive argument can be expressed as follows:

All As are B
C is an A
Therefore C is a B

Replacing the A, B and C with an example, we can produce the following:

All humans are mortal
Grant is a human
Therefore Grant is mortal

The conclusion, that Grant is mortal, follows logically from the two premises. However, a deductive argument might be valid without being true. For instance:

All fruit can fly
A banana is a fruit
Therefore a banana can fly

Whilst the conclusion does follow from the premises, it is not true. This is because one of the premises is false. Therefore, a deductive argument can be valid but not true, or it can be valid and true. If a deductive argument is both valid and true then it is sound. It can only be sound if *every* premise and the conclusion are true. It is possible that the conclusion of an argument is true, even if its premises are false. For example:

All animals have four legs
A pig is an animal
Therefore a pig has four legs

D

The conclusion is true, but the argument is not sound because the first premise is false (spiders have eight legs). But if every premise of a deductive argument is true, then the conclusion must be true. This is because the conclusion does not go beyond the premises. It only states information which could be worked out from the premises. Deduction can be contrasted with induction – a logical argument in which the conclusion goes beyond the premises, often by making generalisations which seem likely to be true based on the premises. This use of generalisations can make inductive conclusions false even if the premises are true.

See also: **fallacy; induction; logic; Popper; scientific method; soundness; validity**
Further reading: Bonevac (1987); Johnson-Laird and Byrne (1991)

Definite descriptions

A definite description is a phrase in the form 'the so-and-so' (such as 'the Queen of England' or 'the bed'). Despite appearing uninteresting, definite descriptions have been subject to a fierce debate over the last 100 years, with strong disagreement over the correct way of analysing them. The classic analysis of definite descriptions is Bertrand Russell's (1903, 1905). Russell was concerned with how some sentences containing definite descriptions could be true, particularly those referring to non-existent objects. How can I say 'unicorns are beautiful' if there is no such thing as a unicorn? Meinong (1904) suggested that things such as unicorns and square circles have a kind of logical being, an existence which is not as full-blooded as the existence of this book or a horse. Russell found this ridiculous and an offence to commonsense. His solution was to provide an analysis of definite descriptions which allowed them to be either true or false without making reference to an existing or non-existing object, thus eliminating the problem. Russell used the sentence 'The present King of France is bald' for his analysis, as there is no present King of France. Russell reveals that what is actually meant by the sentence is:

1. There is at least one King of France
2. There is at most one king of France
3. Everything that is the King of France is bald

Translating this into logical form we get:

1. There is at least one X
2. There is at most one X
3. Everything that is X is B

Nowhere within any of the three sentences is there a referring statement, rather each is a claim about something existing (it is an existential claim). One can see that the 'present King of France is bald' is false because of statement 1, for there is no present King of France.

Despite the popularity of Russell's analysis, Strawson wrote a highly critical essay (1950) in which he claimed that sentences such as 'The present King of France' are neither true nor false. Instead they are incomplete because the speaker has failed to refer to anything. More problematic is Strawson's complaint that Russell fails to take context into account. Applying Russell's analysis to the sentence 'This chair is brown' would generate:

1. There is at least one chair
2. There is at most one chair
3. Everything that is the chair is brown

However this suggests that there is only one chair in the whole universe. When using definite descriptions there is always an understanding between speakers about the context in which the sentence is made. Despite Russell's failure to recognise this context, attempts have been made to adapt his theory accordingly (see Lycan, 2000) and Russell's model remains the dominant way of analysing definite descriptions.

See also: **being; Frege; logic, philosophical; reference; Russell; truth**

Further reading: Lycan (2000); Meinong (1904); Russell (1903, 1905); Strawson (1950)

Deflationary theory of truth

The deflationary theory of truth, also known as the redundancy theory, argues that the concept of truth is dispensable. The idea is that we add nothing to certain propositions by ascribing the property of truth to them (Frege, 1918; Ramsey, 1927). For instance, the sentence 'I see that it is raining' is equivalent to 'it is true that I see that it is raining'. Adding 'it is true' simply provides emphasis rather than changing the meaning of the sentence. From this it can be concluded that truth and falsity are not 'genuine' concepts (Ayer, 1935). The major attraction of the deflationary theory is that it solves puzzles about the metaphysical nature of truth by simply dissolving the problem. Philosophers have frequently stated that truth should be understood as a correspondence with reality or the coherence between a set of propositions. The issue has then been how to understand this correspondence or coherence. According to the deflationary theory, we are mistaken if we view truth as something which has a nature that we can explore and understand. The statement 'birds can fly' is true simply if it is the case that birds can fly. We need not, and indeed cannot, appeal to such notions as correspondence or coherence to make sense of such statements.

See also: **coherence theory; correspondence theory; pragmatism; reality; truth**

Further reading: Armour-Garb and Beall (2005); Ayer (1935); Frege (1918); Ramsey (1927); Soames (1999)

Deleuze, Gilles (1925–1995)

Deleuze is an important thinker within modern continental philosophy. Many of his early works were studies of historical philosophers, including Hume, Spinoza, Kant and Leibniz. Rather than try to produce the 'established' reading of these philosophers, Deleuze created new and alternative interpretations. He was particularly interested in their 'radical' doctrines, such as Hume's empiricism and Spinoza's ontology. Inspired by Spinoza's monist idea that the world is ultimately a single substance, Deleuze writes of a 'plane of immanence' in which everything exists at the same (ontological) level. This idea represents, at least in part, a movement away from 'transcendence', the idea that certain things are 'above' or 'beyond' us. These things would include God or Plato's realm of the forms. We, as subjects, are not somehow 'outside' of the world. Rather, we are embedded within it (situated)

D

and therefore the difference between us and the world is not a genuine, metaphysical difference.

Deleuze's treatment of these thinkers expresses his belief that philosophers are 'creators' (constructionists) and that an examination of an idea or philosopher should (indeed, will always) generate new ideas and concepts. We should not understand thought in relation to grasping truth. Rather, 'truth' is created by thought. Deleuze stressed the importance of difference over identity and argued that reality is dynamic, meaning it is characterised by 'becoming' rather than 'being'. There are links here with vitalism and Deleuze was certainly influenced by Bergson. Like postmodernists such as Foucault and Lyotard, Deleuze is suspicious of 'totalising' theories which claim to capture the 'fact of the matter' and represent a comprehensive account of the object of their analysis. We cannot discover universal or eternal truths, rather we must investigate the conditions under which knowledge is produced and justified. Much of Deleuze's best-known and most highly celebrated work was written in collaboration with Félix Guattari, notably *Anti-Oedipus* (1972) and *A Thousand Plateaus* (1980).

See also: **concept; constructionism; deconstruction; discourse; postmodernism; post-structuralism; vitalism**

Further reading: Colebrook (2006); Deleuze (1953, 1968); Deleuze and Guattari (1972, 1980); Due (2007); Patton (1996)

Democracy

From the Greek *demos* (people) and *kratos* (rule, strength), democracy typically refers to a form of government in which power is indirectly held by the people through an open and fair electoral system. Within this system each individual has an equal vote. More generally it refers to any decision made by a group of individuals with equal decision-making power. It is to be contrasted with anarchy, fascism, communism and absolute monarchies. Advocates of democracy argue that it is necessary because it promotes equality and liberty by ensuring that people are free from control by any one group or person (as all have an equal say in decision-making). Criticisms of democracy include the claim that, because every person has an equal vote, many uninformed people will have an influence on decisions they may know little about. This could result in decisions being taken which, although chosen by the people, are not actually in their best interests simply because the people have been misinformed or chose to vote randomly. Plato (c. 360 BCE) offered an objection along these lines, adding that success will go to people who are adept at winning elections, rather than governing well. Furthermore, individual rights can be over-ridden if the majority so chooses and the minority could end up being oppressed by the majority who may not care for the minority's welfare.

See also: **anarchism; communism; contractarianism; equality; liberalism; liberty; nationalism; Nozick; Rawls; tolerance; utopianism**

Key question: Does democracy inevitably lead to the best possible society? What difficulties might arise from non-democratic decision-making?

Further reading: Blaug and Schwarzmantel (2001); Crick (2002); Dahl (2000); Mill (1861a); Plato (c. 360 BCE)

Deontology

Deontology refers to any moral theory which holds that certain acts are morally right or wrong in themselves, regardless of the consequences they produce. Deontological moral theories therefore demand strict adherence to certain moral laws, which cannot be broken under any circumstance. Deontology is thus strongly opposed to consequentialism, the claim that acts are morally justified based on their positive consequences. The best-known and most influential deontologist is Immanuel Kant. Kant believed that humans, because they are moral beings, are elevated above mere animals, and the reason they are able to be moral is that they are rational. Kant spoke of humans' duty to obey the moral law, for they are rationally bound to do so. This moral law is Kant's categorical imperative for which he offered two different formulations, the best-known being: 'act only in accordance with that maxim through which you can at the same time will that it become a universal law' (1785, 4: 421). This is a sort of calculation which we must perform in order to establish whether our act is morally acceptable or not. The categorical imperative asks us to work out what principle we are acting on (such as 'do not lie'), then to see what would happen if all humans were to act on this principle. The reason we must universalise our principles is that all humans are rational, and therefore they must act on the same rational principles. Let us assume that someone decides it is acceptable to lie in order to achieve their goals. If everyone adopted this principle, then the very concept of lying would be undermined. This is because a lie is only successful if other people assume one is telling the truth. However, if everyone adopts the principle 'it is acceptable to lie' then there is no assumption that other people are telling the truth, thereby preventing the possibility of the concept of 'lying' ever having meaning. It implies a situation in which (a) there is no assumption of truth-telling and (b) an assumption of truth-telling is required. Therefore, the principle 'it is acceptable to lie' produces a self-contradiction and is thus irrational.

For many people deontological theories are attractive because they allow us to formulate universal moral laws, thus avoiding the problems of moral relativism (which implies we cannot make moral judgements about another group/culture/society). Furthermore, unlike consequentialist ethics, deontological ethics can allow us to give special consideration to our friends, family and own goals (provided principles are formulated in such a way that they pass the test of the categorical imperative). However, many philosophers dislike the claim that moral laws cannot be broken. The following famous example offered by Kant provides an interesting means of deciding our feelings towards deontology. Imagine a friend runs up to you and asks for somewhere to hide as he is being pursued by a murderer. After your friend has gone to hide, a man carrying an axe comes up and asks you where your friend is. According to Kant we cannot lie, and so we must tell him where our friend is hidden. However, consequentialists would claim that better consequences would be brought about if we lied, for it would be likely to save our friend's life. One defence of deontology would be to say to the murderer, 'I do not want to tell you the whereabouts of my friend', because we can will such action to be universally adopted. However, it may well be preferable to direct the murderer in the wrong direction as it would save putting our own life in danger. Our personal responses

D

to this example will give a good indication of whether we favour deontological or consequentialist theories.

See also: **categorical imperative; consequentialism; descriptivism; duty; egoism; good, the; impartiality; Kant; morality; moral objectivism; moral subjectivism; prescriptivism; universability; virtue ethics; Williams**

Key questions: Are certain actions always right or wrong, regardless of their consequences? How can we work out what those actions are? Is there, and should there be, a role within deontological theories for personal feelings?

Further reading: Darwall (2003b); Hill (2009); Kant (1785); Lippert-Rasmussen (2005)

Derrida, Jacques (1930–2004)

Best known for his concept of 'deconstruction', Jacques Derrida is associated with postmodern and post-structural philosophy even though he expressed regret at being labelled with a particular theory or concept (including, or even especially, deconstruction). Derrida's writings are often notoriously difficult to understand and opponents have accused him of being too obscure, or even nonsensical. However, others have heralded Derrida as one of the most brilliant thinkers of modern times.

Derrida argues that Western philosophy has been obsessed with searching for the truth as a 'presence', a tangible and graspable 'thing'. Following Heidegger, Derrida argues that we must consider not what 'is' or 'appears' to us, but the conditions under which something (an object, a truth, an experience) appears. Traditional philosophy has privileged or favoured 'speech' over 'writing', a feature which Derrida calls 'logocentrism'. Speech has been seen as representing pure meaning by symbolising our mental experiences whereas written language is a collection of symbols representing the spoken word. Consequently, writing consists of symbols of already-given symbols (words). Therefore, writing is at a greater distance from our thoughts and so less 'pure'. Derrida wants to dissolve this speech–writing opposition, which exists as a hierarchy favouring speech. He argues against logocentric metaphysics in which 'being' (individual subjectivity/consciousness) is equivalent to presence (pure, given, the 'truth') because it is represented in speech.

For Derrida, there is no meaning outside the text (language/the symbol). We are situated within a network of texts that generate our understanding of ourselves and the world. Texts, and thus meanings and truths, are always incomplete and beyond the intentions of the author because a word's meaning is always dependent upon other words, creating an unending chain of 'deferred' meaning. Derrida uses the term 'différance' to represent this idea of constant deferral, because words can only be defined through the ways they differ from one another. Consequently, one never arrives at 'the' meaning, a final point of absolute knowing. Instead, an author can always be understood as saying 'more, less, or something other than what he [or she] *would mean*' (1967a: 158). Derrida 'pulls apart', or 'opens up', texts by reading/revealing their inconsistencies, ambiguities and multiple meanings, moving the focus from discovering the 'fact of the matter' to appreciating the context of interpretation and the plurality of meanings this can generate.

See also: **constructionism; context; continental philosophy; deconstruction; Deleuze; difference; discourse; Foucault; hermeneutics; postmodernism; post-structuralism**
Further reading: Derrida (1967a, 1967b, 1972a, 1972b); Norris (1987); Royle (2003)

D

Descartes, René (1596–1650)

Descartes' writings reflect the times of change and resistance in which he lived, including reforms to Catholicism and Galileo's assertion that the earth revolved round the sun rather than vice versa. Descartes pondered how to justify the objectivity of the sciences and how to overcome extreme scepticism, such as idealism. In particular, Descartes sought to discover foundations upon which all knowledge can be justified. In his *Meditations* (1641) he uses the method of doubt in order to attain necessary truths by discovering what, if anything, he *cannot* doubt. Although he can doubt the existence of the world and even his own body, he cannot doubt that he is thinking and therefore he must necessarily exist as a thinking being. This is his *cogito ergo sum* argument – I think therefore I am. An important feature of Descartes' argument is the separation of the mind from the body, which places him in the dualist school.

Descartes also claims to prove the existence of God, for within his thinking self he discovers the idea of a perfect being, which can only have been created by a perfect being. Since we are not perfect beings, the idea must have been given to us by God (see **ontological argument**). Because God is perfect he cannot be a deceiving being and therefore all Descartes' doubts about the existence of the world can be rejected. Many have detected circularity in Descartes' work. The trustworthiness of his reason is established by his *cogito* argument and the argument for the existence of God. However, both these arguments seem to depend on reason being trustworthy. Despite numerous criticisms of Descartes, his philosophy has had a great influence on Western philosophy. In particular, his introspective analysis of the mind and its contents has formed the major historical understanding of consciousness. The history of phenomenology and much contemporary work in the philosophy of mind can be seen as addressing problems which have arisen from this element of Descartes' work.

See also: **body, the; brain-in-a-vat; certainty; consciousness; doubt; dualism; enlightenment; foundationalism; God, arguments for the existence of; mind–body problem, the; phenomenology; private language argument; rationalism; scepticism;**

Further reading: Cottingham (1986, 1992); Descartes (1637, 1641); Kenny (1986)

Descriptivism (Cognitivism)

Descriptivism, also referred to as cognitivism, is the view that moral statements describe or represent moral reality. This means that a moral judgement, such as 'stealing is wrong', expresses a moral fact and therefore moral utterances can be true or false. Descriptivist theories are thus realist about moral values, for they see them as corresponding to mind-independent features of the world. For some philosophers, descriptivism captures an important feature of morality. When we disagree with someone over their moral views, we are expressing the belief that they are genuinely mistaken (factually wrong). However, many modern moral theories, such as prescriptivism and emotivism, are non-descriptivist (non-cognitivist) and therefore deny that morality has any truth content. Whilst we may disagree with someone over a moral value, neither of us can be said to be 'true' or 'false' in our beliefs. Non-descriptivists often refer to the 'sincerity' and the 'consistency' of a person's moral beliefs, rather than their truth value. Therefore, rather than criticising

D

someone's beliefs for being 'false', we might argue that they do not always adhere to them or that they do not genuinely believe their moral views are justified.

See also: **consequentialism; cultural relativism; deontology; egoism; emotivism; fact/value problem; facts; good, the; Hare; Moore; moral intuitionism; morality; moral objectivism; moral subjectivism; prescriptivism; realism**

Further reading: Hare (1963a); Singer (1991); Timmons (1999)

Determinism

According to determinist principles, each thought or action is preceded by another according to a pattern that is set out by natural laws. However, this presupposes that such laws exist and that, if they do, they can be discovered through empirical means, for example introspection or scientific experiments. Science has itself challenged determinism in the form of chaos theory, although apparently random occurrences can show patterns over time or on a particular scale.

Hard determinists, such as Skinner (1971), suggest that free will is an illusion resulting from a lack of awareness or knowledge of what has caused a particular choice or action. This could imply that someone is not responsible for what they do, demonstrated by the legal plea of diminished responsibility. On the other hand, soft determinists or compatibilists (such as William James) argue that people have freedom to choose between actions and are therefore responsible to some extent for what they do. Plato, for example, believed people would make good choices providing they had sufficient knowledge, without which they were slaves to evil influences; Hobbes distinguished between a voluntary (determined) and a spontaneous (free) action. For his part, Locke proposed that we can make free choices but that depends on having the potential to do as we choose. To illustrate the difference he used the example of a man who opts to stay in a room although, unknown to him, the door was locked while he slept and therefore he did not freely choose to stay in the room. Hume supported the idea of some determinism without which events would be left to chance, although he could not resolve the dilemma of a 'good' God that determines morality as well as sin; Mill also saw determinism and freedom as compatible, suggesting that causation is confused with being made to do something, an example being the difference between giving someone money and handing over money to a robber with a gun.

In Eastern philosophy, determinism can be seen in the Hindu and Buddhist teachings of *karma* – the idea that what happens to us now is determined by actions performed in the past, either in this life or in previous lives. Furthermore, what we do in this life affects our future. However, those actions are chosen by us and thus we are responsible for our destiny. Existentialists are critical of all forms of determinism, arguing that they serve only to deny the absolute freedom and responsibility each of us possesses.

See also: **agency; authenticity; existentialism; freedom; free will;** *karma;* **liberty; unconscious, the**

Key questions: To what extent are our actions determined by things beyond our control? What consequences does this have for the idea of moral and legal responsibility?

Further reading: Billington (1997); Dilman (1999); James (1890); Rose (1997); Skinner (1971)

Dewey, John (1859–1952)

An American philosopher who wrote predominantly on epistemology (the study of knowledge), Dewey sought to defend pragmatism, which analyses truth and knowledge in terms of a person's practical engagement with their environment. He was heavily influenced by Darwin and William James. Dewey believed that previous theories, whether rationalist or empiricist, had unjustifiably divided the realm of thought (the mind) from the world. Instead, he argued for a naturalistic philosophy in which the mind is shaped by its interaction with the environment and in turn reshapes its environment. Understanding arises through an organism's relationship with its environment, and so the mind cannot be described as passively examining the world. This pragmatic approach sees knowledge as a product of an organism's adaptation to, and interaction with, its environment. Echoes of Dewey's ideas can be found in Quine's naturalistic philosophy and Richard Rorty's pragmatism.

Dewey is also regarded as one of the key educational theorists of the 20th century. He argued that social progress is dependent upon schooling. Education should promote democracy by producing children capable of engaging in the democratic system, and this would be achieved by supporting children's interests, enhancing their experiences, encouraging a scientific mindset and instilling a sense of respect for humanity. In effect, a school should aim to replicate the form of democratic life desired within wider society.

See also: **Darwinism; democracy; instrumentalism; James; mind, the; naturalism; pragmatism; Quine; Rorty**

Further reading: Alexander (1987); Dewey (1903, 1916, 1925); Tiles (1988)

Dialectic

In Greek philosophy, dialectic was a method of argument in which two people with opposing views try to refute the other's position. The best-known Greek proponent or supporter of the method is Plato, who used the dialectic method throughout his works. The basic structure consists of a thesis (a proposition, such as God exists) and an antithesis (God does not exist), with either one becoming the accepted position or a new position being formed which is a synthesis of the two (God may or may not exist).

The dialectic model was radically reworked by Hegel. Hegel believed that truth was not static, but rather changes and develops throughout history. It grows and progresses, mirroring the growth and progression of the human mind. The way that truth develops is through a process of conflict and resolution, which Hegel termed 'dialectic'. According to Hegel, the evolution of consciousness towards absolute knowing is achieved through an organic, dialectic process in which an idea (A) proves unsatisfactory under rational analysis, leading to the affirmation of the opposite idea (not A). This opposite idea thus becomes the accepted idea and is then itself subjected to analysis. Once that idea is found to be unsatisfactory, it too is replaced by its opposite. Crucially, the third idea is not simply the original idea but rather a new one, a 'higher' stage of thinking which takes us closer to full awareness (consciousness/self-realisation). This dialectic process is often described using the notion of the 'thesis' (original idea), 'antithesis' (second,

D

oppositional idea) and 'synthesis' (third, new idea). Within Hegel's system, the synthesis will become the thesis in a new dialectic, culminating in the grasping of reality as a totality, at which point no new antithesis is generated and we have attained absolute understanding.

See also: **dialectical materialism; Hegel; Marx; Marxism; Plato; Socrates**

Further reading: Adler (1927); Cooper (1997); Gonzalez (1998); Hegel (1807)

Dialectical materialism

Dialectical materialism is the conception of history which forms the theoretical foundation of Marxist philosophy. It is strongly influenced by Hegel's concept of the dialectic, which Marx connected to his belief in the importance of natural resources and human needs for understanding society. According to Marx, the progression of history must be understood as a product of human activity governed by the material conditions specific to each time and place. Therefore we must view each stage of history, from early nomadic and agricultural societies to feudalism and industrialism, as a series of developmental stages determined by the physical conditions that prevailed at the time. This represents the 'materialist' aspect of dialectical materialism. The 'dialectic' component is revealed by Marx's belief that society is in a constant state of flux, characterised by many 'stages' of societal development. Each new stage (the 'synthesis') is produced by class conflict (between the 'thesis' and 'antithesis') in the previous stage, generated by economic struggles and material needs. For example, in a feudal society one could see the struggle between feudal lords (thesis) and peasants (antithesis) as driving the development of society, which eventually led to the industrial revolution (the synthesis). At this point a new class struggle arises between the bourgeoisie (thesis) and proletariat (antithesis). Marx believed that the natural end point of this historical tension/movement would be communism, in which the proletariat overthrew the bourgeoisie (thus merging the classes) and established a classless society (the final synthesis).

See also: **communism; dialectic; Marx; Marxism**

Further reading: Cornforth (1961); Lefebvre (1968); Marx and Engels (1845)

Difference

D

The term 'difference' ('différance' in Derrida's work) has a variety of important (different) meanings. In its most literal sense, difference is a relational property (one that exists between objects, such as 'taller than') meaning 'non-identical' (different from). Something is different from you if it is not identical to you. Some monists have argued that all difference in the world is illusionary and that ultimately everything is the same, at least in the sense of being elements of one 'substance'. Spinoza argued that the entire universe is God and so we are all aspects of God's existence, thus there is no genuine ontological difference between objects (meaning that they are all part of the same 'thing'). Mystics have often spoken about the 'oneness' of the universe based on the deep interconnections between all things which renders difference meaningless.

In the political sphere the idea of difference is becoming increasingly important. Indeed, the 'politics of difference' can be seen as dominating the current political landscape with its focus on the demand for recognition and respect for differences between people. This is particularly relevant in modern multicultural societies, in which minority groups have argued that their identities, practices and beliefs have been ignored or devalued by the dominant, majority culture. For example, feminists have argued that men have presented a degrading image of women, forcing women to become like men in order to succeed and generating a negative self-image in women. They demand respect for women *as* women. Similar demands have been made by gay and lesbian movements, as well as race activists. The underlying logic of these claims is that human society is characterised by difference and it is wrong to suppose that one particular way of behaving, looking and thinking is better than another. In this respect, the identity of politics is related to cultural relativism, which claims that one must respect the morals and behaviours of other cultures rather than condemning them because they differ from one's own culture. The idea of difference raises important issues for equality and tolerance.

Finally, philosophers associated with postmodern and post-structural theories have often been called 'philosophers of difference'. According to Deleuze, difference is a 'productive mechanism', not simple negation or opposition, which implies a 'swarm of differences, a pluralism of free, wild or untamed differences' (1968: 50). This is because things are constituted *as* difference; they exist in relation to all other things. An object does not have an identity independent of its relations to everything else. Therefore its existence as difference is primary – without difference there would be no object. Seeing the world as 'difference' means recognising the constant processes of change that underlie it. Nothing is static; reality is in a state of 'becoming' rather than 'presence'. Furthermore, every time something is repeated, it is repeated differently and something new is generated. In effect, Deleuze uses the idea of difference to describe reality as 'dynamic', constantly evolving (there is a strong similarity here with vitalism). A similar idea can be found in Derrida's concept of 'différance', which looks at the production of meaning through constant 'deferral' – a word is defined in relation to a chain of other words through the ways they differ from one another, and we can never produce a comprehensive definition for any one word. Furthermore, words are constantly being revised, producing a 'knock-on' effect on the other words in the chain, so meanings are never fixed but evolve. Thus we should see meaning as a 'becoming' without end.

D

See also: **change; cultural relativism; deconstruction; Deleuze; Derrida; equality; essentialism; feminism; identity; monism; postmodernism; post-structuralism; queer theory; rights; tolerance; vitalism**

Key questions: Is equality achieved through respecting all differences, or by trying to eliminate or ignore difference? Similarly, should we tolerate all differences, or do we have/need some way of judging some cultural differences as acceptable and others as unacceptable?

Further reading: Cook (1999); Deleuze (1968); Derrida (1967b); Lowe (2002); Weedon (1999)

Discourse

Derived from the Latin *discursus* (running to and from), discourse refers to spoken or written exchange or debate. Philosophically, it features prominently in poststructuralist philosophy, particularly the works of Michel Foucault. According to Foucault, discourses are regulated sets of statements (bodies of knowledge) which are controlled and used for political purposes. Only certain discourses are permitted within society, and these discourses are the means by which power is exercised by and over people. Discourses typically inform us of what is good or bad, natural or unnatural, normal or abnormal. They are 'normative'; they construct a standard way of behaving and thinking. For instance, the discourse of sexuality has historically (at least, in recent British history) said that it is good, natural and normal to be heterosexual, monogamous and fertile. Those who were not were seen as deviant and abnormal, and were often punished and excluded from mainstream society. Such views were backed up by so-called 'experts' (scientists, philosophers, psychologists, politicians), who were invested with the authority and power to decide what is and is not acceptable.

However, the idea that certain people have better access to the 'truth' is, according to Foucault, just another discourse. All discourses are socially constructed and exist not because they are true or right but because they maintain power and are thus maintained by those to whom they give power. This is why scientists or philosophers who question their own practices are often dismissed or ignored by their peers. The creation and regulation of norms (regarding both behaviours and beliefs) by discourses has been seen as the fundamental act of oppression. For Foucault, the aim of liberal politics should be to deconstruct these discourses by showing how they are contingent, historical constructions with internal contradictions. An effective way of performing this deconstruction is to generate discourses on those who have been silenced. Hence Foucault was very interested in social 'deviants', including homosexuals and the insane. Feminists such as Butler, heavily influenced by Foucault, have used the idea of discourse to explore how gender is constructed and how gender relations/inequalities are maintained.

See also: **body, the; Butler; constructionism; feminism; Foucault; gender; historicism; ideology; postmodernism; post-structuralism; race; subjectivity; truth**

Further reading: Butler (1990); McHoul and Grace (1995); Mills (1997)

D

Doubt

If we want to see if we are sure about something, then a good way of achieving this is to see if we have any doubts about it. This method was most famously used by Descartes in his *Meditations* (1641), when he doubted the existence of the world and even his own body before finding that the only thing he could not doubt was that he was a mind which thinks (in order to be able to doubt, one must be something that *can* doubt). From this single certainty, he proceeded to relinquish all his other doubts.

In its most extreme form, doubt transforms into radical scepticism, which denies we can be certain about anything. Nihilism is the view that there is no justification for our beliefs and the world is devoid of meaning. In a sense this is not a form of doubt for one is sure that there is no meaning, rather than simply doubting it. It is often said that these forms of scepticism seem to rely on an inappropriate sense of 'knowing' which goes beyond our understanding of knowledge. Furthermore, it is psychologically questionable whether we could doubt that there is a world around us, or that we are alive rather than dreaming our existence. In this regard, it is useful to distinguish between philosophical and psychological/everyday doubt. It might be philosophically legitimate to doubt the existence of the external world, but our everyday lives would be impossible if we doubted everything (why get on the bus if we doubt that it is really there?). The opposite of doubt is certainty, though again there are different criteria for what it is to be certain about something. It would seem certain that $2+2=4$, although Descartes did at one point claim even to have doubts about this.

See also: **belief; certainty; Descartes; facts; faith; justification; knowledge; nihilism; scepticism; solipsism**

Key questions: Are there any beliefs which we cannot doubt the truth of? If something can be doubted, then does that mean we cannot be said to have knowledge of it?

Further reading: Descartes (1641); Hecht (2004); Hookway (1990)

Dualism

Dualism is the belief that there are two fundamental kinds of things or categories in the world: the physical and the non-physical. It is typically associated with the mind–body distinction which sees the mind as a separate substance, entity, category or property from the body. Descartes argued that because minds are not extended in space, and all physical objects are spatially-extended, then minds must be non-physical. Dualists also defend themselves through reference to qualia, the conscious experience of what an object is like. It is claimed that qualia, such as the experience of the 'blueness' of blue, cannot be explained through reference to the physical processes of the brain. Therefore there are non-physical aspects of consciousness.

Nonetheless, many contemporary thinkers tend to adopt a form of monism known as physicalism, the claim that mind and body are the same substance. There are a variety of different physicalist accounts, including functionalism and eliminative materialism. A persuasive argument in favour of physicalism is the problem of interaction. How is an immaterial/non-physical mind or consciousness able to interact with the material/physical body? This difficulty is represented neatly by the common image of ghosts (that is, minds) passing straight through physical objects (that is, bodies). However, there is still the problem of explaining how mental experiences fit within a physical world governed by scientific, causal laws.

D

See also: **consciousness; Descartes; eliminative materialism; epiphenomenalism; functionalism; mind, the; mind–body problem, the; monism; physicalism; qualia; self, the**

Key questions: Is dualism the best explanation for the nature of the human mind? Is the problem of how a non-physical thing can interact with a physical thing insurmountable for dualism?

Further reading: Chalmers (1996); Descartes (1641); Foster (1991); Heil (1998); Hofstadter and Dennett (1981); Rozemond (1998); Ryle (1949)

Duty

The concept of duty (being required to do something) is an important feature of moral and political theories. It was most famously used by Kant, who argued that actions only have moral worth if they are performed from a sense of duty. We must never let our desires motivate us to perform an action because they are not concerned with what is morally right. Only a good will, which acknowledges our duty as rational beings to obey the moral law, can be the right basis for acting morally. Consequently, Kant believed the best examples of a morally worthy act are those which go against our desires and so are *only* performed out of a sense of duty. We act accordingly simply because we know it to be right and therefore the action must be performed. Kant's sense of duty is categorical, meaning there is no way we cannot obey it.

Within social contract theories, the idea of duty is captured in our relationship to the state/government. As citizens we have a set of duties to the state, such as respecting the law, and in turn the state has the duty of protecting us and making sure such laws are enforced. It would seem that any act of promising creates a duty, for we are obliged to keep that promise. Society also expects us to observe a set of duties to our family and friends. Philosophers who defend the idea of rights, in particular natural rights, would insist that we have a duty to respect these rights, such as never killing another human/living thing. One interesting issue regarding duties is their relationship to morality. Is the idea of duties subordinate to morality, meaning whatever is moral must be our duty, or is our duty to a family member or the state sufficient to break certain moral principles? Can, and should, a soldier defend killing another human being on the basis that it is their 'duty' to their country? Religions often contain the claim that one's primary duty is to serve God, and all other duties are secondary to this.

See also: **categorical imperative; Confucianism; contractarianism; deontology; Kant; rights; supererogation**

Key questions: Do we ever perform an act simply because we think it is our duty to do so? In which situations, and for what reasons, may we ignore our moral, social and political duties?

Further reading: Pritchard (1968); Rawls (1971); Stratton-Lake (2000)

D

Ego, the

In 1905 Freud began work on what became *Three Essays on the Theory of Sexuality*. He referred to the 'ego-libido' as a mental representation of sexual energy. In *On Narcissism: An Introduction* (1914) he used the term 'ego-ideal' as a standard against which the self is measured and to describe the mechanism that allows inappropriate thoughts to be repressed or pushed into the unconscious. Later, in *The Ego and the Id* (1923), Freud introduced the term 'id' as an instinctive pleasure-seeking force. For the ego, he used the analogy of a man on horseback trying to reign in the stronger force of the horse (id). The pleasure principle of the id is thus tempered by the reality principle of the ego. The ego-ideal now became the super-ego, based on the morality principle, consisting of internalised social expectations of how to behave.

The importance of the ego, rather than the id, was emphasised by Freud's daughter, Anna, and Erik Erikson among others. Anna added to the defence mechanisms by which the ego protects itself and Erikson rejected Freud's emphasis on sexuality, instead developing a theory of ego development that placed the social and cultural environments as key influences. Melanie Klein's theory of object relations has gained prominence. She proposed that good and bad aspects of an object lead to splitting of the ego (paranoid-schizoid position) unless resolved through acceptance of a whole object that can be both good and bad (depressive position). Jacques Lacan, whose work has strongly influenced many feminists, made language central to the ego's development by arguing that it is oppressed through the individual's entrance into a language system within which they can never fully express their experiences and emotions.

Freudian conceptions of the ego are not to be confused with philosophical notions of a conscious, experiencing self visualised by, for example, Kant, Husserl and Sartre. For Kant, a transcendental ego is a self that is assumed to exist because we have conscious experiences. It is a self that is beyond experience. It transcends experience and thus can never be known or observed in its own right. You might think or say 'I can see a cat', but what is the 'I' referring to? It is assumed that there is some experiencing self that we refer to as 'I', which Husserl calls pure ego. The 'I' is the same one involved in, for example, seeing a cat and, a few seconds later, a tree. Sartre, however, rejected the idea of an experiencing self. Although we have consciousness, that does not necessarily mean there is some 'I' beyond that. Consciousness is not a result of 'I' but rather 'I' is a result of consciousness. Sartre consequently rejects Freud's suggestion of a self (id) that is hidden from a conscious one (ego).

See also: **Dasein; Freud; unconscious, the; Husserl; Kant; Sartre**

Key questions: How can we tell whether what we think of as 'I' or 'me' has some substance or whether it is a result of conscious memory? Do we have an ego when we are asleep?

Further reading: Erikson (1963); Freud, A. (1936); Freud, S. (1905, 1914, 1923); Kant (1781); Klein (1952, 1957); Lacan (1968); Russell (2006); Sartre (1937)

Egoism

Egoism comes in several forms, each of which is connected by the assumption that all of us are, or should be, interested only in our own welfare. The two most philosophically-relevant versions are psychological egoism and ethical egoism.

Psychological egoism is the belief that humans are, by their very nature, motivated by self-interest and any act is ultimately driven by selfish desires. Because it is simply descriptive in form, rather than normative (which would claim this is how we *should* act), attempts to refute it are concerned with providing counter-examples. However, the extent to which altruistic actions (those acts which are performed solely for the benefit of others and at a cost to the individual) can be observed in humans is debatable. Nonetheless, there do seem to be genuine examples of altruistic behaviour, such as when parents sacrifice themselves for their children or when a fire fighter suffers serious or fatal injury saving someone from a burning building. As a result of such examples, 'predominant egoism' has arisen (for example, Kavka, 1986), which claims that we rarely act for non-selfish reasons and these actions tend to have small personal cost and large gains for others, or else they are for family and close friends. However, altruistic acts directed at blood-relatives are subject to the evolutionary argument that we act to preserve our genes, and thus ultimately act through self-interest. This is known as kin selection. Similarly, apparently altruistic acts such as lending money might benefit us in the future when we need a favour returned. This is known as reciprocal altruism and is based on the idea that we can gain more over time by co-operation.

Ethical egoism is the normative claim that we *ought* to choose that action which is in our own best interests. An action is morally right if it serves to maximise one's well-being. This does not mean we will necessarily cause harm to other people. Often it is the case that my personal interests are best served by being pleasant to people. If I attack my boss, then I will lose my job and therefore lack the money with which to buy the things I want. However, the demands to, say, help others that are made by other ethical theories, such as utilitarianism and deontology seem far more unconditional. Within ethical egoism, my donating money to charity is conditional upon it serving my interests better than not donating money to charity. However, utilitarianism would argue that we always have a duty to donate money to charity as this will produce, except perhaps in very rare instances, a greater amount of happiness than if we do not. The key feature of ethical egoism is that the only person or thing with a claim to moral consideration is me, rather than all rational or sentient beings, or even just the members of one's family/society/community. For many people, ethical egoism simply seems counter-intuitive. The basis of a moral theory is the formulation of rules/duties which we must follow,

E

regardless of our personal desires. One might argue that the point of morality is precisely to move us beyond egoism.

See also: **categorical   imperative;   consequentialism;   deontology;   morality; prescriptivism**

Further reading: Baier (1958); Gauthier (1970); Kavka (1986); Shaver (1999)

Eliminative materialism

Eliminative materialism is the name given to a theory of the mind principally defended by Paul and Patricia Churchland. Eliminative materialism makes the radical claim that our everyday understanding of the mind (called 'folk psychology') is mistaken, and that many or all the mental states described by ordinary language do not exist. Folk psychology refers to mental states such as hunger, thirst, belief and desire in order to explain the workings of the mind. According to eliminative materialists these inaccurately describe the mind. The proper way of talking about the mind is in terms of neurological processes. Whilst many materialists worry about how we can explain mental states such as fear in terms of physical brain processes, eliminative materialists argue we do not need to explain them because they do not exist. They envisage a future where we cease to talk of our hopes, wishes and such like, instead describing all brain activity neurologically. Rather than saying 'I am happy' we would say something like 'I am in brain state 34X3'.

Eliminative materialists draw an analogy with previous folk explanations of such phenomena as lightning. Historically people may have used magic or God to explain the occurrence of lightning. However, science has eliminated such talk in favour of electrons and charges. We do not worry about how electrons can explain God's role in lightning, because science tells us He does not play a role in it. He has been eliminated from our understanding of lightning. According to eliminative materialists, our commonsense or folk psychology beliefs that mental states constitute the mind should similarly disappear. Eliminative materialism is a version of physicalism, owing to its claim that the mind is just a neurological system and therefore purely physical in nature.

See also: **belief; consciousness; folk psychology; mind, the; mind–body problem, the; physicalism; qualia; reductionism; subjectivity**

Key questions: Could the mind be fully described if we eliminated all talk of mental states such as fear and happiness? Will scientific descriptions of the mind ever be accurate enough to explain all aspects of consciousness?

Further reading: Churchland, P.M. (1981, 1988); Churchland, P.S. (1986); Stich (1983)

E

Embodiment

The term 'embodiment' expresses the idea that our subjective (personal) experience of the world is conditioned by our body. It was brought to prominence by the existentialist Merleau-Ponty, who introduced the idea of the 'phenomenal' body. The phenomenal body is the body experienced as not just a physiological description, but as something particular to me. The phenomenal body is something that walks to the shops, feels warm, is able to laugh and so on. Theories of embodiment suggest that our very understanding of the world is conditioned by our body. For instance, I may experience a tree as fun, fuel and safety because of my ability to climb it, chop it into firewood and hide behind it. A bird, which can fly, would have a very different understanding of the tree because of the body it inhabits. The world is made meaningful through our bodies. Embodiment marks a radical shift from traditional philosophical approaches, which viewed the body as simply a passive bridge to the world, or as something to be transcended or ignored. Descartes, for instance, doubted the existence of his body in his search for clear and certain knowledge. According to theories of embodiment, we cannot separate thoughts about the world from thoughts about the body, for the former is dependent upon the latter.

See also: **body, the; consciousness; experience; extended cognition; Merleau-Ponty; phenomenology; pragmatism; subjectivity**

Key questions: How does our body affect our experience of the world? Is the world made meaningful through our bodily interaction with it?

Further reading: Lakoff and Johnson (1999); Merleau-Ponty (1945)

Emotion

For many of us emotions play a hugely important part in our everyday life. Our actions often seem directed towards achieving emotional states such as happiness, and avoiding sadness, anger or regret. Producing adequate accounts of emotion is therefore a vital task in understanding the nature of the mind and consciousness. There are, however, a number of difficulties with studying emotions. Firstly, and most fundamentally, is the question of what an emotion actually is. One view is that emotions must be understood physiologically as specific bodily feelings. The most famous proponent of this view is William James, who argued that without feeling there would be no emotion. James uses a thought experiment to support his claim. Imagine extracting all bodily feelings, such as our hearts beating faster, from an emotion. There would be nothing remaining, James claims, which we could possibly understand as an emotion. We realise we are angry when we notice certain bodily changes. To give an example, traditionally it is thought that when one is sad, one weeps. James turns this on its head by arguing that one is sad when one weeps.

An opposing view is cognitivism, in which emotions are understood in terms of a person's cognitive processes such as their beliefs or judgements. Cognitivists such as Solomon and Nussbaum argue that my happiness is simply my judgement that something good has happened to me. For instance, I am happy because I believe I have won the lottery. I would not have the emotion 'happiness' if I did not believe a certain thing to be the case. Cognitivists criticise the physiological accounts of emotions by referring to experiments which have revealed that participants report feeling different emotions whilst under the same physiological conditions. For example, raised adrenaline levels can be interpreted as excitement, fear or sexual attraction depending on the context. Furthermore, our emotional lives are hugely complicated. We often feel a variety of emotions at any one time, or emotional states which seem to be a mixture of different emotions. The number of bodily states required to explain every possible emotional state seems huge, if not unlimited. Cognitivist theories of emotion are problematic because they seem to exclude any being which cannot form judgements or hold certain beliefs about emotions. This would seem to deny that babies and animals have emotional states.

Ultimately it would seem that emotions are a complex blend of physiological, cognitive and social factors. This has led some philosophers to argue for an end to attempts at a grand theory of emotion. Each theory of emotion may only explain one aspect of emotion, or one particular set of emotions.

See also: **belief; consciousness; context; emotivism; James; mind**

Key questions: What is an emotion? What beings are capable of experiencing emotions? Is our understanding of the world determined by our emotional states?

Further reading: James (1884); Leighton (2003); Nussbaum (2001); Solomon (2004)

Emotivism

According to emotivists, our ethical judgements are simply expressions of emotion. Morality is a matter of taste, so that my saying 'murder is wrong' is equivalent to 'murder – eugh'. Consequently, emotivists deny that moral values express any sort of fact, thus making it a form of moral subjectivism. Emotivism can be traced back to Hume, who described ethical judgements as a matter of the heart and sentiment, though it was brought to prominence by Ayer and Stevenson. One advantage it has over some other forms of moral subjectivism is that it explains moral disagreements, for they are effectively attempts to change the tastes of other people. However, emotivism does not seem to allow for structured, reasoned moral debate, for there is no reason or rationale for our ethical views. For emotivists, trying to get someone to stop stealing is equivalent to trying to get someone to like carrots.

See also: **Ayer; descriptivism; good, the; Hare; morality; moral subjectivism; prescriptivism**

Further reading: Ayer (1936); Hume (1751); Satris (1986); Stevenson (1944)

Empiricism

The word derives from the Greek word for experience and is used in philosophy to refer to the epistemological belief that *all* knowledge is gained and justified through sensory experience. Rationalists disagree with this view, arguing instead that some knowledge is gained independently of sense experience, for example by intuition or awareness of innate ideas. Locke stated that we have two fountains of knowledge: experiences and introspective reflection on those experiences. Hume constructed a radical empiricist account which appears to deny that we are justified in believing in such things as causation. His reasoning is that, given we never directly experience causation, we have no justification for asserting its existence. The scientific method of observation is founded on empiricist principles; for example, behaviourists recording the behaviour of organisms in controlled environmental conditions.

Logical empiricism (also called logical positivism) is based on a logical connection between what is stated to be true and what is evident from experience. Anything

E

beyond sensory experience, including God and moral truths, is dismissed as meaningless. This is known as the verification principle. The hypothetico-deductive method developed from the principles of logical empiricism. Although logical empiricism can test an assumption by applying rules of logic, it cannot explain how new ideas are created for testing. In the 20th century, the radical empiricism of Hume was celebrated and reworked by Deleuze.

See also: **epistemology; experience; Hume; justification; knowledge; Locke; logical positivism; rationalism; scientific method;** *tabula rasa*

Key questions: Is all knowledge gained through sensory experience? Is the justification of a belief dependent upon its being experienced?

Further reading: Ayer (1940); Deleuze (1953); Gupta (2006); Hume (1748); Locke (1690)

Enlightenment

The term 'enlightenment' has several different meanings. Within Western philosophy the term is most commonly used to refer to a period of radical philosophical developments in the 17th, 18th and 19th centuries known as 'the enlightenment' or 'age of enlightenment', and is associated with the works of Descartes, Locke, Hume and Kant. Enlightenment thought emphasised the rational nature of humans (or, more frequently, just men). Man's reason was capable of discovering the true nature or explanation of all things in the universe, achieved through a scientific, logical, empirical and sceptical approach. Importantly, this approach was often secular and removed God from the explanatory picture of the universe (although it did not necessarily deny God's existence). This reflected the developing scientific description of the universe initiated by scientists such as Newton and Galileo.

In its broader context, enlightenment refers to a realisation. Typically this is sudden and has a religious context, such as a revelation of spiritual insight or experience of God. Within Buddhism, enlightenment is the goal of spiritual practice, the moment when one achieves insight into the true nature of reality and, in doing so, is freed from all suffering. A being who has obtained enlightenment is said to have entered *nirvana*.

See also: **Buddhism; Descartes; empiricism; Hinduism; humanism; Hume; Indian philosophy; Kant; Locke; rationalism; reason; scientific method**

Further reading: Hyland et al. (2003); Kant (1784); Porter (1990); Yolton (1991)

Environmental ethics

Environmental ethics is a recent branch of applied ethics that examines the moral relationship humans have with their environment, and the moral value of the environment itself. Interest in environmental ethics developed in the 1960s and 1970s when it became clear that human activity was adversely affecting the environment with severe consequences for humans and animals. Issues such as depleted resources, damaging farming practices, the massive growth in the human population and the extinction of species posed previously unconsidered ethical dilemmas. Environmental ethics drew attention to the often anthropocentric (human-centred) nature of traditional Western ethical theory, which had given moral value or consideration only to humans. Rarely was the moral status of animals discussed, and rarer still the physical environment.

One major issue is whether the environment has intrinsic or instrumental moral value. If it has intrinsic moral value then it is morally valuable in its own right; treating the environment well is good in itself. If it has instrumental value then we should act morally towards the environment because ultimately it will benefit those things which have intrinsic moral value, such as humans. One influential theory which assigns intrinsic value to the environment is Arne Næss's 'deep ecology' (1973). Næss argues for 'biospheric egalitarianism', the view that all living things are valuable in their own right. The motivation for this theory was Næss's belief that all living things are intrinsically connected, so that each living thing is bound up, or constituted, by other living things. The 'individual' is actually part of the wider environment, and so in order to respect one living thing, we must respect the other living things around it. Many philosophers have found similar ideas within Buddhism and have consequently used it as a basis for an environmental ethic.

Næss's work raises a further contentious issue. Should we assign moral value to just living things, or do non-living things also have moral status? For instance, should we protect mountains from being mined in order to access the resources they house? If so, we must ask whether this is because they have intrinsic or instrumental value. Is a mountain valuable because it is the home of many animals, or is it valuable in itself? Perhaps the aesthetic experience of seeing a beautiful sunset from the top of a mountain gives it moral worth, or perhaps an important moral value is to promote or protect diverse and unique things in the world. Therefore we should work to protect the world's different environments from being destroyed. It is clear that as global warming becomes one of the major political and moral issues facing the world, environmental ethics will become ever more important.

See also: **animal ethics; morality; value; vegetarianism**

Key questions: Does any part of the environment have intrinsic value? Are humans separate from their environment, and if so, how?

Further reading: Light and Rolston (2003); Næss (1973, 1989); Nash (1989)

Epiphenomenalism

Epiphenomenalism is a theory of mind which argues that mental events are produced by physical processes, but do not affect those physical processes. In other words, mental events play no causal role in the workings of the mind. Epiphenomenalism offers a solution to the problem of how mental and physical phenomena are related, given that they appear to be radically different (for instance mental events, such as thoughts, have no spatial location or shape, unlike a neuron in the brain). According to epiphenomenalists the mental features of consciousness are generated by the physical, in much the same way as smoke is produced by fire. William James likened this idea to a shadow being cast by an object. The shadow cannot physically affect the object, but is dependent upon that object for its existence. Early epiphenomenalist theories tended to accept a dualistic view of the mind, but most modern proponents are monists. Epiphenomenalism rests on the belief that mental and physical events are not the same thing, and so a theory of mind cannot reduce the mental to the physical. Epiphenomenalists therefore resist strongly reductionist accounts of consciousness, such as eliminative materialism.

See also: **dualism; eliminative materialism; mind, the; mind–body problem, the; monism; physicalism; reductionism**

Further reading: James (1879); Kim (1993); Robinson (2004)

Epistemology

Epistemology is the study of human knowledge: how we achieve knowledge, what knowledge is, whether we are justified in claiming to possess knowledge and, if so, why (or why not). Empiricism is the idea that all knowledge is gained through sensory experience and reflection upon those experiences. The most famous British empiricists are Locke and Hume. Those who reject empiricism argue that humans can possess knowledge that is not ultimately derived from experience. This could be through awareness of innate ideas or intuition. Scepticism is the belief that knowledge, or some forms of knowledge, are not possible. According to absolute scepticism we can never say we know something, for we can never justify that belief. We are always able to doubt what we know. A particularly distinctive epistemological view is Berkeley's idealism, which claims that all knowledge is an idea and consequently all that exists (or all that we are justified in believing in) is ideas and the minds which possess those ideas. Many philosophers have seen scepticism and idealism as challenges which must be overcome in order to maintain belief in an objective, physical world. However, perhaps we really are all just brains in vats, having all our beliefs generated by a computer.

See also: **belief; Berkeley; brain-in-a-vat; certainty; concept; doubt; empiricism; experience; foundationalism; Hume; idealism; incommensurability; introspection; intuition; justification; justified true belief; Kant; knowledge; Locke; logical positivism; phenomenalism; reliabilism; scepticism; solipsism**

Further reading: Audi (1998); Berkeley (1710); Hume (1748); Locke (1690); Sosa (1991); Sosa and Villanueva (2004)

Equality

The concept of equality is an important feature of many political theories. Literally meaning 'the same' or 'equal', political equality is the non-discriminatory treatment of an individual regardless of their age, gender, race, religion, wealth, class or any other definable characteristic. Political movements which call for justice often use the idea of equality to justify their claims. Within communist philosophy, all individuals have an equal social status and equal claim to the material goods of a society. Within democracy, all individuals have an equal say in the decision-making process. A meritocratic society is one in which all members have an equal chance of success, which is determined by the individual's efforts alone, rather than their or their family's status or circumstances.

Equality is closely related to the concept of justice. Justice is often seen as needing to both respect and enforce equality between individuals. Within many modern cultures an important part of the justice system is that all citizens are equal in the eyes of the law. However, absolute equality in any political system has proven nigh on impossible and may only be a utopian dream. Race, gender, age, physical ability, wealth and appearance all still appear to affect a person's life in ways which seem to clash with the ideal of equality. This raises the issue of whether some inequalities are natural and, if so, whether such inequalities should be accepted. If someone is born with exceptional musical ability, should they be given equal access to musical resources and tuition as someone born with very little musical ability? A highly controversial point is the practice of 'positive discrimination' whereby certain groups in society are given preferential treatment in order to even out socially constructed differences (see Cavanagh, 2002). An example of this would be favouring a student from a state school over one from a private school for university entrance, when both have equal grades.

See also: **democracy; difference; feminism; humanism; Marxism; moral subjects; morality; justice; race**

Key questions: Are all people equal? Are all living things equal? What social practices are justified in achieving equality? Does everyone have equal potential?

Further reading: Cavanagh (2002); Nagel (1991); Pojman and Westmoreland (1998); White (2006)

Essentialism

Essentialism is the idea that there is something (an essence) which a thing must possess in order to be that thing. It is common to distinguish between the essential and accidental properties of a thing or event. These are captured in such common utterances as 'If only I had been two inches taller' or 'He just would not be the same person if he lost his sense of humour'. The former sentence expresses a supposedly accidental property of a thing, whilst the latter expresses a supposedly essential property. An essential property is one which an object has always had and which it cannot cease to have without ceasing to exist itself. In the above example, the person's sense of humour is treated as essential because we are told they would not be the same person without it. Of course, we may think that a sense of humour is not an essential property of a person. Instead it might be an accidental property. An accidental property is a property which an object can cease to possess whilst remaining the same object. For instance, colour would seem to be an accidental property of a car. If we painted our car a new colour we would surely still believe it to be our car (and the self-same car as the one we owned that morning before painting it).

Essentialism regarding objects states that each object has an essential quality, without which it would not be that object. Plato's theory of the forms is one example of this. According to Plato, each individual thing comes to be what it is through partaking in the true 'form' of that group to which it belongs. For instance, a horse is a horse because it possesses the universal property (the form) of 'horseness'. The reason we are able to identify all horses as 'horse', even though they look different, is because of the universal form of horse. One can also be essentialist about the self by arguing that there is some essence to a person which makes them who they are and not someone else. We could remove certain parts of a person, such as a leg, and they would remain that same person. Therefore the leg is not essential to that person. An example of what a person's essence could be is a soul. However, if

E

we deny that there are such things as souls, it is difficult to see just what it is that is essential to a person. Postmodern theories of the self deny that there is any essential property to a person. Sartre famously declared that our existence precedes our essence, meaning we are first born into the world and then define who and what we are. The Buddhist teaching of *anatman* (not-self) is also a non-essentialist account of persons.

Essentialism is often expressed 'modally' by using the idea of possible worlds. An essential property is one which an object possesses in all possible worlds. A property is accidental if an object exists in at least two possible worlds without possessing that property in each one. For example, we often express such thoughts as 'If only I had woken up in time for work today'. According to modal logic, there is some possible world in which I did wake up in time. If there is a property essential to being you, then you must possess that property in both the world in which you oversleep and the world you do not. If a property is non-essential then you may exist in the possible world without having that property.

Forms of essentialism include origin essentialism, which argues that an object could not have been the same object if it had had a radically different origin. For instance, I would not be me if I had been conceived by different parents, or even if it had been a different sperm or egg. Sortal essentialism says that an object could not have been of a radically different kind (grouping of individual things, such as 'carrot' or 'cat') than it actually is. On this view, I could not be me if I were not human. Some philosophers argue that the only property which could be essential to an object is the property of self-identity. However, this is trivial and uninformative as it simply says that 'object X has the property of being X'. Two other theories of an essential property are the necessity of origin and the necessity of constitution (Kripke, 1980). According to the necessity of origin argument, the origin of an object is one of its essential properties. According to the necessity of constitution argument, if an object has an original constitution then this is an essential property of that object. The Ship of Theseus puzzle is useful in considering the essentialist debate because it questions how much an object can change before it becomes a different object. Philosophers who deny that there are any such things as 'essences', arguing instead that all talk of essences simply reflects our ability to impose such ideas on the world, are called conventionalists (Sidelle, 1989).

See also: **being; Buddhism; change; difference; kind, natural; modality; properties; Sartre; self, the; Ship of Theseus, the; universals and particulars**

Key questions: Are there any essential properties of an object? How can we know what is an accidental or essential property of an object?

Further reading: Kripke (1980); Loux (1979); Lowe (2002); Rea (1997); Sartre (1946); Sidelle (1989)

Event

An event is, simply speaking, something that happens. It appears different from such things as objects, properties, facts and beliefs, which do not 'happen'. The philosophical interest in events focuses on metaphysical issues, in particular whether an event is a genuine ontological category. Can an event be seen as some 'thing' existing in the world, or is it a useful concept we create and employ in order to explain things, such as causes and effects. Our everyday language and understanding of the world suggests we do treat events as metaphysically meaningful. We commonly distinguish between separate events and debate the causal relationship between events, such as whether event A affected event B. Furthermore, it would appear very difficult to describe the world without using the concept of events.

One influential view of events is Donald Davidson's 'object–event dualism'. According to Davidson, events should be seen as equivalent to objects. His claim is that an event always occurs at a certain place at a certain time. It is a 'particular', like objects, meaning each event is unique (precisely the same event never occurs twice, just as precisely the same object never exists twice). Furthermore, they cannot be reduced down to some other category (they are 'primitive'). Just as an object such as football cannot be reduced down to some other object, or set of objects, an event cannot be reduced to some other 'thing' (whether another event or an object). Davidson thus describes them as 'primitive particulars' and argues that they should be seen as 'basic' (ontologically fundamental) as objects. One implication of this is that an event's existence does not depend on the objects involved in it.

An opposing view, defended by Jaegwon Kim, is that events are 'property exemplifications' by objects at a certain time. What this means is that events are built out of objects, properties and times. They depend upon these things for their existence. To give an example, the event 'Chris and Steve watched the summer solstice sunrise' is the collection of the objects 'Chris' and 'Steve' which possess the property of 'watching' and a particular time. The 'event' can be understood as the structural relationship between these objects, properties and times. So for an event to take place (exist) particular objects ('Chris' and 'Steve') must have a certain property ('watching') at a certain time ('summer solstice sunrise'). According to Kim's theory, events do not belong to a separate ontological category.

A realist view of events would defend the idea that events are genuinely existing things which the mind perceives in the world. However, an anti-realist position regarding events would claim that events are imposed onto the world by the mind, and cannot be thought of as actually existing in 'reality'. One supporting argument for this anti-realist view is that two people may share the same experience and yet 'perceive' different events. For example, one person may have seen the event 'A is wrestling with B', whilst another sees the event 'A is hugging B'. A realist view of events might have to say that there are two things (two events) occurring in the same place at the same time. This might not be an appealing move, for it is generally assumed that two different things cannot exist in the same place at the same time.

See also: **causation; context; experience; metaphysics; ontology**

Further reading: Bennett (1988); Casati and Varzi (1996); Davidson (2001); Higginbotham et al. (2000); Lombard (1986)

Evil

To describe someone or something as evil is to say it is morally abhorrent. We therefore have to have a definition of what is morally good in order to have a concept of what is morally evil and vice versa. It seems that an act can be immoral without being evil. For instance, it might be immoral to lie but we would not necessarily call a liar evil. So we might want to say that 'evil' is an example of something which is especially immoral (such as rape or murder). In this case, we would need a theory of morality which allowed degrees of right and wrong, so that something could be more right or wrong than another thing.

Evil is commonly discussed in the philosophy of religion, particularly with regard to the problem of evil. A modern problem associated with evil is the extent to which we can condemn the practices of another culture, such as hanging or female circumcision, as evil. Some acts, such as murder, may be considered as a universal evil (wrong in all places at all times), in which case we would be able to criticise other societies if they allow such evil acts.

Utopian visions of future societies often portray a world which is free from evil. However, if we no longer have a concept of evil (since it has been eradicated), would we appreciate that the world is full of good? An important legal and moral issue connected to acts of evil is whether we are able to hold people responsible for them. We often make a distinction between 'mad' and 'bad', thus implying that someone who committed murder could have done so either freely or owing to a psychological defect. This issue rests heavily upon the concept of free will and the degree to which a person's behaviour is determined by their genes and social environment.

> *See also:* **cultural relativism; evil, the problem of; free will; good, the; morality; responsibility; utopianism; Zoroastrianism**
>
> *Key question:* Is it possible to judge how evil an act is and, if so, what criteria would be applied?
>
> *Further reading:* Astley et al. (2003); Baumeister and Beck (1999)

Evil, the problem of

The 'problem of evil' is the question of how a benevolent and all-powerful God could allow there to be evil in the world. If God is benevolent and all-powerful, then He has both the ability and the desire to remove all evil from the world, where evil is most often understood as suffering and anything that produces suffering. Many philosophers believe the problem of evil to be sufficient for rejecting the existence of such a God. One common response to the problem of evil is that God gave us free will as an act of kindness to humanity, and so all evil is performed by humans and not God. Others argue that all evil in the world must be understood over a large timeframe, so that an act or event which seems evil actually, in the long-term, turns out to be a blessing.

However, if God is all-powerful then there seems to be no reason why He should allow evil in the short term when He could just construct the world so that there is no evil whatsoever. The problem of evil relies upon a certain conception of God. Some religions do not ascribe benevolence as a property of God, or they deny that we can meaningfully describe God. Non-monistic religions often contain both good and evil deities, who reflect the balance of good and evil in the world.

An early use of the problem of evil to disprove God's existence, or at least the inconsistency of the idea of God, was produced by Hume. Historically, philosophical exploration of the problem of evil has been condemned by the Church, with those who challenged the existence or benevolence of God being accused of heresy and risking punishment. Alvin Plantinga and Peter van Inwagen have produced important modern defences against the problem of evil.

E

See also: evil; free will; God; God, arguments for the existence of; Zoroastrianism
Further reading: Adams and Adams (1990); Hume (1757, 1779); Plantinga (1974, 1977); van Inwagen (2006)

Evolution

See **Darwinism**

Existence

Existence appears to be a very simple concept. For something to be, or to be real, it must exist. However, there are several troubling issues connected to existence. The first is an epistemological concern over whether we are justified in knowing that something does or does not exist. Scepticism regarding God, the external world, other people's minds or moral laws can cause us to question whether we have any justification for believing they exist. How can we prove, or indeed disprove, the existence of such things? Solipsism is the belief that only I exist, although it is rarely defended by philosophers.

A second concern centres on the use of existence as a predicate. A predicate assigns properties to a thing, such as 'is hot' or 'runs'. Philosophers have debated whether existence is a true property of things. Kant argued that it is not. Were we to write a list of all the properties of Durham cathedral, such as 'is big' and 'is made of stone', we would add nothing by also putting 'exists'. Rather, existence is something a thing must have in order to have properties in the first place. In other words, to say 'I do not exist' makes no sense because I must exist in order to say I do not exist. This debate is particularly relevant to the ontological argument for the existence of God.

A third, related issue is the nature of non-existence. How is it possible to say anything meaningful about things that do not exist? Words are often assumed to have meaning because they refer to things. The sentence 'the tree in my back garden has green leaves' is either true or false depending on whether or not there is a tree which exists in my garden. However, we would want to say that the sentence 'a unicorn has a single horn on its head' is true. Yet how can we say something is true or false if it does not exist? The sentence does not refer to any existing thing, so how can it even be meaningful? Finally, we assign a special meaning to the concept of 'existence' when we apply it to ourselves. When a person dies we tend to say that they have ceased to exist. Yet their body is still present, so what aspect of them has ceased to exist? It is tempting to say that existence in this sense equates to consciousness, but it is far from clear just what consciousness is. Therefore in order to fully understand existence we need a satisfactory account of consciousness.

See also: being; change; consciousness; death; definite descriptions; identity; God, arguments for the existence of; ontology; properties; reference; self, the; solipsism; reality; truth

Key questions: Is 'existence' a genuine property of an object? Must we experience something to say that it exists? When does something stop existing?

Further reading: Kant (1781); McTaggart (1927); Reinhardt (1992); Williams, C.J.F. (1981)

E

Existentialism

Existentialism is a philosophical, political and literary movement chiefly associated with French philosophy. If Kierkegaard is seen as the 'father' of existentialism, then his most famous offspring include Heidegger, Sartre, De Beauvoir, Camus and Merleau-Ponty. Rather than there being a core set of beliefs that all existentialists endorse, existentialists are linked by a set of concerns or areas of philosophical interest. Existentialism begins with an analysis of the human subject rather than the natural object. One key insight into the human subject is Sartre's observation that their existence precedes their essence. This is to say that humans must generate their own meanings in the world. Unlike an object such as a bottle-opener, which is created to perform a specific function, humans have no such purpose. This is why the idea of freedom is so important to existentialism. We have absolute freedom because we begin as nothing and can make ourselves into anything we want. However, humans have rarely enacted this freedom, choosing instead to accept the worldview they are taught by religions or society. Rather than choosing for themselves, they let God or their families choose for them. They therefore live an inauthentic life because they are failing to take responsibility for their own lives by making their own choices. Existentialism is highly critical of transcendental philosophies, which search for objective, universal truths. We must face our specific, contingent existence at this precise moment in history. We always exist at a particular moment in a particular place, and to try and generalise beyond our immediate existence is futile. Owing to these beliefs, existentialism is often seen as an atheistic philosophy. Certainly most existentialists deny God's existence, but Kierkegaard shows how one can combine an existential attitude with a strong Christian faith.

Because existentialism denies that the universe and humanity has any purpose or meaning, it is often seen as nihilistic or a philosophy of despair. However, in encouraging us to take responsibility for our lives and make our own meanings, it could be seen as a philosophy of hope in which there is always the possibility for change. It is also wrong to accuse it of being an immoral or non-moral philosophy. Although existentialism denies any objective moral truths, it insists we must take responsibility for our actions and the effect they have on others. Indeed, respecting the freedom of other people is the cornerstone of existential ethics. To fully accept and embrace the freedom, responsibility and specific situation which one is constantly confronted with is to live an authentic life, which can be seen as the pinnacle of existential philosophy. The importance of freedom also explains the fact that existentialist philosophers, most famously Sartre and De Beauvoir, have been heavily involved in politics, particularly Marxist and socialist movements. Existentialist philosophy has been widely expressed in literary works. Sartre, Camus and de Beauvoir all wrote novels exploring existential issues.

See also: **angst; authenticity; continental philosophy; Dasein; de Beauvoir; embodiment; freedom; free will; Heidegger; Kierkegaard; Merleau-Ponty; nihilism; nothingness; responsibility; Sartre; subjectivity**

Further reading: Camus (1942); de Beauvoir (1944, 1949); Heidegger (1927); Kierkegaard (1843a, 1843b, 1844, 1846); Merleau-Ponty (1945); Sartre (1943, 1944, 1946)

Experience

To experience something is to directly observe it, whether by sight, touch, taste, hearing or smell. According to empiricists, all knowledge is gained through experience. As Locke noted, we are born a 'blank slate' (*tabula rasa*) and all understanding is subsequently gained through experience. However, scepticism questions the accuracy of our experiences. Do they provide a description of how the world actually is, or do they provide a description of the world as we experience it? Reliabilism is a theory of knowledge in which justification for a belief is grounded in the consistency of our experiences and the faith we have in our perceptual system to produce such consistency. Kant claimed that the mind was active in ordering our experiences and it was impossible to experience the world independently of this structuring process.

Certainly our concepts do play an important role in the way we experience things. For instance, if I have the concept of 'affection', but not 'violence', then if I saw two people wrapping their arms around each other I would experience an act of affection rather than violence. On learning about violence, I might revise my memory of the experience and realise I was witnessing a fight. One view of this would be that we did experience a fight (there was a fight taking place independently of my experience of it) but we did not believe we experienced a fight. Another view would be that we did not experience a fight; there was no fight taking place 'for us'. There are certain experiences, such as experiencing our own minds and qualia (the subjective, 'like-thisness' experience of objects, such as the 'redness' of a rose), which seem necessarily private. They are experiences we can never share with, or adequately describe to, another person. However, Wittgenstein's private language argument is an attempt to claim that there can be no 'private' experience. Whether or not we can have an experience of something we do not have a word for is a fundamental debate in the philosophy of language and epistemology.

See also: belief; Berkeley; concept; embodiment; empiricism; epistemology; idealism; justification; Kant; knowledge; linguistic relativism; Locke; logical positivism; private language argument; qualia; rationalism; reliabilism; *tabula rasa*; Wittgenstein

Key questions: Is experience the only source of knowledge and justification? Can all experience be described and understood? To what extent is our experience determined by our beliefs and assumptions?

Further reading: Haldane (1926); Locke (1690); Wittgenstein (1953)

E

Extended cognition

Extended cognition is a theory of mind which challenges the supposed boundary between the mind and the world. Traditionally, philosophy characterised the mind as contained within the body (or even just the brain) and the world as external to this. However, philosophers have begun to explore the idea that we must understand the human mind and human cognition as intrinsically bound up with the environment. This has led Clark and Chalmers (1998: 8) to claim that 'Cognitive processes ain't (all) in the head!' Their reasoning is that there are some parts of the world that function like a process which, if the same process were conducted in the head, would be considered part of human cognition. They argue that there is no reason why those processes in the world should not be seen as part of our cognitive processes. Basic examples of the mind's extension include the use of a pocket calculator for processing sums or an address book for recalling where people live. To boost the plausibility of this theory, imagine implanting a small computer chip into your brain which helps you to multiply numbers. We would think of this multiplication process as part of your cognition. If the computer chip happens to be outside of our mind, why not also think of that as part of our cognition?

Extended cognition has been greatly influenced by developments in neuroscience and artificial intelligence. However, old traditions such as tying a knot in a handkerchief to remind us of something could also be seen as extended cognition. Although not literally a (physical) part of our mind, the knotted handkerchief and the calculator both form an important part of our reasoning processes. Extended cognition should not be confused with embodied cognition (embodiment). According to theories of embodiment, our body is an intrinsic part of the mind and conditions the way we think and perceive. Extended cognition is the more radical thesis that the mind is not just part of the body but also extends beyond the body into the environment.

See also: **cognition; embodiment; mind**

Key questions: Should things outside our mind be considered part of our cognitive processes? If so, how do we decide what these things are?

Further reading: Clark (1997); Clark and Chalmers (1998); Rowlands (1999)

E

Fact/value problem

The fact/value problem, also known as the 'is–ought' problem, is a long-running ethical dilemma first posed by Hume (1739–1740). Although there is a great deal of debate over precisely how to understand Hume's point regarding the issue, he is commonly assumed to be arguing that there is a 'gap' between what is the case (facts about the world) and what should or ought to be the case (evaluation of the world). We cannot validly infer what ought to be done from any set of facts; no ought-statements are entailed by is-statements. For instance, it is a fact that hitting a human causes them pain. However, we cannot infer from this fact that we ought not to hit humans. Therefore we cannot justify the claim 'we should not hit people' simply because of the fact 'it hurts people when we hit them'. We have to add the evaluative claim 'it is wrong to hurt people' in order to justify our ethical belief that harming people is wrong. The key idea behind the fact/value problem is that the world is morally neutral. A factual description of the world will not contain any mention of how we ought to act. The conclusion many draw from this problem is that our moral beliefs can never be grounded in, or justified by, facts about the world. This position is anti-realist because it denies that our moral values are facts. Consequently they are not things which can be true or false; they are not 'truth-evaluable'. Hume's view was that morals were an expression of 'sentiment' (taste).

See also: **anti-realism; emotivism; good, the; Hume; inference; meta-ethics; morality; validity**

Further reading: Hudson (1969); Hume (1739–1740); Moore (1903)

Facts

Facts play an important role in many theories of truth and knowledge. When we use the word 'fact' – as in the proposition, 'It is a fact that the Beatles were a popular English band' – we do so to indicate that the sentence is true. Contingent facts are those that do not need to be the case, such as the above propostion because it is possible to imagine that the Beatles were not a popular band. Other facts, such as '1 + 1 = 2', are said to be 'necessary'. Some philosophers, including Hume and Wittgenstein, have argued that all facts are contingent.

Whether contingent or necessary, it is also important to establish just what facts are. One theory is that they are 'truth-bearers'. A truth-bearer is something which can be true, normally described as a proposition (such as the above proposition about the Beatles). It is typical to think that facts relate to actual things in the world, such as the existence of a band called the Beatles. Difficulty arises when we try to make sense of negative or conditional facts. For instance, the proposition, 'it is a fact that a unicorn has a horn on its head' is conditional on the existence of unicorns, or at least on the existence of such a fictional animal. There is, therefore, nothing in the world itself which makes this fact true. Similarly, we might want to say that it is a fact that if I had missed the bus this morning, then I would have been late for work. Again, how are we to understand whether this is a true fact or not? Finally, moral philosophers have often spoken about 'moral facts', such as 'it is a fact that killing is wrong'. However, it is difficult to understand just what kind of a 'thing' this moral fact would be and how we could ever discover it.

See also: **anti-realism; correspondence theory; definite descriptions; knowledge; metaphysics; moral objectivism; realism; truth; unexplainable, the; Wittgenstein**

Further reading: Armstrong (1997, 2004); Hossack (2007); Neale (2001); Wittgenstein (1921)

Faith

The major question regarding faith is whether it is sufficient justification for holding a belief. I have faith in my friend repaying the money I lent him, but does this mean I am justified in believing he will repay the money? Faith is usually discussed within a religious context. What does it mean to have faith in God, and is this faith justified? Faith is typically contrasted with reason. Reason is assumed to be 'demonstrable'; we can explain how we arrived at our belief based on a set of facts which have been empirically verified, and any rational person would arrive at the same belief based on that set of facts. Faith, on the other hand, does not seem to be demonstrable. It tends to rest on some personal experience, revelation or conviction, which need not be shared by any other person.

The reason or evidence we have for our faith will not necessarily convince someone to share that belief. Descartes observed that, for those with religious convictions, 'it is enough to accept on faith ... that God exists' (1641: 3). For those without religious faith, Descartes felt that rational proofs were required and could be offered. Kierkegaard made the notion of faith central to his religious philosophy. Contrary to Descartes, he argued that reason and rationality were entirely irrelevant to religious belief. Instead, one must make a leap of faith from rationality to God. One does not 'prove' God, instead one 'feels' the existence of God just as one feels one is in love. Furthermore, to choose faith is to give up reason since religious faith 'begins precisely where thinking leaves off' (Kierkegaard, 1843b: 82). We cannot reason that God exists if we have faith that God exists.

The idea of a personal feeling or experience of God is common to many mystical traditions. God cannot be described or understood through words, therefore God cannot be grasped through reason and explanation. Instead one has faith in God based on personal, ineffable (inexpressible) experiences which cannot be communicated to anyone else (see, for example, James, 1902). Religious faith is typically seen as having no place in a scientific view of the world, a view which requires that knowledge is based on observable empirical methods. However, one must wonder whether the insistence that science is a superior method for obtaining a true understanding of the world is not itself a questionable form of faith.

See also: **belief; certainty; doubt; God, arguments for the existence of; intuition; justification; Kierkegaard; knowledge; mysticism; religious belief**

Further reading: James (1902); Kierkegaard (1843a, 1843b); O'Hear (1984)

Fallacy

A fallacy is a flawed argument. It is typically defined as a poor piece of reasoning that *appears* to be a good piece of reasoning. It can therefore be quite difficult to detect a fallacy. Formal fallacies relate to the 'form' or structure of an argument, rather than to the content. It does not matter whether the conclusion is true or false because the issue is whether the form of the argument is correct (valid). An example of a formal fallacy is:

Some musicians do not like playing football
Guy is a musician
Therefore Guy does not like playing football

Although it might appear convincing, the conclusion is not guaranteed by the premises. Only some musicians do not like playing football and we cannot know whether Guy is one of those musicians.

Informal fallacies are problems with the content of an argument rather than its logical structure. An example of this is the common 'gambler fallacy', in which someone misunderstands the nature of probability. Imagine that a fair coin was tossed five times. Even if it landed 'heads' on all five tosses, the chance of it landing 'heads' on the next toss is still 50/50. However, people are liable to think mistakenly that because it has landed 'heads' for the last five tosses, it is more likely to land 'tails' on the next toss. There are many informal fallacies, which a great number of philosophers have been guilty of committing (see, for example, **Descartes**). Important informal fallacies include begging the question, vicious circle, straw man, *ad hominem* and slippery slope.

See also: ad hominem; **begging the question; deduction;; hypothetico-deductive method; induction; justification; logic; slippery slope argument; soundness; validity; vicious circle**

Further reading: Engel (1994); Hamblin (1970); Hansen and Pinto (1995); Walton (1989)

Feminism

Feminists claim that women are the victims of patriarchy, the systematic political and social oppression of women by men. The term 'systematic' refers to the belief that gender inequality is built into the structure of social institutions so that men are inherently favoured over women in employment, education, the legal system and so on. The aim of feminism is to end the oppression of women. Feminist debate focuses on how this is to be achieved. Three main solutions – referred to as 'waves' of feminism – have been defended in turn.

First-wave feminism, also known as liberal feminism, developed during the nineteenth and early twentieth century. Its main focus was women's suffrage (the gaining of political voting power). First-wave feminists believed that women were equal to men, and thus capable of doing all that a man could do. This belief was influenced by the activities of women in England during the World Wars, when women performed many of the tasks normally performed by men who had left to fight. Second-wave, or radical, feminism arose in the 1960s and 1970s when feminists began to challenge first-wave feminism's emphasis on equality. Second-wave feminists argued that first-wave feminism led women to accept the current state of society, rather than to change it. Instead of aspiring to become like men, second-wave feminists set out to create a separate space in which women could express themselves. The solution to women's oppression was a rejection of male-dominated society, rather than first-wave feminism's demands to be accepted into it. The focus of second-wave feminism was on documenting women's experiences and the positive aspects of womanhood. By exploring the essential features of being a woman, which historically had been ignored, distorted and repressed by men, second-wave feminists sought to create a global women's movement founded upon their collective 'womanness'.

From the 1980s onwards, third-wave feminism has questioned the ideas of the universal woman and, indeed, our understanding of gender. Strongly influenced by post-structural philosophy, third-wave feminists challenged the image of the essential nature of 'woman' which, they claimed, represented an educated, middle-class, white understanding of what a woman is. Third-wave feminism seeks to deconstruct the categories of 'man' and 'woman' in an attempt to break down divisions between them. The aim is to multiply gender beyond the binary division of man/woman which represents a male logic of separation. As long as women are perceived as opposite to men, they will always be dominated and oppressed. This is not a return to first-wave feminism's desire for equality between the sexes but an attempt to break down the idea of oppositional/binary sexes and genders.

See also: **Bentham; body, the; Butler; constructionism; de Beauvoir; equality; gender; Mill; performativity; queer theory**

Further reading: de Beauvoir (1949); Chodrow (1978); Daly (1979); Friedan (1963); Koedt et al. (1973); Millett (1970); Spelman (1988); Tong (1998)

Folk psychology

Folk psychology is the term given to theories of mind based upon the idea of mental states such as 'belief', 'happiness', 'desire' and such like. Folk psychology is also known as 'commonsense psychology' because it is based upon our everyday understanding of the mind. According to folk psychologists we can explain, predict and analyse human behaviour by referring to mental states such as beliefs. For instance, we explain our observation of someone drinking a glass of water through reference to their being thirsty, believing that drinking water will get rid of their thirst, thinking that a glass is a good object to put water in, and so forth. Folk psychology has been challenged by eliminative materialism, which argues it is an obsolete and inaccurate description of the mind and must therefore be eradicated.

See also: **belief; consciousness; eliminative materialism; mind**

Further reading: Davies and Stone (1995); Hutto and Ratcliffe (2007)

Formal fallacy

See **fallacy**

F

Foucault, Michel (1926–1984)

One of the most influential and well-known philosophers of the twentieth century, Foucault is a major figure in post-structuralist theory as well as a prominent political analyst. There are several important strands to Foucault's work. One is an interest in the historical development of concepts. In *The History of Madness in the Classical Age* (1961), Foucault traces historical changes in the concept of madness in an attempt to demonstrate that the supposedly objective scientific and psychological understanding of madness is a product of political and social forces. In other words, the idea of madness, and thus reason, are socially-contingent (socially-dependent) constructs which serve to maintain power relations and social inequalities. *The History of Sexuality* (1976) is a similar analysis of sexuality, which has strongly influenced many recent feminists, such as Butler.

The method of uncovering the roots of a concept in order to show how it has been constructed, rather than discovered, is known as a 'genealogical' analysis, which Foucault adopted from Nietzsche's (1887) critique of morality. Underlying these studies is an interest in the way knowledge is used to silence and exclude people. Those people who scientists and psychologists deem to be 'mad' are hidden away, ignored and mistreated. Foucault refers to the experiences and beliefs of the oppressed as 'subjugated knowledges' (1980: 82) and much of his work is aimed at making them heard.

Underlying these ideas is Foucault's notion of 'discourse', which is a regulated body (system) of knowledge that is presented as authoritative and serves to transmit and produce power. Discourses do not aim at, or produce, 'truth'. They control and create behaviour and knowledge. In other words, we, as subjects, are created by, and controlled through, discourse. The discourse of madness is one way in which norms of behaviour and belief (demonstrated by the 'sane') are enforced, with those who challenge it facing punishment. Foucault was sceptical of the idea of an autonomous and rational 'self', believing it to be simply another discourse, and argued that it is impossible to think of ourselves independently of the social power relations and discourses within which we are created and maintained. Foucault even argued that the body itself is an historically and socially contingent entity. It is formed through political and social discourses and cannot be thought of as a 'natural' thing.

See also: **body, the; constructionism; discourse; feminism; genealogy; historicism; ideology; post-structuralism; postmodernism; relativism; self, the; subjectivity**
Further reading: Foucault (1961, 1969, 1976, 1980, 1984); Gutting (2005); Mills (2003)

F

Foundationalism

According to foundationalism, all justified belief ultimately rests upon a foundation of certain knowledge. Much of what we think we know is actually justified by other beliefs or knowledge. For instance, my knowing that Descartes was a philosopher could be based upon my knowing that books written about him are accurate. Such beliefs are 'inferred' because we arrive at them by moving from premises to conclusions. The premises might include something like 'the history book I am reading says Descartes was a philosopher' and 'history books are accurate guides to the past'. The belief that Descartes was a philosopher is an 'inferentially justified' belief.

Foundationalists argue that at least some of our beliefs must be 'basic', that is, non-inferentially justified on the basis of an infinite regress argument. According to their analysis, if all beliefs are inferentially justified then we have two options: (a) each belief must be justified by another, which in turn must be justified by another, *ad infinitum.*, which leaves us with an infinitely long chain of justification in which no belief is unconditionally justified; or (b) the chain of justification loops back on itself, creating a circle in which our justification for believing 'x' ultimately rests upon x itself. Both options lead to an impossible situation in which no belief has any positive justification Descartes famously arrived at his *cogito* (the certain belief that he is a thinking being) as that which was certainly true, and did not rely upon any other belief for its justification. Unlike Descartes, who was a rationalist, most foundationalists are empiricists. They seek to find a basic, non-inferential belief in our immediate sensory (perceptual) experience. There must be some sensory experiences, they argue, which are 'infallible' (cannot be doubted) and can thus act as the necessary non-inferential beliefs needed for a secure foundation of knowledge.

See also: **certainty; Descartes; doubt; empiricism; intuition; justification; knowledge; truth**

Key questions: Must there be a foundation of certain knowledge in order for our beliefs to be justified? How could we discover this foundation?

Further reading: Dancy (1985); Descartes (1641); Rockmore (2004)

Frankfurt School

The Frankfurt School was the title applied to the department for the scientific study of Marxism which opened in the Institute for Social Research in Frankfurt in 1923. A number of important thinkers met at the Institute, bringing with them knowledge from different disciplines such as philosophy, psychology and aesthetics. The early members included Adorno and Horkheimer. Habermas joined the group later. Together they created an inter-disciplinary critical theory of society, which included analyses of culture, consumerism and fascism. These analyses aimed to evaluate the application of Marxist theory to the social context of the time.

See also: **Adorno; Habermas; Marxism**

Further reading: Marxists Internet Archive (http://www.marxists.org/subject/frankfurt-school/index.htm); Wiggershaus (1995)

Freedom

If an individual has freedom, then that individual's actions and decisions are of their own making and thus they are responsible for them. To what extent humans possess, or should possess, freedom is a major issue in political and moral philosophy. It seems difficult to assign moral praise to someone who does not act freely. Similarly, can we justify punishing someone – perhaps by putting them in jail – if they did not act freely? Politically we can differentiate between freedom-to-act (positive freedom) and freedom-from-actions (negative freedom). Possessing freedom-to-act is to have autonomy, to be able to do as one pleases. Freedom-from-actions means that individuals are protected from having their freedom inhibited. For instance, in the UK individuals supposedly have freedom from racial or gender discrimination. The extent to which different political systems promote or erode freedom is often used as a reason for supporting or opposing them.

Another issue is whether it is in the best interests of society and individuals to grant people total freedom, and the extent to which people should be granted civil liberty. For example, should people in institutional care for a mental disability be permitted to form relationships or have children? Anarchists argue for the removal of all authoritative (governmental) power, which they see as inhibiting the freedom of individuals. However, opponents of anarchism argue that society can only function if people are prevented from acting with total freedom. According to existential philosophy, humans possess absolute freedom and so are entirely responsible for every single action or thought. However, many psychological explanations of human action, such as behaviourist and Freudian theories, limit the extent to which humans possess freedom, so human action is determined by such factors as one's upbringing or unconscious thoughts. More recent theories include the role of genetic inheritance in determining behaviour. Post-structuralists, such as Foucault, explore how discourse and social power relations construct who we are, including our desires and beliefs about how we should live. Theories of fate, common to many religions, also appear to limit the extent to which humans possess freedom.

See also: **anarchy; agency; Butler; communism; democracy; determinism; discourse; existentialism; Foucault; free will; humanism; individual, the; karma; liberalism; liberty; Mill; responsibility; rights; socialism; subjectivity; tolerance**

Key questions: Is freedom always a good thing? Should each of us be granted absolute freedom?

Further reading: Brenkert (1991); Carter et al. (2007); Civil Liberty (http://www.civilliberty.org.uk/); Gray (1991); Sartre (1946)

Free will

Free will is different from being free to do whatever we want because we might 'will' ourselves to fly but there are constraints on that being possible. Free will refers to making choices and thus we are responsible for what we do. For compatibilists (see **determinism**) free will means we are free to the extent that we can choose how we act given who we are. We are not controlled by external or internal forces although limits might be imposed by, for example, our height or the weather. Sartre believed we are not constrained by God-given morality, stating that man is condemned to be free: we can do as we choose but the outcome is entirely our responsibility and in that sense a source of anxiety. However, hard determinists such as Skinner claimed free will to be an illusion arising from not knowing the chain of causation leading to a particular behaviour.

See also: **behaviourism; determinism; freedom; reason; Sartre; unconscious, the;**

Key questions: Do we possess free will? What are the consequences for moral and legal responsibility if we do not?

Further reading: Fischer et al. (2007); Kane (1996); Sartre (1943); Skinner (1971)

F

Frege, Gottlob (1848–1925)

Frege, a German mathematician, logician and philosopher, was central to the development of analytic philosophy, in particular modern logic and philosophy of language. His ideas greatly influenced the work of Russell and Wittgenstein amongst others. His most important philosophical contribution was his theory of meaning.

Frege began by distinguishing between 'objects' and 'concepts'. An object is something which can be referred to by name, such as 'Belfast' or 'Duncan'. A concept is the reference of a predicate, and a predicate is what remains of a sentence when all names (objects) have been deleted. So, for instance, the predicate of the sentence 'Duncan is artistic' will be 'is artistic'. In effect, predicates are things which describe names (objects). Frege thought of concepts as 'abstract entities', meaning that they are not something mental (in the mind) but features of the world. So the reference of the concept 'is artistic' will be the property of being artistic, which is possessed by the object 'Duncan'.

Frege proceeded to analyse just how proper names refer to objects. A proper name is one which refers to a single object, such as the person 'Duncan', rather than a group of objects, such as 'cat'. According to Frege, all proper names have both a 'sense' and a 'reference' which allow us to identify them successfully from amongst the objects in the world. To show this, he considered a puzzle concerning an identity claim. The terms 'morning star' and 'evening star' were, in his time, both used to refer to the planet Venus. Therefore, the following statements are true, because they 'denote' (refer to) the same object:

1. The morning star = the morning star
2. The morning star = the evening star

Frege noted that, whilst (1) is known to be true *a priori* (simply by inspecting the sentence itself), (2) is true only through empirical investigation (that is, astronomy). Therefore, a sentence must be taken as having both a sense and a reference. This is the only way that (2) can be informative, because if we took the meaning of a sentence as simply what it refers to then (1) would be identical to (2) because they would express entirely the same information (for they would refer to the same thing). Frege believed that the 'sense' of a proper name is its 'mode of presentation' and it is this which allows us to pick out or identify the particular object. Often this will be some definite description. For instance, a speaker may associate the sense of 'the morning star' with 'is the second planet from the Sun'. Mill and Kripke have both argued against the idea that proper names have senses. They claim that they only have a reference.

See also: **analytic philosophy; definite descriptions; Mill; Russell; reference**

Further reading: Currie (1982); Dummett (1981); Frege (1892a, 1892b)

Freud, Sigmund (1856–1939)

Freud's work strongly affected our understanding of the mind and human behaviour. Influenced by Darwin's theories and an essay by Goethe on nature, he decided to study medicine, later developing an interest in nervous disorders above physiology. He considered religion to be a form of neurosis (see Freud, 1913) and espoused a scientific approach to his work that relied on observation and testing. One of

Freud's major contributions was his theory of the structure of the mind. Although the idea that the mind included an unconscious component can be traced back at least as far as Spinoza and Leibniz, Freud was the first to formulate the theory and its implications comprehensively. Freud used the concept of the unconscious to explain how apparently random acts, such as the dropping of a pen or uttering the wrong word in conversation, actually had causal explanations. Specifically, they were caused by unconscious desires. This allowed Freud to maintain the belief, formulated during the enlightenment, that the world was a rational place, governed by cause–and-effect relations, and wholly subject to scientific explanation.

According to Freud, the mind is divided into three components, the ego, id and superego. The ego mediates between three conflicting demands being made on the mind: (1) the impulsive, pleasure-seeking drives originating in the id; (2) the socially imposed morals forming the super-ego; and (3) the external world (which Freud calls reality). The task of the ego is thus to balance the various pressures placed on each of us, which, in relation to the id, Freud likened to a rider trying to control the movements of a powerful horse. Freud's concept of the mind has very important implications for the notion of free will, for it suggests that many of our actions are not freely chosen but rather result from unconscious processes in the brain. Furthermore, it produces problems for the introspective model of the mind, which originated with Descartes and his legacy of the mind as a 'private theatre'. If we are unaware of many of the workings of our mind, then no amount of introspection will reveal its contents. A full account of the mind and its workings requires more than 'arm chair' philosophy in which one reflects upon one's conscious awareness. Instead, the unconscious must be analysed by symbolically interpreting conscious thoughts and actions. Freud's influence can be seen in the widespread use of psychoanalysis as a reasoned approach to treating mental ill-health.

See also: **Darwinism; ego, the; scientific method; unconscious, the**

Further reading: Erwin (2002); Freud, S. (1901, 1913, 1920); Gay (1995); Gilman et al. (1994); Storr (2001)

Functionalism

Functionalism is a theory of mind inspired by the technological developments in computer programming. Functionalists describe the mind as an organic computer and mental processes as functions performed by neurological patterns in the brain. Just as a computer contains many electronic circuits which run a variety of programs, so a brain has many neurological circuits which produce different mental states. The images produced on a computer screen are analogous to our experience of hunger or pain. Functionalist accounts of the mind tend to be monist, for they see the mind as purely physical. Just as the image of the computer screen is not some ghostly, non-physical entity, so our consciousness is not some soul or non-physical substance.

Functionalism explains mental states by the function they play in the physical system we call the mind. For instance, a functionalist would characterise hunger as a state caused by the stomach being empty of food, which in turn causes the mental belief that something is physically wrong, causing the desire to cure this problem through eating. The functionalist account of mind therefore characterises mental states in terms of causal stimuli such as sensory stimulations and other mental states which can be realised in many different ways. If an alien or animal behaved in the same way as the hungry human then we would ascribe the mental state 'hunger' to that alien or animal.

A major debate arising from functionalism is whether computers could be said to possess mental states if they functioned in a way that we would recognisable as a mental state such as hungry or sad. If a robot winces when kicked in the leg, is this sufficient to label it as conscious? One influential argument against this belief is Searle's Chinese Room argument (see **artificial intelligence**)

See also: **artificial intelligence; belief; cognition; consciousness; dualism; mind, the; physicalism;**

Further reading: Block (1980); Chalmers (1996); Heil (1998)

F

Gadamer, Hans-Georg (1900–2002)

The leading figure in hermeneutic philosophy, Gadamer was highly influenced by Martin Heidegger, under whom he studied, and the later work of Wittgenstein. Hermeneutics is the understanding and interpretation of texts. In Gadamer's view, understanding a text does not involve simply trying to understand the author's meaning (intention), but rather setting up a dialogue between one's own understanding and the text. All understanding is therefore a 'fusion of horizons' (Gadamer, 1960). We impose a particular interpretation on the text, which alters how the text is read, which in turn alters our understanding. This potentially endless circle of interpretation and re-interpretation is known as the hermeneutic circle.

Another key feature of Gadamer's work is his rehabilitation of prejudice. According to Gadamer our understanding and knowledge are bound up with the specific time and place we are born into. Our reading of a text, or understanding of an idea, is already 'prejudiced' by our framework of knowledge because we can only understand using the ideas and concepts of our society. Gadamer was thus keen to emphasise the importance and inescapability of one's tradition. Two criticisms levelled against Gadamer's work are that it falls into subjectivism and that it does not adequately explain how we can differentiate between good and bad interpretations of a text.

See also: **context; Habermas; Heidegger; hermeneutics; historicism; knowledge; Rorty; subjectivity; Wittgenstein**

Further reading: Dostal (2002); Gadamer (1960, 1976, 1981); Grondin (2002, 2007)

Gender

Following the work of Gayle Rubin (1975), feminist philosophers have tended to separate sex from gender. Sex is used to refer to one's physical/biological sexual characteristics (such as having a penis or uterus), whereas gender refers to the cultural and social expressions of difference. Consequently male/female is used to denote sex and masculine/feminine denotes gender. A key feminist insight is that understandings of gender differ across time and place. This has allowed feminists to argue that inequalities between men and women are not a product of sexual (physical) differences, but a social construct created by men which can be changed. The mistake is to assume that gender is determined by sex, and therefore it is 'natural' for women to wash-up, wear make-up, raise children and be subservient to men.

As Simone de Beauvoir (1949) declared, biology is not destiny, meaning being born physically female does not mean one must behave as society expects a woman to behave. A major debate within feminism is whether we should retain the idea of gender and work to change our definition of gender characteristics, or try to open up a plurality of genders, or eliminate the idea of gender altogether. The second two options attempt to move us beyond the idea of having to be either masculine or feminine.

See also: **Butler; constructionism; de Beauvoir; feminism; kind, natural; performativity; post-humanism; queer theory; yin-yang**

Further reading: Butler (1990, 2004); de Beauvoir (1949); Nicholson (1990); Rubin (1975)

Genealogy

Genealogy is a method of analysis first used by Nietzsche and most famously employed by Foucault. To perform a genealogical analysis is to trace the development of an idea, belief or concept throughout history. In doing so, one reveals that there is no single origin of the idea and no essential truth to that idea, but rather that all beliefs are contingent historical products, influenced and shaped by socio-political events throughout history.

Foucault performed a genealogical study of sexuality and madness in order to reveal the different understandings of each concept throughout history and to show that at each point the definitions were used to control and construct individuals. A genealogical study will show how certain experiences and knowledge, which did not fit the 'official' view, were silenced and punished. In other words, genealogy highlights how knowledge is a vehicle for power by linking the development of knowledge to the ability of authority to control members of society. The notions of what is sexually 'right' and who is sane/mad did not arise from an essential truth, but rather developed as a form of social and political control over how the individual should be.

See also: **anti-realism; constructionism; deconstruction; discourse; Foucault; historicism; Nietzsche; post-structuralism; postmodernism; reason; subjectivity**

Further reading: Foucault (1978); Nietzsche (1887); Prado (2000)

Gestalt

See **holism**

God

Whilst the idea of a god or gods is common to almost all human cultures, interpretations and descriptions of 'god' differ considerably. Monotheistic religions claim there is only one god, whilst polytheistic traditions, such as Hinduism and Greek mythology refer to many gods, although some are more powerful than others. Some religions view god as existing within the universe or literally being the universe, whilst others claim god is partly or entirely outside the universe. If a god created the universe, then that god must be independent of it. Within the dominant Western traditions the god in question is described as the all-powerful (omnipotent) and all-knowing (omniscient) creator of the universe. God is also thought to be present everywhere at all times (omnipresent) and morally perfect. Feminists have critically highlighted that God is always referred to as 'He' and represented as a male.

According to deism, a god set the universe in motion and has not intervened since. Deists thus deny such events as miracles and revelations and deists deny that we can assign any attributes to or make any meaningful descriptions of god. Theist religions, which include Christianity, Islam and Judaism, reject this view, arguing that God is actively involved in the universe and reveals Himself through His actions. Interesting Judaeo-Christian philosophical puzzles about God include whether He created the moral laws, or is subject to them. If He did not create them, then they can be changed at any time and therefore the Ten Commandments are only literally set in stone. Another puzzle is whether, if God is all-powerful, he could create an object that is too heavy for Him to be able to lift.

See also: **Anselm; Augustine; Berkeley; creationism; Darwinism; enlightenment; evil, the problem of; faith; God, arguments for the existence of; Hinduism; Kierkegaard; mysticism; paradox; Pascal's wager; religious belief; teleology; transcendence; unexplainable, the; Zoroastrianism**

Further reading: Armstrong (1994); Etienne (2002); Owen (1971)

God, arguments for the existence of

From its very beginnings, philosophy has produced arguments which claim to prove that God exists. There are three major arguments (the Holy Trinity of proofs): the cosmological argument, the ontological argument and the teleological argument. The cosmological argument can be traced back to Aristotle, but its best-known formulation comes from Aquinas. The cosmological argument is based upon the principle that everything has a cause, so that we can trace a chain of causes throughout time which have led to the present moment. However, because it is impossible to have an infinite number of causes, there must be a first cause in the universe, which is God. The ontological argument rests upon the notion of a perfect being. The most perfect being would have to exist, because it would be more perfect than a being that did not exist. Therefore, because we have a notion of the most perfect being, that being must necessarily exist. Influential formulations of the ontological argument have been offered by Anselm, Malebranche, Leibniz, Spinoza and Descartes. A more robust version of the ontological argument using the idea of modality was formulated in the late 20th century (van Inwagen, 1993). The teleological argument, also called the argument from design, is the best known of the three proofs. Essentially, it is the claim that when we examine the universe it appears so ordered that it must have been designed. The only possible thing which could have designed the universe is God, therefore God exists. Darwin's theory of evolution is often used to explain how the apparent order of the universe could have arisen purely through chance. However, defenders of the teleological argument might argue that the conditions required for life to develop are so hugely complex that the probability of them coming about by chance is simply too small. Therefore such conditions must have been designed, by God.

G

Many religious thinkers deny that God is something that could ever be proved through rational argument. Mystical accounts of God claim that it is through a personal, internal experience that one gains belief in, or knowledge of, God's existence. Famous Western proponents of the value of such religious experiences include William James and Kierkegaard, who talked of a 'leap of faith' from rationality and reason into religious belief. Sufism, Buddhism, Taoism and Hinduism all see religious belief as a result of direct personal experience, rather than abstract logical proofs, which is why these religions value techniques such as meditation above scholarly, rational debate. This does not mean that belief in God is irrational, but rather that such belief or knowledge is a different form of knowledge from that produced by logical, rational enquiry.

See also: **Anselm; Augustine; Berkeley; creationism; Darwinism; Descartes; faith; evil, the problem of; faith; free will; God; mysticism; religious belief; unexplainable, the**

Further reading: O'Hear (1984); Swinburne (1979); van Inwagen (1993)

Good, the

In its general use, the term 'the good' refers to positive moral appraisal. To act morally is to act in a 'good' way and so the concept of the good is the basis of all ethical theories. The problem with 'the good' lies in actually defining it. A famous critique of this problem was produced by G.E. Moore (1903) and runs as follows. Assume we are utilitarians, such as Mill, and define 'the good' as happiness. The good is therefore whatever promotes happiness. However, if we define 'the good' as 'happiness' then the moral statement 'happiness is good' would mean the same as the statement 'happiness is happiness', because 'happiness' simply means 'good'. On the basis of this analysis, Moore argued that 'the good' or the property 'being good' is simple and unanalysable. In effect, we can recognise what is good without being able to define it. Despite this, most moral philosophers believe we can give a full account of what is good.

One major dispute is whether the good is an objective or subjective concept. To claim it is objective is to argue that there is some 'thing' in the universe, a moral law, which defines what is good. Plato's theory of the forms is a famous example of this. Plato argued that every feature of reality, from a horse to the colour red, has a true essence which resides in a heavenly realm. We can recognise a horse as a horse because each horse possesses the essence, or form, of 'horseness'. According to Plato, the ultimate form is the form of the good, which resides in everything we recognise as good. A subjectivist would reject the idea that what is good is anything more than a human construct, and so what we think of as 'good' depends on our culture, set of beliefs, or personal tastes. Unlike objectivists, a subjectivist would not see one notion of the good as being any more 'right' or 'wrong' than any other.

See also: **consequentialism; descriptivism; deontology; emotivism; evil; fact/value problem, the; happiness; intuition; Moore; moral intuitionism; morality; moral objectivism; moral subjectivism; Plato;** *summum bonum*

Further reading: Blackburn (2001); Desjardins (2004); Moore (1903)

G

Greek philosophy, ancient

The work of the ancient Greek philosophers has determined a good deal of the topics discussed and methods adopted within Western philosophy. Many of the major philosophical issues discussed today were first raised by the Greeks. This led Whitehead (1929) to claim that the history of philosophy is best viewed as a series of footnotes to Plato. The other major figures of Greek philosophy are Aristotle and Socrates. Ancient Greek philosophers belonged to a number of different schools of thought, including the Presocratics, the Sophists, the Stoics and the Epicureans. There were also many influential thinkers. Thales, often regarded as the 'father' of Greek philosophy, argued that water was the source of all things in the universe. Anaximander declared the basic 'stuff' of the universe to be indefinable and limitless. Heraclitus thought that this basic 'stuff' from which everything developed, and to which it eventually returned, was fire. Pythagoras and his followers believed that the universe could be understood mathematically through discovering the numerical relations and principles that are inherent within the universe. Epicurus was both a hedonist, claiming that the goal of human life was happiness (or absence of suffering), and an empirical materialist, arguing that all knowledge is derived through the senses and that only material things exist (therefore there is neither a soul nor an afterlife). Democritus made the interesting assertion that all material things were composed of microscopic entities, which has striking similarities to the modern idea of 'atoms'. Finally, Zeno composed many fascinating paradoxes, which are still discussed today. Other important figures in Greek philosophy include Anaxagoras, Xenophanes and Parmenides.

As suggested above, the ancient Greeks discussed metaphysical and ontological issues, including the composition of the universe and the possible existence of non-observable entities (such as numbers and universals). They also debated what 'the good' is, how this relates to living the 'good life' and how such a life can be achieved. Other topics of discussion were the epistemological question of what, if anything, we can be said to know and the political issues of justice and government. Finally, the *way* in which philosophy was performed was a major interest of these philosophers. Their use of logical analysis of argument, their emphasis on reason rather than rhetoric, and their attempts to suspend what they believed in order to see if it was justified, have defined the way in which the majority of philosophers believe philosophy should be conducted.

See also: **Aristotle; dialectic; epistemology; good, the; logic; metaphysics; monism; ontology; Plato; Socrates; sophism; stoicism;** *summum bonum*; **Zeno's paradoxes; virtue; virtue ethics**

Further reading: Cohen et al. (2005); Long (1999); Sedley (2003); Shields (2003)

G

Habermas, Jürgen (1929–)

A highly influential German philosopher, Habermas was greatly affected by the rise of Nazi politics in Germany and the failure of German philosophy to provide a satisfactory opposition to it. He is a leading proponent of the Frankfurt School of critical theory, which was founded upon Marxist principles. One of Habermas's major projects is to defend the idea of rationality in the face of postmodernist deconstruction and Gadamer's hermeneutics. Habermas sought to 'rehabilitate' (restore faith in) the enlightenment's belief in reason as emancipatory (liberating), believing that communities should be able to express and evaluate moral and political concerns using rational and logical analysis.

A key aspect of Habermas's thought, which underlies almost all his writing, is his theory of 'communicative action'. This concept describes how members of society use reasoned debate to achieve common understanding, consensus and mutual co-operation. It contrasts with the description of humans as isolated knowing subjects, strategically seeking to fulfil their own goals. Underlying Habermas's model is the belief that language (communication) is necessarily social and rational. We exist as intersubjective beings, meaning that we are necessarily social beings sharing a 'life-world' (community/environment) in which we must work together and communicate in order to achieve our desires and meet our needs. Communicative action is achieved by rational agents freely agreeing that their respective goals are reasonable. This generates coordinated action aimed at achieving these goals. Habermas believes that social cohesion could be grounded in rational discourse, since respecting other people's opinions and differences becomes acceptable if such differences are seen as rational. It is also the basis for Habermas's model of 'deliberative democracy' in which governmental policies and laws are open to public debate, with decisions being based on the most rational conclusions. His liberal model stresses the importance of free speech, though the extent to which such speech is, or can be made, rational is open to debate.

See also: **democracy; Frankfurt school; liberalism; Marxism; postmodernism; reason**

Further reading: Habermas (1967, 1971, 1981a, 1981b); Honneth and Joas (1991); Pusey (1987)

Happiness

According to certain forms of utilitarianism, an action is morally good if it promotes happiness and morally objectionable if it promotes unhappiness. The best acts are those which promote the greatest happiness for the greatest number of people (or sentient beings). According to virtue ethicists such as Aristotle all human action is directed towards a certain goal, which Aristotle termed *eudaimonia*.

Often this is translated as 'happiness', but a more appropriate translation might be 'flourishing' or 'living well', a state which is achieved by cultivating specific characteristics or virtues. Within Buddhist philosophy the way to achieve true happiness is by entering a state of *nirvana*. Following a similar approach to virtue ethics, Buddhism teaches that we must develop ourselves through meditational practices in order to become the kind of person who is capable of enlightenment. Buddhists claim that mere everyday happiness is always fleeting. Eternal happiness can only be achieved through becoming enlightened.

One problem with discussing happiness is that different people have different conceptions of happiness. Some people are made happy by watching a beautiful sunset, whilst a sadist might derive happiness from inflicting pain upon people. Can we say that one person's happiness is 'better' or more akin to 'real' happiness than another? A further issue is whether happiness should be considered a physical emotion, a complex cognitive phenomenon or a social construction.

See also: **Aristotle; Buddhism; consequentialism; egoism; subjectivity;** *summum bonum*; **virtue ethics**

Key questions: Is it possible to experience happiness without also understanding unhappiness? Is a world in which people were only ever happy possible or indeed desirable?

Further reading: Harvey (1990); McMahon (2006)

Hare, Richard M. (1919–2002)

Hare was an important 20th century moral theorist best known for his development of prescriptivism, the view that moral beliefs are universal 'prescriptions' or commands. This offered an important alternative to emotivism, the view that what is morally right is simply whatever our emotions/feelings dictate. Despite being a pacifist, Hare served during World War II. He spent three years as a prisoner of war and this experience helped convince him of the importance of moral philosophy in people's everyday lives, particularly with regard to the daily moral challenges we face.

Hare was influenced by the ordinary language approach to philosophy and formulated his moral theory through an analysis of the meaning of words such as 'good' and 'ought'. Hare's basic idea was that moral judgements are universal prescriptions/imperatives, which indicate what each person ought to do in a given situation. When I say 'do not steal my bag', I am insisting that (1) you should not steal my bag, and (2) no person in a sufficiently similar situation should steal my bag. One important feature of Hare's work was that it did not treat moral statements as 'truth-evaluable', meaning we could not say whether they are true or false. Instead we should examine whether they are sincere, consistent, rational and so on. Hare's work allows us to retain the freedom to make moral judgements based on our personal attitudes – the view which had made emotivism appealing – whilst showing that reason, and not just emotion, has a decisive role to play in constructing our moral beliefs.

See also: **descriptivism; emotivism; categorical imperative; moral intuitionism; morality; moral subjectivism; prescriptivism**

Further reading: Hare (1952, 1963a, 1963b, 1981, 1989)

H

Hegel, Georg (1770–1831)

One of the great German philosophers, Hegel had a strong influence on Marx and, more recently, members of the Frankfurt school, as well as such theorists as Gadamer and Butler. Generally, his reception within analytic philosophy has been lukewarm, though even here attitudes seem to be becoming more favourable. Hegel wanted to generate a comprehensive philosophical system, one that moved beyond his own situation and offered a more 'global' perspective. He attempted to reconcile each particular, historical stage of philosophy by uncovering the 'logic' and 'reason' behind its development. This was achieved through his idea of the 'absolute', the 'whole' within which the world and philosophical thought could be understood as 'parts'.

Hegel believed that history is 'teleological', meaning we can view it as a linear, progressive movement towards a single end point. Within this view, philosophy can be seen as the development of consciousness towards a final moment of 'absolute knowing', which is no longer relative to historical perspective. Truth, according to Hegel, is dynamic, meaning it develops as the human mind develops. When the mind achieves absolute knowing, we will have realised absolute truth. Hegel described truth as a 'dialectic', a process of conflict in which a thesis is set against its antithesis, producing a synthesis. This synthesis then becomes the thesis in the next stage in the logical development of truth.

Within Hegel's grand system, consciousness and the world cannot be thought of as separate. There is no world (or world-in-itself) distinct from consciousness, which is why Hegel is an idealist. Furthermore, each individual consciousness is actually part of the one, universal consciousness or 'spirit' (*geist*). All reality is the product of this single universal spirit, or mind, and each individual is an expression or aspect of this mind. God, according to Hegel, is this universal spirit and the end point of humanity's development will be a full self-realisation in which we become identified with this 'absolute spirit' and thus attain absolute knowing (truth).

See also: **Butler; dialectic; Frankfurt school; Gadamer; idealism; reason; teleology; truth**

Further reading: Beiser (2005); Hegel (1807, 1822); Stern (2002)

Heidegger, Martin (1889–1976)

H

A German existential phenomenologist best known for his work *Being and Time* (1927), Heidegger's ideas have greatly influenced many important thinkers, including Sartre, Gadamer, Arendt and Rorty. Others, perhaps most notably Carnap, have dismissed his confusing style of writing and use of obscure concepts as nonsensical. Heidegger's major project was an attempt to revive the meaning of 'being' (Dasein), which he believed had been ignored by the dominant Western philosophers, Plato, Descartes, Kant and Husserl. Dasein represents an individual's 'being-in-the-world', both how we find ourselves in the world and what allows there *to be* a world for us. Dasein is revealed through anxiety, a state in which one loses all familiarity with the world and nothing holds significance. According to Heidegger this gives one a sense of radical freedom and responsibility, as well as the awareness of one's own mortality. As a result, one can begin to live authentically rather than just following the herd.

Another feature of Heidegger's idea of being is that, in order for us to have any understanding whatsoever, we must already be 'in' the world 'alongside' that which is to be understood. In other words, when we approach something in an attempt to understand it, we always approach it as *something*. For example, if we try to understand a piece of music we must already have some prior understanding of it. At the very least, we understand it as a collection of notes related in a certain way. Heidegger describes this condition of understanding as our 'situatedness' – we must exist in a certain 'situation' (world of meaning) and cannot think of ourselves as somehow independent of, or able to transcend, a particular situation. To give an account of understanding, therefore, is to 'lay bare' the structure of meanings (situation) within which we find ourselves. This idea forms the basis of modern hermeneutics and has particularly influenced Gadamer.

See also: **angst; Arendt; authenticity; being; Dasein; existentialism; freedom; Gadamer; intersubjectivity; nihilism; nothingness; phenomenology; Rorty**

Further reading: Cooper (1996a); Dreyfus (1991); Heidegger (1927, 1953, 1967); Mulhall (2005)

Hermeneutics

Hermeneutics is a term referring to both the skill and theories of interpretation. Originally, hermeneutics was limited to the interpretation of Biblical texts, but Friedrich Schleiermacher and Wilhelm Dilthey expanded its usage to cover all human communication, including history. Schleiermacher argued that we can never assume we shall correctly understand something, such as another culture, and therefore we must approach interpretation with great care and openness and be wary of imposing our own expectations and beliefs onto a text. This suspicion regarding supposedly neutral interpretation was developed by Heidegger, but it is given its most thorough expression in the work of his student, Gadamer.

Gadamer argued that it is through language that the world is made available to us, for without language the world would have no meaning. As a result we are always 'trapped' within our specific inherited language, which is expressed as our culture. In other words, we exist on a particular historical horizon (a 'tradition') from which we view all other times and places. Consequently, a text can never be approached neutrally, nor understood on its own terms. Instead, we regard it from our specific tradition; we understand a text and the world itself using a background of inherited, unconscious beliefs. Interpretation is a dialogue between the interpreter and that which is being interpreted. Since each is only a certain perspective, interpretation is always a 'fusion of horizons'. The aim of understanding a text cannot be to reveal the author's intentions or original meanings, because meaning arises through a process of interpretation. Reading a text, therefore, is not a matter of getting inside the author's head to understand their thought processes. Instead, it sets up a dialogue between the reader as interpreter and the text which is being interpreted.

A further consequence of this theory of interpretation is that a text can only be understood in relation to the whole, for each single interpretation is only possible because of a whole background framework of meanings. However, the whole is constantly being changed by the specific parts. In other words, reading a text is

H

only made possible because of our conceptual framework, but in reading a text we refigure that conceptual framework, in turn changing how we read the text. This is known as the hermeneutic circle, a key consequence of which is that meaning is never total or complete. Habermas has produced an important critique of Gadamer's hermeneutics in which he proposes that tradition is itself subject to reason and so ruptures in tradition (one's horizon) can be brought about by rationality. Furthermore, traditions can be oppressive and it is the power of reason which can offer emancipation or liberation. The power of rationality, Habermas argues, allows one to move beyond one's tradition and achieve a non-historical perspective.

See also: **context; cultural relativism; Gadamer; historicism; linguistic relativism; perspectivism; postmodernism; relativism; Rorty; subjectivity; truth**

Key questions: Is understanding and interpretation always determined by one's 'tradition'? How can we distinguish between a good and a bad understanding or interpretation?

Further reading: Gadamer (1960, 1976); Grondin (1994, 2007); Habermas (1986); Ricoeur (1974)

Hinduism

Hinduism originated in India and its roots can be traced back to at least 2000 BCE. It would be mistaken to think of it as a single religion, because the only essential core belief common to Hinduism throughout its history has been reverence for the *Vedas*, or sacred texts. Furthermore, unlike many other religions, Hinduism does not have a single founder or teacher. One major feature of Hinduism is the caste system, a social hierarchy into which all Hindus are born. Like Buddhism, Hinduism teaches the principle of reincarnation, the cycle of rebirth (*samsara*), which is governed by *karma* (the universal law of cause and effect). The only way of moving position within the caste system is through a positive/negative rebirth.

Although often described as a polytheistic religion, Hindus believe in a single, universal and eternal 'soul' called Brahman, which is the cause and foundation of all existence. The gods of Hinduism represent different aspects of Brahman, the best-known of which are Brahma (the creator), Vishnu (the preserver) and Shiva (the destroyer). Many schools of Hinduism teach that the way of achieving liberation from *samsara* is through realising one's true self (*atman*). This escape from the world of suffering is termed *moksha*.

See also: **creationism; enlightenment; Indian philosophy; *karma*; self, the**

Further reading: Flood (2003); Klostermaier (2007); Knott (2000)

Historicism

'Historicism' is most commonly used to describe the idea that knowledge of humanity is always specific to a particular point in history, and therefore there can be no 'ahistorical' description of human society. It emphasises the importance of context, both with regard to the thing being studied and the person doing the studying. One can only understand and explain human action in the past from the position of the present. There is no reason to assume that, or way to discover whether, our view of the world will match those views held in the past. We can never escape our own particular point in history to neutrally assess other periods in time. Consequently we cannot produce objective, universal principles of human action or thought. Historicist principles bear many similarities to the modern hermeneutic tradition, such as the work of Gadamer. Owing to its insistence that understanding is always specific to a particular point in history (it is always 'situated'), historicism is often identified as a form of historical relativism.

The term 'historicism' has also been applied to theories which describe society as developing according to general, deterministic principles. History is understood as moving inevitably towards an end-point, driven by these principles. This kind of historicism is found in Hegel's philosophy and also in Marxism.

See also: **context; cultural relativism; dialectic; dialectical materialism; Foucault; Gadamer; Hegel; hermeneutics; linguistic relativism; Marx; perspectivism; Popper; relativism; transcendence; truth**

Further reading: Foucault (1984); Gadamer (1960); Hamilton (1996); Popper (1957)

Hobbes, Thomas (1588–1679)

An English philosopher and politician, Hobbes is perhaps best known for his monumental work, *Leviathan* (1651). Unlike many of his contemporaries, Hobbes defended a strict materialism, emphasising the physical world and rejecting dualism (mind–body as separate), thus arguing for the mortality of the soul. However, he is also known for his political and moral philosophy. Hobbes was interested in social order and stability. He painted a rather stark picture of humanity as often self-interested and also highly vulnerable. Consequently, human society (specifically, government) is the result of necessary agreements between individuals who recognise that mutual co-operation is the best means for each of them to achieve their personal desires. Without civil government, humans would exist in a 'state of nature' in which individuals live in constant fear of violence from one another. The only way to maintain social harmony is by installing a government which promises to protect the individual, who in turn agrees to obey the government. Hobbes concluded that we must therefore submit ourselves to the authority of a ruling power. Hobbes' work is one of the best-known versions of social contract theory. His views were no doubt highly influenced by the political unrest in England during his lifetime, which culminated in the English Civil War (1641–1651).

See also: **contractarianism; dualism; Habermas; materialism; political philosophy; Rawls; Rousseau; state of nature**

Further reading: Hobbes (1651, 1655); Martinich (2005); Tuck (2002)

H

Holism

The idea of holism can best be captured by Aristotle's (350 BCE) claim that the whole is more than the sum of its parts. Holistic theories state that individual aspects of a concept, phenomenon or doctrine can only be understood through their position in relation to the other parts of that system. Semantic holism claims that the meaning of a word is determined by its place in the sentence, and that the sentence is only meaningful in relation to the entire language system. Mental holism argues that beliefs can only be understood and analysed through their position within a complex belief system.

An important modern formulation of holism is Gestalt psychology. According to this theory, the whole is not exactly the 'sum' of its parts 'because summing is a meaningless procedure, whereas the whole–part relationship is meaningful' (Koffka, 1935: 176). This has important ontological implications because it implies that the whole has an existence, it is an ontological category which cannot be reduced down to its parts. To give an example, we might see the 'mind' or 'self' as more than a collection of specific neuronal impulses produced by a physical brain. The 'mind' or 'self' is itself a basic category of being (existence). Gestalt theory also emphasises the phenomenology of perception (how things appear to us). Phenomenologically, our experience of, say, a piece of music is quite different from the component parts of notes and instruments (or even periods of silence) that make it up.

Holism stands in opposition to reductionist theories, which aim to explain complex phenomena by analysing the properties of their component parts. A holistic sociological view, for example, would argue that 'society' is more than the sum of each individual member of that society.

See also: **reductionism; semantic holism; supervenience**

Further reading: Esfield (2001); Koffka (1935); Merleau-Ponty (1945); Moran (2000)

Humanism

As the name suggests, humanism refers to the idea that humans, and human experience, are of unique importance. Humanist philosophers see all humans as rational, equal and sharing a common bond. They believe in a universal moral code founded upon reason and applicable to all humans by virtue of their being human. Most humanists reject religious accounts of the world, which make humans subject to a higher power, and also deny that humans should be viewed as simply part of the natural world. Humanists therefore reject a purely biological analysis of humans and human society which reduces humans to the same level as animals. This is demonstrated by Rogers' claim that, 'There is no beast in man. There is only man in man' (1961: 105). The enlightenment period had a profound effect on the development of humanism as it emphasised the power of human reason and rationality, which was common to all of humanity. Humanists therefore highly value education, for example the study of philosophy, which provides the means for humans to realise their cognitive capabilities, as well as freedom of speech, equality, secularism and the arts (which allow expression of the human experience). Important historical humanists include Hume, Voltaire and Kant. Modern humanists include Ayer, Russell, Berlin, Blackburn and Singer.

See also: **Ayer; enlightenment; equality; freedom; Hume; individual, the; Kant; liberty; liberalism; post-humanism; reason; Russell**

Key questions: Should humans, and human experience, be viewed as 'unique'? In what ways are humans different from animals?

Further reading: Lamont (1949); Norman (2004); Rogers (1961); Russell (1927b)

Hume, David (1711–1776)

A strongly sceptical empiricist, Hume is unquestionably one of the most influential thinkers in Western philosophy. Kant himself credited Hume with waking him from his 'dogmatic slumbers' (1783: 6). Hume started with the belief that all human knowledge is derived from experience, and proceeded to divide this knowledge into sensory impressions and ideas. Sensory impressions are what provide us with all our knowledge for they are the information gained through the senses, giving us the *impression* of green grass or a round football. Ideas are formed on the basis of these impressions, allowing us to recall the colour green or imagine a football the size of the earth. Infamously, Hume then asked what *causes* these impressions in us. He answered that we can never know, for we never experience 'cause', only a continuous stream of impressions which the mind constructs into meaningful order. When we see a foot kick a football and then see the football move, we do not 'see' the cause of the football moving; we only see two events on which the mind imposes a causal connection. Thus, we have no empirical knowledge of causes and, as all knowledge is empirical, we have no justification for believing in the existence of causes. Furthermore, the belief that kicking the ball will cause it to move is justified through appealing to the fact that (a) this has always happened in the past, and (b) the future resembles the past. However, the belief that the future will resemble the past is itself justified through appealing to causation and *vice versa* (see **causation**). Hence we have a derived circularity. This is Hume's infamous sceptical account of causation.

Hume also offers a sceptical analysis of religious belief. He criticises the traditional cosmological and teleological arguments for the existence of God. Briefly, the cosmological argument states that there must be a first cause in the universe (God), because something cannot come from nothing. Furthermore, this cause must possess all the things found in the effect because the cause must be greater than the effect. Hume points out that it is neither a contradiction nor an absurdity to think of something beginning to exist without a cause. Therefore, it is entirely possible that the universe just 'popped' into existence. Furthermore, nothing in our experience of causation reveals that the cause must be greater than the effect. Anything may produce any other thing, regardless of the properties each thing has. Hume concludes that, given the limits of our knowledge, we simply cannot say whether the universe had a beginning and, if it did, what brought it into existence. Instead, we must simply treat the universe's existence as a 'brute fact' that we cannot explain further. The teleological argument holds that the universe is so ordered that it must have been designed. Hume points out that there is a great deal of suffering in the world. If a God did create the world, then we could easily suppose that this God had done a rather bad job and therefore is not omnipotent. Worse still, we might think such a God to be morally indifferent, or even evil. Hume's religious works were highly controversial and led to his being denounced as a heretic by the church.

Hume produced a theory of mind which denied there is any such thing as a 'self'. When we examine our minds all we ever see are momentary experiences, there is no continuous 'I' or 'me' beyond these moments of consciousness. The concept of a persisting self is thus a fiction. Morally Hume was an emotivist, claiming that ethical beliefs were simply expressions of personal taste, rather than reflections

H

of God's will or universal moral laws. This idea is reflected in his aesthetic theory, in which he states that our judging something to be beautiful is a matter of feeling (taste) rather than thought. Hume used the term 'sentiment' to describe our feelings. We have already formed our opinion, based on our sentiments, prior to discussing the beauty or goodness of something. Hume's moral and aesthetic views are therefore a form of subjectivism because our moral and aesthetic beliefs are personal to us.

See also: **aesthetics; causation; emotivism; empiricism; enlightenment; experience; fact/value problem, the; God, arguments for the existence of; Kant; knowledge; mind, the; morality; moral subjectivism; scepticism; self, the; subjectivity**

Further reading: Beauchamp and Rosenberg (1981); Hume (1739–1740, 1748, 1751, 1779); Norton (1993); Stroud (1977)

Husserl, Edmund (1859–1938)

The founder of phenomenology, Husserl reacted against the growing dominance of relativism by developing a 'transcendental phenomenology', which would reveal the basic rules, laws or facts of all experience. These laws were to be found in studying human consciousness, rather than in the world or in language. Husserl thus followed Descartes in searching for certain and solid foundations, which he termed 'apodictic knowledge' (that which cannot be doubted). Husserl argued that, whilst we may doubt the existence of the world, we cannot doubt we are having an *experience* of the world. We must therefore 'bracket off' our subjective experience of the world from the objective world itself, distinguishing between our subjective viewpoint (our ego) and the world. This separation is known as Husserl's 'epoché'. Because we can distance the ego from the world, the ego cannot be part of the world itself. Instead, the ego is like a window onto the world, it is what *allows* there to be experience. Therefore it makes no sense to ask if the ego is inside or outside the world, rather it is 'before' the world. Ontologically it is prior to the world; the ego is what makes a world possible. Husserl consequently criticises Descartes for assuming that the ego is a substance in the world. The ego and its structure, which transcends the world, becomes Husserl's apodictic knowledge.

Husserl recognised that we are also psychological beings who function in the day-to-day world and therefore have 'dual' being. We are both a thing (a being in the world), and that for which there are things (a transcendental ego). The idea that the ego is something which constitutes the world and gives it meaning is known as 'transcendental idealism'. One criticism levelled at Husserl, which is also applicable to Descartes' method of doubt, is whether it is actually possible to perform the epoché upon which his entire philosophy seems to rest. Can we psychologically 'bracket off' the world from ourselves in any genuine sense? Husserl was strongly influenced by Kant and in turn deeply affected the philosophies of Heidegger, Sartre and Merleau-Ponty amongst others.

See also: **certainty; consciousness; Descartes; foundationalism; Heidegger; idealism; Kant; Merleau-Ponty; phenomenology; Sartre**

Further reading: Bell (1990); Husserl (1900–1901, 1913, 1931); Russell (2006)

Hypothetico-deductive method

Rather than relying on experiences and data to confirm what we already know, the hypothetico-deductive method is based on falsifiability. For Karl Popper, this distinguishes science from non-science. The method can be contrasted with induction, by which a general conclusion is drawn from limited information. In the hypothetico-deductive model, theorising (which might be a result of induction) leads to the construction of a hypothesis which is tested by an empirical method such as observation. If evidence is found to support the hypothesis, then it can be reasoned that the theory is correct. If counter-evidence is found, then the hypothesis is untrue and must be abandoned or reformulated. Even if there is no counter-evidence, the hypothesis remains falsifiable because there may be different findings in the future and therefore it is unproven. Some ideas, such as the existence of God or the unconscious mind, are not open to testing in this way and therefore would be considered unscientific.

See also: **deduction; induction; Popper; science, philosophy of; scientific method**

Further reading: Godfrey-Smith (2003); Popper (1959, 1963)

H

'I'

'I' is an indexical expression – the truth of its utterance is always determined by the context in which it is uttered. It refers to whoever utters 'I', just as 'now' and 'here' always refer to the moment and place in which they are spoken. The ability to understand and use the term 'I' represents the development of self-awareness and the capacity to separate oneself from the rest of the world. However, there is a major philosophical debate over precisely what the word 'I' refers to.

Descartes famously used the term to refer to himself as an immaterial thinking being, a 'soul'. However, the movement towards material monism (the belief that people are purely physical beings) has required further exploration of the term and its meaning. One view is that 'I' refers to the physical entity we know to be us. Given that the entire body's cells are replaced over a seven-year period, is the one-year-old 'I' the same as the twenty-year-old 'I'? Does the term 'I' refer to the same 'thing' throughout our entire lives, or is one's life made up of a great many 'I's? This latter view has been held by Hume and describes the Buddhist account of mind. The Buddhist teaching of 'not-self' claims that there is no single persisting thing any of us can call 'I'. Instead we are just a collection of individual moments of physical and mental phenomena which have been 'stitched' together.

See also: **Buddhism; change; consciousness; Descartes; dualism; ego, the; Hume; mind, the; personal identity; physicalism; self, the**

Further reading: Hofstadter and Dennett (1981); Parfit (1984); Siderits (2007)

Idealism

Idealism is the belief that the world is mind-dependent and consequently either (a) there is no external world existing independently of our ability to think and perceive it, or (b) if there is an external world we have no way of knowing what it is like. Extreme idealism, such as that offered by Berkeley, claims that the only things which exist are minds and the ideas they contain. Consequently the whole of reality is non-physical. This is a form of 'monism' as it states that reality is made up of one basic kind of 'stuff', which is immaterial.

The major objection to idealism is that the world would surely continue to exist even if there were no conscious beings or minds. However, this depends on what we mean by 'the world'. Certain things, such as the 'blueness' of the sky, seem to exist in the mind rather than in the object itself, for they are, by definition, the experience of an object, and it might be argued that only minds can experience things. Similarly, we could say that concepts such as 'beauty' are things we impose on objects, instead of those objects possessing the property 'beauty' intrinsically.

Idealism is often defended on the grounds that our only access to the world is through our minds, and our analysis of the world depends upon having concepts with which to analyse it. We could not study trees without having the concept of a tree, for otherwise we would not know what to study. However, this does not necessarily (logically) mean that there is no world outside of our minds. Kant's transcendental idealism is the theory that the world we experience (the 'phenomenal' world) is a representation of the actual ('noumenal') world, which is necessarily unknowable. The mind imposes categories and concepts onto this 'pure' world in order for it to appear to us in a meaningful and understandable way. All we can say about the noumenal world is that is must exist in order for us to have representations of it.

See also: **anti-realism; brain-in-a-vat; Berkeley; Husserl; Kant; metaphysics; monism; realism; scepticism; solipsism**

Further reading: Berkeley (1710, 1713); Ewing (1934); Kant (1781); Neujahr (1995)

Identity

The identity of a thing is its properties or features; it is what makes a thing what it is. A distinction is commonly made between qualitative identity and numerical, or quantitative, identity. Qualitative identity is the sharing of characteristics or properties: an elm tree and an oak tree are qualitatively identical because they share the properties of a tree. Numerical identity is a thing's property of 'being itself', or self-identity: the oak tree in my garden is numerically identical to itself and nothing but itself.

Leibniz's law captures our intuitive understanding of numerical identity. If X is identical to Y, then everything that is true of X is true of Y, and nothing more or less is true about X than is true about Y. In other words, two things cannot be numerically the same object if they have different properties. However, this raises a major issue within philosophical discussions of identity – the problem of change. If we paint our car a different colour, we still say it is the same car as the one before it was painted. However, according to Leibniz's law it is *not* the same car as it now has different properties. The problem of change is captured in the puzzle of the Ship of Theseus in which a ship's parts are changed over time until no original parts remain. The puzzle is whether this is still the same ship as the original, and if so, why. A specific set of issues have been raised in relation to personal identity, particularly because of self-consciousness. We are aware of ourselves changing greatly over time, but we still perceive 'me' to be changing. However, just what part of us is this 'me' that persists through time?

See also: **change; difference; metaphysics; personal identity; Ship of Theseus, the**

Further reading: Hawley (2001); Loux (1998); Lowe (2002)

Identity theory of mind

The identity theory of mind is actually a collection of views with the common belief that the mind is identical with the brain. It is thus a form of reductive physicalism, reducing the workings of the mind and consciousness down to physical processes.

Earlier versions of the identity theory, formulated by Place, Fiegl and Smart, sought only to identify certain aspects of the mind with physical processes. It was Armstrong who took identity theory to its logical conclusion by arguing that *all* aspects of mental life could be identified with physical brain processes. To give a simple example, to be happy (or to be having the experience of being happy) is identical to being in a certain brain state (which is simply a set of neurological pathways being activated).

An important distinction must be made between type and token identity theories. A type is a class or group of things, whereas a token is a single instantiation (specific example) of a type. To understand the distinction, consider the sentence, 'On and on and on'. It contains two types ('on' and 'and') and five tokens (the individual words themselves). Similarly, three individual cats are three tokens of the type 'cat'.

The idea that each brain state is equivalent to a pattern of neurological activity is called type-type identity: a type of state (such as confusion) exactly matches a type of activity in the brain (particular neurons firing in a specific sequence for instance). Token-type identity is the idea that a type of state (such as confusion) can match different neurological patterns. In other words, different brain states can match the same mental state. According to token-token identity theories, each occurrence of a brain state matches an individual neurological brain state. Therefore, the instance of the mental state is different each time it is experienced and so is the brain state. In this case, how could two people who refer to being confused be said to be experiencing the same thing?

See also: **consciousness; dualism; mind, the; physicalism; reductionism**

Further reading: Armstrong (1968); Braddon-Mitchell and Jackson (1996); Heil (1998)

Ideology

The term ideology, originally meaning the study of ideas, typically refers to a systematic body of beliefs, often expressing desired political arrangements. Ideology can also refer to the use of knowledge to deceive individuals into false beliefs. For instance, feminists have claimed that the societal belief that it is natural for men to earn money and women to perform domestic duties is a product of a patriarchal ideology, and not an objective description of men and women's natural roles. Rather than reflecting reality, ideologies denote a desired reality or are used to create a particular reality for political means.

In Foucault's analysis, ideologies are the vehicles of social and political power and are thus used to control and coerce members of society. The American Dream could be read as a political ideology which 'tricks' people into believing that they live in a meritocratic society and that their success or failure is determined by them alone, when in actual fact it is only the rich, educated and powerful who have a chance of success. Furthermore, it is only the rich and powerful who realise that the American Dream is simply an ideological, false view of reality, but they maintain the illusion as it best serves their interests. Religions are also often denounced as nothing more than ideologies.

See also: discourse; feminism; Foucault; Marx; political philosophy; post-structuralism; postmodernism; race; utopianism

Key questions: To what extent are we influenced and controlled by ideologies? Are some people more 'fooled' by ideologies than others? What allows us to see through ideologies?

Further reading: Eagleton (1991); Hawkes (1996)

Impartiality

An impartial act is one that is not biased towards a particular outcome. Similarly, an impartial belief is free from prejudice and therefore arises from an objective, rather than a subjective, basis. The most frequent discussion of impartiality occurs in moral and political philosophy. Often a 'moral' point of view is treated as synonymous with an 'impartial' point of view, capturing the idea that moral actions should be decided from an impersonal viewpoint, one that is detached from a person's particular feelings about the situation. For instance, my decision to fulfil a promise should not be affected by whether the promise was made to a friend or an enemy.

It is typically argued that equality requires impartiality. However, impartial treatment does not simply mean equal treatment. If two people are drowning and we can only save one of them, impartial treatment would take into account all the relevant moral facts and decide rationally who to save. Equal treatment would demand that we let both people drown.

Impartiality is a key element of consequentialism, which states that all ethical issues are determined by the extent to which they produce 'good' consequences. Indeed, one criticism often levelled at consequentialist ethics is that they do not allow for personal feelings or interests to determine action. The sole criterion is whether or not our actions promote positive consequences regardless of who the consequences affect. Although the concept of impartiality often seems intuitively appealing, so too does the concept of partiality. Promoting patriotism or showing faithfulness to one's family are commonly held up as morally praiseworthy and yet both require partiality.

Impartiality also plays a central role in many theories of justice, expressed in the idea that 'all are equal before the law'. One major challenge to defenders of impartiality is whether it is psychologically possible. Can we truly be entirely neutral in our appraisal of a situation; can we completely detach ourselves from all personal feelings, desires and emotions? Furthermore, in ignoring such feelings are we not ignoring what makes us human, our individual emotions and beliefs? Another problem is that impartiality seems to require a 'God's-eye' viewpoint, in which all facts about the situation are known and all possible consequences are foreseen. This requirement for absolute impartiality may well be unachievable.

The possibility, or desirability, of impartiality is less often discussed in metaphysics and epistemology, but has important consequences for both. It is generally assumed that reason and logic are impartial, and therefore scientific descriptions of reality, which are based on such reason, provide objective accounts. Scientists are assumed to be entirely impartial in how they conduct their work, as are metaphysicians, psychologists and sociologists. However, the extent to which any of these are able to be impartial is questionable. How can we be sure that we are not imposing our personal expectations of what we will discover onto the process of discovery, thus influencing our findings?

Post-structural and feminist philosophers have argued that all knowledge is a form of power that serves the interests of particular social groups and individuals. The very notion of impartiality is promoted so that people accept, rather than question, political, moral, social and scientific discoveries. Finally, Gadamer claimed that understanding is always formed from within a particular 'tradition'. We can only make sense of things using the meanings and concepts specific to our society. Therefore *all* knowledge is necessarily prejudiced, and is impossible without such prejudice. Partiality is a prerequisite of possessing knowledge.

See also: **consequentialism; context; deontology; difference; duty; equality; Gadamer; hermeneutics; historicism; nationalism; objectivism; post-structuralism; subjectivity; utilitarianism**

Key questions: Is it ever possible to be truly impartial? Should we aim for impartiality? If so, in which situations should we do this?

Further reading: Mendus (2002); Nagel (1991); Sosa and Villaneuava (2004)

Incommensurability

The term incommensurability refers to two or more points of view that have no common ground on which we can compare them. The term is typically associated with Thomas Kuhn's work on scientific paradigms (1962). According to Kuhn, competing scientific theories such as Newtonian physics and Einstein's theory of relativity do not have a single standard by which they can be judged. This is because science is primarily concerned with problem-solving and as scientific theories change so too do the problems which need to be solved. Consequently, because they are trying to solve different problems, we cannot say which theory is the more successful or 'better' one. Each scientific theory defends its value using its particular standard of judgement, thus any attempt to justify a paradigm is necessarily circular. More generally, it may be argued that different times in history are always incommensurable. According to historicism, we can only understand history from our particular moment. We must impose the beliefs and values of our time onto those we are studying because we have no other system of understanding to use. There is no 'ahistorical' (historically 'neutral') viewpoint from which we can judge and compare different points in history. Therefore, there is never any common ground between any two points in time. The system(s) of knowledge for an Iron Age society is/are incommensurable with the system(s) of knowledge in modern, Western society. Each addresses specific problems and needs, and any attempt to compare them will inevitably use the system of knowledge that we have in modern, Western society.

See also: **context; historicism; Kuhn; paradigm; objectivism; relativism; science, philosophy of**

Further reading: Kuhn (1962); Sankey (1994)

Indian philosophy

The three major schools of Indian thought are Buddhism, Hinduism and Jainism. The origins of all three can be traced back to the *Vedas*, a set of texts written around 2000 BCE, and the *Upanishads*, a second body of texts composed around 800 BCE. Central themes to these works include the cosmological questions of where everything in the universe came from and whether the original 'things' (being) came from 'nothing' (not-being), as well as concepts of the *Brahman* (the ultimate Being and source of all things) and *atman* (one's true self). According to some Indian schools, in discovering one's *atman*, one becomes identified with the *Brahman*. However, Buddhists reject the idea of there being any such thing as an *atman*.

Another important concept within Indian philosophies is that of *dharma*, which has several different meanings. Within Buddhism it is used to describe the ultimate truth or reality, discovered at the moment of enlightenment, as well as the body of teachings given by the Buddha. Hinduism and Jainism also use the term *dharma* to refer to the laws of spiritual practice and the understanding one achieves through such practice. The concept of *dharma* is similar to the concept of *tao*, which is common to many Chinese philosophies. There has often been tension between the metaphysically-minded schools of philosophy and the mystic tradition, with the latter arguing that the theoretical considerations of the former are pointless.

See also: **Buddhism; enlightenment; God; Hinduism; 'I'; karma; mysticism; self, the; Zen**

Further reading: Hamilton (2001); King (1999)

Individual, the

In the West the individual has historically been treated as a single, unified person. Christianity teaches that each individual person is a soul located within a body. Ontologically, the individual is indivisible, which is to say that the soul cannot be divided into smaller parts. As secular accounts of the universe arose, the idea of the individual was retained. Each of us is a unique and separate entity, a view of persons which has been called 'atomism'.

Locke described the individual as a *tabula rasa* (blank slate), upon which all knowledge was written through experience. Descartes viewed the individual as a *cogito* (thinking being), which had been furnished with certain ideas by God. Despite such differences, enlightenment thinkers were united in seeing the individual as rational and free. This formed the basis of political liberalism, which insisted upon the importance of individual rights and freedoms. Similarly, moral theories focused on the value of the individual and equated moral rightness with either the amount of good experienced by individuals (consequentialism) or the individual's duties (deontology).

Moving into the 19th and 20th centuries, existentialists spoke of the individual's absolute freedom and their ability to fully determine who they are and what they do. Nietzsche, Heidegger and Sartre described most individuals as simply part of the herd and called for each of us to realise that we are radically free to define ourselves. The 'authentic' individual was that person who had freely chosen to follow their own path. During the mid-20th century a different conception of the individual started to develop as philosophers asked how isolated from one another we really are. The atomistic view of the individual was challenged by descriptions of the individual as fragmented, multiple, fluid and deeply connected to both other people and the world. This account of individuals suggests that we are intrinsically 'bound up' with other individuals, to the extent that the very notion of an 'individual' no longer makes sense. My interests, projects, happiness and choices are intertwined with those of my friends and family. Morally, it does not make sense to talk of harm being done solely to an individual, for the good or harm done to one person affects many other persons. The roots of this may lie in Hegel's idea of intersubjectivity, according to which the individual is constituted through their relations with others. Each person is dependent upon the recognition of other people in order to become a fully-developed individual. The idea that the individual and their interests are subsumed by the interests of society is characteristic of 'collectivist cultures'. In contrast, Western culture, under the influence of liberalist and humanist beliefs, has tended to promote a more 'individualist' culture within which the individual is independent of the whole and cannot be compromised for the greater good of society.

See also: **agency; authenticity; deontology; Descartes; determinism; dualism; empiricism; existence; existentialism; freedom; gender; humanism; 'I'; intersubjectivity; liberalism; mind, the; moral agents; negation; other minds; person; personal identity; post-humanism; postmodernism; responsibility; rights; self, the; solipsism; subjectivity**

Key questions: To what extent, and in what ways, should we think of ourselves as 'individuals'? Is anything more important than the individual and their interests, experiences and desires?

Further reading: Guignon (2004); Kolak and Martin (1991); Martin and Barresi (2006)

Induction

Induction is a form of reasoning in which the conclusion 'goes beyond' the premises. The classic form of an inductive argument is:

Every *A* that has been observed is *B*	(Every swan that has been observed is white)
Therefore all *A*s are *B*	(Therefore all swans are white)

The conclusion does not logically follow (is not 'entailed' by) the premise. Although every *A* that has been observed is *B*, the premise does not say that all *A*s have been observed. Therefore it is possible that there are some *A*s which are not *B*. We know, for instance, that there are some swans which are black. Induction does not guarantee the truth of a conclusion, for it is always possible that the conclusion is false. Induction contrasts with deduction, in which the conclusion is entailed by the premises.

The conclusion of an inductive argument serves as a hypothesis, which can be tested by further observations to see if it is the most reasonable conclusion to be drawn from the premises. A conclusion that 'all swans are white' formed from the premise 'the swan in my local park is white' is not very reasonable because it is based on only one observation (one instance) of a swan. If we observed four million swans and found they were all white, we would be likely to feel confident that our conclusion 'all swans are white' is reasonable.

Scientific research is very often based upon inductive reasoning, for it tries to produce general principles from specific observations. If we test to see whether a metal dissolves in acid, we do not test *every* piece of that type of metal. Instead we test a certain number, and if every one of them does dissolve in acid (having ensured that the conditions for each test were the same) then we conclude that this metal does dissolve in acid.

However, the tendency to use inductive reasoning in everyday life can lead us to jump to unfounded conclusions. For example, if we observe a woman driving slowly, we might reason that all women drive slowly. Inductive reasoning is therefore part of stereotyping and prejudice.

See also: **deduction; fallacy; hypothetic-deductive method; justification; logic; Popper; scientific method; soundness; validity**

Further reading: Holland et al. (1986); Holyoak and Morrison (2005)

Inference

Inference is the movement from one set of assertions to another. When we form an argument we infer the conclusion from the premises. A valid inference is one which is 'reasonable'. In other words, if our conclusion seems to follow from our premises then we have made a valid inference. There are two main types of inference: deductive inference (see **deduction**) and inductive inference (see **induction**). Scientists seek to find the 'inference to the best explanation', that is, the conclusion which best explains what has been observed.

See also: **deduction; induction; logic; soundness; validity**

Further reading: Earman (1992); Gabbay at al. (2002); Lipton (1991)

Infinite regress

An infinite regress is a never-ending chain of propositions. We have all experienced an apparent infinite regress when we stand between two mirrors and see the reflection being reflected *ad infinitum*. Philosophically, an infinite regress occurs when we justify a proposition using a second proposition, which in turn needs to be justified by a third proposition, without ever reaching a proposition which does not need justifying. Children are adept at performing this move by constantly asking 'why' to every response made by an adult. It has been argued that intuition can provide a basic truth which needs no further justification. If something is intuited as true, then it strikes one as immediately obvious and unquestionable.

Many philosophers have denied that infinite regresses are bad, because ultimately no knowledge or belief is self-justifying, and therefore everything can be made into an infinite regress. With regard to this view, Wittgenstein famously wrote, 'If I have exhausted the justifications, I have reached bedrock and my spade is turned. Then I am inclined to say: "This is simply what I do"' (1953: 217). The cosmological argument uses the supposed impossibility of an infinite regress by arguing that if everything has a cause then there must be something which is uncaused, for otherwise we have an endless chain of causes. The only thing which could be uncaused is God, and therefore God exists. One way of rejecting this argument is by denying that time has a beginning and so an infinite chain of causes is perfectly plausible.

See also: **foundationalism; God, arguments for the existence of; intuition; justification; truth**

Further reading: Sosa and Bonjour (2003); Wittgenstein (1953)

Informal fallacy

See **fallacy**

Instrumentalism

Within the philosophy of science, instrumentalism refers to the idea that scientific theories are not literal descriptions of reality but rather are practical tools or instruments for making successful predictions and technological developments. Scientific instrumentalism, therefore, does not attach any 'truth' to scientific theories and the entities of scientific theories (such as atoms or quantum particles) are not assessed ontologically. It is, therefore, irrelevant whether or not science accurately describes reality; what matters is whether or not scientific theories 'work'. Instrumentalism could be viewed as anti-realist, though arguably it is neutral with regard to the realism/anti-realism debate. Instrumentalism is also used as another word for pragmatism.

See also: **anti-realism; Dewey; James; ontology; pragmatism; realism; Rorty; science, philosophy of; scientific realism; truth**

Further reading: Dewey (1925); Duhem (1954); Psillos (1999)

Intentionality

The philosophical discussion of intentionality uses a different meaning from the ordinary understanding of intention as 'meaning to do something' or 'doing something on purpose'. Intentionality, first discussed by Brentano (1874), is seen as capturing an essential feature of consciousness. What makes mental phenomena (the mind) different from physical phenomena is the fact that minds possess intentionality. Thoughts are 'directed': I enjoy looking at the tree in my garden; I believe my friend is happy. In such situations my conscious awareness 'moves towards' or 'searches out' that object. Physical objects, such as a rock or chair, seemingly cannot direct themselves towards other objects in the way that minds can.

If intentionality captures a key feature of consciousness, then a key element in any theory of mind is to account for intentionality. Reductive materialism, which argues that all mental phenomena can be reduced to physical phenomena, must find some way of explaining how intentionality can be explained entirely through non-intentional phenomena. How can purely physical phenomena, such as chemicals or neurons in the brain, which presumably cannot possess intentionality, give rise to minds that do possess intentionality? Intentionality might mark out an unbridgeable gap between the physical and the mental.

See also: **consciousness; dualism; mind, the; physicalism; reductionism**

Key questions: Is intentionality an integral aspect of consciousness? Can physicalist theories of mind satisfactorily explain intentionality?

Further reading: Brentano (1874); Dennett (1987); Heil (1998); Searle (1983)

Interpretivism

In the social sciences, interpretivism refers to the proposal that human behaviour and experiences need to be understood in terms of their meaning to the people (social actors) involved. It is therefore founded on an idealist theory of how we gain knowledge of the world. In relation to the philosophy of law, legal interpretivism refers to the construction of practice by lawyers which is based on values (see, for example, Dworkin, 1986). Legal texts must be interpreted in the light of current norms and practices. The approach offers an objection to legal positivism, whereby laws are based on principles and may or may not be ethical or moral, and natural law, in which right and wrong are based on some form of natural, possibly universal, morality.

See also: **constructionism; hermeneutics; social constructivism**

Further reading: Dworkin (1986); Heshusius and Ballard (1996)

Intersubjectivity

Each person understands the world from their own point of view, that is, subjectively. Having an understanding that other people are experiencing the world in similar ways to you, and that those people share that understanding, creates the possibility of intersubjectivity. Intersubjectivity is philosophically important because it allows us to confirm that the world we perceive can be perceived by others and therefore objectively exists. It is what Husserl refers to phenomenologically as the difference between what is 'for me' and what is 'in itself'. According to Husserl, in order to have empathic relations with other people, we must be able to put ourselves in their shoes in order to 'simulate' their perspective. This can only be done if we assume that the objects we experience from our own subjective perspective exist independently of our perception. They must exist in an objective reality. We could not have empathic relations with others if this were not the case.

A different understanding of intersubjectivity can be traced back to Hegel, who argues that we are fundamentally (ontologically) intersubjective beings. Our very existence as self-aware conscious beings is dependent upon receiving the recognition of other self-conscious beings (who, in turn, depend upon being recognised in order to be self-aware conscious beings). This means that each of us is intrinsically or inextricably 'bound up' with other people in order to develop as self-conscious beings. This theme was further explored by Heidegger, who argued that our existence as intersubjective beings meant that there could be no conception of ourselves as isolated from others. Heidegger hyphenated his term 'being-with-others' to reflect the fact that the very nature of our own being (Dasein) is inseparable from our connection to other people. The 'I' presupposes the 'they'. This could be seen as an argument against solipsism, which is the claim that the only thing we can justifiably know to exist is our own mind.

Sartre offered a highly negative view of intersubjectivity, arguing that our relations with others are always conflictual. According to Sartre, each of us tries to impose our own subjectivity onto others, thus turning them into objects rather than subjects. De Beauvoir criticised this view, claiming that it is through our relations with others that we can fulfil our projects and realise our freedom. An influential modern account of the positive nature of intersubjectivity has been produced by Honneth (1995).

See also: **Dasein; Heidegger; 'I'; individual, the; Husserl; negation; phenomenology; solipsism; subjectivity**

Further reading: Frie (1997); Hegel (1807); Heidegger (1927); Honneth (1995); Williams, R.R. (1992)

Introspection

The word derives from the Latin *intro* meaning 'inside' and *spicere/specare* meaning 'to look at'. Looking inside by reflecting on what we have experienced or are experiencing leads to a different kind of knowledge than can be gained from perception of the outside world. It would seem that introspection gives us a direct view of what is in our minds and, hence, direct control over it. For example, you can direct your thoughts to what you are doing now (presumably reading) and there is apparently nothing between the thought 'I think I am reading' and the action 'I am reading'. It would also seem to be the case that introspection gives us some form of special, private knowledge. For example, if you were to look out of the window and introspection revealed that you were thinking about the colour of leaves in autumn, it would strike you as very odd if someone told you that that was not what you were thinking about. Descartes decided that even if an evil demon had put thoughts in his head, he still had the thoughts and those could not be doubted. Descartes therefore believed that introspection was infallible and debate continues as to whether this is so. Arguments against infallibility might include the selective nature of introspection, where only certain thoughts are attended to or leave consciousness too quickly to be reflected on, the possibility of automatic or unconscious thoughts that are inaccessible through introspection, and the point that thinking-about-thought alters what was being thought about.

The suggestion that introspection allows us some privileged access to ourselves as a source of knowledge has also been questioned. Behaviourists, for example, dismissed introspection as a method of gaining knowledge about human behaviour because it is not available for public inspection and therefore not sufficiently objective to be valid. The idea that we have unique, private knowledge of ourselves, as solipsists would suggest, was rejected by Wittgenstein on the basis that your thoughts can only be expressed in a public, not private, language.

See also: **behaviourism; certainty; Freud; intuition; knowledge; mind, the; other minds; private language argument; solipsism; subjectivity; unconscious, the**

Key questions: Does introspection produce a special form of knowledge? Can anyone else understand the contents of our minds?

Further reading: Armstrong (1963); Elshof (2005); Wittgenstein (1953); Wright et al. (1998)

Intuition

The term 'intuition' is derived from the Latin *intuere*, meaning 'to look closely at'. There are several traditional conceptions of intuition in Western philosophy. Classical intuitionism identifies intuition as the route to an ultimate reality, which is often treated as being superior to reason and outside the realm of ordinary human experience. Rational intuitionism, exemplified by Descartes' *cogito*, views intuition as providing general, self-evident truths that constitute the necessary basis for demonstration and reasoning. Similarly, mathematical intuitionism, derived from the work of Kant, sees intuition as revealing mathematical principles as true *a priori* (they are known to be true without reference to experience). Finally, empirical intuition represents 'common sense' views of the world, such as when we say it is 'intuitively' obvious that the external world exists. In all three traditions intuition represents an introspective form of knowledge that is basic, immediate and self-evident.

Mysticism typically claims that one can possess an intuitive knowledge of God or the universe. Some moral theorists believe we can have intuitions that particular ethical propositions are true, such as 'pleasure is good'. In all cases, intuition is treated as sufficient justification for the truth of a belief. With the rise of logical positivism and critical rationalism, both of which emphasised the importance of subjecting knowledge to empirical testing, knowledge became equated with the scientific method. This was in part motivated by a suspicion of individual knowledge claims, which were seen as lacking the allegedly rigorous objectivity of scientific research. Within these naturalistic, empirically-grounded movements, intuitive knowledge was dismissed as subjective and irrational.

See also: ***a priori*** **and** ***a posteriori***; **certainty; Descartes; foundationalism; introspection; justification; knowledge; logical positivism; mysticism; rationalism; reason; scientific method; subjectivity; truth; Vienna Circle**

Key questions: What things, if any, are known intuitively? Can our intuitions be wrong? How could we know if they are wrong or right?

Further reading: Dummett (1977); Fricker (1995); Moore (1903); Westcott (1968)

James, William (1842–1910)

William James studied physiology, philosophy and psychology. He was a pragmatist, critical of philosophy that did not have relevance for everyday life, calling it 'a kind of marble temple shining on a hill' (1907: 8). According to this pragmatism, 'truth' is to be judged in terms of the practical value it has for us. Something is 'true' if it works for us and allows us to achieve things. James also thought that through experience we come to make sense of what goes on around us which, as babies, appears to us as a 'blooming, buzzing confusion' (1890: 462). He is also known for the term 'stream of consciousness' or 'stream of thought' (1890) which describes the non-stop activity of the mind, whether we are aware of it or not.

James's pragmatism included his approach to religion and truth: 'if the hypothesis of God works satisfactorily in the widest sense of the word, it is true' (1907: 143). However, James also defended a 'mystical' account of religious belief. Mystical experiences, James says, are ineffable (indescribable) and yet convey genuine, special knowledge which cannot be attained via any other means. These experiences are real and should be made central to our understanding of religion and its justification. Finally, James proposed a theory of emotion according to which emotions are equated with bodily feelings. Without any physical feeling, he argues, there would not be any emotion. This would imply that we do not shed tears because we are sad, but rather, we are sad because we shed tears. James's writings on knowledge and truth influenced the thinking of Dewey and Rorty amongst others.

See also: **consciousness; Dewey; emotion; experience; mysticism; pragmatism; Rorty; truth**

Further reading: Gale (1999, 2005); James (1879, 1884, 1890, 1897, 1902, 1907)

Justice

Justice is central to moral and political philosophy, representing the principle of moral rightness and the upholding of what is 'just'. Typically justice has been equated with fairness and the idea that each person should get what they deserve. Corrective justice refers to the imposition of punishments which are in proportion to the action. This is summed up by the Biblical expression 'an eye for an eye, and a tooth for a tooth' (Matthew 5: 38). Distributive justice refers to fair allocation of resources in proportion to what is available. Many philosophers see justice as an essential condition of society. Without an effective justice system, they argue, society could not successfully function. Rawls (1971) defines justice as those principles to which everyone would rationally agree to be subject. For instance, we might not want to be subject to capital punishment (the death penalty), and so capital punishment should not be part of corrective justice. Justice is closely linked to the law, which defines what behaviour and, in some societies, values are acceptable. Justice can be seen as enforcing the laws. However, whilst laws may change over time, the idea of justice as equal treatment before the law seems far more fixed.

See also: **contractarianism; equality; impartiality; morality; political philosophy; Rawls**

Further reading: Rawls (1971); Reiman (1990); Sandel (2007); Westphal (1996)

Justification

The concept of justification has two distinct meanings. (1) In epistemology, justification refers to whether or not one has good reasons for holding a belief. There are many different ways in which a belief can be justified, such as by deduction (reasoning about a specific instance from many similar ones), induction (reasoning about instances from a specific one), or *prima facie* (when something seems self-evident on first appearances). For example, knowing that the world is spherical could be justified by deduction from the curved horizon, the shape of other planets, pictures from space and so on. Alternatively it could be induced from seeing that the moon is spherical and therefore assuming all other planet-like objects are also spherical. Finally, it could be justified on the grounds of *prima facie* evidence, although in the case of the earth that might depend on being able to see it from a space ship. Scepticism states that our beliefs can never be justified as our reasons for holding them can always be doubted. Foundationalist theories hold that all beliefs are justified by a basic set of non-inferential beliefs. A non-inferential belief is knowledge that is self-justifying and does not rely on our having any other knowledge. Examples of this might be our immediate sensations or our perceiving that '1 + 1 = 2' is true. Descartes' concept of the *cogito* is a classic account of foundationalist thought. Coherentist theories of justification reject foundationalism, arguing instead that beliefs are justified through their relations to other beliefs within a web of knowledge. A belief is justified if it coherently 'fits' with other related beliefs and helps support the structure of our belief systems. No one belief is more 'basic' or foundational, because our beliefs are not like branches growing from a single trunk.

(2) In ethics, justification refers to whether or not an action is morally right. Each ethical theory provides different criteria for the justification of an action. Emotivism implies that no justification can be given for an action. Instead an action is merely an expression of taste akin to saying potatoes are good because we like them. It has also been argued that our knowledge of moral truths is intuitive, meaning we directly perceive that something such as killing is wrong. Both theories suggest that no discussion can take place regarding the justification of an act, beyond stating that one believes it to be right or wrong. This is often used as a good reason for rejecting emotivism and moral intuitionism.

See also: **certainty; coherence theory; correspondence theory; context; Descartes; deduction; doubt; emotivism; epistemology; foundationalism; induction; inference; intuition; meta-ethics; reliabilism; relativism; truth**

Key questions: Are there some beliefs that cannot be justified and, if so, why? What justification might there be for believing that moral truths are intuitive?

Further reading: Singer (1991); Sosa and Bonjour (2003); Swinburne (2001)

Justified true belief

Philosophers have often wondered about the sufficient conditions for knowledge. In other words, what are the requirements which allow us to say that someone 'knows' something? A common response has been that we may assert that a person knows X (for example, grass is green) if someone has a 'justified true belief' about X. This can be expressed as follows:

P knows that X if and only if:
1. X is true
2. P believes that X
3. P is justified in believing that X

In a famous paper, Gettier (1963) claimed to have shown that a justified true belief is not sufficient for knowing something. He provided two examples to prove this claim, the second of which is presented in this way:

Imagine that a man named Smith has good reason to believe the following proposition about his friend, Jones:

Jones owns a Ford car

Also imagine that Smith has another friend, called Brown, whose whereabouts Smith is totally ignorant of. Smith selects three locations at random, and constructs three propositions:

(A) Either Jones owns a Ford or Brown is in Boston.
(B) Either Jones owns a Ford or Brown is in Barcelona.
(C) Either Jones owns a Ford or Brown is in Brest-Litovsk.

On the basis that Smith believes that he has good evidence to believe Jones owns a Ford, he believes (A), (B), (C). Since Jones owns a Ford car entails (A), (B) and (C), we must say that Smith is justified in believing all three propositions. In other words, Smith holds a justified true belief. Now, let us add two more conditions. Firstly, as it happens, Jones does not own a Ford (he is currently driving a rented car). Secondly, Brown is actually in Barcelona (although Smith is totally ignorant of this fact). So it turns out that Smith does not actually know that (B) is true, even though (i) (B) is true; (ii) Smith does believe that (B) is true; and (iii) Smith is justified in believing that (B) is true.

In this example, it does not appear that we would want to say that Smith's belief is an example of knowledge. It is sheer chance that his belief (B) turns out to be true (because he has no idea where Brown is). Therefore, Gettier concludes, the three conditions for a justified true belief (truth, belief, and justification) are not sufficient to say that we possess knowledge. The extent to which Gettier's argument forces us to give up the idea of justified true belief as knowledge, or whether it just means we must adapt it, is a much debated matter and remains far from settled.

See also: **certainty; justification; knowledge**

Further reading: Gettier (1963); Goldman (1979); Nozick (1981)

Kant, Immanuel (1724–1804)

Kant was possibly the greatest enlightenment philosopher, and it is hard to over-state his influence on modern philosophy. Uniquely, Kant is heralded by both the analytic and continental traditions. His metaphysical work begins with a distinction between analytic and synthetic truths. Analytic truths are statements in which the information being offered is contained within the sentence: 'Trees have branches' is an analytic truth because having branches is part of what it means to be a tree. A synthetic truth is a statement which cannot be proven to be true or false through analysis of the words being used, such as 'There are three trees in my back garden'. Kant also distinguishes between *a priori* and empirical (*a posteriori*) judgements. An *a priori* judgement is one that is necessary: one's knowledge that, for example, 2+2=4 cannot be wrong. Empirical knowledge (for example, it is raining) is not necessary and is therefore contingent (it might not be raining).

A major concern for Kant was how *a priori* synthetic knowledge is possible. The origin of this concern was Hume's sceptical analysis of causation, in which he de-nied we can ever justify our belief in causation. To overcome Hume's scepticism, Kant makes a distinction between the 'noumenal' world and the 'phenomenal' world. The noumenal world is the reality beyond experience, the 'things in them-selves' of pure metaphysics, which includes knowledge of God, immortality and the infinite. The phenomenal world is the world as it appears to us, through expe-rience, which can be scientifically studied and understood. Kant's novel idea was that the mind is active in shaping the phenomenal world. The mind does not pas-sively reflect reality; rather, it renders it meaningful by organising it into principles and categories. This is the only explanation for how the world appears in a regular, structured and temporal way. Constructing our minds as rational and organising allowed Kant to conclude that concepts such as causation are built into a human's cognitive framework. Kant's theory produced a revolutionary shift in the philo-sophical approach to truth and reality. It is the mind which orders the (phenom-enal) world, not the (phenomenal) world which orders the mind. We can thus see that, with regard to the empirical (phenomenal) world of experience, certain beliefs (such as causation) are necessarily true even though they are not analytic truths.

Kant also produced a highly influential ethical theory called deontology, based on the principle that man is bound by reason (indeed, according to Kant reason is what sets us apart from mere animals) and therefore all moral actions must be ra-tional. This idea is captured in Kant's categorical imperative, which states that we can only act on a principle that we can accept every other rational person adopting. For instance, if we lie then we say that every other person may lie. Yet if this were the case, there would be no use in lying because no one would assume we were telling the truth (as everyone could be lying). Indeed, the concept of lying requires the assumption that we are telling the truth and without this assumption then the concept of lying could never arise. The principle implies a world in which there cannot be an assumption of truth-telling and yet there must be an assumption of truth-telling. Therefore, the principle that it is acceptable to lie is self-contradictory and thus irrational.

Finally, Kant analysed aesthetic judgements, arguing that they are both 'subjective' and 'universal'. By 'subjective' he meant that the objects we find beautiful do not intrinsically possess the property 'beauty'. Instead, the judgement of beauty is imposed onto the object by our minds. By 'universal' he meant that we demand that all other rational beings agree with our judgement that a particular object is beautiful.

Kant's legacy cannot be overemphasised. His discussion of the world as it appears to us and is organised by us has profoundly influenced the development of phenomenology, which seeks to characterise the structure of *experience*. Meanwhile, his emphasis on rationality and the importance of the logical analysis of concepts and principles has been celebrated by the analytic tradition.

See also: **aesthetics; analytic philosophy; analytic/synthetic distinction; categorical imperative; continental philosophy; deontology; duty; ego, the; enlightenment; idealism; intuition; reason; universability**

Further reading: Broad (1978); Guyer (1992); Hill (2009); Kant (1781, 1783, 1785, 1788, 1790); Seung (2007)

Karma

Based on the principle of cause and effect, *karma* is common to many Indian philosophies including Hinduism and Buddhism. The law of *karma* is the fundamental principle of the universe, stating that nothing happens which has not been caused. Applied to living beings, it becomes a moral theory explaining why good and bad things happen to people. If someone has a negative experience it is because they performed a bad action at some point during the past. Because Buddhists and Hindus believe in reincarnation (*samsara*), the bad action need not have been performed in this life. A person builds up a great deal of *karma* through countless lives. It is said that when he became enlightened, the Buddha realised the true nature of *karma*. Some, but not all, Buddhist accounts argue that we can only become enlightened when we have 'used up' all our previously accumulated *karma*, which can only happen if we stop generating negative karma through immoral actions and thoughts. The type of reincarnation that a person experiences, whether as an ant, human or God, is the result of their *karma*.

See also: **Buddhism; determinism; enlightenment; Hinduism; Indian philosophy**

Further reading: Flood (2003); Harvey (1990); Knott (2000)

K

Kierkegaard, Søren (1813–1855)

The greatest figure in Danish philosophy, Kierkegaard is best known as a founder of existentialism and a critic of traditional Christianity. Kierkegaard's primary motivation was the desire to rehabilitate or regenerate Christian belief and he was particularly scathing of the dogmatic way in which Christianity was preached in churches. Kierkegaard did not think religious belief was simply a matter of going to church, repeating doctrines and following rituals. Such mindless following of religion lacked passion, the key feature of religious belief. Each individual must come to 'feel' God and to develop their individual faith and this could not be done through rational argument or 'proofs' of God's existence. Nothing can compel a person to believe except their own subjective passion-filled faith.

Kierkegaard went as far as rejecting the notion of objective truth in favour of subjective, personal truth. This is summarised in his 'leap of faith' in which one moves beyond the realm of rationality. Because God is personal, each individual bears the responsibility for cultivating the true religious self on which they will be judged by God. This self-making is done freely, so the individual must make their own lives. Angst is the feeling which arises from realising this responsibility and freedom, neither of which can be escaped. Kierkegaard's notions of individual responsibility, choice and angst were central themes in the later existentialist writings of Heidegger (1927) and Sartre (1943, 1946). What marks Kierkegaard's existentialism as unique are his religious convictions.

See also: **angst; authenticity; existentialism; faith; freedom; Heidegger; religious belief; Sartre**

Further reading: Gardiner (2002); Grøn (2008); Kierkegaard (1843a, 1843b, 1844, 1846); Rée and Chamberlain (1998)

Kind, natural

The term 'kind' is used in philosophy to refer to a grouping of things. A natural kind is a grouping which is not created by humans, but rather reflects a division in nature that can be discovered by humans. The realist view is that natural kinds exist independently of how humans describe the world and can be identified objectively. The idea of natural kinds implies a form of 'essentialism' because there must be some essential property which defines which things are, and are not, included as members of a natural kind. Chemical elements, such as silver and nitrogen, are said to be natural kinds, as are the categories of animal, mineral or plant. Some supposed natural kinds are more controversial than others. For instance, whether animal species are natural kinds is a matter of much debate within the philosophy of biology.

It has been argued that there are no natural kinds whatsoever, because the world can never be examined independently of a particular scientific framework that determines the way it is categorised (Dupré, 1993). Adherents of this view tend to make the anti-realist claim that science does not present a neutral picture of reality. Instead it actively constructs that reality. Recent feminist and race theories have argued that the supposed natural kinds of gender and race are actually artificial divisions. There is no such thing in nature as 'woman' or 'black', and any attempt to define their essential features will always fail.

See also: **anti-realism; constructionism; gender; race; realism; science, philosophy of**

Key questions: Are there any natural kinds? If so, what are they and how can we identify them?

Further reading: Dupré (1993); Ellis (2002); LaPorte (2004)

K

Knowledge

Knowledge is a fundamental concept in philosophy. Indeed, the history of philosophy can be seen as a debate over what it is possible to know. Can we ever have knowledge of God, or other people's minds, or even the world? Scepticism is the view that we are not justified to claim we have knowledge of certain things, whilst extreme scepticism states we can never justifiably know anything. Foundationalists claim that some knowledge is self-evident and therefore does not rely on anything else for its justification. Such foundational knowledge, or 'basic belief', is often associated with empiricism. Our immediate perceptual experiences are treated as infallible, meaning they cannot be doubted. Descartes' *cogito* is an example of non-empirical foundationalism. Coherentism is the argument that knowledge is self-supporting and so we are justified in believing something is true if it neatly fits into the intricate web of connected beliefs which we call knowledge.

A major distinction is made between *a priori* and *a posteriori* knowledge. *A priori* knowledge does not depend on experience. For instance, we do not have to check on the truth of '2+2=4' or 'a square has four sides' each time we say or think it. Such sentences are true by virtue of the meaning of the words used. *A posteriori* knowledge, on the other hand, does depend on experience: 'it is raining at the moment', 'Tony Blair was prime minister'.

Bertrand Russell (1912) distinguished between knowledge by acquaintance and knowledge by description. Knowledge by acquaintance is gained 'first hand' through direct experience, such as knowing that ice is cold because we are holding a lump in our hand. Knowledge by description is 'inferred', meaning it is gained from other sources such as knowing ice is cold because we read it in a science textbook.

A final important distinction is between propositional knowledge and practical or purposive knowledge. Propositional knowledge comes from 'knowing that': knowledge accurately expressed through propositions, such as 'the earth is the third heavenly body from the sun'. Practical or purposive knowledge consists in 'knowing how': knowledge which cannot be expressed easily, or at all, through propositions. Knowing how to ride a bike or how to play a musical instrument is very difficult to explain in words. Memorising every textbook on bike-riding or playing the clarinet would not be much help when we first sit on a bike or pick up a clarinet.

See also: anti-realism; *a priori* and *a posteriori*; certainty; constructionism; context; deconstructionism; Descartes; discourse; doubt; empiricism; epistemology; experience; foundationalism; hermeneutics; historicism; idealism; ideology; introspection; intuition; justification; linguistic relativism; logical positivism; objectivism; private language argument; realism; scepticism; solipsism; truth; unexplainable, the;

Key questions: How is knowledge possible? What makes something count as 'knowledge'? Are there different 'kinds' of knowledge? Is one form of knowledge more important or valuable than another and, if so, why?

Further reading: Audi (1998); Russell (1912); Sosa (1991); Sosa and Villanueva (2004)

Kripke, Saul (1940–)

Kripke is a key figure in contemporary philosophy of language, logic and metaphysics. He rejects descriptivist theories of proper names, which state that we know to apply a proper name to an object if that object meets a set of definitions attached to the name. For instance, we can identify the object known as 'Barack Obama' through such definitions as 'the president of America', 'a former law professor', 'born in 1961'. Kripke argues that descriptivism is false, pointing out that if Descartes had died at the age of five, then the name 'Descartes' would still refer to the same object. In place of descriptivism, Kripke offers a causal theory of reference which holds that a proper name refers to an object through a causal connection that begins with an original 'baptism'. In other words, the name 'Barack Obama' refers to the object that was given the name 'Barack Obama' at birth and has continued to be referred to as that by a community of language users who passed the name on to one another.

See also: **definite descriptions; Frege; logic; logic, philosophical; metaphysics; reference; Russell**

Further reading: Hughes (2004); Kripke (1980, 1982)

Kuhn, Thomas (1922–1996)

One of the most influential philosophers of the 20th century, Kuhn's work radically altered how scientific theories are viewed. Kuhn argued that science is essentially a problem-solving activity. A scientific theory develops through the solution of a set of problems for which science must develop certain practices, instruments and theoretical entities and concepts (for example, atoms and gravity). Once a successful theory is established, it becomes a 'paradigm' and defines the rules (the scientific method) which scientists must follow. Over time new puzzles will be generated, which scientists then solve using the methods prescribed by the current paradigm, until they come across a puzzle which cannot be solved by the existing paradigm. A radically new solution will be developed which overthrows the existing scientific beliefs and sets up a new paradigm. Crucially, each new paradigm creates new puzzles and new rules by which the puzzles are to be solved.

According to Kuhn, we can only assess a paradigm using criteria provided by that paradigm. No single, objective assessment of a theory exists independently of that scientific theory. This is his idea of 'incommensurability', which states that we have no common standard to which we can compare different scientific theories. Since each paradigm contains different entities and concepts (quantum particles did not 'exist' in Newton's scientific theory), Kuhn has been interpreted as arguing that those who live during different paradigms *literally* live in different worlds. This would be a form of radical ontological relativism, and it is by no means certain that Kuhn ascribed to this view.

K

See also: **anti-realism; coherence theory; context; impartiality; incommensurability; instrumentalism; paradigm; relativism; science, philosophy of**

Further reading: Bird (2000); Hoyningen-Huene (1993); Kuhn (1962, 1977, 2000)

Language game

The concept of a language game was developed by Wittgenstein in his *Philosophical Investigations* (1953) and has had a strong influence within philosophy, anthropology and social science. Wittgenstein, in his later work, moved from viewing language as representation to understanding language in terms of its use. This means that words do not get their meaning from 'mapping onto' the world, but simply from the way they are used. Therefore the world 'tree' can come to mean anything, depending on how it is put to use. This accounts for the shifting and multiple meanings of words such as 'gay' and fixes the meaning of words to the contexts in which they are uttered. Each particular way and context in which words are used form a language game, so we may have a language game of buying clothes, or a language game amongst a street gang. The term 'game' reflects Wittgenstein's belief that language is essentially rule-following. To use language correctly we must follow the rules of its use. If we are walking in a park and a child points at a tree and utters the sound 'bird' then they have incorrectly followed the rule of when to use the word 'bird'. To be able to play a game, we must learn to abide by the regulations. Similarly, we take part in a language game by learning its rules.

See also: **context; linguistic relativism; private language argument; Wittgenstein**

Further reading: Kripke (1982); Lyotard (1979); Wittgenstein (1953)

Leibniz, Gottfried (1646–1716)

With Descartes and Spinoza, Leibniz is one of the three great rationalist philosophers of the enlightenment period. Fundamental to his ideas is the concept that the universe and everything in it is a 'mirror of God', a unified (monistic) creation reflecting an omnipotent and benevolent (all good) creator. The world is therefore the best of all possible worlds. One of his suggestions for overcoming the difficulty of sin or unpleasant occurrences within our ideal world is that our ideas of how we might theoretically improve the world would in fact make it worse. This is due to our limited, imperfect perspective.

Metaphysically, Leibniz proposed that the world is made up of 'monads' that are the basic substance of all things. (The concept of monads is similar to that of atoms but monads cannot be divided because they are the basic level of matter.) The term comes from the Greek for unity, reflecting Leibniz's theory that everything is a harmonious whole. Monads also have mental or soul-like properties and form a hierarchy, according to how they perceive the world, of bare monads, souls and spirits. Monads connect apparently disparate phenomena, such as mind and matter. The idea of monads allowed Leibniz to resolve the problem of how the immaterial mind and physical body can interact.

Leibniz also proposed an identity of indiscernibles (known as Leibniz's law), which stated that if A and B are identical, then everything that is true of A must be true of B, and there cannot be something that is true of A that is not also true of B. Leibniz was a skilled mathematician and is attributed with the development of calculus.

See also: **difference; enlightenment; God; metaphysics; monism; ontology; rationalism; substance**

Further reading: Jolley (1995, 2005); Leibniz (1675–1715, 1704, 1710); Rescher (2003)

Lewis, David K. (1941–2001)

Lewis was a highly original philosopher who made his most significant contributions in metaphysics. Lewis defended modal realism, the theory that possible worlds are not just concepts but actual existing universes. For every way we can conceive the world as being different, such as grass being blue or my currently drinking a cup of coffee rather than tea, there is a corresponding actual universe in which this is true. These universes are causally isolated, meaning that there is no way of connecting any one universe to another. Our universe is not the 'actual' universe, for all universes are equally real. Every universe in which the phrase 'actual universe' is uttered is the actual universe (just as the expression 'I' always refers to whoever says it).

Lewis used his modal realism to explain counterfactuals. A counterfactual is an expression of what might have been the case, such as 'If I had not drunk so much alcohol last night, I would not have a headache'. Lewis claims that what makes counterfactuals true is the existence of a possible world in which I did not drink alcohol last night and in which I do not have a headache this morning, and that world is more similar to this world than one in which I did not drink last night and do have a headache. Lewis also defended a version of the theory of temporal parts, sometimes called 'perdurantism' (see **change**).

See also: **change; conditionals; metaphysics; modality**

Further reading: Lewis (1983, 1986a, 1986b, 1998); Nolan (2005)

Liberalism

L

Liberalism emphasises the importance of liberty and the need to protect it. It can be traced back to enlightenment philosophers' portrayal of humans as rational and free beings. Indeed, it is reason itself that allows humans to be free because it provides them with the ability to choose and prevents them from being guided by mere impulse or social pressure. Political and legal institutions were justified to the extent that they defended this freedom. There are two ways in which this is achieved. Negative liberalism is the view that government must protect liberty through preventing one person's liberty from being limited by another. Positive liberalism is the view that a person is only free if they are able to think and act autonomously, and consequently government must do all it can to enable this. Positive liberalism stresses the importance of providing education and sufficient material resources to make possible the freedom to think and act. Liberalists defend freedom of speech, freedom of thought, freedom of movement and equality of opportunity.

See also: **enlightenment; equality; freedom; individual, the; liberty; nationalism; Nozick; political philosophy; Rawls; reason; rights**

Further reading: Bentham (1789); Mill (1859); Rawls (1971); Sandel (1982)

Libertarianism

According to libertarianism, each person owns their life and their property. Libertarianism therefore emphasises both personal and economic liberty. The only role that government should play in the economy is protecting individual property rights. Libertarianism also makes the individual the basis of social analysis; only individuals make choices and are entirely responsible for their actions. Libertarians reject the intervention of government to redistribute resources through measures such as taxation. They are also heavily critical of any political action which limits the freedom of the individual. Certain forms of libertarianism argue that all government intervention is unjustified. This approach would see state education replaced by home education and all wage control being abolished, in addition to an absence of state control in the allocation and use of natural resources.

See also: **freedom; individual, the; liberty; Nozick; political philosophy; Rawls; responsibility**

Further reading: Machan (1982); Narveson (1988); Otsuka (2003); Vallentyne and Steiner (2000)

Liberty

The concept of liberty is closely linked to the idea of freedom. Defending and/or promoting liberty rests on the idea of individuals being in some sense free. If the entire universe, both past and future, were entirely determined then there would be no point in speaking of liberty. The concept of liberty gained prominence during the enlightenment period when philosophers described man as rational and self-governing. Rather than being determined by God, 'animal' instinct or superstition, man's ability to reason allows him to freely choose his actions and beliefs. The development of liberty is therefore closely linked to secularism. Governments are justified to the extent that they protect and promote a person's liberty.

It is questionable whether political models such as communism and anarchy, which seek to overthrow the state, are consistent with the principle of liberty. A further question is whether granting liberty is the best way to secure the well-being of individuals. Perhaps individuals do not know what is best for them and should instead allow authority, at least partly, to dictate or limit their actions, which is precisely what parents do in raising their children.

Indian traditions, such as Buddhism and Hinduism, teach the principle of *karma*, which, amongst other things, causes all the good and bad things that happen to a person during their life. However, an individual can generate positive and negative *karma* so the idea of liberty can be seen as consistent with *karma*. In Chinese philosophy a person is encouraged to live in accord with *tao* (the way), which will guide a person's actions to produce the best possible results. Whilst a person may be at liberty not to search for the *tao*, they will live the best life if they do discover it, and helping individuals to discover the *tao* has more importance than liberty *per se*.

See also: anarchism; Bentham; Chinese philosophy; communism; democracy; determinism; freedom; free will; karma; liberalism; libertarianism; Mill; Nozick; Rawls; reason; responsibility; rights; tao; tolerance; utopianism

Key questions: Does each of us have a right to liberty? Are there any occasions when it is justifiable to compromise a person's liberty?

Further reading: Gray (1991); Mill (1859); Miller (2006); Nozick (1974); Rawls (1971)

Life

Life is the property of living things. The problem with this definition is that it is circular and does not give a guide to what things may possess life, or what it is that makes a thing possess life. One view is that life is associated with having a mental life: thoughts and conscious experiences. This raises the question of whether computers and robots are capable of being alive if they exhibit conscious traits. A different view associates life with biological processes such as reproduction, cell-replication or possessing DNA. However, many people do not want to grant trees the same 'kind' of life as humans or, arguably, animals. They claim that trees are not capable of sentience (feeling) and so do not have as full a life as organisms which can love, hurt, hope and so on.

The distinction between mental life and physical life is captured by talking of someone 'living a life' and of people in a coma being in a 'vegetative state'. The question of what is, can be and should be, included in the circle of life is far from resolved. An extreme account is the Gaia theory developed by James Lovelock (1979), which describes the Earth as a single living organism. Another issue is whether life is inherently valuable and should be protected at all costs. The view that human life is invaluable is used to criticise abortions and euthanasia. This argument is typically religious in nature and uses the idea of a 'soul' as a special kind of life. One argument in favour of abortion is the claim that in the early stages of development a foetus cannot be considered a 'living thing', again raising the issue of just what it means to possess life. Arguments in favour of euthanasia typically rest upon the idea that each person owns their life and has the right to choose what to do with it, even if that involves taking it.

Finally, many philosophers have seen their task as revealing the meaning or point of life. These theories are teleological; they teach that there is an endpoint to living which we should strive towards and that this endpoint is not a human construct. Although we may wish to deny any intrinsic meaning to life, this does not mean we are incapable of creating meanings and thus living a purposeful and rewarding life.

See also: animal ethics; bioethics; consciousness; death; dualism; environmental ethics; existence; humanism; individual, the; nihilism; rights; self, the; teleology; vitalism

Key questions: What things are capable of possessing a 'life'? Does a person have complete control over their life? Is there an inherent point to life, or must we decide this?

Further reading: Baggini (2004); Fry (2000); Lovelock (1979); Rosen (1999)

L

Linguistic relativism

Linguistic relativism holds that perception and thought are influenced by the language that is used to describe them – language does not merely describe thought but shapes it. A well-known theory of linguistic relativism is the Sapir-Whorf (or just Whorfian) hypothesis. Whorf makes the point that differences in language have implications for metaphysical understanding. His discussion (1956) uses the example of the Native American Hopi Indian language which does not have past, present and future tenses but rather the manifest (subjective/present and past) and unmanifest (objective/future and what we might call supernatural). This usage contrasts with English, which has a two-dimensional restriction to space and time, thus limiting English speakers' understanding of the world in a temporal (past, present and future) and spatial (here, there, near, far) way.

The strong version of linguistic relativity supports the idea that perception and thought are limited by language. If that were the case we could not adequately see, hear, taste or think about something that there was no word for. The weak version states that language has an influence on our perception and thought. Evidence for weak-version linguistic relativity includes differences in the ability of English and Zuni (a Native American tribe) speakers to recall colours. The Zuni language does not have different words for yellow and orange so Zuni speakers appeared to be restricted in their ability to remember visual information (Lenneberg and Roberts, 1953). That does not mean that they could not see that there were two different colours as the strong version would imply.

See also: **context; constructionism; cultural relativism; Derrida; experience; hermeneutics; language game; perception; private language argument; sign; Wittgenstein**

Key questions: To what extent does our language determine our experience? Can we experience things that we cannot describe linguistically?

Further reading: Gumperz and Levinson (1996); Whorf (1956)

Locke, John (1632–1704)

An English philosopher and politician, Locke ranks among the greatest thinkers of the 17th century. He was greatly influenced by the scientific discoveries of Newton and Boyle and the newly developed atomism. Locke was one of the first empiricists, arguing that each mind at birth is a *tabula rasa* (blank slate) onto which all knowledge is written by experience. There are two kinds of experience: sensation and reflection. Sensation is our bodily perceptions and provides us with knowledge about the world. Locke called this type of knowledge 'simple ideas'. Reflection is the mind's ability to combine simple ideas into 'complex ideas'. All our knowledge is built upon simple ideas, which come solely from experience of the world and are not created by the mind. A fascinating critique of Locke's theory of knowledge was offered by Bishop Berkeley.

Locke defended both the existence of the self and God, for which he provided a cosmological argument as proof. Put simply, Locke claimed that something must always have existed in the universe because something cannot be created from nothing. Given that humans are knowing and perceiving beings, this eternal thing must also be knowing and perceiving in order to have created us. This led Locke to the conclusion that there is an eternal, most-powerful and most-knowing being, namely God. However, it is hard to see how knowledge of the self and God can fit into Locke's theory of knowledge, for we have no simple idea (direct experience) of either. Locke's political writings offer an early version of liberalism and an attack on the monarchy's claim to divine right and absolute power. Locke was also one of the first thinkers to produce a social contract theory, according to which government is justified only to the extent that it protects the individual interests and well-being of its citizens.

See also: **Berkeley; contractarianism; determinism; empiricism; epistemology; experience; God, arguments for the existence of; liberalism; personal identity; properties; substance;** *tabula rasa*

Further reading: Chappell (1994); Locke (1689a, 1689b, 1690); Lowe (2005)

Logic

Logic is the systematic analysis of arguments. It looks at the reasons (premises) offered for a conclusion, and whether these premises justify the conclusion. If an argument follows the agreed rules of inference (the movement from premises to a conclusion), then it is valid. If an argument is valid and both the premises and conclusions are true, then it is sound. The form of an argument is its logical structure. An example of a valid argument, with the logical form in brackets, is:

Premise 1	All animals are able to grow	(all X are Z)
Premise 2	A stone is able to grow	(Y is Z)
Conclusion	Therefore, a stone is an animal	(therefore Y is X)

The conclusion follows from the premises because the argument states that anything which is able to grow is an animal and a stone is able to grow, therefore a stone is an animal. However, the argument is not sound because Premise 2 is false. If a conclusion follows from the premises, then the argument must be valid, but if one of the premises is false, then the conclusion must be false. Therefore an argument can be valid but not sound.

A sound argument would be:

Premise 1	All animals are able to grow	(all X are Z)
Premise 2	A cow is able to grow	(Y is Z)
Conclusion	Therefore, a cow is an animal	(therefore Y is X)

The argument is sound because it is valid, all the premises are true and the conclusion is true.

The two main forms of logical argument are deduction and induction. A deductive argument is one in which the conclusion is 'entailed by' (logically follows from) the premises. Because it does not 'go beyond' what is stated in the premises, the conclusion of a deductive argument *must* be true if its premises are true. The example of a sound argument given above is a deductive argument. An inductive argument is one in which the conclusion goes 'beyond' the premises. Therefore, the conclusion is only probably true if the premises are true and the argument is valid. A fallacy is an error in reasoning, and many famous philosophers have

L

accidentally included fallacies in their arguments. For instance, Descartes is accused of constructing a 'vicious circle' by requiring the existence of God to justify his belief in clear and distinct ideas, whilst justifying God's existence on the basis of his clear and distinct ideas. The rules of logic are believed to be universal, so that a sound argument will be accepted by any rational being.

See also: **conditionals; deduction; Descartes; fallacy; induction; inference; infinite regress; logic, formal; logic, philosophical; paradox; soundness; validity; Zeno's paradoxes**

Further reading: Gabbay et al. (2002); Guttenplan (1997); Howson (1997); Tomassi (1999)

Logic, formal

Formal logic is the study of the structure (form) of arguments. It is not concerned with what an argument is saying (its content), only with its underlying logic. The advantage of looking at the form of an argument is that one is not distracted by its content, and it allows easy comparison of arguments. It also prevents someone using rhetoric to win an argument. Within logic, a 'simple statement' is one which does not contain another statement as a part of it. They are represented by single letters: for example, *S* is the simple statement, 'the sky is blue'. A 'compound statement' contains two or more simple statements: for example, 'the sky is blue and the grass is green'. In order to look at the structure of an argument philosophers use a system of symbols to create compound statements. Table 1 lists some common logical symbols and their usage.

Table 1 Common symbols used in formal logic

P represents the simple statement 'it is raining'
Y represents the simple statement 'it is sunny'

Symbol	Meaning	Example
~	Negation (it is not)	~ P (it is not raining)
∧ or • or &	Conjunction (and)	Y ∧ P (it is sunny and raining)
∨	Disjunction (either … or)	Y ∨ P (either it is sunny or raining)
→ or ⊃	Implication (if … then)	Y → P (if it is sunny, then it is raining)

See also: **induction; deduction; fallacy; logic; logic, philosophical; soundness; validity**

Further reading: Guttenplan (1997); Howson (1997); Jeffrey and Burgess (2006)

Logic, philosophical

Philosophical logic is neither a particular system of logic nor an examination of that system. Rather, it refers to the study of those notions which are central to understanding rational thought: truth, reference, identity, necessity and existence. By examining these topics, philosophers hope to make clearer the structure of thought, and the interrelationships of thoughts with each other and the world.

Modern philosophical logic was developed by Frege, Russell and the early work of Wittgenstein. Later important figures include Kripke and Quine. Philosophical logic is seen as the major concern of analytic philosophy.

See also: **analytic philosophy; analytic/synthetic distinction;** *a priori* **and** *a posteriori;* **being; causation; change; conditionals; deduction; definite descriptions; essentialism; existence; facts; fallacy; Frege; identity; induction; inference; infinite regress; justification; Kripke; logic; logic, formal; metaphysics; modality; ontology; Quine; reason; Russell; soundness; truth; validity; Wittgenstein**

Further reading: Gabbay at al. (2002); Goble (2001); Grayling (1997); Jacquette (2002)

Logical positivism

Logical positivism, also known as logical empiricism, is a school of philosophy with its roots in the ideas of the Vienna Circle, as well as Russell and Wittgenstein. As the name suggests, logical positivism/logical empiricism is heavily influenced by empiricism (which emphasises that all knowledge is gained through sensory experience) and positivism (which advocates the methods of science in all areas of investigation, including philosophy). Perhaps its most famous advocate is Ayer. Logical positivism sought to radically redefine philosophy by eliminating many of its traditional concerns and problems, in particular those relating to metaphysics.

Logical positivism is guided by the 'verification principle', which asserts that only those statements which can be verified empirically (through experience, in particular through scientific examination) are treated as meaningful. Statements which cannot be subjected to empirical investigation – those about God and abstract entities such as moral truths and Plato's forms – are dismissed. Logical positivists thought they could solve many of philosophy's long-standing problems by simply dissolving them. Underlying logical positivist theory was the belief that language was the key to understanding the world, and that through a thorough, logical analysis of language we could work out what was meaningful and what was not. One problem for logical positivism is that it is actually very difficult to reduce statements down to those which are or are not empirically verifiable. Another alleged problem is that the truth of logical positivism is itself not subject to the verification principle and therefore, by its own criterion, it is false and/or meaningless.

See also: **analytic philosophy; Ayer; empiricism; epistemology; experience; justification; knowledge; materialism; metaphysics; positivism; reality; Russell; truth; Vienna Circle; Wittgenstein**

Further reading: Ayer 91959); Friedman (1999); Hanfling (1981a, 1981b); Rescher (1985a)

L

Lyotard, Jean-François (1924–1998)

Lyotard was an influential French philosopher who played a major role in developing and promoting postmodernist theory. Lyotard famously defined postmodernism as 'incredulity towards metanarratives'. A metanarrative is a totalising story (narrative) that presents itself as the sole explanation of history and human activity. In claiming to be truth, it is used to justify cultural values and norms as both right and necessary. Examples of metanarratives include the progress of society towards emancipation and the promise of science to objectively explain everything. Lyotard links knowledge to power so that whoever has power defines what knowledge is, and whoever has knowledge also has power. This is particularly important in the digital age (post-industrial societies which are becoming ever more computerised) as the amount of and speed at which information can be stored and exchanged is increasing rapidly. Because of his resistance to metanarratives, Lyotard emphasises the plurality, difference and fragmentation of knowledge. He employs Wittgenstein's concept of the language game to reveal the multiplicity of meanings to be found within different contexts and the effect this has on our understanding of truth and attempts to legitimise theories.

See also: **context; discourse; Foucault; knowledge; language game; postmodernism; truth; Wittgenstein**

Further reading: Benjamin (1989); Lyotard (1979, 1985, 1988); Malpas (2003)

L

Mm

Machiavelli, Niccoló (1469–1527)

Machiavelli was a politician in the independent city-state of Florence who is best-known for writing *The Prince* (1513). It is a practical guide to how rulers can attain and maintain power, which he wrote in order to gain favour with the ruling Medici family. *The Prince* is a realist account of political life which stresses the importance of cunning, violence and ruthlessness in achieving political power. Such traits were called princely *virtù*, although they bear very little resemblance to Aristotle's virtues or any other form of virtue ethics.

Whether or not Machiavelli should be considered immoral or simply amoral perhaps depends on whether he genuinely advocated these *virtù* or prescribed them only if one wanted to win power within the political system of his time. Furthermore, Machiavelli claimed that political action was only justified to the extent that it served the interest of the population (an early form of consequentialism). In his later work, *Discourses* (1531), he provides a defence of liberty and argues in favour of a Republic in which citizens play a key part in public administration. Despite this shift in his thinking, his name was used to coin the term 'Machiavellian', referring to the use of deceit and cunning.

See also: **consequentialism; liberty; political philosophy; virtue**

Further reading: Machiavelli (1513, 1531); Skinner (2000); Viroli (1998)

Marx, Karl (1818–1883)

Karl Marx is one of the leading figures in political theory who is attributed with founding the socialist movement. Marx was greatly influenced by the philosophy of Hegel, from which he developed the idea of communism as the end of history, the *telos* of human striving. For Marx, the pressing issue was the realisation of absolute freedom and the benefits to human life that would accompany it. One step towards achieving human freedom was the abolition of 'religious consciousness', the removal of all forms of religion as well as the conditions under which religions develop. Marx's famous statement that religion is the opiate of the people expresses the belief that religion is both an expression of suffering and a means of escaping it.

Marx's principal solution to the ills of society was 'revolution rather than evolution' (Russell, 1918: 11). With Engels, he wrote the *Communist Manifesto* (1848), which contains the same themes as Marx's major economic work, *Capital* (1867). Marx and Engels painted a relentlessly negative picture of society, a rhetoric intended to stir up the workers to unite against the capitalists. There are three main principles or themes in their work. The first is the problem of materialism; the economy of a society governs who has control over resources and how they are distributed. Marx predicts inevitable revolution against the unfairness of private ownership by the few who have economic control over the many. The second theme is the concentration of capital which Marx thought should be distributed to many people in a multitude of enterprises. Marx outlined the historical tendency towards a distillation of ownership so that increasingly fewer people are in control of and benefit from resources. However, the owners' power becomes weaker as their numbers decline, strengthening the hand of the 'ordinary' people without ownership who only have their labour to sell (the proletariat). The third theme is the class war which will occur when the tensions between those who work to make the money and those who have ownership lead to a revolutionary change. The workers will then take an organised approach to overthrowing the capitalists and restore ownership to themselves in an equal society.

See also: **alienation; communism; dialectic; dialectical materialism; equality; Frankfurt School; freedom; Hegel; justice; liberty; Marxism; materialism; political philosophy; socialism; teleology; utopianism**

Further reading: Marx (1844, 1859, 1867); Marx and Engels (1845, 1848); Singer (2000); Wood (2004)

Marxism

Marxism refers to both the philosophy of Marx and the subsequent systems of social theory and criticism inspired by Marx's work. An important philosophical element of Marxism is its materialism (as opposed to idealism); human understanding is seen as a product of a structuring world, rather than that which structures the world. In order to understand humans we need to understand the historical circumstances in which they have developed. Marxism interprets the development of societies as a continual conflict between classes, a process which will inevitably lead to the replacement of capitalism with communism. This theory is known as historical determinism.

A key theme within Marxist philosophy is alienation, an unnatural separation of parts that belong together and an indifference to others. For example, workers are separated from meaningful work, and parts of society are separated by their roles in the economic system. Similarly, the concept of 'reification' is used in Marxist theory to describe the experience of workers who are turned into mere 'cogs' within capitalist modes of production (labour/work). The institutions and ideologies of capitalist society have the power to dictate human behaviour and so become like concrete 'things' acting upon us. Marxist thinking reveals the hidden processes (ideologies) in society that shape us. We are manipulated to accept a particular view of society (promoted as 'reality') by the bourgeoisie (ruling, capitalist class), by presenting us with a distorted version of events or highlighting individual achievement or shortcomings, for example.

See also: **Adorno; alienation; communism; determinism; dialectical materialism; equality; Frankfurt school; freedom; idealism; ideology; Marx; materialism; political philosophy; socialism; utopianism**

Further reading: Curtis (1998); Kolakowski (1981); Marxists Internet Archive: http://www.marxists.org; McLellan (1988)

Materialism

Materialism is the view that everything which exists is material (physical). The traditional understanding of the term 'material', influenced by Descartes, is of an object being 'spatial'. Only objects which are extended in space exist. Materialism is often used interchangeably with the term 'physicalism', particularly in the philosophy of mind. According to materialists, the mind is a purely physical thing, whereas dualists, such as Descartes, argue that the mind (or at least part of it) is a non-physical thing. Materialism is commonly linked with naturalism, which is the view that the methods of science are the best way of investigating all aspects of reality, and, therefore, should become the methods of philosophy. Marx produced a 'materialist' conception of history, known as dialectical materialism, according to which the development of societies must be understood in terms of how humans collectively meet their basic needs. He proposed that changes in society are driven by the conditions of material life, such as the need for food and shelter and that, to analyse history, we must analyse the concrete (material) conditions of that time.

See also: **dialectic materialism; dualism; eliminative materialism; Marx; mind, the; monism; naturalism; physicalism; reductionism; supervenience**

Further reading: Rosenthal (2000); Singer (2000)

Merleau-Ponty, Maurice (1908–1961)

Merleau-Ponty was a French existentialist and a friend of Jean-Paul Sartre and Simone de Beauvoir. He was strongly influenced by, and often critical of, Husserl and Heidegger. Merleau-Ponty is best-known for his major work *Phenomenology of Perception* (1945), in which he attempts to restore the 'primacy of perception' to phenomenology. For Merleau-Ponty, humans are essentially 'beings-in-the-world' and the purpose of phenomenology is to give an account of lived experience, an account of the world as we experience it in perception. We do not exist as a pure consciousness or ego, as Husserl and (according to Merleau-Ponty) Sartre had claimed. Rather, we are fundamentally perceiving-subjects and therefore, because all perception is grounded in the body, we exist as embodied beings. Merleau-Ponty argued that philosophers had previously ignored the importance of the body, often viewing it simply as a passive object controlled by the mind (or soul) – which he called 'intellectualism' – or as the means of gaining knowledge about the world – empiricism.

According to Merleau-Ponty, the way we perceive the world and the meanings the world has for us are conditioned by our being body-subjects. When we look at an object, such as a chair, we do not simply see a lump of matter of a certain shape, size, colour and so on. Instead, the object appears as something that can be sat on, hidden behind, fallen over and so on. In other words, we always encounter objects as they relate to us as embodied beings; their appearance to us is conditioned by our existence as body-subjects. This experience of the world is more basic than previous scientific and rational accounts of the world.

An important part of Merleau-Ponty's work was to challenge the assumed dualisms which have run throughout Western philosophy: mind/body; subject/object; inside/outside; self/world. Merleau-Ponty believed that these supposed opposites

M

are actually strongly intertwined. For instance, the subject (that which sees) and the object (that which is seen) produce and affect one another. Our ability to see (our existence as embodied beings) generates the way objects are seen, and that includes ourselves as bodies. The idea that the 'mind' is fundamentally inseparable from the 'body' challenges Descartes' model of mind and body as two separate substances and offers a new way of thinking about ourselves and our relation to the world.

See also: **body, the; de Beauvoir; dualism; embodiment; existentialism; Heidegger; Husserl; individual, the; mind, the; perception; phenomenology; Sartre; subjectivity**

Further reading: Diprose and Reynolds (2008); Merleau-Ponty (1942, 1945, 1964); Priest (2003); Taylor and Hansen (2005)

Meta-ethics

The term 'meta' (beyond, after) reveals that meta-ethics is the philosophical examination of ethics, or questions-about-ethics. It looks at the metaphysical and epistemological issues connected with ethics and ethical belief, such as whether morals are facts, what kind of facts they might be, how we are able to have knowledge of morals and whether certain morals are universal or relative to a time and place. Meta-ethics also addresses the question of who (or what) must obey moral laws and who (or what) has moral value.

A particularly important division in meta-ethics is whether morals are objective or relative. The objective account of morality denies that morals are created by humans. Just as the laws of mathematics, such as '2+2=4', are universal, objective truths, so too are the moral laws. No matter what humans desire, they cannot change the fact that 2+2=4 and nor can they change morality. A major problem with this view is just what kind of 'thing' morality is. If it is not a purely human concept then it must be a part of the universe. Plato spoke of the moral laws as abstract entities existing in the realm of the forms. Alternatively, we can draw an analogy with physics and say that moral laws are like the laws of gravity or motion, but how are we to recognise or discover these moral laws? We have no empirical evidence for where or what the moral laws are, so how and on what grounds can we say they exist? One response is moral intuitionism, which argues that certain moral truths are self-evident. The statement that killing is wrong strikes us as true in the same way that '2+2=4' does. Many philosophers favour subjective accounts of morality, arguing that morals are a human construct. This view is termed 'moral relativism' and includes a large number of opposing theories such as social contract theory, which sees morality as an 'agreement' between individuals, and emotivism, which sees morality as the expression of personal tastes.

A related meta-ethical issue is the 'is/ought' problem generated by Hume. It arises from the fact that no amount of observation will give us any information about what we ought to do. For instance, investigating every feature of pain will not reveal when we should or should not inflict pain. We must add an evaluative claim if we want to say that pain is bad, but such a claim is not logically inferred from the facts about pain. It is an additional, non-empirical statement regarding pain and cannot be justified on the basis of the facts about pain. This suggests that the universe is morally neutral (amoral) as it contains no information about what we ought to do.

A religious response to this problem would be to say that God has actually provided information about what is right and wrong, such as the Ten Commandments in the Judaeo-Christian belief system. Despite the obvious problem of whether these actually are the words of God, there is another meta-ethical puzzle. Does God command what is right because it is right, or is it right because God commands it? In other words, is God subject to moral laws or did He create them? If He created them, then He can also change them. This means that at any point it is possible for God to will that killing is right, which would mean we should all start killing each other. However, if God simply tells us what is right or wrong because he is all-knowing, then we still need to explain where these moral laws come from (as they are not created by God or humans) and we can question why we should obey them.

See also: **animal ethics; anti-realism; constructionism; contractarianism; cultural relativism; descriptivism; emotivism; fact/value problem, the; good, the; intuition; Moore; moral agents; morality; moral objectivism; moral subjectivism; universability**

Further reading: Horgan and Timmons (2006); Moore (1903); Russ (2008); Singer (1991)

Metaphysics

In its broadest sense, metaphysics is concerned with the fundamental structure of reality. The term 'fundamental' reflects the fact that metaphysics searches for a single true and accurate account of all reality. We may wish to deny that such an account of reality exists, but it is still a metaphysical view because it is an argument about the nature of reality. The term 'structure' reflects metaphysics' concern with what exists and how these things are related. Finally, metaphysics investigates 'reality' rather than 'the world' because it asks whether there are things which exist outside this world (such as parallel universes).

Many of the topics within metaphysics overlap with physics. Both subjects explore the nature of time and space, the nature of objects existing within time and space and how these things interact. However, metaphysics is not essentially an empirical subject. Metaphysicians do not typically conduct experiments. Instead they are interested in conducting logical, abstract analyses of these topics. For example, in discussing the possibility of time travel, a metaphysician would consider whether it is logically possible, whereas a physician would consider whether it would be physically/scientifically possible.

'Logical possibility' refers to our understanding of what could logically happen in reality, such as whether an event in the future can affect an event in the past and whether two things can be in the same place at the same time. This reflects the fact that many things in the world appear to be contingent. For instance, you might have been born a day later or with different coloured hair; London may not have been the capital of England. Metaphysics is interested in establishing what could be as well as what is the case.

Metaphysics is also concerned with things which cannot be empirically investigated. These include the nature of abstract entities, such as numbers, facts and propositions, and those parts of reality which might exist outside space-time. Finally, metaphysics is interested in our concepts and how these relate to possible reality. Such concepts include ideas about time, space, change, identity, individuals, events and causes.

See also: **anti-realism; being; causation; change; coherence theory; conditionals; correspondence theory; definite descriptions; deflationary theory of truth; dualism; essentialism; existence; facts; foundationalism; Frege; idealism; identity; knowledge; logic, philosophical; modality; naturalism; ontology; pragmatism; properties; realism; reductionism; reference; relativity theory; science, philosophy of; Ship of Theseus, the; substance; thought experiments; time; truth; universals and particulars; vagueness; Zeno's paradoxes**

Further reading: Loux (1998); Lowe (2002); van Inwagen and Zimmerman (1998)

Mill, John Stuart (1806–1873)

An English philosopher and radical politician, Mill was one of the founders of utilitarianism, a staunch defender of the concept of individual liberty and an early advocate of women's rights. Mill rejected all innate differences between people. Like his father and teacher, James Mill, John Mill believed in 'perfectability', the idea that with the right moral and intellectual education any person could be improved to near (or total) perfection. This was developed from their belief that all human characteristics are formed through experience.

Unlike many of his contemporaries, Mill applied this idea to women, arguing that even the strongest differences between men and women could be explained by upbringing rather than natural capacities and therefore women must be viewed as entirely equal to men (1869). Mill was a radical empiricist who rejected the intuitionist, *a priori* account of knowledge, arguing instead that all truths, even mathematical and logical truths, are grounded in experience. There is no proposition which is necessarily (logically) true.

In *Utilitarianism* (1861b) Mill sets down one of the classic formulations of utilitarian ethics: the single moral principle which must guide all actions is whether or not such an action promotes happiness. His reasoning for this claim is that happiness is the only thing which all beings desire 'intrinsically', meaning happiness is an end in itself and everything else (such as money, fame, family, friends) are means to attaining happiness. Mill developed Bentham's earlier formulation of utilitarianism by introducing the idea of higher (intellectual, aesthetic and moral) pleasures and lower (bodily) pleasures, a response to the criticism that playing with sticks in the mud should be as highly valued as the Pyramids, providing they promote the same amount of happiness.

M

Mill's radical political views focused on the idea of liberty, which he sought to both defend and promote. He argued that the sole principle which should guide society's or government's treatment of people is the 'harm principle', according to which 'the only purpose for which power can be rightfully exercised over any member of a civilized community, against his will, is to prevent harm to others'

(1859: 51). As long as our actions and interests do not harm another person, we should be free to pursue them.

See also: *a priori* and *a posteriori*; **analytic/synthetic distinction; Bentham; consequentialism; empiricism; feminism; freedom; happiness; liberty; morality; other minds; political philosophy; scientific method; tolerance; utilitarianism**

Further reading: Donner (1993); Mill (1843, 1859, 1861a, 1861b, 1869); Skorupski (1989, 1998)

Mind, the

Understanding the nature of the mind is one of the central concerns of philosophy. A basic division exists between dualists, who argue that the mind is an immaterial substance, and materialists, who argue that the mind is physical. If the mind is an immaterial substance, then we must give some account of how it is able to interact with the physical body. This has proved a serious problem to resolve, but, equally, it is far from clear how a purely physical account of the mind can explain our subjective experiences of consciousness and phenomena such as beliefs, intentionality and qualia. When we open up a person's head we see a mass of grey matter, not a 'mind'. Nagel commented that there seems to be an irreducible element to the mind, namely a 'what-it-is-likeness'. For every experience I have, there is a sense of what it is like for me to experience it, and it is difficult to describe and explain this feature of the mind. Eliminative materialists have attempted a radical solution to the problem of the mind by denying that such mental states as beliefs, desires and intentions exist. Radical idealists, such as Berkeley, argue that only ideas and minds capable of having these ideas exist. This solves the problem of mind–body interaction, but at the expense of our belief in a physical world.

Traditionally, the 'mind' has been conceived as something 'private' and contained within one's head. Such a conception raises the problem of other minds: if only I can know about the existence and contents of my mind, what justification is there for the belief that other people have minds like mine? How could we distinguish between a zombie who is physically and behaviourally identical to a person with a mind, and an actual person with a mind? A related idea is that of the unconscious. It seems that a great deal of one's mind, and how it works, is hidden even from oneself. A great deal of our conscious experience, from our emotional state to solving a crossword puzzle, might be hugely determined by unconscious activity.

The idea that all meanings and experiences are private to an individual has been challenged by Wittgenstein's private language argument, which aims to move meaning and understanding from the private to the public sphere. Theories of embodiment have drawn attention to the fact that the 'mind' is not just in the head, but spread throughout our entire body. The way we think, the desires we have, the very nature of experience, is determined by the physical body we inhabit. Extended cognition takes this idea further by arguing that certain objects and processes external to our physical body (such as a diary or calculator) must nonetheless be seen as literally part of our mind's cognition. Finally, researchers in artificial intelligence, inspired by advances in neurobiology and electronics, have attempted to replicate aspects of the mind in computers. However, whether a computer could ever be

M

said to possess a mind is a contentious issue and rests upon many assumptions, not least the assumption that the mind is purely physical in nature.

See also: **artificial intelligence; behaviourism; Berkeley; belief; cognition; consciousness; Descartes; dualism; ego, the; eliminative materialism; embodiment; emotion; epiphenomenalism; extended cognition; folk psychology; functionalism; idealism; identity theory of mind; intentionality; introspection; mind–body problem, the; naturalism; other minds; physicalism; private language argument; qualia; solipsism; subjectivity; supervenience;** *tabula rasa;* **unconscious, the**

Key questions: Is the mind purely physical in nature? How much do we know about the workings of our own minds and the minds of other people? What things are capable of possessing a 'mind'?

Further reading: Chalmers (1996); Heil (1998); Lowe (2000); Lycan (1989); Nagel (1979)

Mind–body problem, the

The mind–body problem arises from the question of how a seemingly non-physical thing (the mind) can interact with the physical body. It can be traced back to Descartes' substance dualism, according to which we exist as two separate substances, a material body and a non-material mind (soul). If the mind is non-physical in nature, then it is not clear how it can have any effect on the physical. For many philosophers this problem of interaction is intractable and thus sufficient reason to reject any form of dualism.

Alternative theories are those of metaphysical idealists, who would claim anything physical to be a product of the immaterial mind, and physicalists (materialists), who take the opposite view that the mind is entirely physical in nature. Both of these are monist solutions to the problem because they argue that both we and the world we inhabit are composed of one type of substance. However, physicalism still faces the problem of explaining how conscious experiences, such as thinking about eating a sandwich, map onto, and can be explained by, the physiology of our nervous systems.

See also: **artificial intelligence; Berkeley; consciousness; Descartes; dualism; idealism; mind, the; naturalism; physicalism; reductionism; supervenience**

Further reading: Baker and Morris (2002); Crane and Patterson (2000); Heil (1998); Lowe (2000); Lycan (1989); Rosenthal (2000)

M

Modality

Modality refers to the concepts of possibility, necessity and contingency. Since Aristotle and Plato, philosophers have distinguished between necessary and contingent truths. It is also a common feature of everyday language. To say 'If only I had worked harder, I would have got a better mark for my essay' is to think modally, because, while it is true that you got a mark of 68, it is not a necessary truth. You could have got a mark of 67 or 83 or 21. Therefore the fact that you got a mark of 68 is a contingent truth. The concept of modality reflects an important feature of human cognition, the ability to conceive of ways in which the world might have been.

The idea of 'possible worlds' is a very useful and common way of understanding modality. A possible world is a way the world might have been. The term 'world' refers not to earth, but the totality of the universe. There are possible worlds in which you did get a mark of 83, and others in which you got a mark of 21, as well as ones in which grass is blue and humans have five legs. If something is possible, it is true in at least one possible world. If something is necessary, it is true in all possible worlds.

Despite the usefulness of the idea of possible worlds, philosophers strongly disagree over how we should understand them. Specifically, what is it that makes statements about possible worlds true? There are two responses to this question. Concretists claim that each possible world is as real as our world. The most famous proponent of this view is David Lewis. Actualists claim that this world is the only one there is and so whatever the nature of possible worlds (such as linguistic propositions), they exist within this world. Using possible worlds to understand modality has been put to important use in many areas of logic, such as explaining the relations between natural laws, analysing counterfactual truths and understanding universals. They have also been used to construct a new, arguably more powerful, version of the ontological argument for the existence of God.

See also: **conditionals; God, arguments for the existence of; Leibniz; Lewis; possibility; truth**

Further reading: Lewis (1986a); Loux (1979); Lowe (2002)

Modernism

Defining modernism is very difficult because there is little agreement on what 'modernism' actually is. It should not be understood literally as meaning 'that which is modern', for this would mean anything that is contemporary. The beginnings of modernism have been linked to the enlightenment period (17th to early 19th century), starting with Descartes' quest for certain, self-evident knowledge. On this view, modernism is characterised by a faith in human reason, foundationalist and realist views of truth and the world, and belief in the progressive nature of society and knowledge. These views were inspired by European exploration of the 'New World', which developed feelings of cultural superiority, coupled with the advances in science and technology, which promised to increase human happiness and well-being.

However, modernism is also seen as beginning in the 19th and early 20th centuries when philosophers (most notably Nietzsche) started to challenge enlightenment thinking. This period is characterised by a rejection of tradition and the disruption, rather than development, of social norms and values. Notably, philosophers started to challenge foundationalism and realism. Karl Marx typifies this movement by rejecting the existing systems of thought as bourgeois ideology which lacked any 'truth' and merely served the aims and needs of the ruling class. Whilst notions of progress still existed, such progress had become revolutionary. Inherited ideas were discarded as philosophers sought new, radical systems of meaning and thought. This is mirrored by the modernist movement in art, which self-consciously rejected the past as a model for what art is, what it represents and

M

how it is represented. Modernist artists include Picasso, Kandinksy, Munch, Dali and Rothko.

See also: **certainty; Descartes; enlightenment; foundationalism; ideology; Marx; Nietzsche; postmodernism; realism; reason; scientific method; truth**

Further reading: Cahoone (1996); Cascardi (1992); Eysteinsson (1990); Kolocotroni et al. (1998); Neville (1992)

Monism

Monism is the view that everything which exists is ultimately only one thing or substance. Spinoza argued that there is just one infinite substance, which makes up all bodies, minds and things. This substance is God and so everything is part of God. The Taoist claim that all things exist in, and depend upon, *tao* could also be seen as the monistic view that ultimately everything is *tao*. In early Greek philosophy, the single substance which constituted the whole of reality was identified as water by Thales, as fire by Heraclitus and as air by Anaximenes. Another Greek philosopher, Anaximander, described it as 'primordial stuff', an idea which bears many similarities to the modern-day theory of atoms. The most common version of monism is materialism, which says that the universe is entirely physical. Berkeley's radical idealism, which claims that the universe is composed entirely of minds and ideas, is an example of immaterial (non-physical) monism. Monism is opposed to dualism, the claim that the universe is made up of both physical and non-physical substances, and pluralism, which argues that the world is made up of many different substances.

See also: **being; Berkeley; difference; dualism; Greek philosophy, ancient; idealism; metaphysics; ontology; physicalism; reality; substance; Spinoza; *tao*; Taoism**

Further reading: Berkeley (1710); Cohen et al. (2005); Spinoza (1677)

Moore, George E. (1873–1958)

Moore was a British philosopher who worked alongside Russell and Wittgenstein, during what has been described as the 'Golden Age' of Cambridge philosophy. Moore defended a commonsense realism, the view that our ordinary, 'everyday' understanding of the world is generally correct. Moore is best-known for his work in ethics, articulated in his influential *Principia Ethica* (1903) in which he attacks 'ethical naturalism', the view that ethical values such as goodness can be expressed through apparently natural terms such as happiness or pleasure. Imagine we define 'good' as 'happiness', then assert that happiness is good. All we are stating here is 'happiness is happiness', which is a tautology and is entirely uninformative. This is Moore's 'naturalistic fallacy': the mistake of thinking that moral properties, such as goodness, are definable in natural terms. According to Moore, the good (or 'goodness') is *sui generis*, which means it forms its own category and cannot be 'reduced' to any other category. Furthermore, the good is basic, meaning it is indefinable and unanalysable. This suggests that ethical knowledge is separate from scientific, psychological or metaphysical knowledge, and that 'the good', for example, cannot be explained by these disciplines. Instead, our knowledge of ethics is intuitive; we

M

recognise certain ethical truths as self-evident, just as when we see '2 + 2 = 4' we just know it to be true. We cannot explain such intuitive truths, they just are.

See also: **analytic philosophy; good, the; happiness; intuition; meta-ethics; moral intuitionism; morality; naturalism; realism; Russell; Wittgenstein**

Further reading: Baldwin (1990, 1993); Moore (1903, 1912); Schlipp (1942)

Moral agents

A moral agent is someone who should, or must, act and think morally. However, it is not clear precisely what it is that makes someone a moral agent. We generally do not think that very young babies or animals are moral agents. Kant argued that it is human reason that makes us moral agents and separates us from animals. This includes the ability to ignore or overcome our feelings and impulses. The Kantian model would seem to prevent many humans, such as the mentally handicapped, from being moral agents. Another view is that simply being able to obey certain moral rules, such as 'do not kill', is sufficient to be considered a moral agent. This means that we would not have to avoid killing for moral reasons because it is sufficient just to follow the command, even if you do not understand why you do not kill. Under this view, we punish and reward young children, and even animals because we recognise their ability to follow the moral laws or, at least, their ability to 'choose' between at least two possible actions.

Moral agents must be distinguished from moral subjects. A moral subject is anything which is worthy of moral consideration. Again, just what this includes is a matter of debate. Whilst a baby is not often seen as a moral agent, it is clearly a moral subject. It is less clear whether fish or trees are moral subjects. The matter rests on the criteria for being a moral subject. The sentience view is that any being capable of feeling is a moral subject. If a fish can experience pain or pleasure, then it is a moral subject as it can be treated well or badly. Kant's model denies animals are moral subjects because they are incapable of being rational. A further issue is whether moral subjects have intrinsic or instrumental value. If they have intrinsic value, then they have moral value in their own right and must always be given moral consideration. If something has instrumental value, then this means it is only morally valuable because it serves the moral interests of something with intrinsic moral value. Kant argued that harming animals can be wrong not because it is intrinsically wrong to harm animals but because harming animals may lead us to harm humans. Therefore it is only wrong to harm animals (which have instrumental value) because of the effect it has on humans (who have intrinsic value). Vegetarianism and environmentalism are often justified on the grounds that animals and the environment have intrinsic value. In other words, even if there were no humans or moral agents in the entire universe, an animal or tree would still have moral value.

See also: **agency; animal ethics; Bentham; bioethics; consciousness; environmental ethics; Kant; life; meta-ethics; Mill; rights; reason; value; vegetarianism**

Key questions: What things are capable of being moral agents and moral subjects? Is it possible to choose not to be a moral agent?

Further reading: Arpaly (2003); LaFollette (2002); Singer (1979)

Moral intuitionism

Moral intuitionism (often just 'intuitionism') comprises a set of beliefs about the nature of morality. These beliefs are (a) that 'good' or 'the good' is indefinable; (b) that objective moral truths exist, meaning what is right or wrong is independent of the mind; and (c) that a rational mind is capable of directly perceiving/understanding these moral truths. Owing to these assumptions, intuitionism is an example of descriptivism (cognitivism), which states that moral beliefs can be true or false. Intuitionism implies that rational human beings have some kind of 'moral faculty', which allows them to intuit what is right or wrong. We cannot reason about this, nor can we arrive at these insights through any process of logical analysis or scientific research. When we look at the statement '2+3=5', we are struck by the truth of it. Similarly, knowing that 'murder is wrong' is a basic, intuitive piece of knowledge.

According to intuitionism, our moral faculty allows us to understand the moral features of a situation, such as when an action could have an immoral consequence. Our intuition cannot tell us what to do in each situation, we must apply the self-evident moral truths to help us calculate that. One consequence of this theory is that those who disagree with the correctly intuited moral truths are objectively wrong, rather than simply 'different' (as moral relativists would argue). Critics of intuitionism question this apparent 'moral sixth sense', arguing that it simply provides a neat way of defending one's moral beliefs. Furthermore, just how we are able to know that we have correctly intuited moral truths is far from clear. Indeed, it would seem impossible to describe how this occurs, other than saying that we simply know. Another objection is that there is little agreement over self-evident moral truths. Finally, when a moral disagreement does occur, it seems difficult to have any further discussion if each side declares their belief to be an intuited moral truth.

See also: **descriptivism; epistemology; fact/value problem, the; good, the; intuition; justification; meta-ethics; Moore; morality; moral objectivism; moral subjectivism**

Further reading: Dummett (1977); Moore (1903); Singer (1991); Sinnott-Armstrong (2006)

Morality

Morality is a system of rules telling us what is right for us to think and do. It sets the limits of behaviour by determining which actions are acceptable and which are not. It should not be confused with the legal system, which is informed by morality but not determined by it. Some laws are non-moral, such as the age at which we can vote, whilst other laws can be considered to be immoral, such as capital punishment. A moral agent is someone who must obey morality. Not all humans are necessarily moral agents and not all moral agents are necessarily human. It is unlikely that a young baby would be expected to understand morality, whilst it is possible that chimpanzees or robots could be taught to act morally and so become moral agents. A moral subject is something which has value within morality. If there is a moral rule against torturing animals, then animals would be moral subjects.

A moral theory is the attempt to explain and justify morality. Influential moral theories include contractarianism, deontology, consequentialism, emotivism and virtue ethics. Morality may either be objective, meaning it exists independently of humans, or subjective, meaning it is a human creation. Religious morality, which claims morality is the word of God or part of the laws of the universe, is an example of objective morality. If morality is objective, then it is universal and so a single moral system will apply to all moral agents in the world. Currently, morality is rarely described as universal. Moral relativism accepts the idea that each society has its own system of morality, and within each system there will be much disagreement about what is and is not morally right. The subjective view of morality sees it as a human construct which is often claimed to be necessary for the maintenance of society and the well-being of individuals.

See also: **Aristotle; animal ethics; anti-realism; Bentham; bioethics; categorical imperative; consequentialism; contractarianism; cultural relativism; descriptivism; duty; egoism; emotivism; environmental ethics; equality; evil; fact/value problem; facts; freedom; good, the; happiness; Hare; impartiality; justice; Kant; karma; liberty; meta-ethics; Mill; Moore; moral agents; moral intuitionism; moral objectivism; moral subjectivism; prescriptivism; responsibility; rights; Rousseau; Singer; Socrates; supererogation; tolerance; universability; value; virtue; virtue ethics; Williams**

Further reading: Benn (1998); LaFollette (2002); Singer (1991)

Moral luck

The concept of moral luck has important implications for ideas of moral responsibility and moral judgement. An instance of moral luck occurs when a moral agent is subjected to moral praise or blame, even when part of what is being praised or blamed is beyond their control. Imagine two people, one who has murdered someone and the other who has attempted to murder someone. The only reason that the second person failed in their attempt at murder is that their gun jammed and thus would not fire. In this instance, the 'successful' murderer would face far harsher moral judgement than the 'failed' murderer, even though the only difference between them was something beyond their control. Examples of moral luck seem to contradict the principle that moral agents should be assessed only on thoughts and actions which are within their control. This principle could be used to argue that the two people in the above example should have faced the same penalty. However, another commonly held principle is that those who cause greater harm should face greater punishment, and therefore the successful murderer should be treated differently from the failed murderer.

The idea of moral luck can be extended beyond such events as a gun failing to fire or instances of simply being 'in the right place at the right time'. More generally, we may wonder at the extent to which our entire moral character is down to luck. Perhaps we were born with a calm, generous, honest and peaceful character, which has made it easy for us to act in a morally praiseworthy way. Similarly, if we are born into a family that is very disadvantaged and perhaps relies upon stealing or violence to survive, what chance do we have of developing our moral character? Kant's theory attempts to avoid the problems of moral luck by highlighting the importance of a good will. According to Kant, what makes someone morally praiseworthy is their possessing a good will, the desire to do what is right solely because it is right. Whilst accepting that all actions may be affected by

M

circumstances beyond our control, we must focus nonetheless on the intention to do what is right, regardless of the consequences of the action. Consequentialism, which judges moral value in terms of the consequences of an action, seems committed to accepting the influence of moral luck. For example, if a person failed in their attempt to murder but, in so failing, managed to save a child's life by mistake, then their act would appear to be a morally good one.

See also: **consequentialism; deontology; determinism; karma; morality; responsibility; utilitarianism**

Further reading: Nagel (1979); Statman (1993); Williams, B. (1981)

Moral objectivism

Moral objectivism is the view that whatever is right or wrong is not determined by what an individual or group believes is right or wrong. It is the opposite of moral subjectivism, which proposes that morality is an individual judgement. Moral objectivists might be moral realists and propose that moral values are mind-independent 'facts', similar to the facts of science. A moral judgement is true if it gets the facts right. This means that we discover rather than create moral values such as 'murder is wrong'. Alternatively, moral objectivists can be moral universalists and claim that a moral system is universally valid without referring to moral 'facts' to justify this claim. One may derive what is right from examining human nature or human rationality.

All moral objectivists agree that whatever is right and wrong does not change across time and place. Providing each being is capable of realising what the moral laws are, there should be no moral disagreements. Such thinking can be seen in the Universal Declaration of Human Rights. Critics of moral objectivism argue that, given the apparent variety of moral beliefs, which often conflict with one another, it is simply absurd to assert that there is one 'correct' set of moral values. Furthermore, even if the moral laws were independent of human thought, it is not clear how we would know if we have discovered them.

See also: **categorical imperative; cultural relativism; descriptivism; difference; deontology; facts; good, the; meta-ethics; Moore; moral intuitionism; morality; moral subjectivism; universability; utilitarianism**

Further reading: Gowans (2000); Harman and Thomson (1996); Sayre-McCord (1988); Shafer-Landau (2003); Singer (1991)

Moral realism

See **descriptivism** and **moral objectivism**

Moral relativism

See **cultural relativism** and **moral subjectivism**

Moral subjectivism

According to moral subjectivism, moral values are a product of thought and therefore do not represent an objective, mind-independent feature of reality: each of us decides what is right or wrong. However, 'divine command theory', the belief that God dictates what is right, is also an example of moral subjectivism. The idea that morality is a product of human thought forms the basis of modern moral relativism, according to which the concept of what is right or wrong is relative to a particular society. According to moral subjectivism each of us has our own set of moral values and if we disagree over a principle, such as whether abortion is right or wrong, then there is no neutral way of settling the disagreement. The belief that morality is determined by a group, rather than an individual, is known as cultural relativism (or occasionally moral relativism, or just relativism).

One common criticism of moral subjectivism is that it implies our moral judgements are infallible; as long as we are sincere about our beliefs then we can never be morally wrong. However, it appears that we are occasionally wrong in our moral judgements; we tend to change our moral beliefs, actions and judgements over time or we may feel that we have been hasty in making a moral judgement and come to regret it. At the very least, many people do not want to give up the option of saying that someone else's judgements are wrong.

Another criticism is that moral subjectivism seems to ignore the process by which we form our moral beliefs. If morality is simply a matter of personal taste, then there can be no genuine discussion over what is right and wrong, we can only state what each of us feels to be right. In fact, many of us try to find reasons for asserting something is right or wrong, often based on empirical evidence (such as whether an action causes someone pain). However, one version of moral subjectivism, known as emotivism, does hold that all moral judgements are purely a matter of personal taste and, therefore, no genuine moral debate is possible.

See also: **consequentialism; cultural relativism; deontology; descriptivism; duty; egoism; emotivism; good, the; Hare; meta-ethics; morality; moral objectivism; rights**

Further reading: Benn (1998); Mackie (1977); Midgley (1991); Singer (1993)

Moral subjects

See **moral agents**

Mysticism

Broadly speaking, the term mysticism refers to any doctrine which claims that there is a form of knowledge which cannot be acquired through ordinary sense-perception or rational thought. Such mystical knowledge is gained through direct apprehension, often by entering a certain state of consciousness. Owing to its personal nature, it is very difficult to communicate the experience or to provide justification for the newly-attained belief. This has led many philosophers, particularly those who advocate empirical and scientific approaches, to view mysticism with great scepticism. Nonetheless, mystical knowledge is common to many religions, including Judaism, Christianity, Islam, Buddhism, Hinduism and Taoism. Meditation, prayer, dance, fasting and the use of psychoactive substances are common ways of inducing mystical experiences.

Debates about mysticism focus on whether mystical experiences are universal, meaning the same experience is had by people across time and place although

M

it may be expressed differently by each individual, or whether there are different types of mystical experience. In addition, it is far from clear whether, and if so how, it is possible to misunderstand or misinterpret a mystical experience. The belief that religious knowledge is beyond reason and science has been held by many philosophers and theologians. Kierkegaard wrote that religious faith 'begins precisely where thinking leaves off' (1843b: 82). An influential defender of mysticism was William James, who argued that personal, mystical experience is central to religion and provides real knowledge, unattainable via other pathways. James's work, *The Varieties of Religious Experience* (1902), describes the key mark of mystical knowledge as 'ineffability' or indescribability. Mysticism therefore presents an important challenge to theories of knowledge which insist on the empirical and linguistic basis of understanding and justification.

See also: **Buddhism; consciousness; enlightenment; faith; God, arguments for the existence of; Hinduism; intuition; introspection; James; Kierkegaard; knowledge; religious belief; unexplainable, the; Zen**

Key questions: Do mystical experiences provide genuine knowledge about the world? Is it possible to tell when a mystical experience is accurate or inaccurate?

Further reading: Harmless (2007); James (1902); Katz (1978, 1983); Yandell (1993)

M

Nationalism

Nationalism refers to the political belief in the fundamental importance of the nation, which raises the immediate issue of defining a 'nation'. Typically, a nation is formed out of those people who share a common ethnicity and culture. There is thus a strong historical dimension to nationalism, for ethnicity and culture are rooted in characteristics, beliefs and practices inherited from our predecessors. Nationalist sentiment describes the feelings produced when members of a nation feel their nation's interests are being harmed or furthered. A nationalist movement is created when sentiment motivates members of a nation to act. Generally, this will result from nationalist anger at a perceived harm being done to the nation. Nationalists argue that states should map onto nations. Taken to the extreme, this means that a state should be made up of all, and only, members of a given nation and must only serve the nation's interests. The state cannot, for example, accept partial rule by foreign powers, as in the UK's introduction of European Union legislation. Membership of a nation is often seen as involuntary, a result of being brought up in a particular place. However, the idea of nationality is made more complex by those who have dual nationality, or those who feel a connection to, say, their parents' nationality, implying that national identities can be chosen to some extent.

Issues connected with nationalism include the extent to which an individual is able to, and should, criticise their own nation. Similarly, what should be done with those individuals who do not identify with the national identity? Another moral issue facing nationalism is when, if ever, one should care about one's nation and national identity, and the extent to which one should care. Can we justify prioritising the nation's interests at the expense of the rest of the world? Related to this we must consider how far a nation may go in defending its interests. The aggressive nationalism of the 1930s, which was associated with Nazi Germany, Mussolini's Italy and Franco's Spain, revealed the violent effects it can have. However, more moderate versions of nationalism may limit the methods of nation-protection to more peaceful means. Finally, is it ever possible to identify a 'national identity'? Some philosophers have argued that all supposed national identities are simply ideologies created to control people's beliefs and actions. Alternatively, multiculturalists may argue that (a) ethnicity and culture are too vague and fluid to allow clear lines to be drawn, and/or (b) a state which contains a plurality of ethnicities and cultures will be a more enjoyable and productive place to live.

See also: **anarchism; communism; contractarianism; cultural relativism; democracy; freedom; identity; impartiality; liberalism; political philosophy; race; socialism; tolerance**

Further reading: Gellner (2006); Hall (1988); Hastings (1997); McKim and McMahan (1997)

Naturalism

Naturalism is the view that the natural world is all that exists. It rejects supernatural entities, such as God or spirits, and insists that features of the world, including the mind and morality, should be investigated using scientific methods and instruments. Naturalism is closely linked to materialism, the view that reality is composed solely of physical things. Naturalism emphasises the importance of empirical, evidence-based justification for our beliefs and explanations. Darwin's theory of evolution is an example of a naturalistic explanation of the origin of diverse species, which challenges supernatural/religious accounts.

Naturalism may be applied to different areas of philosophy. Ethical naturalism is the view that ethical beliefs and actions can be analysed empirically by the natural and social sciences. What is morally good or right can be explained through the scientific study of humans and nature, an approach which treats 'the good', or goodness, as a natural property. An example of ethical naturalism is the claim that what is right is whatever conforms to a thing's proper function. Therefore, what is right for humans is whatever they are naturally meant to do or experience, such as reproduction or happiness, and this will be discovered by scientific investigation. Ethical naturalism was famously critiqued by Moore.

See also: **Darwinism; dualism; epistemology; good, the; kind, natural; logical positivism; materialism; mind, the; Moore; morality; physicalism; positivism; reality; reductionism; scientific method; supervenience**

Key questions: Does science offer the best way of studying and explaining all aspects of the world? How do we decide whether something is natural or supernatural?

Further reading: Craig and Moreland (2000); Harman and Thomson (1996); Heil (1998); Moore (1903)

Naturalistic fallacy

See **Moore**

Necessity

See **modality**

N

Negation/nihilation

The process by which one understands oneself as separate from the rest of the world is called 'negation' or 'nihilation'. It is through negation that we realise we are ultimately alone, for only we can experience our consciousness, make decisions and experience the consequences of such decisions. This process of negation has important consequences for our relationships with other people. In negating something we see it as an object separate from our consciousness. Therefore, in interacting with another person we 'objectify' them as external to ourselves and thus turn them into an object. However, because they are also negating us, we are locked in a constant power struggle with other people in our attempts to turn the other into an object and thus become a subject. This is described in Sartre's play

Huis Clos (1944), where he famously writes, 'Hell is other people'. Sartre has been criticised, originally by de Beauvoir, for portraying human relationships as essentially conflictual and thus ignoring the positive aspects of interaction.

See also: **de Beauvoir; intersubjectivity; Sartre**

Further reading: Frie (1997); Honneth (1995); Sartre (1943)

Nietzsche, Friedrich (1844–1900)

A flamboyant, controversial and distinctive personality, Nietzsche was a German philosopher who is best-known for his attacks upon traditional morality and Christianity, as well as his anti-foundationalism. Nietzsche famously declared the death of God, referring to the impending nihilism he predicted would arise from the demise of the Christian worldview and Christian morality. Nietzsche's philosophy can be seen as an attempt to produce a radical rethinking of the world, free from any religious content. Nietzsche feared that society had become like a herd, blindly accepting and following Christian teachings which preached the importance of meekness, modesty, subservience and acceptance of one's situation. Instead, Nietzsche emphasised the need to take responsibility for one's own life and to strive to achieve one's full potential. He characterised this concept in the *Übermensch* ('overman' or superman).

Another important feature of Nietzsche's philosophy is his rejection of objective truth and absolute knowledge. Nietzsche claimed that all knowledge is 'perspectival', meaning it is limited to subjective points of view. There is no God's-eye view of the world which is absolute and objective. Indeed, Nietzsche denies that there is such a thing as truth and a world to which truth corresponds. At best, there are many truths and many worlds, relative to each society and time period. A key method of Nietzsche's work is his 'genealogy', charting the history of specific ideas, which formed a major part of Foucault's philosophy. Nietzsche is often described as an early existentialist and has inspired such philosophers as Heidegger, Freud, Sartre, Deleuze, Derrida, Foucault and Butler.

See also: **anti-realism; authenticity; existentialism; foundationalism; genealogy; God; Heidegger; knowledge; Marx; modernism; morality; nihilism; objectivism; perspectivism; self, the; truth**

Further reading: Bernd and Higgins (1996); Hollingdale (1973); Nietzsche (1882, 1885, 1886, 1887)

N

Nihilism

From the Latin *nihil*, meaning 'nothing', nihilism is the denial of any foundation or justification for our beliefs. Often this is linked to a strong scepticism and describes the world as meaningless. Epistemological nihilism denies the possibility of justified knowledge and truth. Consequently, one viewpoint is seen to be as good as any other, regardless of its content. Ethical nihilism denies the existence of moral facts and rejects the possibility of justifying moral theories and values. Existential nihilism denies that there is any ultimate meaning to life.

Although nihilism is typically associated with despair, destruction and negation, it is mistaken to thing that all nihilism is purely negative. Indeed, why should we despair if there is no point or meaning to life? This seems to be imposing a value onto the world, which a nihilist might argue is always unjustified or as justifiable as celebrating nihilism. Existential nihilism encourages a person to make their own meanings in life, rather than accept what God, political leaders or our family tell us we should do or be. The philosopher most commonly associated with nihilism is Nietzsche. Although Nietzsche rejected the idea of absolute truth, inherent meaning and the existence of God, his philosophy was aimed at preventing the world from falling into nihilism, rather than trying to spread nihilism. For some, nihilism is a philosophy of freedom as it denies there is anything we should or must be doing, and so reveals the world as pure possibility. A more negative reaction to nihilism (or rather, what it is like to be a nihilist in a particular society) is portrayed by Camus in *The Outsider* (1942).

> *See also:* **angst; certainty; doubt; epistemology; existentialism; foundationalism; freedom; Heidegger; justification; knowledge; morality; perspectivism; relativism; scepticism; truth**
>
> *Key questions:* Does life have any intrinsic meaning? Is nihilism depressing or liberating? Is it possible to live nihilistically in our everyday lives?
>
> *Further reading:* Camus (1942); Nishtani (1990); Rosen (2000)

Non-descriptivism (Non-cognitivism)
See **descriptivism (cognitivism)**

Nothingness

The concept 'nothingness' has both metaphysical and existential connotations. In metaphysics, the idea of nothingness has been discussed since Parmenides (5th century BCE), who wondered whether an empty world was possible; could there be a universe with no matter in it whatsoever? A related question is whether it is possible for something to come from nothing? If we accept that the universe is finite, and so had a beginning, then we must wonder where everything in the universe came from and what there was, if anything, 'before' the universe came into existence.

Existentialists, most notably Heidegger, have employed the term 'nothingness' to refer to a fundamental aspect of our experience. According to Heidegger, in moments of 'angst' the world becomes an unfamiliar, even 'alien', place. The objects of the world are suddenly presented to us precisely as objects, free from their everyday meanings and functions. In being disconnected from our environment, which has become a strange, unsettling place, we are confronted with 'nothingness'. Therefore, rather than referring to a literal absence of things, existential nothingness is more akin to a total lack of familiarity, sense or meaning in the world around us. This 'nothingness' reveals that the world is devoid of any intrinsic significance and the meanings we do assign to the world are arbitrary and contingent.

N

See also: **angst; existentialism; God, arguments for the existence of; Heidegger; nihilism**

Further reading: Cooper (1996a); Lowe (2002); Heidegger (1927)

Nozick, Robert (1938–2002)

Robert Nozick was one of the most important political theorists of the late 20th century. His seminal work, *Anarchy, State, and Utopia* (1974), ignited a major debate between himself and his supporters on one side, and John Rawls and his supporters on the other. Whilst Rawls defended left-wing liberalism, Nozick (at least in 1974) argued for libertarianism, which demands a global free market, minimal interference from the state and absolute property rights. According to Nozick, one has absolute ownership of oneself and one's property. Furthermore, only free market exchanges of owned goods can respect or treat people as equals (what Nozick calls 'ends in themselves'). Liberal arguments for controlling the distribution and exchange of goods, such as by differential taxation and the welfare state, are rejected by Nozick, even if such intervention would increase overall well-being. According to him, the state's existence is justified only to the extent that it protects the individual's rights and their property.

Unfortunately perhaps, Nozick moved his attention elsewhere after writing *Anarchy, State, and Utopia* so criticisms of that work have not received a systematic response in print. He criticised utilitarianism on the grounds that its definition of good as the greatest amount of happiness experienced by individuals would imply we would all want to be plugged into machines which could generate a life-like experience of every possible desire we have. Nozick claims that our negative response to such an idea reveals that we care about more than simply experiencing happiness. Nozick also explored epistemology, developing a 'tracking theory' of knowledge according to which, someone can be said to have knowledge if their belief 'tracks' (follows) the truth. This means that for someone to know there is a cat in the room, the following conditions must be met: (1) there is a cat in the room; (2) they believe there is a cat in the room; (3) if there were not a cat in the room, then they would not believe there was a cat in the room; and (4) if there were a cat in the room, then they would believe there was a cat in the room. Conditions (3) and (4) represent the 'tracking' element of the theory, for they indicate that a person's belief must follow the facts.

See also: **anarchy; communism; contractarianism; epistemology; freedom; justice; knowledge; liberalism; libertarianism; liberty; political philosophy; Rawls; rights; socialism**

Further reading: Nozick (1974, 1981, 1989, 2001); Schmidtz (2002); Wolff (1991)

N

Objectivism

Objectivism is the view that some, or all, knowledge is an accurate picture of the universe. Moral objectivism is the view that certain moral propositions, perhaps 'murder is wrong', are justified independently of human thought. This means that moral values are not created by humans; they are discovered and apply universally across space and time. Objectivism in science states that scientists paint an accurate picture of the world. Such things as atoms and quantum particles really do exist because science is able to provide a true theory of the universe. Metaphysical objectivism is the belief that statements about the world capture how the world really is. If I say that the table in my room is brown, this means it is actually brown. If no one were alive or able to see the table, it would still be brown. If two people disagree about the colour of the table, then objectivism holds that one person is right and the other is wrong. Objectivism reached its zenith during the enlightenment, when the celebration of human reason and science promised to provide an authoritative and accurate description of reality. Subjectivists reject these arguments, maintaining that our knowledge of the world, or some part of it, is created (not discovered) by humans. This may not mean that we deny that a table has a colour. Instead, the subjectivist would say we could never get outside of our subjective perceptions to say what that 'true' (objective) colour is.

See also: **anti-realism; constructionism; enlightenment; epistemology; facts; idealism; impartiality; knowledge; metaphysics; moral objectivism; perspectivism; realism; relativism; science, philosophy of; scientific realism; truth**

Key questions: Is objective knowledge possible? How can we distinguish between objective and subjective beliefs?

Further reading: Daston and Galison (2007); Harman and Thomson (1996); Machan (2004)

Ockham's razor

William of Ockham, a 14th century Franciscan monk and philosopher, has become associated with the phrase '*Pluralitas non est ponenda sine necessitate*', meaning 'do not put forward more than one suggestion for something without necessity'. For William of Ockham, God was the only required explanation for all reality. The term 'razor' was attached to his name because of his tendency towards simplicity. Ockham's razor – also known as the principle of parsimony – is nowadays used to choose between two competing theories. It states that if two or more theories about a particular phenomenon are otherwise equal (they explain all the same facts), then we should choose the simplest theory. The 'simplest' theory is the one which contains the fewest premises or the least number of ontological entities (things that exist in the world). One reason for this is that the simpler the theory, the less there is to justify and less that can be found to be flawed. To give an example, if we are trying to explain how I am able to raise my right arm, then a physicalist theory which explains it in terms of bodily processes may well be preferable to a dualist theory which explains it in terms of a soul causing bodily processes to happen.

See also: **dualism; justification; physicalism; science, philosophy of**

Further reading: Ariew (1976); Rodríguez-Fernández (1999); Spade (1999)

Ontology

Ontology is the branch of metaphysics which studies 'being'. It considers what types of things there are in the world and what 'parts' or 'substances' the world can be divided into. An ontological analysis aims to discover the basic, individual things from which other things are built, and the way in which these things are related to each other. In order to conduct an ontological analysis, we must also explore what makes something an individual thing and how these individual things interact. An ontology of the mind might define emotions, beliefs, intentions and feelings as on-tologically distinct categories. We then must explore whether these features of the mind are physical, non-physical, or both. If the mind is seen as both physical and non-physical, then we need to examine how these two aspects interact. Ontology also addresses the existence of more abstract concepts, such as events, numbers, facts, causes and possible worlds.

See also: **being; causation; dualism; event; existence; facts; metaphysics; mind, the; modality; monism; reality; supervenience**

Further reading: Lowe (2006); Reinhardt (1992); Steward (1997); Worrall (1994)

Other minds

The concept of other minds is normally presented as the *problem* of other minds. Namely, how do we justify the belief that other minds exist and are very much like our own minds? The problem arises from the 'private-access' or 'theatre' view of the mind, upon which you, and you alone, can know about the contents of your mind. Mental life is necessarily an inner, private life. If we open up a person's head we do not see the beliefs, feelings and memories which make up our mental lives. Instead we see a mass of grey matter we call the brain. On what basis can we assert that others have a mind?

An early solution was offered by Mill, who drew a link between behaviour and mental states. Certain behaviours are linked with certain mental states. Every time I scratch myself it is because I have the sensation of an itch. When we observe other people scratching, we can assume that they too are experiencing an itch. Because the itch is always an internal experience, we can expect all other minds to be internal and therefore necessarily private. Mill's argument is seen as a version of the analogical inference argument that people are very similar to me in all physical and behavioural respects. Therefore, if I experience mental states, and use this to explain why I behave the way I do, then it makes sense to infer that other people also have mental states which explain their behaviour. The belief in other minds is the best explanation for people's behaviour. Some have criticised this argument because it is an inference from one single case to many millions of cases. A sceptical challenger may ask how we know that other people are not all zombies or robots who behave and look just like humans but are completely devoid of a mind. The problem is that the conclusion of the analogical inference argument is necessarily untestable; we simply cannot empirically prove the argument.

A somewhat different analysis is associated with Wittgenstein's private-language argument that language, and therefore meaning, is necessarily public. As a result, meanings (and therefore minds) are not 'in the head'. Sensations do not exist privately in our mind's theatre, which we, as detached viewers, watch. In order to have sensations we must have words to describe these sensations, and these are obtained through a public language. Although this may not prove that other minds exist, it could change how we think about minds in such a way as to destroy the foundations upon which the problem of other minds was built.

Existentialists, most notably Heidegger and Sartre, have approached other minds in a very different way. Within Heidegger's philosophy, our own existence (Dasein) is intrinsically connected to the existence of others. This 'being-with-others' suggests that our own existence is imbedded within a world shared by other people. They are a part of the foundations of our being and it does not make sense to think of ourselves in isolation from other people. According to Sartre, it is through other people that we get a sense of ourselves. In a famous example he describes being caught in a shameful act. Our feeling of shame is bound up with being seen by another person and at that moment we are painfully aware of the existence of this other consciousness which has made us an object of shame. Both Heidegger and Sartre characterise the existence of other minds as 'basic'; we directly know it to be true, though we could not justify or explain this belief. It simply makes no sense to think that other minds do not exist, as our every experience with other people tells us that they do.

See also: **behaviourism; belief; consciousness; Dasein; Descartes; Heidegger; inference; intersubjectivity; individual, the; introspection; mind, the; private language argument; Sartre; scepticism; solipsism**

Key questions: Can we ever know whether other people have minds like ours? Do we need to prove that other minds exist? How could we prove that a person has a mind but a zombie or robot does not?

Further reading: Avramides (2001); Buford (1970); Heidegger (1927); Sartre (1943); Wittgenstein (1953)

o

Paradigm

From the Greek for a pattern or model, the word paradigm was used by Kuhn (1962) to describe a scientific approach that becomes accepted in terms of theory and practice. Crises in scientific understanding may lead to revolution when what has been accepted as normal science is challenged. Kuhn foresees three possible outcomes if that happens:

1. normal science is able to solve the problem;
2. normal science remains whilst acknowledging that there is something that cannot be solved (yet);
3. a new paradigm competes and, if successful, changes the rules of what had been accepted as normal.

Science may appear to be a linear, cumulative process because that is how it is presented in scientific texts. However, the development of scientific knowledge has tended to consist of episodes of normality and revolution. A well-known example of a paradigm shift is that between Ptolemy's theory that the earth is at the centre of the universe and Copernicus' proposal that the sun is central to our galaxy.

See also: **context; historicism; incommensurability; Kuhn; science, philosophy of; quantum mechanics**

Further reading: Bird (2000); Gutting (1980); Kuhn (1962, 1977)

Paradox

A paradox is an apparently sound piece of reasoning that produces a contradictory conclusion. Paradoxes are very useful for revealing faulty assumptions or flawed logical reasoning. Interest in paradoxes dates back to Zeno (5th century BCE). Zeno's paradoxes are still discussed today, of which the best-known focuses on motion. For instance, imagine you are walking towards a friend who is standing 100m away. Suppose you walk half way towards them, so you are 50m away. Then you walk half-way from there, leaving you 25m away. You carry on halving the distance between yourself and your friend. Yet because you can always halve the distance between the two of you (even if just 1cm away, you could halve it to 0.5cm, then halve 0.5cm to 0.25cm, *ad infinitum*), you never actually reach your friend.

Modern interest is in semantic paradoxes, which focus on notions of truth and definability. The most famous is the Liar Paradox, which dates back to Epimenides (6th century BCE), who pronounced that 'all Cretans are liars'. Given that he himself was a Cretan, if what he says is true, then he is a liar and hence what he says is false (if it is true). Strictly speaking, this is not a true paradox because someone

153

who is described as a liar does not lie *all* the time. Modern formulations escape this problem with statements such as: 'this sentence is not true'. When we assign a truth value to it we get the following conclusion: S is true if and only if it is false (and *vice versa*, so if we take S to be false, then we conclude that it is true). Hence we derive a contradiction, which is an unacceptable conclusion. What has troubled philosophers is that this contradictory conclusion is derived from apparently sound (good) reasoning and acceptable use of language (breaking no grammatical or semantic rules). Solutions include: accepting contradictions as acceptable conclusions; dropping the principle of bivalence, which states that a meaningful statement must be either true or false; radically revising our understanding and use of English. None of these seem particularly attractive, which is why paradoxes have drawn such attention.

A final interesting set of paradoxes is to be found in religious views of God as omnipotent (all-powerful) which are designed to show that the idea of omnipotence is incoherent. For example, if God is omnipotent, can he create a stone that is too heavy for Him to lift? If God can do this, then there is something He cannot do (lift a particular stone). If God cannot create this stone, then that is something He cannot do (create the stone). Therefore the idea of God being omnipotent produces a contradiction which demonstrates that God cannot be omnipotent.

See also: **logic; God; reason; truth; Zeno's paradoxes**

Further reading: Clark (2002); Rescher (2001); Sainsbury (1995); Sorenson (2005)

Particular

See **universals and particulars**

Pascal's Wager

Pascal's Wager refers to a unique argument for believing in God, which was formulated by the French philosopher Blaise Pascal in his *Pensées* (1660). Rather than try to prove God's existence, Pascal gives us reason to believe in a God regardless of whether God does or does not exist. Indeed, Pascal explicitly states we cannot know whether God exists. Given that God might exist, Pascal argues, it is worthwhile wagering that God does exist and therefore following God's teachings. His reasoning is that, if God does exist, then we will be rewarded with infinite happiness in Heaven for obeying Him, whereas, if we choose not to believe in God and God does exist, then we will be punished with eternal suffering in Hell. Now, if God does not exist, then it does not matter whether we choose to believe or not (although Pascal says we will live better and happier lives if we do believe in God). Given the possible rewards and punishments, the only sensible wager is belief in God. Importantly, if God does exist then the rewards and punishments are eternal and therefore infinite. This means that even if the chance of God existing is tiny, the enormity of reward or punishment we receive from each option makes it worth the wager of God existing. This argument is relevant to all of us because we *have* to play this game; we are using our lives as the wager and only we can choose what that wager will be.

There are numerous criticisms of Pascal's Wager. Firstly, it implies that we should believe in every possible God and therefore follow every religion on Earth. Secondly, it assumes that God is just and will suitably reward or punish us when we die. If God is entirely good, it is possible He would not be able to inflict suffering. Thirdly, God is very likely to be aware that we are only choosing to believe in Him for our own selfish desires. We do not really believe in Him but instead we just choose to follow the Bible in the hope of getting a reward. Such cold, calculated reasoning does not count as true faith. If anything, we are more likely to be punished for trying to trick God than for simply remaining undecided about His existence. In his defence, Pascal did argue that after going to church, reading the Bible and following God's teachings, we would discover a true and genuine faith in His existence. Nonetheless, there remain serious philosophical doubts over the persuasiveness of Pascal's Wager.

See also: **faith; God; God, arguments for the existence of; religious belief**

Further reading: Jordan (1994); Pascal (1660); Rescher (1985b)

Patriarchy
See **feminism**

Perception
Perception is the ability to gather information from the world through our senses (sight, touch, hearing, smell and taste). According to empiricists such as Locke, there is no innate knowledge and so all knowledge is ultimately derived from our perceptions. The major philosophical problem with perception is whether it provides an accurate account of how things really are. We can be deceived in our perceptions, such as when hallucinating or seeing an illusion, and therefore how can we know when we are perceiving correctly? Furthermore, are qualities such as colour or heat part of the object itself or part of our perception of the object? When we put our hand in very cold water and then touch a warm piece of metal, the metal will feel much hotter than if we had had our hand in a very hot bath. Similarly, when we go into a room having been outside in bright sunshine, the room appears darker to us than if we had been in a dingy cellar. Finally, two people looking at a table from different angles and in different light levels will see a different shape and colour. In all these cases, is it possible to say what the actual colour or shape or temperature of a thing is? Sceptics argue that we can never get beyond our subjective perceptions in order to experience an object as it really is. A further issue is whether this means we should or should not speak of objects existing in an external world. Perhaps, as Berkeley argued, everything exists in our minds and the mind of God.

P

See also: **Berkeley; empiricism; experience; idealism; knowledge; Merleau-Ponty; perspectivism; reliabilism; scepticism; solipsism**

Further reading: Berkeley (1709, 1710; Merleau-Ponty (1945); Robinson (1994); Russell (1912); Schwartz, R. (2004)

Performativity

The concept of performativity was developed in the speech–act theory of J.L. Austin (1962a). Austin distinguished between two forms of speech. Constative utterances, such as 'it is raining', express facts and can be true or false. Performative utterances, such as 'close the door' or 'thank you for this meal', express or bring about actions. They can be neither true nor false, instead they are judged on their success (performance). However, the idea of performativity was transformed by Judith Butler, who made it central to her theory of gender, sexuality and identity. According to Butler, gender is performative, meaning it is an identity constructed over time by a series of acts. Gender is not a feature of our being with which we are born and which explains why we act the way we do. Rather, the way we act gives rise to the idea of gender. Gender is nothing more than a set of social rules for how to think, behave, talk and look. The mistake is to think that these social rules are justified by gender, when in actual fact they are used to justify gender. Butler stresses the fact that gender performativity is not the same as a performance. This is because Butler denies that we are the 'actors' behind our expressions (performances) of gender. Rather, each of us is constructed through and by performativity.

This idea is adapted from Nietzsche's claim that there is 'no "doer" behind the deed, no "being" behind the doing' (1887: 25). Nietzsche uses the analogy of a flash of lightning to demonstrate his point, arguing that people are mistaken if they separate the lightning from the flash and claim that the flash is an *effect* of a subject called lightning. The flash is the lightning, just as we are our actions rather than some 'thing' which performs them. This rejection of a substance we call 'I' is similar to the Buddhist teaching of *anatman* (not-self), which says that each of us is just the collection of actions and thoughts we label 'Tom' or 'Nava'. There is no 'self' existing over and above our actions. Although Butler has been criticised for removing the possibility of agency from her account of identity, she says that there is always the chance of altering how gender is performed. Given that identity consists of a series of isolated acts, these acts can be changed and therefore the possibility of new identities is opened up. Butler's concept of performativity has become central to queer theory, particularly the exploration of 'deviant' identities such as homosexuality, transsexuality, transgenderism and drag, all of which reveal the way gender is performatively created by re-performing gender in new ways.

See also: **Austin; Buddhism; Butler; change; constructionism; feminism; gender; 'I'; personal identity; queer theory; self, the; speech-act**

Further reading: Austin (1962a); Butler (1988, 1990, 2004); Jagger (2002); Salih (2002)

Persistence
See **change**

Person

The concept of a person is particularly important in relation to ethical issues. Although we use the term without problem in our everyday lives, there are difficult questions surrounding the idea of a person. First and foremost, what does it mean to be a person? What makes something a person? This issue of personhood has often been linked to concepts such as agency (particularly moral agency), reason and rationality, language, or a feature of the mind such as intentionality, self-awareness or intelligence. Within religious accounts, a person is often seen as someone possessing a soul.

However, each of these suggestions raises problems. To what extent do they apply to babies, the mentally handicapped, animals, foetuses, robots or those in a vegetative state? We often assign special moral status to persons, treating them as moral agents and giving them certain rights, such as liberty, freedom from harm and legal representation, which are not given to non-persons. Issues such as abortion, euthanasia, infanticide and vegetarianism all rest, to some degree, on what we regard as persons. A major criticism of the idea of personhood has been its frequent anthropocentrism, the idea that humans are somehow special, privileged beings and the related tendency to understand the world in human-centred ways. To overcome this, we could either extend the idea of persons to include some or all living/sentient beings, or we must give up the notion of a person altogether.

See also: **agency; animal ethics; artificial intelligence; bioethics; Dasein; death; dualism; ego, the; existence; 'I'; individual, the; life; mind, the; moral agents; other minds; personal identity; reason; self, the; solipsism; subjectivity; vegetarianism**

Key questions: What makes something a 'person'? Should being a 'person' give you special moral or political value and rights?

Further reading: LaFollette (2002); Martin and Barresi (2003); Noonan (2003); Parfit (1984)

Personal identity

The concept of personal identity refers to the identity of a person over time. This means quantitative identity, something being numerically the same thing, rather than qualitative identity, which is something having the same properties or characteristics. We change qualitative identity all the time, such as when we cut our hair or acquire a tan. Despite this we tend to think of ourselves as maintaining quantitative identity. It seems obvious that when we meet a friend on two separate occasions we are meeting the same person, or when you see a photo of yourself aged three it is you and not a different person that you are looking at.

Nonetheless, the persistence of a person over time is philosophically puzzling and has been explained in a variety of ways. An early account of personal identity was formulated by Locke who argued that what secures the identity of a person over time is memory, which can unite various actions, thoughts and experiences into a single, persisting concept we call 'I' or 'me'. The memory theory is one version of the popular psychological continuity thesis, which states that some psychological relation is necessary for a person to persist. This means the 'you' of ten years ago is the same as the 'you' now if the current 'you' inherited certain psychological features (memories, rationality, feelings, experiences, and so on) from the past 'you'. An alternative approach is to base persistence on physical continuity so that a person is the same if there is a causal connection between a body ten years ago and a body now. Given that every cell in a person's body will have been replaced every seven years, physical continuity must refer to cell-regeneration of

P

the organism. You and the three-year-old you are the same if the three-year-old body has produced your current body. A third view of personal identity would argue that a person persists by being a single, unchanging soul. The problem is actually experiencing this soul to know whether, for instance, it is the same soul we met yesterday. All we ever seem to experience are physical bodies and psychological phenomena, not souls.

A useful way of assessing these theories of personal identity is through thought experiments. For instance, imagine that you experienced total amnesia and had no recollection of the past. Do you think you would be the same person as the person before the amnesia? Or imagine your brain was transplanted into a new body and a replacement brain was put into the old body. Which of the two people are you? Perhaps both are you or perhaps neither is you. The issue of personal identity has been complicated by scientific developments which offer the possibility of an entire person's memory being stored on a computer or the cloning of an entire organism.

Interest in personal identity is not restricted to Western philosophy. Buddhists argue that a person is a series of individual things connected in a causal way. In other words, each moment a 'new' you comes into existence, and the concept of a person is the name given to those momentary 'slices' which are connected in a causal chain. The current 'you' gives rise to the next 'you' through cell-regeneration and psychological features such as desires. For instance, the desire to have a drink connects the 'you' which was sitting at home with the 'you' now sitting in a café. The Buddhist view therefore bears similarities to both the psychological and physical continuity theories. The difference lies in its denial that there is anything special about each person. Because all things, to some extent, interact causally, all persons are interconnected. The idea of a person has practical advantages, but there is nothing (ontologically) significant about labelling a certain set of people-slices 'Henry' or 'Isobel'. Western ideas of personal identity tend to view a person as a meaningful, individual 'thing', which explains the desire to provide a satisfactory account of personal identity. Buddhism would appear to be content if all talk of people persisting were abandoned.

See also: **Buddhism; body, the; change; consciousness; Dasein; ego, the; essentialism; 'I'; identity; individual, the; intersubjectivity; mind, the; responsibility; self, the; subjectivity**

Key questions: What is it, if anything, that makes you aged five the same person as you aged sixty-five? How much could your physical and mental features change before you became a different person? If it became possible to fully clone a person, what, if anything, would make the clone a different person to the original?

Further reading: Martin and Barresi (2003); Noonan (2003); Perry (2008); Siderits (2007)

Perspectivism

Perspectivism is the belief that there is no single, authoritative 'truth' but rather a host of individual or collective perspectives. The theory is chiefly associated with Nietzsche, who denied the possibility of a 'God's-eye view' of the world and reality in which everything is seen from a neutral and all-knowing position (1887: Section 12). This does not mean that every viewpoint is equally valid; instead claims to truth and knowledge are restricted to particular historical and cultural contexts. Furthermore, certain beliefs may be more suitable to certain practical aims and interests than others. The key point is that there is no transcendental (detached/outside/God's-eye view) position from which the world can be surveyed, described and explained. Nietzsche's theory has influenced the development of pragmatism and can be seen as similar to Deleuze's concept of immanence. Perspectivism was developed by Ortega y Gasset, who claimed that reality is always 'my life' and thus what is real is real only so far as it real for me. Truth is made relative to each person's perspective and the only necessarily false claim is that there is an absolute truth.

See also: **context; cultural relativism; Deleuze; experience; hermeneutics; historicism; impartiality; incommensurability; objectivism; pragmatism; reality; relativism; truth**

Further reading: Hales and Welshon (2000); Nietzsche (1887); Ortega y Gasset (1923)

Phenomenalism

Phenomenalism is the theory that the world and knowledge are reducible to the way the world appears to us through our senses (phenomena). To say that an object exists is to say that we would experience certain sensations with regard to that object. If I say there is a carrot in the next room, I am saying that if you walk into that room you will, under the right light conditions and so forth, have the sensations of seeing, smelling and touching a carrot. An important feature of phenomenalism is its commitment to the world as it appears. There is no mysterious reality 'beyond' the senses, for this world is necessarily unknowable as all knowledge is founded upon sense-data. An early version of phenomenalism was formulated by Mill, who described all matter as 'the permanent possibility of sensation' (1865: 183). Phenomenalism's emphasis on sense-experience as the condition for justifying knowledge was adopted by the logical positivists, who argued that the only meaningful statements are those which can be verified empirically (through our senses).

See also: **experience; knowledge; Mill; perception; reality; reliabilism; Vienna Circle**

Further reading: Ayer (1936, 1940); Mill (1865)

Phenomenology

Broadly, phenomenology is the study of structures of consciousness and experience from the subjective (first-person) viewpoint. It examines how the world appears to us and our place within that world. In actual fact, phenomenology is not a single, systematic doctrine. Rather, it is a general philosophical trend away from scientific, naturalistic philosophy towards a theory of 'being' (Dasein), a term referring to our situation as self-aware, intentional beings (beings for whom being is an issue, to use Heideggarian terminology). The phenomenological movement began with Husserl and was developed in various directions by Heidegger, Sartre, Merleau-Ponty, de Beauvoir, Arendt and Gadamer.

One key feature of phenomenology is the intentionality of consciousness. Experiences are always directed towards something, such as a belief about an object in the world. Furthermore, our experiences are dependent upon certain conditions such as embodiment, culture and language. The world is always a 'world-for-us'; we are intrinsically bound up in a 'life-world', which means we must explore our practical engagement in the world and the meaning the world has to our particular projects, goals and beliefs. Phenomenology therefore resists the reductive approaches of science and psychology to understanding and explaining both human beings and the world. In turning back to our direct experiences of the world and our place within it, phenomenologists believed they were returning to the fundamental issues from which philosophy had strayed.

See also: **angst; Arendt; body, the; consciousness; Dasein; de Beauvoir; embodiment; experience; Gadamer; Heidegger; Husserl; intentionality; Merleau-Ponty; reductionism; Sartre; subjectivity**

Further reading: Dreyfus and Wrathall (2006); Moran (2000); Smith and Thomasson (2005)

Physicalism

As the name suggests, physicalism (sometimes called materialism) is the view that everything is physical. This is occasionally treated as the claim that everything can be explained through physics and science. More generally, it is the belief that whatever exists must be physical in nature. This includes the laws of physics, such as gravity, which are explained through energy, which is treated as a physical thing. Physicalism is mainly discussed within the philosophy of mind because it is the mind which appears, of all things in the world, the hardest to 'reduce' to a physical explanation.

Physicalists reject the dualist claim that humans are both a physical and a non-physical substance. Whatever consciousness is, it is ultimately purely physical and can be explained through the physical processes of the brain. To draw an analogy, the images on a computer screen are generated by computer chips built into the central processor. Although the screen is separate from the computer (we see an image of a cat, not a computer chip), it is ultimately reducible to the computer chip. Similarly, the images of conscious experience are not separate from the workings of the brain. Although when we look at a brain we do not 'see' consciousness, this does not mean that consciousness is some 'thing' separate from the brain. Ryle dismissed such a dualistic notion by declaring there is no 'ghost mysteriously ensconced in a machine [our body]' (1949: 21).

The major attraction of physicalism is that it fits well with a scientific, reductive view of the world, which seeks to explain everything through scientific laws and principles, as well as allowing for empirical testing and observation. Despite this, many philosophers have objected to it for two fundamental reasons: qualia (the subjective, 'like-thisness' of conscious experience, such as the 'redness' of a rose) and intentionality (the 'aboutness' of thoughts, the fact that they are directed towards objects in the world). Another issue is that, if physicalism were accepted as true, it would imply two things: firstly, consciousness could one day be entirely described, analysed and recorded; secondly, it is possible to produce consciousness by designing a sufficiently complex machine. Unlike dualism, physicalism is therefore compatible with the creation of a sentient, intelligent robot that would be as 'human' as humans. The rejection of physicalism does not necessarily mean some form of dualism or idealism is correct. It could be that there are certain features of the world, consciousness being one of them, that simply defy explanation. For instance, Nagel has argued that there is an irreducible component of consciousness, described as 'what it is like', the subjective viewpoint of experiencing the world from the first person. This sets the limit of possible explanations of the mind, without implying that there is (or is not) a non-physical substance such as a soul.

See also: **artificial intelligence; behaviourism; belief; consciousness; dualism; eliminative materialism; functionalism; 'I'; identity theory of mind; intentionality; mind, the; monism; naturalism; phenomenology; qualia; reductionism**

Key questions: Can every feature of the world, including human consciousness, be explained in purely physical terms? If not, is that because science and technology are not advanced enough yet or because some features of the world are necessarily unexplainable in physical terms?

Further reading: Heil (1998); Lowe (2000); Rosenthal (2000); Ryle (1949)

Plato (429–347 BCE)

It is nearly impossible to overstate the influence that Plato has had on the development of philosophy in the West. Plato was a student of Socrates, who deeply affected his thinking, and the teacher of Aristotle, who later rejected Plato's views. A key theme of Plato's philosophy was his belief in a realm of 'ideas' or 'forms' (the two terms are generally used interchangeably). The forms are the true nature of things, a 'pure' reality, which stands beyond the everyday world of appearances. Rather than being mental ideas or concepts, the forms are more real than the concrete world. They are the essence of all things. For every object and idea on earth, there is a corresponding form. When we see a horse or say something is beautiful, we are recognising the form of 'horseness' or beauty in those objects. This is why we can recognise many objects as being the same thing, even if they appear superficially different. For example, although no two horses are exactly alike, we are able to identify them all as horses. This is because they possess (instantiate) the form of 'horseness'.

The same analysis applies to ethics – the enlightened philosopher is able to recognise the form of the good (the 'highest' form) and thus know what is virtuous and right. Plato's theory of the forms has been accused of 'reification' (literally 'thing-making') on the ground that it is a fallacy (piece of flawed reasoning) to assume that concepts, such as beauty, exist independently of the objects which possess them and to treat them as concrete 'things'. Plato was a deeply political philosopher and his best-known work, *The Republic* (c. 360 BCE), is a description of the ideal state governed by the 'philosopher-king'. This philosopher-king is able to rule through his knowledge of the forms and demonstrates Plato's dislike for the 'rule of the many', which he blamed for causing the death of Socrates. Plato also believed that gaining knowledge is a matter of 'recollecting'. We, as souls, resided in the realm of the forms before inhabiting our current bodies. In this state we had knowledge of the true nature of the forms, but forgot much of it when entering this world. Understanding the true nature of reality is therefore remembering what we once knew.

P

Plato's characteristic use of dialogues has also been very influential. His characters debate particular issues, such as the true nature of 'virtue', with his chief protagonist Socrates often leading the discussion. The dialogues frequently create a sense of puzzlement by showing the apparent contradictions or strange conclusions certain beliefs can lead to. However, they also show a strong desire to subject our everyday assumptions to rigorous, logical analysis. This relentless, systematic examination of issues in the pursuit of truth is one of the hallmarks of Plato's philosophy and seems to owe much to Socrates' method of inquiry.

See also: **aesthetics; Aristotle; beauty; democracy; dialectic; good, the; Greek philosophy, ancient; knowledge; metaphysics; political philosophy; properties; rationalism; realism; Socrates; truth; universals and particulars; utopianism**

Further reading: Benson (2006); Cooper (1997); Desjardins (2004); Gonzalez (1998); Plato (c.360 BCE)

Political philosophy

Political philosophy is the theoretical analysis of society and an individual's relationship to it. It applies ethical concepts such as justice, rights and freedom to the study of societies in order to determine how societies should be structured. Dominant schools of political philosophy include liberalism, conservatism, socialism, communism, anarchism and totalitarianism. More recently, environmentalism and animal ethics have developed in response to the belief that politics must concern itself with non-human interests too. Feminists have drawn attention to the potentially 'patriarchal' nature of political discussion. They argue that politics has traditionally been (perhaps continues to be) conducted largely by men and reflects their interests, beliefs and desires, which has produced societies which are structured to favour men at the expense of women.

See also: **Adorno; agency; anarchism; animal ethics; Arendt; Bentham; communism; Confucianism; conservatism; contractarianism; democracy; dialectical materialism; discourse; environmental ethics; equality; feminism; Frankfurt school; gender; Hobbes; ideology; impartiality; justice; liberalism; libertarianism; liberty; Locke; Machiavelli; Marx; Marxism; materialism; Mill; nationalism; Nozick; race; Rawls; rights; Rousseau; socialism; state of nature; subjectivity; tolerance; utopianism; value**

Further reading: Adams and Dyson (2007); Farrelly (2004); Knowles (2001); Strauss and Cropsey (1987)

P

Popper, Karl (1902–1994)

Popper was born and brought up in Austria. His interests were influenced by his parents and the dominant theories of the time, including music, Freudian and Marxist ideas, and Einstein's theories. It was the latter, combined with his reading of philosophers such as Hume, that influenced Popper's thinking on the importance of falsification as opposed to verification (that is, demonstrating that something is not true rather than looking for evidence that it is) and led to his dissatisfaction with logical positivism.

One of Popper's major contributions was to the philosophy of the scientific method. In *The Logic of Scientific Discovery*, Popper questioned the use of induction: 'no matter how many instances of white swans we may have observed, this does not justify the conclusion that *all* swans are white' (1959: 4). He referred to this as the problem of induction, which may lead to a logically invalid conclusion. His solution was to apply empirical methods that depend on deductive reasoning, with the aim of searching for counter-evidence to a theory. If no non-white swans can be found, then we are justified in holding the belief that all swans are indeed white. However, this is not proof that all swans are white and we remain open to the possibility that a swan of a different colour might be found.

Popper was also influential in politics. He rejected the deterministic nature of 'historicism', the view that history unfolds according to certain principles which drive society towards an inevitable end-point. Popper argued that society is no more than the sum of its individual members. Political and historical analysis should focus on these individuals and their ability to critically examine society, rather than searching for general, deterministic laws acting on a 'group' which is treated as a single entity separate from the individuals within it.

See also: **Freud; historicism; Hume; induction; Marxism; science, philosophy of; scientific method; validity**

Further reading: Levinson (1982); Popper (1957, 1959, 1963, 1992); Stokes (1998)

Positivism

The term positivism was coined by Comte (1856), who emphasised the role of science in transforming society. Although Comte's positivism was more concerned with political philosophy, positivism is generally associated with advocating the methods of science in all areas of investigation, including philosophy. The positivist movement sought a new metaphysics which would admit only what was empirically and scientifically verifiable. The culmination of this was logical positivism, also known as logical empiricism. According to logical positivists, the only meaningful statements are those which could be empirically verified. Consequently religious and ethical statements, which are unverifiable, were dismissed as meaningless. Despite its popularity during the 1920s and 1930s, logical positivism is rarely, if ever, defended. One major philosophical criticism was that the doctrine of logical positivism was itself unverifiable empirically, and so according to its own criteria it is meaningless.

See also: **Ayer; empiricism; experience; knowledge; metaphysics; naturalism; phenomenalism; scientific method; truth; Vienna Circle**

Further reading: Comte (1856); Hanfling (1981a); Laudan (1996); Popper (1959)

P

Possibility

The concept of possibility is very important in philosophy. It allows us to deal with what could or should be the case (what is possible) and not just with what is the case (what is actual). For example, whilst physics is the scientific study of the actual universe and its laws, metaphysics reflects on what is physically possible, even if it is not the case. Metaphysics may ask whether the current universe could have been other than it is, or whether it is possible to travel back in time. By exploring the limits of what is possible, philosophy is able to influence future investigation. If it could be shown that time-travel is impossible, then science need not spend time and money trying to build a time machine. Political philosophy examines possible ways of organising society and reflects on the potential benefits of these systems. Epistemology examines the possibility of attaining knowledge and the justification for believing such knowledge. Finally, moral philosophy assesses the possible effects of a moral theory on individual behaviour and the promotion of goodness, justice and happiness.

The ability of the mind to conceptualise possible, rather than actual, events is an important feature of cognition. Philosophers have wondered how to make sense of statements about what is possible, rather than actual. How can we say an expression of possibility is true, when it is necessarily not real (being only possible). Modality is a recent branch of logical and metaphysical philosophy which seeks to make sense of possibility, necessity and actuality. Philosophical study of possibility reflects our daily attempts to work out what options are open to us and how we can go about achieving these possible goals. In deciding how to live our lives, it is vital to work out what it is possible to do.

See also: **cognition; conditionals; epistemology; knowledge; metaphysics; modality; political philosophy; truth**

Key questions: Is it possible to determine what is and is not possible? How would this be done?

Further reading: Gendler and Hawthorne (2002); Loux (1979); Lowe (2002)

Post-humanism

The concept of post-humanism is a recent development influenced by scientific, medical and technological advances. Confusingly, there are several varieties of post-humanism which are almost antithetical (in opposition) to one another. One version of post-humanism refers to the rejection of humanism, the theory that humanity is of unique importance and should not be viewed as simply part of the natural world. Secondly, post-humanism is also a theory about ways in which the human can be enhanced, particularly through medicine and technology. In this form (also called transhumanism), post-humanism focuses on such possibilities as radically extending human life, increasing human cognitive capacities (such as greatly increased memory), and heightening sense capabilities (such as an enhanced sense of smell or the ability to see infra-red light) (see, for example, Savulescu and Bostrom 2009). The third formulation of post-humanism is aimed at deconstructing and ultimately eliminating the notion of 'the human'. This version of post-humanism begins by challenging the concept of the human as meaningful and stable, and a key feature of this theory is the exploration of the boundaries between human/machine and human/animal. Haraway's work (1991) on the Cyborg, a creature which crosses the boundary between human and machine, critiques the idea of the 'human' by arguing we are all (becoming) Cyborgs. This is particularly clear in contemporary mass-society in which people merge ever more with the machinery around them. Basic examples include glasses, hearing aids and prosthetic limbs. As technology develops, people will increasingly integrate with machinery to produce organisms that are unidentifiable as simply 'human' or 'machine'.

This last form of post-humanism also points to the fact that humans are not meaningfully different to animals and so the stability and justification of the human/ animal distinction is challenged. One could also see this theory as challenging the division between 'natural' and 'artificial' as the supposedly 'natural' human organism is fused with the 'artificial' machine. Furthermore, we are strongly 'bound up' with our environment, to the extent that we cannot make sense of ourselves without understanding our relationship to the world around us. This challenges the treatment of humans as distinct entities, which can be studied and understood as if they were individual, isolated organisms. One of the goals of the third form of post-humanism is an abandoning of the importance of 'the human', rather than the improvement of it as advocated by the second form of post-humanism.

See also: **bioethics; cognition; extended cognition; humanism; 'I'; individual, the; mind, the; person; queer theory; self, the; subjectivity**

Key questions: Are we becoming post-human? Is post-humanism desirable?

Further reading: Badmington (2000); Gordjin and Chadwick (2008); Gray (2001); Haraway (1991); Savulescu and Bostrom (2009)

Postmodernism

Postmodernism is a philosophical, political, artistic and literary movement which developed during the second half of the 20th century. It is associated with writers such as Lyotard, Foucault, Barthes, Derrida, Baudrillard and Rorty. The term was first used by Lyotard, who defined it as 'incredulity towards metanarratives' (1979: 7). However, a consistent theme amongst postmodernists has been their refusal to produce definitive definitions and to accept particular labels. Indeed, the resistance to stable, unambiguous definitions is a key feature of postmodern philosophy.

Generally speaking, postmodernism is the challenging (or 'destabilising') of truth, objectivity, progress, identity, certainty, stability, meaning, authorial intention, the subject and binary oppositions. This is achieved using the methods of deconstruction and genealogy, and the exploration of concepts such as difference, simulacram, hyperreality and multiplicity. As the name suggests, postmodernism takes a particular (critical) stance towards modernism, but it also takes a particular stance towards itself. According to postmodernists, philosophy has sought to 'totalise' knowledge, producing grand theories which claimed to authoritatively explain everything. These theories are called 'metanarratives', and it is a major concern of postmodernism to challenge them. This means that postmodernism must also resist becoming a metanarrative itself, which is why it often frustratingly appears to refuse to give definitive answers and clear definitions.

Postmodernism emphasises the historical nature of knowledge and truth, arguing that our understanding must always be linked to a particular context. There is no 'ahistorical', absolute perspective on truth, reality and knowledge. Indeed, the very notions of 'truth' and 'reality' are but one way of approaching and describing the world. They are the metanarratives of modernism, which postmodernism seeks to undermine. Despite its heavily theoretical nature, postmodernism is a deeply political theory. It explores and celebrates that which has been ignored, oppressed and pushed to the margins – those things which do not 'fit' with the dominant

P

metanarrative. Foucault's examination of madness and sexuality are the two best-known accounts of how knowledge is used as a vehicle for power by enforcing certain ways of being (such as 'sane', 'rational' and 'heterosexual'), which are presented as 'right' and 'natural'. By studying the history of concepts, called the genealogical method, Foucault was able to show how what is considered right and natural is constantly changing, shaped by the political power-struggles of history, and does not reflect an enlightened and 'true' account of reality.

See also: anti-realism; Butler; context; constructionism; continental philosophy; deconstructionism; Deleuze; Derrida; discourse; enlightenment; Foucault; Gadamer; genealogy; Habermas; hermeneutics; historicism; ideology; knowledge; language game; Lyotard; modernism; post-humanism; post-structuralism; queer theory; relativism; Rorty; subjectivity

Further reading: Butler (2002); Connor (2004); Docherty (1993); Natoli and Hutcheon (1993)

Post-structuralism

Beginning in the 1960s, the term refers to the ideas of a number of theorists who were opposed to the structuralism of thinkers such as Saussure and Levi-Strauss. Post-structuralists reject the existence of a single determining, universal structure that, although we are not aware of it, shapes and explains our behaviour. Furthermore, they deny the possibility of ever discovering such structures, should they exist. This is because we are 'situated' within specific discourses, understood as historically-specific bodies of knowledge which generate our understanding of the world. An important figure in post-structuralism is Derrida, who used deconstructive methods to demonstrate that texts can contain multiple meanings, rather than possessing some underlying structure or truth. He even deconstructed the idea of a structure. Post-structuralism reflects what Lyotard (1979) referred to as the 'postmodern condition', in which grand theories and metanarratives are rejected. Other important post-structuralists are Foucault and Kristeva.

It should be noted that there is much debate over the distinction between 'postmodernism' and 'post-structuralism'. Often the terms are used interchangeably and the same philosophical ideas are associated with both. Furthermore, writers such as Derrida and Foucault are commonly labelled as both 'postmodern' and 'post-structural'. One way of introducing a distinction is that, historically, the development of postmodernism is related to artistic movements which consciously challenged 'modernist' aesthetics. In this sense, the musician John Cage and the director David Lynch are two important postmodernists.

See also: anti-realism; context; constructionism; continental philosophy; deconstructionism; Deleuze; Derrida; discourse; enlightenment; Foucault; Gadamer; genealogy; Habermas; hermeneutics; historicism; ideology; knowledge; language game; Lyotard; modernism; post-humanism; post-structuralism; queer theory; relativism; Rorty; structuralism; subjectivity

Further reading: Finlayson and Valentine (2002); Harland (1987); Sarup (1989); Young (1981)

Pragmatism

Pragmatism is an American school of thought that was developed by Peirce, James and Dewey at the end of the 19th and beginning of the 20th centuries. These philosophers reacted against seemingly unsolvable philosophical puzzles, such as whether or not there exists a 'hidden world' behind the world of appearances (as Plato and Kant asserted in different ways). They urged a down-to-earth approach by insisting that a theory should be judged on its practical value, rather than our acceptance or rejection of it. According to pragmatism, scientific and philosophical theories are ultimately 'tools' or 'instruments' for dealing with the world (reality). Knowledge is essentially 'problem-solving'. Rather than representing objective, absolute and foundational truths, knowledge is a set of hypotheses which are formulated with respect to specific, practical and concrete problems that we face in the world.

This pragmatic theory of truth and knowledge was greatly influenced by Darwin's theory of evolution. Humankind was viewed as a developing, contingent organism, deeply connected to its environment. As a result, human cognition (theories, truth and knowledge) is strongly affected by one's environment, and it is only within the context of nature and our environment that we can understand human thought. Pragmatism rejects the model of the mind as a private realm, completely detachable from the world and our body. It is precisely *within* the context of the world that we can understand the mind. Despite the efforts of James and Dewey, pragmatism was largely ignored by philosophers until a revival in the second half of the 20th century. The most notable of the neo-pragmatists is Rorty.

See also: **cognition; Darwinism; Dewey; instrumentalism; James; Kant; knowledge; mind, the; naturalism; Plato; Quine; Rorty; truth**

Further reading: Haack (2006); James (1907); Rorty (1982); Shook and Margolis (2006)

Prescriptivism

Prescriptivism is a moral theory proposing that moral statements are 'prescriptions' or 'imperatives' rather than expressions of truth. For example, the principle 'it is wrong to murder' does not represent a fact and is not subject to being true or false. Instead, our moral principles are akin to imperatives (commands) such as 'close the window!'. According to Hare, the leading figure within prescriptivism, moral statements, unlike other imperatives, are characterised by being 'universalisable'. This means that any moral judgement implies (a) you should do this, and (b) every other rational person in the same (or very similar) situation should do this. If we express the moral view that having an abortion 25 weeks into a pregnancy is wrong, then we are making the claim that you should not have an abortion 25 weeks into a pregnancy and neither should any other person in this situation, regardless of time and place.

Prescriptivism moves away from moral realism (the view that there is a set of objective, mind-independent moral truths) whilst avoiding emotivism (morality is essentially a matter of personal 'taste') and subjectivism (what is right is simply what is right for me). Prescriptivism allows for rational discussion and investigation

P

in the construction of our moral values and also captures the common belief that our moral values should be adopted by other moral beings. Further, it expresses the importance of moral consistency. We would generally find it odd if a person was constantly changing their moral views on an issue, and prescriptivism argues that a key element of a moral judgement is that it remains the same in each situation that is sufficiently similar to the original situation in which the judgement was made. One potential difficulty for prescriptivism is specifying to what extent the situation must be similar (given that, logically, no two situations can ever be identical) and what it means to be 'sufficiently' similar. Another objection is that prescriptivism gives up any commitment to moral truths. Therefore we are unable to say that a person is factually wrong in believing that murder is acceptable, because there is no such thing as knowledge of moral truths.

See also: **Ayer; categorical imperative; consequentialism; deontology; descriptivism; emotivism; egoism; Hare; morality; moral subjectivism; universability; utilitarianism**

Key questions: How consistent are our moral principles? Do we always expect others to behave in the same way as we do when in similar situations? Do we sometimes have one prescription for ourselves and one for other people?

Further reading: Gensler (1998); Hare (1952, 1963a, 1963b); Singer (1991)

Private language argument

The influential private language argument was formulated by Wittgenstein in his *Philosophical Investigations* (1953). Wittgenstein defines a private language as words which 'can be known only to the speaker' because they refer to his 'immediate, private, sensations…[s]o another cannot understand the language' (1953: Section 243). According to Wittgenstein, the idea that one could construct such a language is a necessary feature of the view of the mind as a private realm of inner experience and meaning. Wittgenstein aims to show how a private language is impossible because the use of language is necessarily a public activity. Wittgenstein uses the example of trying to keep a diary of the recurrence of a certain sensation, which we note in the diary as *S*. Wittgenstein makes the point that every time we use *S* we cannot know that we are using it in the same way. We cannot say that it has 'rightly' referred to the same sensation on each occasion, because 'right' here will only mean 'right to me'. We need some independent verification that the same meaning has been assigned to *S* each time, but this is precisely what we lack in a private language. As Wittgenstein puts it, 'In the present case I have no criterion of correctness… And that only means that here we can't talk about "right"' (1953: Section 243). We cannot both formulate the rule and judge that it has been followed.

The key point is that language is rule-based and we learn how to use it correctly by understanding its 'rules' and 'obeying' them. For example, imagine that a baby sees a tree and makes a sound. If it is the right sound (similar to the word 'tree') then it is told it has correctly obeyed our language rules. If it makes the wrong sound then it is corrected until it makes the right sound. The same applies to our inner sensations; we learn to apply the right word to the right sensation. Imagine a young child crying and uttering the word 'happy'. It would be taught to use the word 'sad' and in doing so understands the meaning of what it is to be sad. This interpretation of Wittgenstein's ideas puts the meaning of psychological phenomena within the public sphere. That is, there must be a public criterion for what a sensation is in order for us to be able to have any meaningful words about sensation. Consequently meanings are not just 'in the head', and understanding the mind is not a matter of simple introspection.

See also: **Descartes; introspection; knowledge; mind, the; solipsism; Wittgenstein**

Further reading: Jones (1971); Kripke (1982); Mulhall (2007); Wittgenstein (1953)

Properties

The concept of properties is central to metaphysical and ontological debates about objects and the world. A property is an attribute or quality of a thing. Commonly accepted properties include colour (X is red), shape (X is round) and taste (X is spicy). More controversial are the questions of whether something like 'standing in the rain' or 'being a cat' can be true properties of an object. The importance of properties is that they are used to explain the truth of statements about objects, for instance 'This football is round' is true if and only if the object we call a football has the property 'being round'. They also explain how we can speak meaningfully about the similarities between different objects. For instance, to say that two footballs are both round is to say that they both have the one property 'being round'. Properties are sometimes distinguished from relations, which are things that hold between two objects. Relations include 'is bigger than' or 'is closer to', such as 'an elephant is bigger than a mouse'.

There is much debate over how to understand properties, beyond the description just given. A fundamental dispute is whether properties are universal or particular. A universal is something which can exist in more than one place at any one time, meaning it has many 'instances'. A particular is something which cannot have more than one instance. The bike outside my house is a particular, for it cannot be both outside my house and in Australia at the same time. If properties are universal then the very same property is present (instantiated) in the red apple and the red pepper which are currently in my kitchen. If properties are particulars then there are two different properties in my kitchen, one instantiated by the apple and the other by the pepper. They may resemble each other exactly in colour, but they are still different things. Philosophers who believe in universals are called realists, and those who believe properties are particulars are called nominalists.

Another issue regarding properties is whether a property can exist even if it is not instantiated. For instance, can we say there is such a thing as the property 'being a flying pig', when clearly there are no pigs which fly? Finally, are the properties of an object essential or accidental? If a property is essential then it means that the object would cease to be that thing if it did not possess that property. It would seem that 'having four sides' is an essential property of a square. However, 'having brown hair' does not seem to be an essential property of a person, because a person with brown hair would still be that same person even if they no longer had brown hair. The ontological argument for the existence of God relies on the belief that existence is an essential property of a perfect being. It has been argued that no properties are essential to an object and that existence cannot act as a 'property' of a thing.

P

It is also a matter of much debate whether the properties of an object are intrinsic to it. If properties are intrinsic then they belong entirely to the object. So the property 'redness' is actually something in the red object. However, it is often argued that properties are partly, or wholly, external to an object and exist in the mind of the person who is experiencing the object. For instance, when you have very cold hands and you touch something warm, that object appears warmer than if you had very warm hands. Therefore it seems that the property 'being hot' does not wholly belong to the object but is in some way dependent upon the observer. Locke makes the distinction between primary and secondary qualities. Primary qualities, or properties, are those which remain part of the object even if it were divided up into smaller parts. Examples include being 'moveable' and 'solidity', properties that are part of both a whole grain of wheat and a grain of wheat that has been cut up. Secondary qualities are non-essential properties of the object; rather they cause some sensation, such as the prickly texture of wheat. Other secondary qualities would be the colour or temperature of something. Sceptics argue that we can never say what the properties of an object are, only what we perceive them to be. Taken to its extreme, scepticism denies there is any reason to think objects have properties at all.

See also: **aesthetics; anti-realism; beauty; Berkeley; change; epistemology; essentialism; facts; God, arguments for the existence of; identity; Locke; metaphysics; modality; ontology; perception; substance; supervenience; universals and particulars; vagueness**

Key questions: Are properties intrinsic to an object? Do universals exist? Can objects possess essential properties? If an object is something separate to its properties, what is it and how can we know it?

Further reading: Loux (1998); Lowe (2002); Mellor and Oliver (1997)

P

Qualia

Qualia (singular 'quale') represent the subjective elements of experience. They are the features of consciously experiencing something, the qualitative 'like-thisness' of objects. Qualia include the itchiness of itches, the pinkness of a rose, the sweetness of an apple, or the loudness of a drum kit being played. Qualia appear to be an essential part of conscious experience, and so any account of the mind must satisfactorily account for them.

Physicalist theories, which reduce the mind to a purely physical explanation, argue that all facts about the mind are facts about the physical world. The problem qualia pose for physicalism is that they seem to defy physical explanation. We cannot scientifically observe and measure the experience of tasting an apple. If we open up a brain we see a lump of grey matter, we do not 'see' the experience of biting into a piece of fruit. Qualia appear to be a necessarily private and subjective affair, to the extent that we find it difficult (perhaps impossible) to describe qualia to other people. To get a sense of this, imagine capturing in words the precise experience of watching a sunset and then re-reading that description to see if it matches what it was like to directly experience the sunset.

The most famous thought experiment regarding qualia was formulated by Frank Jackson in a paper entitled 'What Mary Didn't Know' (1986). Imagine a scientist called Mary who has spent her entire life in a black and white room. She has never experienced any other colours, but has spent her entire life studying everything there is to know about colours. One day she is released from her room, looks at the sky and says, 'So that is what blue looks like'. Now, do we say that she has gained anything upon leaving the room? If she has, then it suggests that the physicalist view of the world is incomplete. For Mary knew everything physical about colour perception, and yet seemingly gained some new information. Therefore there is something about mind that physicalism cannot account for.

Another interesting critique of qualia is presented in Nagel's 'What Is It Like to Be a Bat?' (1979), in which he argues for a non-reducible, subjective element of consciousness that defies physical (scientific) explanation. A final interesting question considers precisely which things are capable of possessing qualia. Do cats, fish or spiders have qualia? Is it possible for a machine to have qualia? Responses to these questions, which relate to whether or not there is 'something it is like' to be these things, will depend on the nature of mind and consciousness.

See also: **artificial intelligence; consciousness; dualism; knowledge; mind, the; naturalism; physicalism; reductionism; subjectivity; thought experiments**

Key questions: Can qualia be explained by physicalism? What things are capable of possessing qualia?

Further reading: Chalmers (1996); Heil (1998); Jackson (1986); Nagel (1979)

Qualities

See **properties**

Quantum mechanics

Quantum mechanics refers to the physical laws governing the behaviour of sub-atomic particles, those that make up the atom such as electrons. It poses challenges to many deep-rooted metaphysical assumptions. For example, it has often been assumed that an object cannot be in two incompatible states at the same time. However, quantum particles behave like both particles and waves, even though the properties of waves and particles are incompatible. It is only by measurement that we can ascribe the property of particle or wave, or even existence, to a quantum particle. This has led some physicists to conclude that the particle is not 'real' until it is measured; the act of measurement brings the particle into existence. The well-known thought-experiment, Schrödinger's cat, demonstrates this problem. A cat is placed in a box with a container of poisonous gas that will be released if radioactivity is detected. There is a 50/50 chance of this happening, which leads, mathematically, to the conclusion that the cat is in a mixture of states and thus both dead and alive. Until the box is opened and the outcome observed, the cat remains in both states.

Another interesting feature of quantum particles is that they seem to interact at a distance. It has long been assumed that for object A to affect object B they must be in the same location. However, the behaviour of one quantum particle can apparently affect another particle's behaviour even if they are separated by an unreasonably large distance. Furthermore, it seems that quantum particles can exist in several places at the same time. This conflicts with the basic assumption that an object can exist in a single location at any point in time, a belief which has been used to argue against the possibility of time travel because that implies the same object being in two places at the same time.

The probabilistic nature of quantum particles means we can never be certain that they will behave in a particular way. In everyday science, as in life, we assume that causation is consistent: if A has caused B in the past then we assume that, under the same conditions, A will cause B in the future. Quantum mechanics therefore forces us to revise certain fundamental metaphysical beliefs, at least with regard to objects at a sub-atomic (quantum) level. This is particularly interesting because it is commonly assumed that some metaphysical truths are true *a priori* (independent of our experience of the world), but quantum theory suggests that all logical and metaphysical truths may have to be discovered empirically, even that the act of measurement alters them. Although the quantum world is nothing like our everyday experience of the world, this very world is built of quantum particles so the potential influence of quantum mechanics on philosophy cannot be dismissed or ignored. Furthermore, in the same way that quantum theory presented a completely new concept of reality, or parts of reality, to explain observations which did not fit traditional scientific theories, it continues to demonstrate how scientific explanation can differ radically from our 'commonsense' understandings of the world.

See also: causation; empiricism; incommensurability; Kuhn; metaphysics; relativity theory; science, philosophy of; scientific realism; relativism; time

Further reading: Baggott (2004); Healey (1991); Messiah (1999)

Queer theory

Describing queer theory is problematic because it self-consciously defines itself as whatever is at odds with the normal, the legitimate and the dominant, and as such there is nothing in particular to which it necessarily refers. Jagose (1996: 21) observes that, 'Queer itself can have neither a fundamental logic, nor a consistent set of characteristics'. Queer theory grew out of the lesbian and gay movements of the 1970s. It rejected the logic of group identity and similarity which underpinned feminist, lesbian, gay and racial theories, emphasising instead a politics of difference. Queer theorists can be seen as reflecting a general characteristic of post-structuralism. The focus on the constructed, contingent and unstable character of subjectivity, identity, social relations, power and knowledge is common to both.

The term 'queer' is representative of the theory it denotes. Whereas the terms 'gay' and 'lesbian' have become fixed and excluding, 'queer' seems more ambiguous. The word lacks a fixed reference and has had multiple meanings. It is just as at home in 19th-century drawing rooms as when employed as a recent term of political empowerment. Owing to its use throughout various historical periods, 'queer' produces nothing but confusion (a feature which queer theorists celebrate). Queer theory seeks to question the unity, stability, value and practical importance of sexual identities. It works to deconstruct the notions of sexuality and gender, often through exploring alternative ways of expressing sexuality and gender which cross boundaries and confound expectations, such as transgenderism and drag. Judith Butler is described as the most famous queer theorist, though she does not refer to herself as one. Other philosophers whose works are celebrated by queer theorists include Haraway and Bornstein. Philosophers influential in the development of queer theory include Foucault, Derrida, Cixous, Irigaray and Kristeva.

See also: Butler; deconstructionism; Derrida; feminism; Foucault; gender; performativity; personal identity; post-humanism; subjectivity; tolerance

Further reading: Butler (1990); Jagose (1996); Morland and Willox (2005); Sullivan (2003)

Q

Quine, Willard V.O. (1908–2000)

One of the foremost logicians of the 20th century, Quine was supervised by Whitehead (who worked with Russell at Cambridge) and is seen as a leading figure of modern analytic philosophy. Quine (1953) is famous for his rejection of the analytic–synthetic distinction on the grounds that even analytic truths (those true by virtue of their meaning) were only justifiable on empirical grounds. This reflects Quine's strict empiricism, according to which all knowledge is gained through sensory/perceptual experience. Influenced by the pragmatism of William James and John Dewey, Quine also defended 'naturalised epistemology', the idea that all human knowledge must be understood in the light of humans being a species of animal.

We have developed through the entirely natural processes of evolution and therefore epistemology (the theory of knowledge) must be situated within an awareness of the cognitive capacities and capabilities for creatures such as us. Related to this naturalism is his thoroughly physicalist view of the world, according to which all that exists is physical in nature and physical in explanation.

See also: **analytic philosophy; analytic/synthetic distinction; Darwinism; Dewey; empiricism; James; logic; naturalism; physicalism; pragmatism; semantic holism**

Further reading: Gibson (2004); Hylton (2007); Quine (1953, 1960)

Q

Race

The term race can refer to a group of humans, the human race in general, and a particular species. Distinguishing different races amongst humans is done on the basis of biological descent and is identifiable through characteristics such as skin colour, hair colour, facial features and body shape. Different personality traits, as well as cultural norms and values, have also been linked to particular races. Race is a highly contested concept, both politically and philosophically. The political dimension of race relates to its use as a form of discrimination. Typically this is associated with the anti-slavery campaigns and, more recently, the racial politics of the 1960s and 1970s inspired by Martin Luther King, Malcolm X and the Black Panthers. These movements all claimed that people were unfairly treated, solely on the basis of their race, and that the identity of their race had been intentionally distorted. The colonialist image of blacks as lazy, stupid and even less than human was challenged and rejected. Race continues to be a major political issue, as witnessed by the 2001 riots in Oldham, Burnley and Bradford, and the ongoing local and national government initiatives to improve inter-community relations.

However, more recently, philosophical analyses of race have attempted to challenge the very notion and meaningfulness of race. The biological basis of race has been refuted by evidence that there are no 'racial' genes which account for physical and cultural aspects of each 'race'. Furthermore, the realisation that there has been constant historical 'mixing' of races makes it impossible to identify a 'pure' or single race (apart, perhaps, from undiscovered tribes in rainforests). This has led to the claim that the division of people into races is purely contingent and arbitrarily constructed. For instance, one country's classification of people as 'black' differs from another's. The concept of race is situated within networks of power and redefined as a 'discourse', created to maintain unequal social relations. Finally, the increase in global migration and growing racial tolerance have produced many 'mixed races', which serve to blur the boundaries between racial groups and to undermine the idea of unique racial characteristics. Consequently, racial theorists have started to argue that the very concept of race should be abandoned altogether, rather than demand improved rights for any one particular race.

See also: **difference; equality; justice; kind, natural; nationalism; political philosophy; post-humanism; rights; tolerance; utopianism**

Further reading: Appiah (1992); Appiah and Gutmann (1996); Bell and Blumenfeld (1995); Bernasconi (2001); Frederickson (2002);

Radical feminism

See **feminism**

Rationalism

Rationalism is the claim that some important forms of knowledge are acquired independently of sense experience. It is opposed to empiricism, which is the view that all knowledge is gained through the senses. One version of rationalism holds that intuition (rational insight) is one route to knowledge. Sometimes we just 'see' that a certain belief is true and justified, such as intuiting that God exists or that '2+2=4'. We do not arrive at the belief from any empirical observation or sense experience; it just strikes us as genuine knowledge. Another version of rationalism claims that we are born with some beliefs or concepts as part of our rational nature. This is commonly identified as knowledge of God's existence, although innate knowledge inherited through our genes and knowledge acquired in past lives have also been identified. Plato's theory of knowledge as recollection is a strongly rationalist position. According to Plato, we already 'know' everything that we come to learn, but we have forgotten this knowledge because of the traumatic experience of being born. Descartes described our knowledge of God as innate (the 'Maker's Mark' argument). Rationalism emphasises the importance of reason (rationality) in providing non-empirically justified belief. Important historical critics of rationalism include Locke and Hume. More recently, Ayer and the logical positivists have insisted that the only meaningful concepts and propositions are those which can be empirically verified.

See also: **Ayer; certainty; Descartes; enlightenment; epistemology; experience; Hume; intuition; justification; knowledge; Plato; reason; truth**

Key questions: Is some knowledge attained non-empirically? If so, how is it gained?

Further reading: Cooper (1997); Cottingham (1984); Descartes (1641); Kenny (1986)

Rawls, John (1921–2002)

Rawls is one of the most influential modern political theorists and a defender of liberalism. Rawls' major concern was what a just society should be and how this vision could be justified. In his seminal work *A Theory of Justice* (1971), Rawls offers an alternative to utilitarian theories of justice, which he criticises for allowing the sacrifice of the individual for the collective good. Rawls is therefore situated within the liberal humanist tradition, which emphasises the importance of the individual, their liberty, and equality between all individuals. Rawls works out his ideal just society by way of a thought experiment. Imagine a group of people coming together to form a society (termed the 'original position' by Rawls, which is similar to Hobbes' 'state of nature'), none of whom has any idea what their position in this society will be (they are behind a 'veil of ignorance'). What kind of society would any rational person construct if in such a situation? Rawls believed that they would select a society in which (1) 'Each person is to have equal right to the most extensive, basic liberty compatible with similar liberty for others', and (2) 'Social and economic inequalities are to be arranged so that they are both (a) reasonably expected to be to everyone's advantage, and (b) attached to positions and offices open to all' (1971: 60). He reasoned that an individual, given that they necessarily do not know what position in society they will occupy, will opt for the 'best worst' principle. They will make the worst position in society bearable, even if this means limiting life at the top. Thus Rawls assumes each person will calculate how society should be by using a logical cost–benefit analysis.

The advantage of Rawls' theory, which is part of the social contract tradition, is that it provides a fair and just system for every member of society. To use an analogy, when dividing food among people, we would not want the person dividing the food to know which portion will be theirs. One criticism levelled at Rawls is that he equates being a rational individual with being self-interested and materialistic. He ignores the importance of non-commercial goods, as well as the value of friendship, aesthetics and family. In effect, Rawls is accused of fixing the rules of the game to produce his vision of justice, that of individualistic, liberal capitalism. Furthermore, it is debatable to what extent we could actually perform the thought experiment outlined above. Can we genuinely imagine ourselves without any of our current ideas, beliefs, characteristics, and so forth?

See also: **contractarianism; equality; Hobbes; justice; liberalism; liberty; Nozick; political philosophy; reason; Rousseau; state of nature; thought experiments; utilitarianism**

Further reading: Davion and Wolf (1999); Freeman (2003, 2007); Rawls (1971, 1993, 1999)

Realism

Realism is the belief that the existence and nature of a certain thing is independent of people's beliefs, language, perceptions, concepts, and so on. Furthermore, we are able to understand these things accurately. Typically, realism is adopted with regard to a particular area of philosophy. Scientific realism states that the world is as science describes it, thus science provides an accurate and objective picture of the world rather than a construction of how we think of it. Ethical realism is the view that there exist ethical facts in the world, or that certain morals are objectively right. Our moral principles relate to truths about the world, not truths about human activity. Metaphysical realism argues that there is an independently existing world, and when we state truths or facts we refer to the way the world actually is. Within metaphysical realism there are many different views about what actually does or does not exist. Alternative worlds, events, numbers, causation, time and facts have all been defended by realists. Realism in aesthetics is the claim that some things are objectively beautiful, rather than beauty being in the eye of the beholder. Scepticism, relativism, anti-realism, pragmatism, idealism, perspectivism and nihilism all represent doctrines which question the basic realist belief that the world is independent of human activity.

See also: **aesthetics; anti-realism; constructionism; context; critical realism; cultural relativism; deconstructionism; experience; facts; hermeneutics; historicism; idealism; incommensurability; instrumentalism; kind, natural; language game; linguistic relativism; metaphysics; moral objectivism; objectivism; perspectivism; post-structuralism; pragmatism; reality; relativism; scepticism; scientific realism; solipsism; truth**

Key questions: What features of the world, if any, exist independently of our thoughts? How would we discover what these things are?

Further reading: Alston (2002); Devitt (1991); Gupta (2002); Putnam (1983); Searle (1995)

R

Reality

Reality, in the most basic sense, can be understood as 'what is real'. However, it is far from clear just what we should consider as 'real'. A commonly drawn distinction, at least historically, is between 'appearance' and 'reality'. Metaphysics can be seen as an attempt to grasp the true, fundamental reality beyond mere 'appearances'. This idea can be traced back to Plato's theory of the forms. According to Plato, the everyday world we encounter is not the 'real' world. There exists a realm of the forms, which is unchanging and eternal, and the world around is a mere imperfect representation of this realm. On this view, reality is not simply what exists but is connected with discovering the fundamental, true and objective features of the world.

Certain forms of idealism argue that we can only ever experience our ideas of the world, and not the world itself. This suggests that there is a 'real' world, but that we can never know it. There has been increasing hostility towards the idea that there is an 'objective' reality and the associated notion of objective truths. Postmodernists, for instance, argue that there is no single 'true' reality. Rather, our idea of what is real is conditioned by our language and historical circumstances. We can never get beyond our particular perspective to achieve a 'god's-eye view' of the world from which we could determine what reality actually is. Therefore it is more appropriate to speak of 'realities' rather than 'reality', or even to refrain from speaking of 'reality' at all.

See also: **anti-realism; being; constructionism; enlightenment; epistemology; existence; facts; hermeneutics; idealism; incommensurability; instrumentalism; intuition; Kant; linguistic relativism; metaphysics; naturalism; objectivism; ontology; phenomenalism; physicalism; Plato; postmodernism; quantum mechanics; realism; reductionism; relativity theory; science, philosophy of; scientific realism; sign; transcendence; truth; vitalism**

Further reading: Bradley (1893); Cooper (1997); Greco and Sosa (1999); Potter (1996); Russell (1912)

Reason

The concept of reason has two different philosophical meanings. Firstly, a reason can be equated with a cause, so that to ask for the reason for something is to ask why it happened. Reasons can contain both desires and beliefs, so my reason for going to the fridge is the desire for a drink and the belief that there is something to drink in the fridge. The difficulty with treating reasons as causes is the gap between mental states and physical explanations of causes.

Secondly, reason can refer to logical, rational cognition. To reason about something is to reflect on it in a systematic and objective way. Our reason(s) for holding a belief is linked to having sufficient justification for that belief. The reason for believing that grass is green could be (a) faith in the accuracy of perception, and (b) the perception of some grass which looks green. Two major forms of reasoning are induction and deduction. Scepticism is the view that we never have sufficient justification for a belief, and therefore there is never enough reason to accept it. The only reasonable position is a suspension of belief. Often, what is considered reasonable or a good reason for a belief is strongly disagreed upon. Information which one person interprets as good reason to believe in God, another person interprets as reason to believe in evolution. Feminists (such as Lloyd, 1984) and post-structuralists have tended to criticise the notion of reason as the only acceptable way to think, because it imposes systems of thought and belief on people and punishes those who show a lack of reason. This is particularly noticeable in Foucault's critical examination of the concept and treatment of 'madness' (1961)

See also: **artificial intelligence; belief; certainty; cognition; deduction; doubt; Foucault; hypothetico-deductive method; induction; inference; justification; justified true belief; scepticism**

Further reading: Foucault (1961); Guttenplan (1997); Lloyd (1984); Scriven (1976); Sosa and Bonjour (2003)

Reductionism

Philosophical reductionism refers to the view that complex phenomena can, or should, be understood at a more basic level. There are ontological, methodological and epistemic (knowledge) implications. Ontologically, for example, a human can be viewed as a conglomeration of molecules and their consciousness consisting of activated neurons. Methodologically, phenomena should be investigated at the simplest level, specifically methods associated with physics that in turn give rise to chemistry and biology. Epistemically, what we know about humans is best understood in terms of their physical components (for example, depression is a result of a neurochemical imbalance). Other forms of reductionism have been identified. For example, behaviourism denies the relevance of mental states in favour of studying stimulus–response associations and, in sociology, Durkheim attempted to reductively explain society in terms of individuals and their relations. Rose's (1997) criticism of philosophical reductionism includes the point that its assumption that the smallest element should be studied is likely to be false because the part gives rise to the whole. Holists would point out that the whole is frequently very different from the parts that make it up.

See also: **behaviourism; dualism; holism; mind, the; naturalism; Ockham's razor; ontology; physicalism; science, philosophy of; semantic holism; structuralism; supervenience**

Further reading: Jones (2000); Sachse (2007)

R

Reference

Theories of reference are primarily concerned with the relationship between names and the things they name, as well as predicates and the properties they convey (such as the predicate 'is green' and a green leaf). When we use the words 'Tony Blair' or 'my bike' we meaningfully refer to specific objects in the world. Philosophers have puzzled over what it is about certain words (definite descriptions, proper names, kinds) that enable them do this. The focus has tended to be on proper names. According to Frege, names have both a sense and a reference. This means that there is a unique definition for each name that allows it to refer to that object in the world. The 'sense' of the name 'Tony Blair' could be something like 'former prime minister, married to Cherie Blair, graduate of Oxford' and so on. Frege's view explains why a statement about a person's identity involving two different proper names can be informative. If I say 'George Orwell is Eric Blair' I convey a new piece of information. However, if proper names only referred, without having a sense attached to them, this sentence would have the same meaning as 'George Orwell is George Orwell'.

Kripke (1980) criticised Frege's view on the basis that people often use proper names without having any uniquely identifying information about that person. For instance, you may assert that Diego Maradona was a famous footballer who scored the 'Hand of God' goal without being able to identify which particular footballer he was from a set of footballers. Furthermore, supposing it turns out that we had been tricked all along and it was actually Pele who scored the goal. Frege's theory implies that the whole time we have been using the name Maradona, we have actually been referring to Pele because we have uniquely identifying information that refers to Pele alone. However, clearly we have not been referring to Pele, we have been referring to Maradona.

Kripke's view is that proper names are purely referential devices, a view also held by Mill. According to Kripke, proper names do not have a unique set of identifying features, they simply form a 'causal chain' from the original naming ('baptism') of the object which is passed on from speaker to speaker. All that is necessary to refer successfully to an object is that we intend to refer to the same object as other people, from whom we learn what is being referred to. Evans and Altham (1973) criticise Kripke's theory because it cannot easily allow for the changing of names over time. Imagine two newly-born identical twins, christened 'Sarah' and 'Jane'. After a week or two they are accidentally swapped in their cots, so that whenever we refer to 'Sarah' we are actually referring to 'Jane'. Kripke's theory implies that all our beliefs about Jane are false, because they are actually about Sarah. The reason for this is that no new naming has occurred and so they must still bear the original names they were given. However, it would seem plausible that at some point they will simply adopt their new names and so switch from Sarah to Jane. If it were later discovered that they had been switched in their cots, perhaps from watching CCTV footage, then they could revert back to their original names.

See also: **being; correspondence theory; definite descriptions; Frege; Kripke; Russell; sign**

Key questions: On what basis does a word successfully refer to an object? How do words successfully refer to non-existent objects?

Further reading: Evans and Altham (1973); Hughes (2004); Kripke (1980); Moore (1993); Russell (1905)

Relativism

The term 'relativism' applies to any theory which argues that certain concepts or judgements are relative to other things, rather than representing an objective or absolute account. Ethical relativism is the idea that moral judgements and beliefs relate to particular cultures, societies, groups or individuals. Moral theories which identify a universal goodness or rightness are actually only expressing a social norm or value. Given that morality is said to be relative to humans, there are no moral facts which exist independently of human thought. Epistemological relativism argues that knowledge about the world, ways of thinking and/or ways of reasoning are relative to different groups. This suggests that there is no ultimate 'fact of the matter' and that to speak of something being right or true is only to speak of 'rightness' or 'trueness' within a body of knowledge. Aesthetic relativism can be summed up by the statement 'beauty is in the eye of the beholder'. Linguistic relativism claims that our ideas of the world are constrained by the language we have to describe and understand the world.

Interestingly, physics has also incorporated the idea of relativity. Einstein's special theory of relativity states that the measurement of time is dependent on (relative to) the frame of reference (such as an observer). Relativism does not imply that there are no such things as truth or facts or beliefs. Instead it claims that we cannot speak of them as absolute, objective, neutral or 'ahistorical'. We cannot move from one particular set of beliefs and truths, such as modern, Western, liberalist, capitalist society, to the conclusion that all societies are and should be like this. The major challenge of relativism is how we are to conduct international legal, moral and metaphysical discussions. If we have no single standard of truth, how are we to judge between competing views and claims? Whilst relativism teaches respect and tolerance of other people's views, it is not clear how it supports the idea of intervention. For instance, should practices such as stoning people to death or female circumcision be challenged by the West?

See also: **anti-realism; constructionism; context; cultural relativism; discourse; experience; Foucault; Gadamer; hermeneutics; historicism; incommensurability; knowledge; Kuhn; language game; linguistic relativism; moral objectivism; perspectivism; postmodernism; post-structuralism; realism; relativity theory; scientific realism; sign; truth**

Further reading: Baghramian (2004); Harman and Thomson (1996); Kirk (1999); Nola (1988)

Relativity theory

Einstein's theory of relativity has had a profound influence on our understanding of the universe. Newton had described time and space as 'absolute'. Time was an independent 'thing', which passed at a constant rate. Even if nothing whatsoever happened in the universe, time would still pass. Similarly, space was an independent substance in which objects existed. If there were no objects in the universe there would still be 'space'. If an object moves a metre, it moves a metre relative to space itself. In contrast, Einstein's work describes space and time as 'relative' or 'relational'. This means that we must specify time, location and motion in relation to something (an object or perspective). To say 'the earth is moving' is like saying the 'earth is bigger'. We need to identify it as moving in relation to something, just as we must say what the earth is bigger than. Furthermore, Einstein conceived of space and time as a single entity, called the space–time continuum. Essentially, space and time are intrinsically linked, meaning that we cannot move through space without also moving through time. One consequence of this idea is that very large objects in the universe (such as stars) can exert an influence on the 'fabric' of space–time, affecting not just physical space but also the passing of time.

R

Einstein's theory of relativity is usually divided into two parts. The special theory of relativity concerns the structure of space–time and claims that the laws of physics are only the same if all observers are in uniform motion relative to one another. For example, the laws of physics will be the same for every observer on the surface of the Earth. However, they will be different for someone travelling at a different speed in relation to the Earth, such as an astronaut heading into deep space. This means, for example, that the measurement of time is relative to the frame of reference. Someone travelling at very high speeds will measure the passing of time differently from someone travelling at a relatively low speed, and the effect increases with the difference in relative speeds. Imagine the occurrence of two solar flares. One person, observing from the Earth, may see the two events ten days apart. The person in the space rocket, moving relative to the first person, will measure a different time interval between the flares. Both are right, relative to their frame of reference. Similarly, the length of an object is also relative to the frame of reference, so two people travelling at different speeds will measure the same object differently. The special theory of relativity holds that the speed of light is absolute, and that nothing can move faster than it. This differs from Newtonian physics, which had viewed the speed of light as relative.

Einstein's general theory of relativity is a theory of gravity, which unifies special relativity with Newton's universal law of gravitation. It deals with the effects of massive bodies in the universe, such as suns and very large planets, which 'bend' space–time. This explains why light bends when it passes close to the sun. Although light is travelling in a straight line, it does so along a curved surface (space–time). Einstein's general theory of relativity successfully predicted such things as the existence of black holes.

The theory of relativity clearly has very important implications for how we understand the nature of time and space. This, in turn, affects such things as the possibility of time travel (see **time**), the experience of time passing and the measurement of objects. It implies that what is 'true' of objects is relative to how they are experienced. Furthermore, it shows how our everyday experiences and commonsense understanding of the world do not always match with the descriptions of the world given by science.

See also: **context; experience; metaphysics; perception; quantum mechanics; reality; science, philosophy of; time**

Further reading: Bohm (1965); Kenyon (1990); Russell (1925)

R

Reliabilism

Reliabilism is a theory of knowledge and justification which says that a belief is justified if it is the result of a reliable psychological process. The term 'reliable' does not mean 'infallible' (never wrong); rather it indicates that most of the beliefs produced by the process are true. Randomly generated truths, such as guessing the colour of the walls in my living room, are not as reliable as the process of directly perceiving the walls under normal light conditions whilst in a conscious and sober state. First suggested in a note written by Ramsey (1931), which was seemingly ignored by philosophers at the time, reliabilism developed during the 1960s,

1970s and 1980s. Dretske, Goldman and Nozick have produced influential forms of reliabilism.

See also: **belief; epistemology; experience; justification; knowledge; Nozick; perception; scepticism; truth**

Further reading: Dretske (1981); Goldman (1986); Nozick (1981); Ramsey (1931)

Religious belief

Religious belief is, broadly speaking, a way of understanding and explaining the world which includes some reference to the supernatural. This can take many forms. Typically it is the belief in a single God (monotheism) or set of gods (polytheism), although spiritual and mystic doctrines may emphasise a general 'life force' or worship nature as divine. One could also classify atheism and agnosticism as religious beliefs, the former being a denial of the existence of any supernatural being(s) and the latter a denial that we can know one way or the other.

A major issue concerning religious belief is the justification for it. Since Aristotle, Western philosophy has produced arguments intended to prove the existence of God. The traditional three proofs are the ontological argument, the cosmological argument and the teleological argument (see **God, arguments for the existence of**). Theologians disagree over whether religious belief is rational, irrational or non-rational. Natural theologians attempt to prove God's existence through reason and argument, and therefore see religious belief as essentially rational. Mystics describe religious belief as non-rational, arguing that it is a form of knowledge gained through revelation, intuition or enlightenment. Atheists often claim religious belief is irrational as there are no good reasons for believing in God(s). Marx famously described religion as the opium of the masses, indicating that religious belief served only to comfort and console people who are suffering. Commonly this is achieved through promising salvation and happiness in the next life (for example, Heaven), providing people accept, rather than try to change, their misfortunes in this life.

See also: **Ayer; belief; creationism; God; God, arguments for the existence of; Hinduism; intuition; justification; logical positivism; Marx; mysticism; reason; Vienna Circle**

Key questions: Is religious belief rational? How we do decide when a religious belief is and is not justified?

Further reading: Harmless (2007); Peterson et al. (2008); Swinburne (1979)

R

Responsibility

If we say someone is responsible for something, we take it to mean that the person was the cause. It was their 'fault'. It is often the case that we will search for a person who can be held accountable for an occurrence. People may be praised for good outcomes and blamed or punished for bad ones. Causal responsibility can be particularly problematic when events are not easily associated with one person, for example economic crises. There are times when people 'take responsibility' for an event, whether they were the cause or not. The implication is that responsibility is a material quality that can be passed between people. It has also been proposed that responsibility can be diluted among several people, known as diffusion of responsibility, sometimes to the extent that no one acts because there is an unspoken understanding that another person could equally take action. Well-known examples include the murder of Kitty Genovese who was repeatedly stabbed outside a block of flats in 1964. Although the attack was prolonged and reportedly observed by more than 30 residents, no one made a serious effort to intervene.

Issues of moral responsibility are a consequence of philosophical debate over the extent to which we are determined to act or have free will. Moral responsibility is associated with free will and therefore agency. If we can choose what we do, then we can be said to be responsible for our actions. Coercion, for example, being told to do something under threat of punishment, might be seen as reducing our responsibility. The suggestion that we are not responsible if carrying out orders is the basis of the Nuremberg Defence, taken from the Nuremberg trials of Nazi war criminals after the Second World War. Legally, responsibility is assumed, although it is possible to claim diminished responsibility. The plea, which reduces murder to manslaughter, became admissible in the UK after the 1957 Homicide Act. It rests on the assumption that not all states of mind are equal. Those with reduced mental functioning as a result of injury, disease, or developmental difficulties are held to be less responsible. However, this approach was criticised by Szasz (1960) for assigning a special non-responsible status to those who are not coping with the pressures of society. A key element of existential philosophy is that one is always entirely responsible for one's life. No one can lighten this 'burden' of responsibility that each of us must bear. We are free to choose to do anything and are wholly responsible for our actions. Any attempt to deny or escape responsibility is an example of inauthenticity and results in a life lived in 'bad faith'.

See also: **agency; authenticity; bioethics; evil; existentialism; freedom; free will; individual, the; justice;** *karma;* **moral agents; moral luck; personal identity; unconscious, the**

Key questions: Must we possess free will in order to be responsible? Are there occasions when we can justifiably deny that we are responsible for our actions?

Further reading: French et al. (2005); Szasz (1960)

Rights

Rights refer to what may or may not be done. They form an important part of many historical and modern political and ethical theories. Legal systems represent systems of rights which describe what an individual is allowed to do and what they are protected from. For instance, in UK law citizens have the right to own property and the right to freedom from racial discrimination. One issue surrounding rights is whether they are universal or relative. Do all humans share the same set of rights and, if so, should these rights be enforced in countries which do not recognise them? Another issue is which beings or things are capable of possessing rights. Animal rights movements claim that animals possess certain rights, such as freedom from suffering, which must be legally and socially acknowledged and enforced. There are similar debates regarding whether foetuses, people in a vegetative state and the environment have rights, and, if so, just what these rights are.

Philosophical concern about rights often focuses on when rights come into conflict. For instance, can we balance the right to freedom of speech and the right to protection from terrorism if individuals use public speeches to promote terrorism?

See also: **animal ethics; bioethics; contractarianism; cultural relativism; democracy; environmental ethics; equality; feminism; freedom; humanism; justice; liberty; life; moral agents; person; race; vegetarianism**

Key questions: Are rights natural and/or universal? What things are capable of possessing rights?

Further reading: Campbell (2006); Ivison (2008); Orend (2002); Paine (1791)

Rorty, Richard (1931–2007)

Rorty was a controversial and influential American postmodern philosopher. He is best-known for defending pragmatism and attacking the idea that truth is objective and that knowledge is an accurate representation of a mind-independent world. Following in the footsteps of Dewey and James, Rorty argued that thought and language are not ways of representing the world; rather, language is a tool which allows us to cope with, not copy, the world. Knowledge is a matter of 'knowing how', not a case of 'knowing that'. Consequently, we cannot speak of anything being more 'in touch' with reality or truth; the very idea of there being a 'true' reality is dissolved. Rorty applied this approach to literary criticism, arguing that there is no 'right' or 'wrong' way of reading a text; different readers in different contexts will generate different meanings. The world and the text both offer multiple – perhaps infinite – ways of reading them, none of which should be considered more accurate than any other. These philosophical ideas are reflected in his political views. Rorty argued that the key feature of politics is freedom, for only within a thoroughly free framework can different viewpoints and beliefs be discussed openly. He was a self-professed liberal whose major desire was the spread of solidarity. Through becoming sensitive to the experiences of others, particularly those who suffer discrimination and injustice, we begin to identify with them and give greater moral and political consideration to their views, experiences and needs.

See also: **context; Dewey; freedom; Habermas; hermeneutics; James; knowledge; liberalism; liberty; pragmatism; postmodernism; post-structuralism; truth**

Further reading: Brandom (2000); Malachowsky (2002); Rorty (1979, 1982, 1989)

R

Rousseau, Jean Jacques (1712–1778)

An important figure of the enlightenment period, Rousseau wrote influential books on education, morality and political philosophy. Rousseau rejected Hobbes' view that humanity was ultimately selfish, arguing instead that humans were essentially good. It is the effects of society and politics which have corrupted people: 'Everything is good as it leaves the Author of things [God]; everything degenerates in the hands of man' (Rousseau, 1762b: 37). Rousseau therefore went against the common enlightenment belief that developments in the arts and the sciences would inevitably improve people's lives. However, Rousseau did follow Hobbes in formulating a social contract theory of society, stating that society is a human construct and the original nature of humans can only be understood by stripping them of all socialisation. Rousseau's educational treatise, *Emile* (1762a), secured his fame but led to his exile from France and Switzerland. He argued that, owing to the corrupt and damaging political environment of his time, the only educational solution was to withdraw the child from society and teach them independently. The key aim in raising children should be to maintain the inherently good and rational nature we are all born with. The criticisms aimed at Rousseau include his alleged utopianism, sexism and elitism.

See also: **contractarianism; enlightenment; Hobbes; state of nature; utopianism**

Further reading: Dent (2005); Riley (2001); Rousseau (1750, 1762a, 1762b)

Russell, Bertrand (1872–1970)

Arguably the leading English philosopher of the 20th century, Russell was one of the founders of analytic philosophy and made important contributions to many areas of philosophy, most notably logic. Throughout his life Russell was driven by one question: can we know anything with certainty? Russell was committed to using a scientific methodology in tackling philosophical problems and, having rejected the idealism he advocated when a student, rigorously defended realism. According to this view, objects in the world (such as tables, teacups and trees) exist independently of being experienced. More specifically, given Russell's emphasis on scientific knowledge, it is the atomic particles (nowadays the sub-atomic particles, such as quarks and quantum particles) which make up these objects that exist outside of human thought.

Russell believed that natural language was a vital means of understanding reality. A proper logical analysis of language, which would reveal its underlying 'logical form', would in turn reveal insights into the structure and content of reality. This approach is best demonstrated in Russell's analysis of definite descriptions, which attempted to resolve problems generated by sentences which refer to non-existent entities (unicorns, flying pigs, three-sided squares). According to Russell, definite descriptions such as 'the present king of France' are not actually referring expressions but rather can be analysed into statements about existence.

Another important idea was Russell's distinction between knowledge by acquaintance and knowledge by description. Knowledge by acquaintance is knowledge gained by immediate perception and is 'intuitively true', meaning we simply cannot doubt the truth of it. Knowledge by description is knowledge built up using information from our immediate perceptions. Russell's analysis of knowledge reveals the assumption, inherited from Descartes, that the proper starting point for investigating knowledge is the individual's experience. There has subsequently been a strong movement against this point of view, with many philosophers arguing that it traps us in a solipsistic and sceptical viewpoint (specifically, that we cannot be said to know anything about another person's mind). The proper starting place for enquiries into knowledge, they argue, should be the public domain and shared language use.

Russell was also a highly controversial political figure. His pacifist beliefs led him to campaign against the First World War (which resulted in a six-month prison

R

sentence) and, later, the Vietnam War. He spoke out against the spread of nuclear weapons (resulting in a second spell in prison) and was founding president of the Campaign for Nuclear Disarmament (CND).

See also: **analytic philosophy; being; certainty; definite descriptions; empiricism; Frege; humanism; idealism; knowledge; logic, philosophical; private language argument; metaphysics; realism; reference; scientific method; scientific realism; Wittgenstein**

Further reading: Grayling (1996); Griffin (2003); Russell (1903, 1905, 1912, 1948); Russell and Whitehead (1910)

R

Sartre, Jean-Paul (1905–1980)

The best-known proponent of existentialism, Sartre has a hugely important place in 20th century philosophy as well as being a celebrated writer and social commentator. Sartre was strongly influenced by Husserl and Heidegger, as demonstrated by his masterpiece *Being and Nothingness* which pays homage to Heidegger's *Being and Time*. Sartre emphasised the radical freedom of each individual, stressing that we must take full responsibility for all our actions. To assume full responsibility for our lives is to live authentically, which is the key existentialist 'virtue' or moral principle. Indeed, living authentically and respecting the authenticity of others is the essence of Sartre's ethics.

Owing to his emphasis on freedom, Sartre was critical of psychological theories, such as Freud's psychoanalysis and behaviourism, which explained humans as a product of instinctive drives and social conditioning, respectively. In Sartre's view, such accounts were merely excuses for people's thoughts and actions which they could hide behind. Each of us is entirely responsible for choosing how we live; we must carry the weight of the world on our shoulders. To say that something I do is not my fault, but rather the result of my upbringing, is to live in 'bad faith'. It is to deny the absolute freedom and responsibility we possess with regards to our lives.

Sartre's emphasis on individual freedom is summed up by his view that, for humans, existence precedes essence. By this Sartre means that humans are not created with any purpose, rather each person first comes into existence and then has a purpose created for them. This is different from man-made objects such as knives, which are first thought of ('I need something to cut up this mammoth with') and then created. The essence or purpose of the knife precedes its coming into existence. Given Sartre's claim that God does not exist, we cannot have been created with any purpose. It is up to each of us to create our own meanings, goals and purpose. We cannot let another person or theory dictate who we are and what we do. Nevertheless, Sartre recognised that freedom is constrained by such circumstances as our age, bodily health and our past actions. Therefore freedom is always within a situation, although Sartre stresses that we must seek to change that situation if we dislike it.

According to Sartre, humans are a combination of two forms or modes of being. The in-itself (*en-soi*) and the for-itself (*pour-soi*). The in-itself state is non-conscious being. It is being which is solid, identical with itself and unified, such as the being of a stone or a chair. For-itself is conscious being, which can reflect upon itself and be aware of itself as something which is existing. Humans are unique in possessing such being, for they can reflect on their own existence and therefore create a distinction between themselves and the world. This separation of ourselves from the world is known as 'negation' or 'nihilation'. Relations between people are characterised by negation. Each of us asserts our own subjectivity by turning others into objects within our consciousness, rather than seeing them as a separate consciousness. In turn, others try to objectify us in order to assert their own subjectivity. Philosophers have argued that Sartre's account of human relations as essentially a battle is too negative. Indeed, the original criticisms came from his wife, Simone de Beauvoir. More generally, some see his philosophy as one of despair and isolation, although Sartre saw it as one of hope and freedom in which we have the chance to make anything of ourselves and the world.

See also: **angst; authenticity; consciousness; continental philosophy; Dasein; de Beauvoir; determinism; existentialism; freedom; Heidegger; Husserl; negation; nihilism; phenomenology; responsibility; subjectivity**

Further reading: Howells (1992); Levy (2002); Sartre (1943, 1944, 1946, 1958)

Scepticism

Broadly stated, scepticism is the view that we are not justified in saying we know something. Strong scepticism, similar to nihilism, is the belief that no knowledge is justified and therefore we cannot say we know anything at all. More commonly, philosophers adopt a sceptical approach to specific areas of philosophy. Most frequent is scepticism regarding the external world. Solipsism is a sceptical position which denies that we can know anything exists outside of our own mind. There is no good reason to assume the external world exists. The brain-in-a-vat theory is the claim that we cannot have knowledge about the external world because we cannot be sure we are not brains sitting in a vat having the entire world generated for us by a computer. Such a possibility has been explored by science fiction, most famously in the *Matrix* films. Religious scepticism is the view that we do not have sufficient justification for believing in a God or Gods. Epistemological scepticism argues that our senses cannot be relied upon to provide an accurate picture of the world. For instance, we are tricked by our senses into believing a stick is bent when it is put into water or that there is an alien in the room when hallucinating.

One response to scepticism is to redefine what we take to be sufficient justification for knowledge. Perhaps sceptics are demanding a level of certainty that is never achievable. If so, then this means that we can still claim to be justified in believing something, even if one can theoretically have doubts about it. Therefore, we do not have to rule out the possibility (no matter how small) that, for example, we are brains-in-a-vat, in order to say we have knowledge about the external world. Alternatively, we might point out that scepticism about such things as the external world appears impossible in our everyday interactions with it. We are compelled to trust our senses and it would not be possible to live if we genuinely doubted the reliability of our perceptions. Finally, even if the sceptic is right and we cannot justifiably know anything at all, or the whole world is just a computer simulation, does this actually change anything? We can seemingly go on living our lives as we always have done, without worrying about such sceptical challenges to our experience.

See also: **anti-realism; belief; brain-in-a-vat; certainty; doubt; epistemology; experience; Hume; justification; knowledge; morality; nihilism; perception; religious belief; scientific realism; solipsism; unexplainable, the**

Further reading: Grayling (2008); Hookway (1990); Williams (1991)

S

Schopenhauer, Arthur (1788–1860)

Schopenhauer was a German philosopher whose central idea was that of the 'will', an instinctive force, energy or drive which is fundamental to all things. Out of this 'world-will' arises the world of appearances or representations, as well as human intellect, reason and understanding. The world of 'reality' is the world of will, whilst the world of appearances is the subjective experience of the world of will. As humans we can understand our bodies as both appearance and will. When you move your arm you experience both the internal, subjective willing of your arm to move and the external, objective movement of the arm. This concept of the 'will' had a strong influence on Nietzsche, who initially accepted much of Schopenhauer's philosophy but later became highly critical of it.

Schopenhauer painted a pessimistic view of humanity, describing how our nature as willing beings leads us into conflict, frustration and violence. Echoing Buddhist philosophy, which he was very attracted to, Schopenhauer declared that daily life is suffering and the ultimate route to salvation is through renouncing our will and consequently the attachments and desires which our will produces in us. Tranquillity and peace is achieved through developing an ascetic mindset (one governed by self-control and abstinence) which has quietened the will and the demands it makes upon us. Schopenhauer emphasised how certain artists, particularly musicians, are able to achieve will-free perceptions and create works which lift one out of individual, will-based experiences into objective, universal experiences of the world. Salvation is consequently an overcoming of human nature through renouncing or giving up our individual will. Schopenhauer's ethics reflect his concept of humans as naturally egoistic for he emphasises the importance of compassion for overcoming the tendency towards selfishness, which generates conflict and sufferings.

See also: **Buddhism; morality; Nietzsche; state of nature; vitalism**

Further reading: Janaway (1999); Magee (2002); Schopenhauer (1813, 1818, 1840)

Science, philosophy of

Historically, science can be seen as developing out of philosophy. The ancient Greek philosophers made no distinction between the two areas. Aristotle wrote works on what we would nowadays call biology and physics as well as more 'philosophical' topics such as ethics, logic and politics. Many of the great modern philosophers, such as Descartes, Locke, Bacon, Hume and Leibniz, were strongly influenced by scientific developments and often contributed to them. The enlightenment period of philosophy was characterised by the belief that scientific methods of investigation would lead to objective and comprehensive knowledge of the universe and humanity. By the early part of the 20th century science had become an independent subject area, and many philosophical movements, such as existentialism and phenomenology, had become concerned with concepts outside of scientific discourse.

The philosophy of science developed as a critical assessment of the sciences. The focus is on analysing the methods of science and the results obtained by these methods. A major debate within the philosophy of science is between scientific realists and anti-realists. Scientific realists argue that science provides an accurate reflection of the world, whilst anti-realists claim that scientific theories in some way construct, rather than mirror, the world. The philosophy of science also examines the nature of experimentation, what counts as evidence, what is proved by such evidence, how to decide between competing theories, the nature of probability and certainty, and the role of induction, deduction and hypotheses.

Recently, feminists have begun to examine the ways in which science has contributed to the oppression of women. They ask, for example, whether science is an essentially male, or masculine, subject and whether the traditional description of women given by science (as essentially child-bearing, weaker, less rational beings) is accurate. A related critique of science comes from postmodernism, which explores how science is used to transmit power and maintain social inequality. Rather than producing objective and universal knowledge, post-structuralists argue that science creates a certain picture of the world which serves the interests of particular social groups and individuals, and thus excludes others. Science claims to produce authoritative and truthful descriptions of the world and humans. Anyone who disagrees with, or deviates from, this picture is dismissed as wrong and potentially punished (such as putting 'mad' people in asylums).

See also: anti-realism; causation; creationism; Darwinism; enlightenment; hypothetico-deductive method; impartiality; incommensurability; induction; inference; instrumentalism; kind, natural; Kuhn; metaphysics; naturalism; objectivism; paradigm; physicalism; Popper; positivism; postmodernism; quantum mechanics; reductionism; relativity theory; scientific method; scientific realism; time

Further reading: Bird (1998); Boyd et al. (1991); Curd and Cover (1998); Kuhn (1962); Newton-Smith (2000)

Scientific method

The scientific method refers to a general approach to finding out about the world. It shares some features with methods we apply every day when trying to explain phenomena. Both involve identifying a problem through observation (such as why objects fall down rather than moving in any other direction) and formulating one or more possible solutions, or hypotheses (for example, objects fall down because they are being pushed or pulled in that direction). Our analysis of the problem will involve inductive and deductive reasoning. Inductive reasoning, which takes an observation and applies it to the general situation, will be used in formulating the hypothesis:

I have seen an object fall down, therefore all objects fall down.

The hypothesis would then be tested by deduction, which involves taking a general principle and applying it to a specific situation (hypothetico-deductive method):

All objects fall down, therefore this object will fall down.

The distinction between scientific methods and our 'non-scientific' attempts to solve problems lies in the techniques used to test the hypothesis or hypotheses. In order to test our everyday theory about falling objects, we might simply drop various items, or make a note every time we see something fall. This can lead to 'confirmatory bias', the subjective tendency to notice only those phenomena which support our theory. The experimental (scientific) method aims to offer an objective way of measuring cause and effect. A range of objects might be dropped under controlled conditions, in a laboratory perhaps, and the results analysed statistically to find out the probability of the hypothesis being true.

The term 'scientific method' implies that there is an agreed way of gaining information. This is not the case in practice and, as Kuhn pointed out, a scientific paradigm can change. For example, introspection was considered scientific in the 19th century whereas later it was rejected as subjective and therefore unscientific. Consequently, some techniques are considered 'more scientific' than others.

See also: **causation; conditionals; deduction; experience; hypothetico-deductive method; impartiality; induction; inference; intuition; introspection; Kuhn; paradigm; Popper; science, philosophy of**

Further reading: Gauch (2003)

Scientific realism

Scientific realism is the belief that science produces an accurate image of the world and that the entities described by scientific theories really do exist. The atoms and molecules of modern scientific theory are real and were discovered, rather than created, by scientific investigation and theory. Scientific realism is often equated with a 'commonsense' view of science, because people typically accept science as stating facts about reality. However, several important challenges are raised against scientific realism. One concerns the problem of unobservable entities (also called theoretical entities). Unobservable entities are posited or put forward by scientific theories to explain certain facts, but they are not directly perceived by the scientists. For instance, scientists may claim to be measuring quantum particles by producing a machine which detects them, but how can they be sure that the machine is detecting quantum particles rather than some other type of particle? Scientists may argue that their machines are carefully designed to detect quantum particles. The problem is that the machine was built to prove the existence of quantum particles by detecting them, so anything it detects will be interpreted as being a quantum particle. Given that quantum particles were first thought up theoretically and then the experiments to prove their existence were designed, there is no independent evidence for assuming the existence of quantum particles. In this view, all science and scientific instruments are theory-dependent; they depend on a theory to make sense but there is no independent means of assessing that theory.

A related challenge is the empiricist claim that we are only justified in believing in those things which can be empirically verified. Given that we can never experience unobservable entities we are not warranted in claiming that unobservable entities exist. Some anti-realists, such as instrumentalists (also called pragmatists), allow science to use unobservable entities if they help us to achieve things (in other words, if they have instrumental value). For instance, if assuming that quantum particles exist allows us to build powerful computers, then we may include quantum particles in scientific theories, but we cannot claim that they actually do exist. Post-structuralism and postmodernism have also challenged scientific realism. According to these theories, notions such as truth, reality and knowledge are social constructions. They are limited to particular social and historical situations, rather than being universal. Science, therefore, does not reflect a single, objective world existing independently of human understanding. Instead it helps to create what we think of as real. As science and culture change, so too does the world we assume to be real.

See also: **anti-realism; causation; constructionism; context; incommensurability; instrumentalism; justification; kind, natural; Kuhn; naturalism; objectivism; paradigm; quantum mechanics; realism; relativity theory; science, philosophy of**

Key questions: Does science present an accurate account of the world? If it currently does not, is it possible that one day it will? How would we know when science has produced an accurate account of the world?

Further reading: Curd and Cover (1998); Kukla (1998); Psillos (1999); van Fraassen (1980)

Self, the

The idea of the self has played a central role throughout philosophy's history. An inscription at the Ancient Greek site of Delphi reads 'know thyself' and in Plato's *Phaedrus* Socrates states that he has no time to consider theology whilst he is yet incapable of knowing himself. This search for self-understanding and self-knowledge was also present in early Indian philosophy, which emphasised the importance of discovering one's *atman* (true self). The rise of Judaeo-Christianity in Western culture generated an idea of the self as an immaterial soul. The idea was particularly useful as it helped to settle the question of life after death, for one's self was able to survive the physical body's demise. Two of the great Christian theologians, St. Augustine and Aquinas, stressed the importance of inner reflection and cultivation of one's soul/self in order to connect with God and earn a place in Heaven.

During the enlightenment period, the self continued to develop into an individual, distinct entity. Descartes famously separated his self from both his body and the world. That he existed as an immaterial, thinking self was the one thing he could not doubt. The self became a 'subject', isolated from the rest of the world, from which the world was understood. A further important development regarding the self was initiated by Freud, who split the self into a conscious, accessible part and an unconscious, hidden part. The concept of the self as a centre of subjectivity, a point from which we experience the world, was developed by existential philosophers such as Sartre.

Recently, however, scepticism has arisen towards the idea of the 'self'. Although many self-help programmes, spiritual organisations and therapists encourage us to 'discover our true self', philosophers are increasingly challenging the idea that the self is a meaningful notion. Where is this 'self' we are meant to be discovering? How can we distinguish between our true self and our false self? One solution is that our self is our genetic code, but many people are unhappy equating themselves with a purely biological description of who they are. The increasingly secular view of the world has also turned against the idea of the self as a soul which inhabits the body. Postmodernists often talk of the self as multiple, fluid and ever-changing. It is a constantly shifting collection of feelings, memories, experiences, beliefs

S

and physical experiences, no one collection of which is more 'true' or more 'real' than another. Interestingly, this picture of the self bears similarities to the Buddhist teaching of *anatman* (not-self). According to this view, there is no real, unchanging self which each of us possesses. The self is simply a label given to all the physical and mental processes which make up a person. The analogy of a chariot is used to make this point. If we broke a chariot up into its individual pieces, we would never find 'the chariot'. We would have some wheels and spokes and some reins, but we would never have some 'thing' which is the chariot. Rather the chariot is a name given to a collection of individual things, just as the self refers to the individual parts of a persona and not some special thing residing in that person.

See also: **Aquinas; Augustine; Buddhism; consciousness; Dasein; death; Descartes; dualism; essentialism; Freud; holism; 'I'; individual, the; personal identity; postmodernism; Sartre; subjectivity; unconscious, the;**

Key questions: What is the self? If we possess a self, how do we understand what and where it is? If you can know what your self is, does this mean that it is in some way separate from 'you'?

Further reading: Gallagher and Shear (1999); Guignon (2004); Harvey (1990); Taylor (1989)

Semantic holism

Semantics is the study of meanings, and semantic holism argues that the meaning of a symbol only makes sense in relation to the entire system of which it is a part. In order to understand a word we cannot study it in isolation, for it has meaning only in the context of a whole language. Similarly, a paint mark on a canvas has meaning in relation to the whole picture and a particular desire can only be understood within a whole system of beliefs. Modern advocates of semantic holism include Davidson, Quine and Searle. Semantic holism stands in opposition to resemblance theories of meaning, which argue that a symbol's meaning is secured by its resembling that thing in the world. For instance, the idea of a tree is derived from, and made meaningful by, it successfully resembling a tree (we have the mental image of 'a tree'). This theory is called semantic atomism, and is generally rejected by modern philosophers.

Many philosophers have criticised semantic holism. One implication is that when two people with different systems of knowledge use the same word, they mean different things by it. Given that each of us will know and believe slightly different things, is it ever possible for two people to mean the same thing? Poststructuralists have adapted this idea to claim that there is no single fact about the meaning of a text. Semantic holism must also explain what is meant by an 'entire system'. It may not be possible for someone to master the entire system of English language, but they can still converse in English with relative ease. Furthermore, if any one word is meaningful only in relation to a whole system of words, then how can we begin to learn a language in the first place?

See also: **context; Davidson; language game; post-structuralism; Quine**

Further reading: Davidson (1984); Fodor and LePore (1992); Quine (1953)

Sense

See **reference**

Sex

See **feminism**

Ship of Theseus, the

The Ship of Theseus is a puzzle about identity, which can be traced back to the Ancient Greeks. A basic version of the puzzle runs as follows. Imagine a famous ship, let us call it S, which is kept in a harbour. Over time parts of the ship start to rot and so they are replaced. Eventually we reach a point where every part of the ship has been replaced. Let us call this ship R. The question is whether S is the same ship as R (is S identical to R?). If it is, then we need to explain how some thing (R) can be composed of entirely different matter to another thing (S) and yet be considered the same thing. If we say that R and S are different ships, then we need to specify when S stopped existing and R came into existence. The Ship of Theseus was elaborated by Hobbes (1655). In this complex version of the puzzle we are asked to imagine that each of the original parts of the ship is kept in a storeroom after being removed. Once every original part of the ship has been replaced, all the original parts are taken from the storeroom and used to build another ship, let us call it N. In this example, is N or R the same ship as S? Perhaps neither is, or perhaps they both are. If we say only one of them is, then we must have good reason to justify which one it is. The Ship of Theseus clearly raises interesting issues regarding the persistence of an object over time, and the change that an object can and cannot undergo whilst remaining the same thing. In everyday practical terms, this is particularly relevant to such problems as legal claims over the ownership of objects.

See also: **change; difference; identity; metaphysics; ontology; thought experiments**

Further reading: Brown (2005); Garrett (1998); Lowe (2002)

Sign

The 'sign' is a key term within structuralist analyses of language. Linguistic signs are essentially the words of a language, such as 'tree' or 'cat', which convey meanings. According to structuralism, the meaning of a sign is a combination of two things: a signifier and a signified. The signifier is the 'sound image' of the word; it is the impression the word makes upon us. The signifier is both the sound of speaking a word and the effect of thinking about a word. Both produce in us an understanding of what that word is. The signified is the object in the world to which the sign refers. For the sign 'cat', the signifier is the meaning of the word and the signified is the physical object called a 'cat'.

There are many different signifiers for each signified. For example, each language has a different word for 'cat' (*chat* in French, *katze* in German and so on). According to structuralists such as Saussure, the connection between the signifier and the signified is arbitrary. This means there is no necessary connection, natural law or logical relation which states that the sound 'cat' must refer to the physical objects we know as cats. The importance of this idea is that it rejected the previously accepted view that language is directly mapped onto the world, and thus the key to understanding reality is to analyse language. Structuralism's analysis of the sign was used to argue that the relationship between words (signifiers) and the world (signified) was ambiguous and ever-changing because the connection between the two is arbitrary and therefore it can always be altered. It also generates the idea that our understanding of reality is socially constructed and will differ depending upon which system of signs we are using.

See also: **correspondence theory; deconstruction; Derrida; language game; post-structuralism; Russell; structuralism**

Further reading: Chandler (2002); Holdcroft (1991); Saussure (1916)

Singer, Peter (1946–)

Peter Singer, perhaps the best-known modern moral philosopher, is a strong defender of utilitarianism and has been particularly influential in the area of applied ethics. His first major work, Animal Liberation (1975), has played a central role in the development of the modern animal welfare movement. According to Singer, any sentient being (a being capable of experiencing pleasure or pain) must be given equal moral consideration. To ignore the interests of a sentient being simply because it is not human is dismissed as 'speciesism', which is akin to forms of discrimination such as racism and sexism. Speciesism expresses the belief that there is no morally relevant or significant difference between humans and non-human animals. Traditional criteria, such as intelligence, rationality or self-awareness, are not necessarily appropriate measures of the superiority of humans. It can be argued that some animals (such as chimpanzees) possess higher levels than very young babies and some mentally-handicapped adults.

In his controversial work, Practical Ethics (1979), Singer developed his utilitarianism by considering how the interests of different beings should be weighed up. He applied a utilitarian analysis to practical ethical issues, arguing in favour of abortion, euthanasia and vegetarianism (although there are careful qualifications regarding each one). Singer is also highly critical of the economic gap between the rich and poor. He argues that if we can do something to help alleviate poverty and starvation, without sacrificing something of comparable significance, then we are morally bound to do so. For example, if we have two wardrobes full of clothes, then we should donate a bag of clothes to a charity appeal. The sacrifice of one bag of clothing will not leave us without any clothes and will greatly help someone in desperate need of clothing. True to his principles, Singer reportedly donates 25 per cent of his salary to charity.

See also: **animal ethics; bioethics; consequentialism; environmental ethics; morality; utilitarianism**

Further reading: Jamieson (1999); Singer (1973, 1975, 1979, 1995, 1997)

Slippery slope argument

The slippery slope fallacy is a criticism against an apparently acceptable action or principle because of an unacceptable consequence that would follow. As the name suggests, it is like sliding inevitably towards an undesirable outcome. For instance, it may be argued that we must not allow people to abort severely handicapped foetuses because it will lead to people having abortions for any reason they like. Similarly, a deeply religious country may object to evolution being taught in schools because this will lead to the abandonment of religion, which in turn will produce an immoral society. Although one may not object to the action itself, one thinks it will necessarily lead to an unwanted state of affairs and therefore the action cannot be justified. The slippery slope argument is also used to justify intervention with regard to a certain chain of events. Suppressing a riot may be justified on the basis that it stops other riots beginning in nearby cities, which could lead to the whole of society descending into anarchy. These slippery slope arguments rely on consequentialist ethics, which analyse moral rightness in terms of the consequences of an act. Often these arguments use very questionable causal claims by saying that there is a necessary connection between two vaguely related events. As a result, the slippery slope argument is classified as a fallacy. Nonetheless it is an argument which is very frequently used in ethical and political debates.

*See also: **ad hominem**; **begging the question**; **fallacy**; **straw man**; **vicious circle***

Further reading: Engel (1994); Hansen and Pinto (1995); Walton (1992)

Social constructionism

See **constructionism** and **social constructivism**

Social constructivism

The terms 'social constructionism' and 'social constructivism' are frequently used interchangeably. Social constructionism emphasises the creation of cultural norms of understanding that are often assumed to relate to essential properties. Gender is one example because there are widespread beliefs about the differences between males and females that go beyond physical characteristics. Social constructivism refers to the process by which people come to understand the world, specifically through social interaction with others. Therefore, truth and knowledge are what is produced and agreed upon by the social context and, as a consequence, one's knowledge is relative to the culture that one is raised in. As Vygotsky wrote, 'Every function in the child's cultural development appears twice: first, between people (interpsychological) and then inside the child (intrapsychological) ... All the higher functions originate as actual relationships between individuals' (Vygotsky, 1978: 57).

*See also: **context**; **cultural relativism**; **constructionism**; **gender**; **knowledge**; **linguistic relativism**; **truth***

Further reading: Burr (1995); Herskovits (1972); Kukla (2000); Vygotsky (1978)

Social contract
See **contractarianism**

Socialism

Socialism is an economic theory advocating the creation of societies in which the government controls all means of production. Socialism developed in response to perceived injustices arising from private ownership of the means of production, which was characteristic of early industrialism. Within such societies wealth was unevenly distributed and the majority of workers were poorly rewarded for their labour. Socialists stress the need for radical, often revolutionary, action in which the state assumes full control of property and wealth is distributed equally amongst citizens. Socialists wish to replace individual self-interest with collective goals which benefit all members of society rather than the few with power and wealth. A socialist society would eradicate class as all people would stand in equal relation to the collective economic resources. The most famous socialists are Marx, Engels and Lenin, and the most famous attempt to construct a socialist state was the former USSR, which collapsed into a totalitarian regime. A major problem for contemporary socialists is how to prevent such a failure and also how to overcome, and subsequently resist, the continued dominance of global capitalism

See also: **communism; conservatism; dialectical materialism; equality; liberalism; libertarianism; Marx; Marxism; political philosophy; utopianism**

Further reading: Hann (1993); Jennings (2003); Newman (2005); Stiglitz (1994)

Socrates (469–399 BCE)

Socrates occupies a hugely important and revered position in the history of Western philosophy, despite the fact that nothing he may have written has been preserved. Our knowledge of Socrates and his philosophy comes from three main sources: Plato, whose dialogues feature Socrates as the main character, the historian Xenophon and the playwright Aristophanes. Traditionally, Plato is treated as the authoritative source for our knowledge of Socrates, though the extent to which Plato's Socrates represents the philosophy of the man himself is far from clear. It is generally agreed that Socrates was something of a social non-conformist, who walked around the city barefoot, somewhat dishevelled in appearance, engaging anyone he met in philosophical debate. He was sentenced to death by an Athenian court, having been found guilty of corrupting the youth of Athens and denying the existence of Athenian Gods. Despite being offered the chance to escape, he chose instead to poison himself with hemlock.

The image of Socrates conjured by Plato is of a man fascinated with the idea of virtue (*aretê*). Many of Plato's dialogues focus on Socrates' attempt to understand what virtue is and how it can be achieved. One view often associated with Socrates is that if someone knows the nature of virtue, then they will always do virtuous things. The way to leading a moral life is to understand precisely what the 'good' (virtue) is. This means we must always interrogate someone about their conception of virtue, because if it is deficient then it will lead to them doing bad things.

S

His acceptance of death, rather than life as a fugitive, could be seen as the ultimate example of his dedication to what he felt was the virtuous life.

Rather than bestowing a particular set of philosophical beliefs, Socrates' legacy was the Socratic Method. This method, which forms the basis of what we commonly take to be the essence of philosophical investigation, can be described as a systematic enquiry into knowledge, a search for self-understanding, a willingness to engage and challenge our current beliefs, a refusal to simply accept what we are told, and an attempt to ascertain the consequences of our ideas. This was achieved through a dialectic process in which two opposing views were debated, with either one being accepted and the other rejected, or a new view arising as a result (a synthesis of the two original views). Socrates, then, is associated with the fundamental desire to search for the truth for truth's sake, as well as the conviction that we must stick to our principles if they are right. Socrates' commitment to this philosophy may have caused him an early death, but it has also cemented his place in history.

See also: **dialectic; Greek philosophy, ancient; morality; Plato; virtue**

Further reading: Brickhouse and Smith (1994); Cooper (1997); Taylor (2000)

Solipsism

The term 'solipsism' is derived from the Latin *solus ipse*, which means 'oneself alone'. Solipsism is the radical claim that 'I am the only thing which exists'. It is based on the idea that all existence is experienced by me. All I know, and can know, is the contents of my own mind. Therefore I have no reason to suppose that anything exists, other than my own mind. I cannot know whether you are simply a figment of my imagination. Solipsism is often discussed in relation to the problem of other minds. Specifically, what reason do we have to believe that other minds exist? Given that all we see is a physical brain, rather than a 'mind' or 'consciousness', why should we assume that other people have minds? Many philosophers have celebrated Wittgenstein's private language argument as a conclusive refutation of solipsism. According to Wittgenstein, it is impossible to have a purely private experience of one's mind. In order to experience pain, one must have learnt what it is to be in pain and when to use the word 'pain' to express this experience. We can only successfully learn how and when we are in pain through social interaction with other people; therefore it does not make sense to think that only I exist. The argument rests upon Wittgenstein's claim that it is logically impossible to construct a private language for describing the contents of one's mind.

Another line of argument against solipsism might be to point out that there was clearly a time before I existed. Therefore the world cannot simply be the contents of my mind because otherwise I could not have come into existence. In response the solipsist might say that I still have not experienced a time before I existed and thus have no justification for believing it. I only experience my own mind, regardless of its contents.

See also: **consciousness; doubt; experience; intersubjectivity; introspection; justification; mind, the; other minds; private language argument; scepticism; Wittgenstein**

Further reading: Descartes (1641); Johnstone (1991); Malcolm (1971); Wittgenstein (1953)

Sophism

Based on the Greek word for 'wisdom', the sophists were teachers in the 5th century BCE who were paid by Greeks who wished to gain knowledge but more particularly hoped for political success. Their teaching included a variety of subjects according to what their customers wanted, for example history, physics and rhetoric (persuasive use of language). They were not philosophers as such and indeed were viewed sceptically by thinkers such as Plato and Aristophanes who disapproved of the practical nature of sophists' teachings, considering it to be lacking in virtue. In particular, the use of rhetoric to persuade people to think in a particular way, not unlike today's spin-doctors, was frowned upon. The negative view of sophism is demonstrated by the later use of the word to describe an invalid, although apparently valid, argument. In the 13th century, a philosopher by the name of Richard the Sophister wrote a list of sophisms under the title *Abstractiones*. Examples include: nothing is true about nothing; if you know that you are a stone you do not know that you are a stone.

See also: **Greek philosophy, ancient; Plato; Socrates; validity**

Further reading: Guthrie (1971); Waterfield (2000)

Soundness

See **logic**

Speech-acts

The concept of speech-acts arose from the realisation that language does many more things than simply describe reality. Asking questions, making promises, or demanding actions are all examples of speech-acts. Speech-acts are not limited to speaking; holding up one's hand to make someone stop or smiling encouragement are non-verbal examples of speech-acts. The best-known theory of speech-acts was developed by Austin, which influenced philosophers such as Derrida and Butler. A key feature of speech-acts is that they must be understood within the context they were uttered. The words 'I do' could be a response to someone asking if you enjoy playing football or they could be uttered as part of a marriage ceremony. The way we use and understand language depends upon a background of social conventions and expectations, none of which are fixed, and therefore the meaning of a word can change depending on where, how and for what purpose it is used.

See also: **Austin; Butler; context; Derrida; language game; performativity; sign**

Further reading: Austin (1962a); Grewendorf and Meggle (2002); Holdcroft (1978); Searle (1969); Tsohatzidis (1994)

Spinoza, Baruch (1632–1677)

Baruch Spinoza, also known as Benedictus de Spinoza, was a radical political and religious thinker, as well as a highly celebrated philosopher. His major work is the *Ethics*, which is as much an exploration of metaphysical issues as it is a moral treatise. Spinoza argued that there is only one infinite substance and that all the things in the world, including minds and bodies, are attributes of this one substance. No person and object in the world is a separate 'thing' existing independently and in its own right, but rather they are all part of the one universal substance. According to Spinoza, God is also part of the universe. Indeed, he says they are one and the same thing. Consequently, God did not create the universe because He *is* the universe, and the universe/God has existed forever. Spinoza therefore breaks with the traditional belief, traceable to the ancient Greeks, that there must have been a beginning to the Universe (a first cause) and that that first cause was God. Equally radically, Spinoza denied that the universe has any purpose and that God plays any active role in the world. He also defends a strong form of determinism, which leads him to dismiss the idea of free will. The universe must be the way it is, and there is no other way it could be. One consequence of this idea is that our world is the best of all possible worlds. Owing to the extremely controversial nature of his views, Spinoza was considered to be a dangerous person to associate with and so he could not easily discuss his ideas with his fellow philosophers of the time, such as Locke, Newton and Leibniz.

See also: **determinism; enlightenment; free will; God; modality; monism; teleology**

Further reading: Allison (1987); Della Rocca (2008); Garrett (1996); Morgan (2002); Spinoza (1677)

State of nature

The concept of the state of nature is commonly used in political philosophy, particularly social contract theories. A state of nature describes the state humans would be in if there were no society. It is a hypothetical reflection on what humans would be like if they were devoid of the socialising effects of society and government. Typically, the state of nature is used to (a) understand what the basic nature of humans is, and (b) to justify the existence of government and civil society as the means of escaping this state of nature.

According to Hobbes, who produced the term, the state of nature would be a terrible place. Humans, he argued, are essentially self-interested, weak, nasty and solitary. The creation of a government is necessary to drag people into a co-operative, productive and peaceful existence. Rousseau criticised Hobbes, arguing that humans are timid and peaceful. According to Rousseau the effects of society can often be damaging, producing morally corrupt individuals. Contemporary interest in social contract theory and the state of nature was ignited by John Rawls' work. He uses the term 'the original position' to refer to the state of nature, arguing that principles of justice can be worked out and justified by imagining what principles of social justice and law we would agree to if we were placed in a state of nature and had to construct a society. The idea of the state of nature has been criticised for being a purely hypothetical conjecture that is too abstract to be of any relevance or value. Some philosophers go further and argue that it is impossible to imagine ourselves genuinely being in a state of nature.

See also: **contractarianism; Hobbes; Rawls; Rousseau; thought experiments**

Further reading: Chriss (2007); Hobbes (1651); Rawls (1971); Rousseau (1762b)

Stoicism

The word derives from the Greek for a porch, *stoa*, because Zeno of Citium (c.300 BCE) (not to be confused with the 5th century BCE Zeno of Elea who constructed many famous paradoxes) taught from a particular porch. Although none of Zeno's writings survive, the principles of stoicism have been pieced together to reveal three interrelated aspects: physics, ethics and logic. Diogenes used similes to demonstrate this connection: for example, 'like an egg' in which physics forms the yolk, ethics is the white and logic is the shell. In logical terms, Stoics distinguished between what we know through our senses (empirically) and what we know to be true of those sensations by rationalising our impressions. Stoics' logic is not reducible to the modern sense of logic because it refers to both rhetoric (persuasive use of language) and dialectic (reasoning or argument to reach a conclusion). They used propositions (*axiomata*) to test the validity of knowledge using five forms of syllogism (for example, 'If A then B' and 'If not A and B but A, then not B'). They also used puzzles to test logic, such as 'I am a liar, true or false'.

With regard to physics, the stoics viewed the world as a whole, living system, surrounded by a void (empty space) but without any void within it. The majority of the system consists of bodies (and that includes non-physical aspects like justice as part of a corporeal soul). The four non-bodily components of the world are *lekta* (roughly equating to statements about the world), place, time and void. The elements of fire and air are seen as active in comparison with the passive ones of water and earth. The combination of the active elements creates *pneuma* (breath) that forms the basis of life and development.

Given the stoics' view that human purpose is directed towards living in harmony with the nature of the world/cosmos (as opposed to a more restricted view of nature as plants and animals) there is an ethical element to their version of physics. Ethically, stoics are virtue ethicists and subscribe to Aristotle's teleological idea that the end-point of life is *eudaimonia* ('flourishing' or 'living well'). However, in order to reach that state, it is only necessary to have tried to live healthily or virtuously because our destiny is god-given. The acceptance of one's state has become associated with people who 'put up with things', although the intended meaning is more positive than that, being similar to the Taoist belief that the 'best life' is achieved through living in accordance with *tao*.

See also: **Aristotle; dialectic; empiricism; epistemology; Greek philosophy, ancient; logic; paradox; rationalism; Taoism; validity; virtue ethics**

Further reading: Inwood (2003); Long (1986)

Straw man

The straw man fallacy refers to the criticism of an imaginary argument (a 'straw man'), rather than an opponent's real argument. Philosophers often misrepresent a view they disagree with in order to make it easier to refute. For example, if we criticise agnostics for denying the existence of God, then we are committing the straw man fallacy. This is because agnostics are actually saying we can neither prove nor disprove the existence of God, which is arguably a more difficult position to refute.

*See also: **ad hominem; begging the question; fallacy; logic; slippery slope argument; vicious circle***

Further reading: Cedarblom and Paulsen (2006); Engel (1994); Walton (1989)

Structuralism

Structuralism developed during the second half of the 20th century and was particularly popular in France. Structuralists are interested in the underlying structure of such things as languages, societies, religions, the sciences and stories/myths. They conceived of such phenomena as systems which could be analysed in terms of 'units' and 'rules'. For instance, the units of the English language are the words (or, strictly speaking, the 31 phonemes from which all words are formed) and the rules are the grammatical system which determines how words are put together. The actual meaning of specific words does not matter; what is important is identifying the underlying structure of a language. For instance, we can identify 'The bed kicked a story into the goal' as a sentence, although nonsensical, because it conforms to the rules of our linguistic system.

A structuralist analysis of literature examines the units and rules which govern a text. The reason that we can easily read lots of different books is because they conform to the same structural system. There are usually 'units' such as a hero or heroine, an evil character, a friend of the hero/heroine, whilst the rules include 'the main character falls in love', 'the hero/heroine learns an important lesson', 'bad people do not succeed'. From a structuralist perspective many fairy tales are the same because they have the same underlying structure. According to structuralism, the underlying structure of all these systems is not inherent in the world but is imposed by the human mind. This means that the orderly nature of the world is a product of the mind's ability to organise systems, rather than a reflection of the world itself.

See also: **idealism; language game; post-structuralism; sign**

Further reading: Hawkes (2003); Lane (1970); Robey (1973); Sturrock (2003)

Subject, the
See **subjectivity**

Subjectivity

The idea of subjectivity, a person's experience and understanding of the world, is important in several areas of philosophy. Within the philosophy of mind, the idea of subjectivity is used to challenge reductionist models of consciousness which try to characterise the mind in purely cognitive, physical terms. According to theorists such as Nagel and Searle, there is an irreducible subjective element to consciousness. This is the 'what it is like to be me' aspect of experience: the way we experience the world from our individual perspective and how the world appears to us. Such experiences include the tasting of an apple or the splendour of a sunset. It also refers to the fact that our attempts to understand the world are always rooted in our own experiences. In Nagel's example, if I consider what it is like to be a bat,

I can only ever consider what it would be like *for me* to be a bat. Descriptions of the mind must account for both objective facts about conscious states (I am in a state of pain) and the subjective experience of that pain (what it is like to be in pain).

The term 'subjectivity' is also used to refer to theories of the subject/self and how they are formed. Whereas the thinkers of the enlightenment described people as free, autonomous individuals, more recent theorists have explored the ways in which subjects are continuously created. Marxist theory described the way in which ideology formed one's idea of self and identity. Feminists have explored the ways in which subjectivities can be gendered, whilst theorists such as Lacan argue that the subject is essentially produced by language. Foucault's influential works have investigated how the subject is formed by power relations in society. Our understanding of who we are and how we experience the world is produced by historically contingent discourses which claim to represent the 'truth' about us. Such discourses, which include biological and psychological theories of the individual, serve to construct, rather than reflect, reality. Recently, theorists such as Haraway have explored the impact of technology on subjectivity. The idea is that humans are becoming increasingly merged with machines, producing post-human (cyborg) subjects. This offers a radical rethinking of subjectivity, from greatly enhanced vision and hearing to robotic limbs and computer chips in a person's brain which could hugely increase cognitive abilities.

See also: **Butler; consciousness; discourse; dualism; embodiment; experience; feminism; Foucault; gender; 'I'; ideology; intersubjectivity; Marx; Marxism; mind, the; other minds; physicalism; post-humanism; postmodernism; qualia; reductionism; solipsism**

Further reading: Butler (1990); Cascardi (1992); Hall (2004); Mansfield (2000); Nagel (1979); Zahavi (2006)

Substance

The concept of 'substance' derives from Aristotle's works on metaphysics. In his *Categories*, Aristotle used the word substance to refer to the basic 'stuff' out of which the world is composed. What is unique about substances is that they are independent, meaning they do not depend on anything else. All other 'things' in the world, such as qualities (colour, heat, taste, and so on) and quantities (size, number), depend upon substance. Colour, for example, is always the colour of a substance. In Aristotle's view, then, primary substances are real individual things such as a tree or a rabbit. Secondary substances, which are 'less real', are the groupings of these primary substances such as the species 'rabbit' or the group of things referred to as 'trees'.

Aristotle discussed how to characterise substance at great length. One definition of a substance is something which is the subject of a sentence (basically, this means nouns are substances). Another definition is to say that substances are things that possess properties. A substance can be hot or cold, blue or black, heavy or light. These properties can change but the substance remains the same; my house is still the same house even if I paint it a different colour. Confusingly, Aristotle presents another analysis of substance in his *Metaphysics*, arguing that substance is best equated with 'form', by which he means the type of thing an object is. Many philosophers have been puzzled by this shift in Aristotle's thought because the form of a thing appears to be a universal property, such as the form 'horseness', of which each individual horse is an instance. Consequently Aristotle has been accused of presenting two radically different definitions of substance.

Locke's view of substance has similarities to Aristotle's original ideas, for he defined a substance as the part of a thing which possesses properties. Interestingly, this suggests that we can never know substance, because all we ever experience are a thing's properties, not the substance itself. Descartes claimed there are two kinds of substance: material bodies, which are physical, and immaterial minds, which are non-physical. Spinoza's radical view was that there is only one single substance, and the entire universe, including God, is an expression of this single substance. Spinoza's theory implies that there are no such things as 'individuals', because everything is part of the single substance. Hume's sceptical analysis of substance denied that there is any such thing as substance, describing the belief that there is an underlying substance which exists through change as illusion. We are mistaken when we think that a table or a tree has a substance which continues through the many changes the objects undergo. Within Hume's analysis, the term substance refers to a series of momentary bundles of properties, which we combine in our mind into the concept of a single, persisting thing. The term 'substance' is rarely used nowadays and recent developments in physics, such as quantum theory and string theory, have radically reshaped the understanding of the basic 'stuff' of the universe.

See also: **Aristotle; Descartes; dualism; Greek philosophy, ancient; Hume; Leibniz; Locke; metaphysics; monism; ontology; physicalism; properties; qualities; quantum mechanics**

Key questions: What, if anything, is 'substance'? What kinds of substance exist? If a substance is that which has properties, can we ever experience it (rather than experience its properties)?

Further reading: Aristotle (350 BCEa); Hoffman and Rosenkratz (1994, 1997); Wiggins (2001)

Summum bonum

A Latin term meaning 'the greatest good', the concept of *summum bonum* is used to describe that which is of ultimate importance. Within ethics, it is that thing which determines all moral considerations. *Summum bonum* is that which all actions are ultimately directed towards, meaning it is an end in itself rather than a means to an end. If we think that having lots of money is the greatest good then all our actions are performed in order to get more money. Religious thinkers often speak of leading a pious life, obeying the laws and serving the glory of God, as the greatest good. In Buddhism and Hinduism the *summum bonum* is achieving enlightenment. In many Chinese philosophies, particularly Taoism, it is learning to live in accord with *tao*. Many philosophers are sceptical about being able to identify a single good which all humans should strive towards. A major reason for this is that what is considered 'good' differs greatly between cultures.

S

See also: **Aristotle; Augustine; Buddhism; Chinese philosophy; Confucianism; cultural relativism; enlightenment; good, the; happiness; Hinduism; moral objectivism; Plato; Taoism; teleology; utopianism; virtue ethics**

Further reading: Harvey (1990); LaFollette (2002); Singer (1991); Smith (1991)

Supererogation

Supererogation refers to those actions which are seen as morally good but not morally necessary. It is a recent topic of ethical debate, tracing back to Urmson's article 'Saints and Heroes' (1958) in which he argues that the traditional classification of moral actions excluded the action that is good to do and not bad not to do. The idea of supererogatory acts is captured by the phrase 'above and beyond the call of duty'. Just what acts may be considered beyond our moral duty depends greatly on what we consider our moral duty to be (assuming there is such a thing at all). For example, one might see charity as a supererogatory act. We may not be morally required to donate money to charity, but to do so is certainly a morally praiseworthy action. Others might disagree and state that we are morally obliged to give some proportion of our income to charity, in which case giving above that limit would then be supererogatory.

Often heroes and saints are seen as demonstrating supererogatory deeds. However, a sceptic may point out that modern-day heroes, such as the brave fire-fighter or soldier, are merely doing their job. Indeed, whilst we may heap praise on such figures, it is not uncommon to hear their response that they were simply doing what they had been trained to do. Some would argue that there can be no such thing as a supererogatory act on the grounds that if an act is morally good then it must be performed. Utilitarianism, according to which the right action is the one with the overall greatest positive outcome, does not seem to leave much room for supererogatory acts. If we are able to perform an action which has greater overall consequences than the one we were intending to perform, then we must change our course of action. The logical end-point of such a stance could be donating all our money, food, clothing and so on, except that which is needed for our own survival (assuming that there is at least one person in the world with less than us). One interesting aspect of supererogation is whether it could have an inverse, namely acts which are bad to do but not good not to do (so, allowable wrong-doings).

See also: **duty; egoism; morality; utilitarianism; Singer**

Further reading: Heyd (1982); Urmson (1958)

Supervenience

The concept of supervenience can be summed up as 'no A-difference without a B-difference'. What this means is that if a set of properties, A, supervenes on another set of properties, B, then two objects with the same A properties cannot have different B properties. The A properties are dependent upon the B properties and so a change in the A properties can only happen if there is a change in the B properties. For example, it is common to think that the colour, weight, shape and texture of an object depend upon the microphysical properties of the object (such as the arrangement of atoms). Assuming that the physical properties of an object depend upon its microphysical properties, then two objects with exactly the same microphysical properties cannot have different physical properties. The idea of supervenience is common to many areas of philosophy. Generally speaking, any form of reductionism seems to require the concept of supervenience. This is because reductionists argue that one set of properties can be reduced down to (supervenes onto) another set of properties. For instance, within the philosophy of mind it has been argued that mental properties supervene on physical properties (often, more specifically, neurophysiological properties). This suggests that two people with the same brain activation should have the same mental experience.

See also: **materialism; metaphysics; mind, the; naturalism; physicalism; reductionism**

Further reading: Kim (1993); Preyer and Siebelt (2001); Savellos and Yalçin (1995)

S

Tabula rasa

The term *tabula rasa* (literally meaning 'blank slate') is a central concept in Locke's epistemology (theory of knowledge). He claimed that all humans are born with minds like a blank slate and that all knowledge is gained through experience. Locke attacked the rationalist theories of Plato, Descartes, Spinoza and Leibniz, which claimed that certain ideas could be gained without appeal to experience. Locke's main argument against innate ideas is that if there were such ideas, then they would be universally known by all humans. However, Locke claims that there are no principles which are universally agreed upon and, even if there were such principles, it does not prove that these ideas are innate rather than gained by experience. It is much debated whether anthropological study of various cultures supports Locke's view or provides evidence for universal principles. For instance, the French structuralist Claude Levi-Strauss argued that underlying all societies was a basic set of structures. In the field of linguistics, Noam Chomsky has famously suggested that humans possess an innate capacity for grammar, which can explain the speed and ease with which a young child learns a language. Chomsky also argues that this linguistic structure shapes the way we think and explains the similarity of human thinking across all cultures. The idea of *tabula rasa* is central to the behaviourists' theory of learning in which the environment is entirely responsible for shaping a person's psychological development.

See also: **behaviourism; Descartes; empiricism; epistemology; experience; introspection; intuition; Leibniz; Plato; rationalism; Spinoza; structuralism**

Further reading: Gupta (2006); Leibniz (1704; Locke (1690); Stich (1975)

Tao (dao)

Tao, generally translated as 'the way', is a very important concept in Chinese philosophy. It is the central feature of Taoism, in which it refers both to a path to be walked, or way of living one's life, and the guiding force behind the development and change of all things. The *tao* of Taoism is the nature of all things, the way the world works, and also the way we should act in the world. The Taoist sage is one who acts in accord with *tao*, letting it guide his actions, and who sees *tao* in all things. According to Taoism, *tao* is ineffable and therefore unable to be captured in words; the only way to understand it is by directly experiencing it. For Taoists, the route to *tao* involves throwing off the shackles of socialisation and enacting one's natural spontaneity. Confucianism also stressed the importance of acting in accord with *tao*. However, Confucius argued that the means to achieve this was by living a virtuous life, which he defined as correctly observing the traditional rites and rituals of society. For Confucius, the route to *tao* was scholarly development and self-cultivation.

See also: **Chinese philosophy; Confucianism; summum bonum; Taoism**

Further reading: Chan (1973); Kupperman (2001); Waley (1987)

Taoism (Daoism)

A Chinese philosophical and religious tradition founded around the 5th century BCE, Taoism is typically associated with the writings of Lao Tzu (Old Master) and Chuang Tzu (Master Chuang). The best known Taoist text is the *Tao Te Ching*, also known as the *Lao Tzu*. Said to have been written by Lao Tzu, it is now commonly believed to be a collection of sayings by various thinkers. Along with Confucianism, Taoism represents a dominant philosophical school of thought within Chinese philosophy. The central feature of Taoism is the concept of *tao*, meaning 'path' or 'way'. Although *tao* is common to many Chinese philosophies, including Confucianism, it takes centre stage in Taoist philosophy. Within Taoism, *tao* refers to both the way to live one's life and the guiding force behind the development and change of all things. According to Taoists the way to live well is to model oneself on the workings of *tao*, largely achieved through reflecting upon nature and cultivating one's mind through meditative practices.

Taoists argue that *tao* is beyond the understanding of the intellect; it is that which cannot be spoken or understood through verbal descriptions. This is made clear in the first line of the *Tao Te Ching* which states that the *tao* that can be spoken is not the eternal *tao* (at least, this is one common interpretation as there are numerous translations of the original Chinese). One must realise the nature of *tao* through practice, just as a musician develops musical knowledge through playing their instrument rather than simply studying descriptions of it. Although Taoists accept that words are useful, they deny that they can capture ultimate reality, understood as *tao*, and warn against becoming obsessed with intellectual discussions concerning the meaning of words. This is the major theme of Chuang Tzu's philosophy, which appears to argue for a radically relativist position. Chuang Tzu describes all viewpoints as equally valid as there is no objective viewpoint to refer to in deciding between them. Consequently, the Taoist should try to rise above the act of judgement-making, as they have no reason to believe their judgement is better than another's. This idea is captured by the Taoist idea of 'silent teaching', in which understanding is communicated non-verbally. There are strong similarities between Taoism and Buddhism, particularly Zen Buddhism.

See also: **Buddhism; Chinese philosophy; Confucianism; knowledge; monism; mysticism;** *tao***; yin-yang; Zen**

Further reading: Chan (1973); Coutinho (2004); Graham (2001); Waley (1987); Yu-Lan (1948)

Teleology

Teleology is the study of goals, ends or purposes (derived from the Greek *telos* meaning 'purpose' or 'goal'). Aristotle offered a teleological account of the universe, arguing that all things had their own internal purposes which were part of their essence. The key to understanding the nature of things is grasping what their function is. The reason for a stone falling to the ground when dropped from a height, or the reason for a horse having hooves, is explained by their purpose. Each thing has its right 'place' in the universe and a set of functions to fulfil, such as the stone 'belonging' on the ground and a horse running on hard ground.

Religious accounts of the universe are often teleological. Theologians, such as Augustine, argue that a person's purpose is to serve the glory of God. Creationism holds that humans were designed by God and therefore they have certain functions they must fulfil. Darwin's theory of evolution has been seen as undermining the view that nature is designed, by explaining how the world developed through the blind, causal process of natural selection. The fact that there are birds, humans and cats is contingent, and if history were replayed, then things could have turned out very differently indeed. Hegel constructed a teleological theory of history as an inevitable, logical movement towards an end-point of 'absolute knowing'. Hegel's philosophy influenced Marx's teleological belief that communism was the inevitable end-point of society and that the history of society represents the necessary stages in this movement towards communism. Most modern philosophers are sceptical about speaking of the function or purpose of things. Sartre famously claimed that a person's existence precedes their essence, meaning we are born with no purpose and must instead create our own goals to fulfil. Foucault's analysis of knowledge and history was designed to show how our beliefs about what is right, true and natural are contingent, constantly changing constructions. There is nothing in the world that tells us the true purpose of things.

See also: **Aristotle; Augustine; Aristotle; creationism; Darwinism; dialectical material-ism; Foucault; Hegel; historicism; Marx; nihilism; Sartre;** *summum bonum*

Further reading: Bekoff and Lauder (1998); Johnson (2005); Rescher (1986); Woodfield (1976)

Thought experiments

Thought experiments have played a vital role throughout the history of philosophy. They are imagined, hypothetical situations which are used to test theories by seeing what these theories would say about that situation. The important point is that the situation need only be imagined, rather than actually constructed and experienced. Historical examples of thought experiments include Descartes' Evil Demon and the Ancient Greeks' Ship of Theseus. Powerful, modern thought experiments include John Searle's Chinese Room Argument (see **artificial intelligence**), John Rawls' Veil of Ignorance and Frank Jackson's Mary the Scientist (see **qualia**). Despite their ubiquity, some philosophers have worried about the value of thought experiments. One criticism is that they are often too far removed from what is likely or possible to be of relevance. Another criticism is that we can only assess them by using already accepted, commonsense beliefs and therefore our analysis of thought experiments will be necessarily conservative as it relies upon established beliefs (which may well be false). For example, our response to thought experiments regarding the structure of the world would be radically different depending on whether we were alive in a time before or after Magellan's expedition proved the world was round by circumnavigating it.

See also: **artificial intelligence; Descartes; intuition; qualia; Rawls; Ship of Theseus, the; state of nature;**

Further reading: Cohen (2005); Horowitz and Massey (1991); Sorenson (1992); Tittle (2005)

Time

The concept of time is philosophically intriguing. Although we all use the word 'time' without any problem, such as when we say 'it is time to go home' or 'I ran out of time to finish my essay', the nature of time is far from clear. One major debate is whether time is something which exists independently of events. Imagine if the entire universe suddenly froze so that nothing changed whatsoever. Is it possible for time to pass whilst the universe is in such a state? If we say yes, as Plato and Newton did, then time exists independently of events. One consequence is that it is possible that the world has just been in such a frozen state for a thousand years between the time you read *this* and *this* word. Many philosophers, including Aristotle and Leibniz, have argued that time does not exist independently of events. On this view, time can be reduced to the temporal relations between events. This means that time is not a kind of empty container which exists regardless of the events that take place in it. Rather, time simply is the occurrence of events and we could never know time if we did not perceive things to be changing.

Another debate takes place between eternalism, presentism and the growing universe theory. According to eternalism, things in the past and the future exist just as much as things in the present moment. This is meant literally, so that Aristotle and Queen Elizabeth I should be included in the list of things that currently exist. The difference between Aristotle and you is that you are present whilst Aristotle is not. Although this sounds strange, we can draw an analogy with space to help make sense of it. Imagine time as a 'block' extending all the way into the past and future, just as space extends all the way to the edges (if there are any) of the universe. Just as all space is existing now, so too all time is existing now. Which part of time/space you experience depends on where you are. However, just because a distant galaxy is not spatially present to you whilst you read this book, it does not mean it does not exist. Similarly, just because Aristotle is not temporally present to you, it does not mean he does not exist. The growing universe theory partly accepts eternalism, but argues that only objects in the past and present exist, not the future. This means that the 'block' of time is constantly growing as more things and events occur and pass into the past. Presentism rejects both these views, arguing that the only things which exist are those which are currently present. There can be no non-present objects in a list of all the things which exist.

Although presentism may appear to be more intuitively plausible, there are several problems with it. Firstly, it is hard to know how to make sense of talk such as 'Aristotle was a Greek philosopher'. If there are no non-present objects, then how is talking about Aristotle meaningful? We want to say it is *true* that Aristotle was a Greek philosopher, but for something to be true it seems to require a truthmaker

T

(something which makes it true), and it is not clear what the truthmakers are for non-present objects and events. We might appeal to history books and to Aristotle's own works for proof of his existence, but then we have no reason to believe these sources without referring to that existing thing we call Aristotle. Also, it implies that if all reference to Aristotle were erased, then no statements about Aristotle could be true. But we would like to think that truths about him remain true regardless of what people do or do not think about him.

The concept of time has been radically changed by the development of relativity theory. According to this view, measurement of the passage of time is relative to the frame of reference. This means that two people moving at different velocities could experience the passing of time in different ways. The possibility of time travel also challenges commonsense ideas of time as linear. Many philosophers believe that travelling backwards or forwards in time is metaphysically possible. One consequence of this is that time travel is only possible if we accept an eternalist, rather than presentist, theory of time. The idea of time travel raises such issues as whether time 'moves' in one direction (from past to future) or not. We experience the passing of time in a single direction (even if it passes differently relative to different people), but this does not mean it is impossible to experience it in a backwards direction for example. It is worth reflecting on the extent to which time is dependent on human perception. Is time 'all in the mind' or is time part of the structure of the universe? Finally, could there ever be a beginning and an end of time? If so, what happened or will happen before and after that point, or is this a meaningless/unanswerable question?

See also: **change; identity; personal identity; metaphysics; relativity theory; thought experiments**

Key questions: Does time exist independently of events? Does the past, present and/or future exist? Is time travel possible? Is there an objective 'time', separate to our personal experience of time?

Further reading: Harper (1997); Le Poidevin and McBeath (1993); McLure (2005); Savitt (1995); Tooley (1997)

Tolerance

Tolerance is an important element of many contemporary political and ethical theories. Philosophical discussion of tolerance can be traced back to the 17th century, especially John Locke's *A Letter Concerning Toleration* (1689b). The concern was primarily religious tolerance because the major conflicts of the time were religiously motivated. Locke stresses the importance of religious tolerance in generating a free and voluntary society and thus promoting the ideal of individual liberty. The concept of tolerance has since been expanded to include tolerance of racial, sexual, social, age, mental and physical differences. The importance of tolerance has been highlighted by the increasingly multicultural nature of modern societies, which brings with it greater diversity and therefore the need for greater tolerance in order to maintain peaceful and co-operative social relations. Tolerance is a key element in liberalism and moral relativism. The major philosophical disputes concerning tolerance are how to decide what should and should not be tolerated, and how tolerance can be enforced. For instance, can we tolerate another society's treatment of women and should we tolerate the application of Islamic law in the UK? If it is decided that a practice or belief cannot be tolerated, what measures can be taken to stop this practice and are they consistent with general principles of tolerance?

See also: **Bentham; democracy; equality; evil; gender; impartiality; justice; liberalism; liberty; Locke; Mill; morality; nationalism; race; rights**

Key questions: Should everything be tolerated and, if not, what justification is there for accepting one practice or situation above another other than personal preference? Do people expect to be treated tolerantly more than they expect to tolerate other people, and, if so, does this imply that tolerance is related to selflessness?

Further reading: Cohen-Almagor (1994); Fiala (2005); Locke (1689b); Mendus and Edwards (1987); Mill (1859)

Transcendence

The concept of transcendence is derived from the Latin term *transcendere* meaning 'to climb over or beyond'. The idea of transcendence was first used by Western philosophers to describe God as existing outside and independently of the world. This view, defended by Aristotle, claimed that God must have created the world and so cannot be part of the world itself. The concept of transcendence also refers to arguments over whether or not we can have knowledge of things beyond our immediate experience, such as God, souls, substance and the minds of other people. Within Plato's philosophy, we must transcend the earthly realm in order to experience the realm of the forms, the true and unchanging reality. Mystical philosophers also teach that true knowledge is gained through transcending our bodies and the world in order to achieve real, albeit indescribable, knowledge.

Kant's transcendental idealism is the suggestion that we cannot have any knowledge of the realm beyond the empirical/the senses. According to Kant, the mind actively shapes the objects we experience and it is impossible to experience things independently of the way that the mind shapes them. Our faculty of reason imposes order and structure on the world, and we cannot know or understand something without imposing this structure. Therefore transcendental knowledge is impossible. This does not mean that there is not a world independent of our mind, but it does mean that it is necessarily unknowable in itself. All we have is the 'phenomenal' experience of it – the way it appears to us.

Transcendence is an important feature of many Asian philosophies. Within Buddhism (especially Zen Buddhism) and Hinduism one must transcend the world of appearances, which is changing and impermanent, in order to experience enlightenment and escape the cycle of rebirths (*samsara*) in which we are caught up. Taoism teaches that *tao* is both beyond and within all things. It cannot be captured by words, but it is nonetheless real and can be directly experienced or 'channelled' by achieving certain states of consciousness in which the mind does not try to rationalise, analyse and describe.

See also: **Aristotle; Buddhism; creationism; enlightenment; experience; God; Hinduism; intuition; Kant; other minds; perception; Plato; solipsism; substance; Taoism; Zen**

Further reading: Faulconer (2003); Holmes (1995); Schwartz, R.M (2004); Smith (1991)

Trope

See **universals and particulars**

Truth

Truth is one of the most important and yet problematic topics in philosophy. It seems obvious that most philosophers aim at 'the truth' of a topic. If we want to investigate the nature of grass or morality or the mind we want to discover the truth about them. However, just what constitutes the nature of this 'truth' has produced much discussion. There are four major theories regarding the meaning of 'truth': the correspondence theory, the coherence theory, the pragmatic theory and the deflationary theory.

The correspondence theory of truth claims that something is true if it correctly corresponds to reality. According to classical correspondence theories, a sentence, such as 'cows have four legs', is true if it corresponds to an actual fact about the world. This relies upon there being entities called 'facts' to which true beliefs correspond. If there are no facts in the world, then there can be nothing which can make something true. The coherence theory of truth claims that something is true if it is part of a coherent system of beliefs. Our beliefs are like a huge web which support and justify each other. Unlike the correspondence theory, the coherence theory does not see truth as mapping onto the world. Instead truth is a belief-to-belief relation rather than a belief-to-reality relation.

The pragmatic theory of truth, also called instrumentalism, is that truth is what 'works' and arises from specific, practical questions and needs. The truth of a belief is judged by whether it leads to practical success and beneficial results. Beliefs about the world are 'true' if they allow us to make good decisions which produce good outcomes. True beliefs are like 'instruments' for action and engagement with the world. Finally, the deflationary theory of truth argues that to assert that something is true is simply to assert that thing. For instance, to assert 'it is true that grass is green' is simply the same as stating 'grass is green'. We cannot say anything more about the truth of 'grass is green'; we add nothing to 'grass is green' by saying 'it is true that grass is green'. The mistakes that the other three theories of truth make are in assuming that there is something more to truth than simply asserting a proposition and that we can explain and understand its nature through philosophical enquiry. Theories of truth are looking for something which simply is not there and so they will inevitably be unsuccessful.

The realist/anti-realist debate is very relevant to discussions of truth. According to realism, there is a world which exists independently of how we think about it, and our beliefs and thoughts are about that world. The correspondence theory of truth relies upon a realist conception of reality, for if we cannot say what the world is like beyond our own understanding then there is nothing (no 'facts') to which our beliefs can accurately and correctly correspond. The coherence theory and pragmatic conceptions of truth are compatible with anti-realism, because neither talk of a relation between our beliefs and the real (objective, independent) world.

See also: **analytic/synthetic distinction; anti-realism;** *a priori* **and** *a posteriori*; **Ayer; belief; certainty; coherence theory; conditionals; constructionism; context; correspondence theory; deflationary theory of truth; discourse; doubt; facts; foundationalism; Hegel; historicism; idealism; incommensurability; instrumentalism; intuition; logic; metaphysics; mysticism; Nietzsche; objectivism; paradox; perspectivism; Plato; pragmatism; postmodernism; rationalism; realism; Rorty; scepticism; scientific realism; soundness; subjectivity; transcendence; truthmaker; unexplainable, the**

Key questions: Is there such a thing as truth? What makes something true? Are there objective truths in the world? How do we know when we have arrived at the truth?

Further reading: Blackburn (2005); Horwich (1998); Lynch (2001); Schmitt (2004)

Truthmaker

A truthmaker, as the name suggests, is that 'thing' (for instance, an entity or a fact) which makes a proposition true. It can be distinguished from a 'truthbearer', which is that thing (such as a proposition) which is made true by a truthmaker. If there exists a truthmaker for a proposition, such as 'there is a tree in my garden', then that proposition must necessarily be true. This does not mean that the truthmaker 'causes' the proposition to be true in the way that my hitting a window causes it to break. Rather, the existence of a truthmaker for a proposition 'entails' (necessarily means) that the proposition is true. However, the relation of 'entailment' has been criticised for being too strong and therefore some philosophers propose that a proposition is true 'in virtue of' the existence of a certain truthmaker. Truthmaker theory is appealing because it provides a response to the intuition that truth should be 'ontologically grounded', meaning truth should relate to genuine features of the world (those grounded in reality). This realist vision of truth, which argues that truth is independent of the mind, fits well with the truthmaker assertion that there exist certain entities in the world which guarantee the truth of our propositions.

However, there is much debate amongst those in favour of truthmakers. One major issue is whether every truth has a truthmaker. For instance, do negative truths ('there is not a tiger in my bedroom') have a truthmaker? Is the truth of this proposition guaranteed by the absence of a truthmaker, or the existence of a negative truthmaker? Another issue, which will help address the previous one, is just what kind of 'thing' a truthmaker is meant to be. It has been called an 'entity', but it is not clear what is meant by this. Finally, how are we able to recognise when a truthmaker is successfully making a proposition true? Armstrong, an important proponent of truthmakers, has called them 'states of affairs'. States of affairs are complex entities, composed of a unified number of objects, properties and relations. For instance, the state of affairs for the proposition 'this leaf is green' would be something like the leaf, the property 'being green' and the relation between them.

Truthmaker theory has strong parallels with the correspondence theory of truth, which argues that truth is a relation between a proposition and some feature of the world which makes that proposition true. One could see the truthmaker theory as an attempt to explain just what the relevant 'feature of the world' is; namely, truthmakers. However, whilst the correspondence theory implies a truthmaker theory, a

T

truthmaker theory does not necessarily imply a correspondence theory. One could hold that truthmakers are the relations between certain propositions (rather than between propositions and the world), which would fit with coherence theories' identification of truth with the coherence between propositions. Nonetheless, realists are drawn to truthmaker theory because it is generally phrased as discussing what the relevant features of reality are that make things true.

See also: **coherence theory; correspondence theory; facts; metaphysics; realism; truth**

Further reading: Armstrong (2004); Beebee and Dodd (2005); Lowe and Rami (2009)

T

Unconscious, the

The idea that there are processes going on in our mind that we are unaware of was made popular by Freud. However, the importance of unconscious material in the form of dreams has a much longer history and Leibniz discussed the idea of unconscious representations 200 years before Freud. A philosophical difficulty is how to be certain that there is an unconscious mind if it is not directly available to consciousness. For example, although people report dreams when they wake up, it is not certain that what they report occurred when they were in an unconscious state. All references to unconscious processes are presented by a conscious mind. However those references do not necessarily imply that there is an unconscious mind. In other words, the unconscious must be inferred from our conscious information. The idea that part of the mind is 'hidden' has important implications for introspective accounts of consciousness. Since Descartes there has been a view of the mind as a 'private theatre', to which we have personal access by simply reflecting on the contents of consciousness. However, this model will never reveal the unconscious and its workings. Therefore, examination of the mind requires more than the process of introspection, if indeed there is an unconscious part of the mind.

For Freud, the unconscious mind contained repressed experiences and thoughts which could be made conscious through psychoanalytic techniques such as free association or dream analysis. Dreams have a manifest (what they seem to be about) and latent (what they are actually about) content and could therefore be an indication of an unconscious desire (Freud, 1900). An advantage of assuming the existence of an unconscious is that it provides rational explanations for seemingly random events. This reveals Freud's desire to continue the spirit of enlightenment thought, in particular the belief that all events have a cause and the entire world is subject to scientific principles and explanations. Jung (1933) agreed that we have a personal unconscious but added the idea of a collective unconscious, that is, knowledge and desires that are shared with other humans now and in the past. The collective unconscious is represented by archetypes such as a horse which, in myths and dreams, has the meaning of a long-suffering mother figure. Such views are compatible with Eastern philosophy and the notion that meditation, as well as dreams, make unconscious thoughts available.

See also: **consciousness; ego, the; enlightenment; Freud; inference; knowledge; Leibniz; mind, the; reason**
Further reading: Freud, S. (1900); Jung (1933); Smith (1999)

Unexplainable, the

Philosophy has sought to explain the nature of such things as the world, the mind, morality and truth. However, it must be considered whether every aspect of reality is explainable, or whether some parts of it are beyond explanation. With the modern physicalist view of the universe, in which everything that exists is assumed to be physical in nature, science promises to one day explain every feature of the universe. However, certain apparent features of reality seem to evade scientific explanation. The most striking example is consciousness. Philosophers of the mind have struggled to adequately describe and explain certain elements of consciousness, such as intentionality and qualia. Some philosophers, such as Paul and Patricia Churchland, have produced eliminative materialist theories of the mind, which argue that consciousness is ultimately a myth and the idea of mental states must be eliminated. In other words, the reason we cannot explain consciousness is that it is not really real. Other philosophers, such as Thomas Nagel, have suggested there is an irreducible, subjective element to consciousness which can never be fully explained or described. A person's subjective experience of the world, 'what it is like to be me', is real but impossible to capture in scientific and philosophical theories. Finally, it is also argued that the problem lies with our current level of understanding and that as the sciences progress they will make sense of every aspect of the mind and the world.

Another possible feature of reality which may escape explanation is God. One view of the unexplainable is that it is our limited cognitive capacity which lacks the ability to explain it. Another view is that no living thing or machine could ever explain it, because it is necessarily unexplainable. Within Eastern philosophies, Taoism has long declared the concept of *tao* to be ultimately unexplainable. Although one can experience it and attempt to describe it, one cannot fully explain the workings of *tao*. It is possible that there is a paradox in talking about the unexplainable, for even in using the word we are offering some kind of explanation of what it is – namely that it is unexplainable.

See also: **consciousness; eliminative materialism; God; knowledge; mind, the; mysticism; physicalism; qualia; reductionism; subjectivity; Taoism; truth; unconscious, the**

Key questions: Are some things ultimately unexplainable? If so, what are those things? If something is unexplainable, is it something to do with our limited understanding or because the thing itself is necessarily unexplainable?

Further reading: Chan (1973); Harmless (2007); Lycan (1995); Nagel (1979)

Universability

The idea of universability is chiefly associated with Kant's 'categorical imperative'. According to Kant, we may act only on those principles which we can rationally will to be universally adopted. In other words, we are only allowed to perform actions which we would accept every person performing. If we tell a lie, we are saying all other people should adopt this principle. This idea of universability was later developed by Hare, whose principle states that whatever is right for one person will be right for another person in the same situation. This captures a common understanding of ethics according to which two rational, moral people should perform the same action if presented with the same situation. More generally, if morality is objective, then there will be certain moral laws which all people across all space and time should obey. However, many philosophers have argued that no moral rules have this feature of universability and therefore there are no moral laws.

See also: **categorical imperative; cultural relativism; deontology; descriptivism; Hare; Kant; moral objectivism; prescriptivism; relativism**

Further reading: Hare (1952, 1981); Kant (1785); Paton (1947)

Universals and particulars

Universals are general properties which apply to particular objects. The debate surrounding universals concerns the ontological status of properties. Realists believe that universals exist, whilst nominalists deny there are such things. Consider the sentence, 'This hat is brown'. Realists argue that it involves two different things, a particular (the hat) and a universal (the property 'brownness'). Unlike particulars, universals can have several instances – the colour brown is possessed by many different objects at the same time. Therefore if we have two brown hats we have three entities: the two hats and the one universal of brownness. The most famous account of universals is Plato's theory of the forms. The defence of universals is often grounded in the structure of language. It is argued that a sentence such as 'This hat is brown' can only be true if some 'thing' (brownness) exists which the hat possesses. Furthermore, we mean the same thing each time we describe different objects as being brown. Therefore, the word 'brown' must always refer to the same thing, namely the universal 'brownness'.

Nominalists agree that particulars can have properties such as brownness, but deny that there are such things as universals. They argue that talk of universals can lead to such absurd observations as something 'getting closer to itself'. For example, when two blue cars approach each other the realist would have to say that the blueness is approaching itself. Nominalists believe that the brownness of a hat is an entity particular to that specific hat, known as a trope. According to nominalism, if we have two brown hats we have four entities: the two hats and two brown tropes. However, nominalism must give an acceptable account of the similarity between objects with the same property without reference to a universal. How can we say that both Kate and Socrates are wise, without reference to the common property 'wiseness'? Ockham's Razor is often invoked to justify nominalism as it offers an effective account of properties using only particulars, rather than requiring that universals exist as well. Nominalism thus assumes fewer 'ontological entities' (actual things existing in the world) than universalism. It is more 'parsimonious' (ontologically 'economic') and therefore the more favourable theory.

Despite the above disagreements, some metaphysicians (for example, Price, 1953) argue that there is nothing to choose between nominalism and realism in terms of their ability to explain an object's possession of properties; they are two different ways of describing the same thing.

See also: **aesthetics; Aristotle; beauty; good, the; metaphysics; Ockham's razor; Plato; properties**

Key questions: Do universals exist? Can we satisfactorily explain properties without using universals?

Further reading: Armstrong (1978, 1989); Campbell (1990); Moreland (2001); Price (1953)

Utilitarianism

Utilitarianism, the major form of consequentialism, is an ethical theory which argues that an act is morally right if it best promotes the good (utility). This principle of utility is the basis of all versions of utilitarianism, although just what the good is taken to be differs greatly amongst utilitarians. The classic formulations of utilitarianism are those by Bentham (1789) and Mill (1861b). Both philosophers advocated a form of utilitarianism known as hedonistic act-utilitarianism. This means that the good was defined as happiness, and that an act is morally right if it produces the maximum overall amount of good (happiness). The classic form of utilitarianism can be summed up in the saying 'the greatest good for the greatest number'. In order to conduct this utility calculation, we must assess how much happiness is produced in all people involved in the act, take away all the suffering that is produced, and see whether this act produces more net happiness than any other action. Critics of this form of utilitarianism have questioned: the possibility of calculating, or in Bentham's case quantifying, happiness; comparing the happiness of different people; and working out just who is affected by the action. Furthermore, it requires great foresight to be able to predict all likely consequences of an action. Another criticism, which was aimed at Bentham's formulation of utilitarianism, is that it does not allow different kinds of happiness. His theory implies that playing with sticks is as good as creating an artistic masterpiece if it creates as much happiness. This was a problem addressed by Mill, who defended the idea of higher (such as intellectual) pleasures having far greater value.

In addition to hedonistic act-utilitarianism, there are several other important forms of utilitarianism. Rule-utilitarianism states that we should follow those rules which would have the best consequences if followed by everyone. Rule-utilitarianism avoids the impracticability (perhaps impossibility) of deciding in each situation on the single best act to perform. However, this means that we might not always choose an action with the best possible consequences in a specific circumstance. For instance, by following a set rule, a rule-utilitarian might produce less good than an act-utilitarian: in breaking the rule 'do not steal' Robin Hood actually produced a greater overall amount of happiness. The rule-utilitarian could respond by highlighting other rules, such as 'give as much money as you can spare to charity', which would (if followed by everyone) prevent the Robin Hood scenario ever arising because there would not be such unequal levels of wealth. An alternative response by rule-utilitarians could be to make their rules ever more specific. For example, we could have the rule 'do not steal unless it is (a) from someone who is very rich, and (b) to give to someone very poor' and so on. Indeed, this seems a necessary thing for a rule-utilitarian to do, because the more specific rule will produce better consequences. However, this seems to reduce rule-utilitarianism to act-utilitarianism, because the rule ends up being tailored to suit all possible situations. Indeed, it has been argued that Mill was a rule-utilitarian rather than an act-utilitarian. The rule would also be indefinitely long. Many philosophers have rejected rule-utilitarianism on the basis of these problems.

Negative utilitarianism insists upon minimising of what is bad, rather than the promotion of the good. If we take suffering as intrinsically bad, then negative utilitarianism recommends those actions which most reduce and prevent suffering. However, a common criticism of negative utilitarianism is that the ultimate way to

U

remove suffering is to painlessly kill all beings capable of suffering. Other general criticisms of utilitarianism include the fact that a person's intentions are treated as irrelevant to the moral assessment of an act and that there is neither room for personal feelings (it is an impersonal morality) nor special considerations for family and friends. Finally, it is often very difficult, perhaps impossible, to decide what all the consequences of our act or rule would be. Therefore, it is argued, utilitarianism demands a calculation of consequences which can never be made.

See also: **Bentham; consequentialism; deontology; equality; good, the; happiness; impartiality; Mill; moral agents; morality; supererogation**

Further reading: Bentham (1798); Mill (1861b); Scarre (1996); Smart and Williams (1973); Singer (1991)

Utopianism

A utopian theory is one which describes the best possible way of constructing a society in which to live. Plato's *Republic* is an early example of utopianism, which describes how the ideal state should be and why this would best benefit citizens of that state. Thomas More's *Utopia* (1516) is a classic utopian account of an ideal society governed by reason. His representation of society in Utopia contrasted with the conflictual state of politics of his time and provided a vehicle to criticise the *status quo*, an important feature of utopianism. Following More's work, utopian visions reject the current social system and offer idealistic alternatives to it. Critics of utopianism claim that these visions are too unrealistic and deviate too strongly from the current situation ever to be achieved.

Karl Marx praised utopianism for revealing the undesirability of current society, but nonetheless rejected utopianism for failing to address the actual situation. Consequently, a division has been made between abstract and concrete utopias. Abstract utopias are idealised visions of a perfect society, constructed without reference to the realities of social life. Concrete utopias are created from critical social theory and therefore focus on visions of how society can be radically transformed, rather than creating a totally new society. Concrete utopias include the feminist vision of a society free from gender inequality and the civil rights struggle for racial equality. In *Walden Two* (1948), Skinner outlines how the application of behaviourist principles could increase a society's happiness. The rapid technological developments of the 20th century led to utopian claims that suffering, material lack and physical deficiencies could all be eliminated through scientific intervention. However, science has also inspired apocalyptic (dystopian) visions of a world destroyed by technology, captured in such science-fiction films as *The Matrix* and *Blade Runner*. The power of utopianism lies in its ability to motivate political activists and theorists by offering an idealised goal to fight for.

See also: **anarchy, communism; feminism; Marx; Plato; political philosophy; post-humanism; race**

Further reading: Geoghegan (1987); Kumar (1991); More (1516); Olson (1982); Sargisson (1996); Skinner (1948)

U

Vagueness

The world appears full of vagueness. At what point does a person with greying hair become 'grey haired'? When does a kitten become a cat? At what moment does night turn to day? There are many things in the world which are not clearly separated and have borderline cases, ones which do not neatly fit into any one category or can fit into more than one. Vagueness must not be confused with ambiguity, which is when a thing has two different meanings. For instance, 'punch' can be ambiguous – it could refer to hitting a person or a drink– or vague – in its first sense, a certain movement of the hand might or might not be a punch (it might be a slap or a push).

The philosophical interest in vagueness is that it gives rise to interesting paradoxes. For example, a cat that is one week old (call this y) is a kitten. A cat that is $y+1$ days old is still a kitten. Applying this principle, we can derive the conclusion that there is a 4000-day-old kitten. Another debate regarding vagueness is whether objects themselves are vague, or whether it is merely our way of describing them that is vague. In other words, is reality vague or is language vague? For example, Ben Nevis might be a vague object; it is unclear whether or not some rocks are part of Ben Nevis. If it is a vague object then it is not the fault of language, the name 'Ben Nevis', but something about the mountain itself. The nature of the mountain causes linguistic vagueness. The idea of vague objects assumes a correspondence between language and reality, with words 'mapping onto' the world. Many philosophers tend to see language as constructing, to some extent, our idea of the world. Therefore, we cannot say whether reality is or is not vague, because we cannot get outside our language in order to check this.

More practically, vagueness poses difficulties in the legal system, so that apparently clear-cut laws pose challenges when deciding what offence has been committed and what sentence should be handed down. Examples include the difference between murder and manslaughter or between careless driving and dangerous driving.

See also: **constructionism; correspondence theory; linguistic relativism; metaphysics; paradox; realism**

Key questions: Are there genuinely vague things in the world? If not, how could we resolve all examples of vagueness?

Further reading: Endicott (2000); Keefe (2000); Keefe and Smith (1996); Smith (2008); Williamson (1994)

Validity

An argument possesses validity if it follows the formal rules of logic. A statement (such as 'All cats are furry') cannot be valid, only an argument which is made up of two or more statements can be valid. The most common form of a valid argument is a deductive argument, in which the conclusion is a logical consequence of the premises. This means that if the premises (P) are true, then the conclusion (C) must also be true because the conclusion follows (is entailed by) the premises. An example of a deductive argument, with the logical form next to it, is:

P1	All cats are furry		P1	All As are B
P2	Thomas is a cat		P2	C is an A
C	Therefore, Thomas is furry		C	Therefore, C is B

An argument may be valid without being true. For instance, it might be the case that not all cats are furry, but as long as the argument follows the laws of logic then it is valid. If an argument is valid *and* happens to be true, then it is sound.

See also: **deduction; induction; fallacy; inference; logic**

Further reading: Guttenplan (1997); Howson (1997); Tomassi (1999)

Value

Value is a central feature in much moral and political philosophy. Certain things appear to possess value, not in a strictly economic sense of being worth money, but because they are seen as 'good'. For instance, we tend to value our friends and family, as well as valuing honesty and generosity. The problem with 'value' is that it is not something which can be quantified or analysed scientifically. One view is that value is a relation between human desires, needs or tastes, and certain objects and events. Alternatively, it could be a special kind of property which we can detect in things, though it is hard to explain just what kind of property it is and how we can experience it.

If we take an objective attitude towards value then we hold that certain things are of value regardless of our attitude towards them. The subjective view of value is the belief that humans decide what has value and if different people value different things there is no way of saying which things *actually* have value. This means that something has value if we choose to value it, rather than the objective view which states that we value something because it has value. If something possesses intrinsic value, then this means that it is valuable in itself. For example, we might say that happiness has intrinsic value because it is an end or goal we strive towards. We do not want happiness in order to achieve a further goal; rather, happiness is an end-point of our actions. Something has instrumental value if it is merely a means to an end. A good example is money. Many people believe that money is of value, but this is only because of what it allows one to do (such as become happy, although some would disagree that money leads to happiness). Therefore, money has instrumental rather than intrinsic value. A final issue surrounding value is whether there is ultimately only one basic, fundamental value. For example, a hedonist might argue that the only thing of (intrinsic) value in the world is happiness. All other value is instrumental in that it allows us to obtain happiness. The

V

alternative view is that there is more than one thing of intrinsic value; for example, beauty, knowledge and religious piety.

See also: **animal ethics; anti-realism; Aristotle; beauty; environmental ethics; good, the; happiness; moral agents; morality; moral objectivism; realism; relativism; *summum bonum***

Key questions: What things are capable of possessing value? Do we decide what has value? If so, how do we decide?

Further reading: Gaus (1990); Hall (1952); Lemos, N.M. (1994); Lemos, R.M. (1995)

Vegetarianism

Philosophical interest in vegetarianism, the refusal to eat meat, dates back at least two thousand years. The Pythagoreans, followers of Pythagoras' philosophy, refused to eat meat because they thought that humans and animals shared a soul. Another reason, seemingly shared by Plato, was that vegetarianism was a more healthy diet. Plutarch's *On the Eating of Flesh*, written around 100 CE, is a justification of vegetarianism based upon the well-being of animals. There was little interest in vegetarianism during the medieval and enlightenment periods of philosophy, owing to the common belief that animals had no soul and therefore could not suffer. Descartes observed how interesting it was to see animals (complex, unfeeling machines) reacting as if they were in pain when being tortured. Kant suggested that it may be worthwhile to avoid harming animals because otherwise we may become insensitive to suffering and thus start harming humans.

It was not until the 1970s that widespread support for vegetarianism developed. Several different arguments were put forward. One was based on health, with advocates of vegetarianism claiming that a non-meat diet is better for us. A second argument focused on the environmental effects of eating meat. For instance, animal farming is highly energy-intensive and requires a lot of food to produce a small amount of meat. Hunger and starvation could be radically reduced if the food given to animals were given straight to humans. Another environmental concern is the razing of jungle and forest to produce land for animals to graze on. Finally, there is a set of arguments focusing on the moral standing of animals. If animals have a right to life or a right to avoid suffering, then animal farming methods should be radically altered or abandoned altogether. This argument was aided by the publicising of, and subsequent public outcry against, inhumane (mostly intensive) farming methods such as battery farming and the treatment of veal calves. The belief that humans are morally superior to or more valuable than animals has been described as anthropocentric. Peter Singer uses the term 'speciesism' to describe this view, just as racism and sexism are used to describe unjustified discrimination based upon race or sex. According to Singer's influential view, all sentient beings must be given equal consideration of interest and the suffering or happiness of an animal cannot be viewed as less important than a human's

In Eastern philosophies, particularly Buddhism and Hinduism, there has been a long tradition of vegetarianism. The principle of rebirth teaches that we have all been animals at some point in the past and that our cat or dog could have been a family member or friend in a past life. Therefore we should treat all sentient animals well. Furthermore, because the distinction between different beings is arbitrary, we should practise universal compassion for all living things. Similarly, Jainism, another Eastern philosophy, teaches non-violence and thus demands we avoid harming any living creature. This is why Jainist monks sweep the path as they walk, to avoid stepping on any living creature.

See also: **animal ethics; Buddhism; environmental ethics; moral agents; morality; Hinduism; Singer**

Further reading: Hill (1996); Spencer (2000); Walters and Portmess (1999)

Vicious circle

A vicious circle is a fallacy (error in reasoning) constructed when a premise is needed to prove a conclusion, but that conclusion is needed in order to justify the premise. For example, 'I have my umbrella with me because I know it will rain ... I know it will rain because I have my umbrella with me'. Philosophers have commonly been accused of constructing a vicious circle. For instance, part of Descartes' proof for the existence of God rests upon his possession of 'clear and distinct ideas'. However, his justification for possessing such ideas seems to require that God exists.

See also: *ad hominem*; **begging the question; Descartes; fallacy; logic; slippery slope argument; straw man**

Further reading: Engel (1994); Hansen and Pinto (1995); Ralph and Blair (1994); Walton (1989)

Vienna Circle

The term 'Vienna Circle' refers to a group of philosophers based in Vienna, Austria, who shared a similar philosophical outlook. The Vienna Circle, which met weekly between 1924 and 1936, was central to the development of logical positivism, a theory which rejected metaphysics as meaningless on the grounds that the only meaningful sentences are those which can be empirically tested. This strongly scientific approach sought to revolutionise philosophy and the social sciences by applying the methods of science to all areas of investigation. Issues such as God and the soul, which could not be empirically analysed, were dismissed as meaningless and having no place in a thoroughly modern, rational and scientific world. The main members of the Vienna Circle included Moritz Schlick, Otto Neurath, Rudolf Carnap, Hans Hahn and Phillip Frank. They were strongly influenced by Wittgenstein's early work, the *Tractatus*, Karl Popper's philosophy of science, and the developments implemented in logic by Frege and Russell. Much of the philosophy advocated by the Vienna Circle was quickly criticised and support for their work rapidly died out. However, their work has been re-assessed recently and more sympathetic studies have rekindled interest in their projects.

V

See also: **Ayer; empiricism; God; knowledge; logical positivism; metaphysics; Popper; positivism; Russell; scientific method; truth; Wittgenstein**

Further reading: Ayer (1936); Carnap (1928); Schlick (1979a, 1979b); Stadler (1997, 2003)

Virtue

The concept of virtue is the key element in virtue ethics. The Greek word for virtue is *areté*, which also translates as 'excellence'. *Areté* refers not only to moral qualities, but also to something being 'good' or 'valuable'. Thus we might say of a wrestler that he has the virtue of being strong. The specific virtues which we should cultivate differ greatly from philosopher to philosopher. Aristotle listed many virtues, some of the most important being courage, temperance, liberality, justice, practical wisdom, sincerity and modesty. During the medieval period, the importance of religious virtues such as piety, faith, charity, meekness and hope was emphasised. Such virtues were famously criticised by Nietzsche as representative of a 'slave morality' which produced passive, weak and herd-like individuals. Interest in virtues as the central concept in moral theories was minimal from medieval times to the middle of the 20th century. Since then an increasing number of moral philosophers have developed new versions of a moral theory grounded in the idea of virtue. Often this is a response to dissatisfaction with the established deontological and utilitarian models of morality. Feminists have examined how many supposed virtues, such as strength, competitiveness and intellectual success, have been associated with men. Historically, women have been discouraged or prevented from developing them. Even today, women are often criticised for 'unfeminine' behaviour when displaying 'masculine' virtues, even though these virtues are often essential for success in the job market.

See also: **Aristotle; deontology; feminism; morality; Socrates; utilitarianism; virtue ethics**

Further reading: Brady and Pritchard (2003); DePaul and Zagzebski (2003); Fairweather and Zagzebski (2001); Zagzebski (1996)

Virtue ethics

A virtue ethic is one in which judgements of character are the basis of assessing moral goodness. The focus is upon becoming a certain type of person by cultivating a specific set of virtues. This approach is contrasted with both deontological theories, which emphasise one's rights or duties, and consequentialist (utilitarian) theories, which focus on the results of actions. Virtue ethics is chiefly associated with Aristotle, although Epicurus and the Stoics also produced versions of a virtue ethic. For Aristotle, morality cannot be captured in, and expressed by, rules for action. Instead, morality is a matter of developing and demonstrating the appropriate virtues. These allow us to respond with the correct action in each unique situation. The person who has fully cultivated his virtuous character is said to live a life of *eudaimonia* ('flourishing' or happiness), which is the ultimate goal of human action.

The idea that morality cannot be 'codified' (set down in a set of definitive rules, such as the Ten Commandments) has appealed to many recent moral theorists, who have begun to revive interest in virtue ethics after the dominance of deontological and utilitarian theories. They argue that moral rules can only be understood and properly applied by those who have developed a virtuous character. Key to this is practical experience, which refines one's moral sensitivity and judgement (Aristotle's *phronesis*).

However, virtue ethics has been criticised precisely because it fails to offer any specific rules for action. A response to this would point out that to develop a 'charitable' character is to do charitable things, therefore we have the rule 'be charitable' as a concrete guide to action. If there is only one eudaimonic life (only one way of living that is the best), then it seems there would be a single set of virtues which all people should develop. This leans towards an objective, rather than a subjective, account of ethics. However, if we accept that different cultures will value different virtues and the idea of the 'good life' will vary across time and place, then it seems that virtues are subjective. This would be a relativist theory of morality. Important modern virtue ethicists include Elizabeth Anscombe, Phillipa Foot, Rosalind Hursthouse, Amelie Rorty and Michael Slote.

See also: **Aristotle; consequentialism; cultural relativism; deontology; Greek philosophy, ancient; morality; moral objectivism; stoicism; summum bonum; virtue**

Further reading: Annas (1993); Aristotle (350 BCEb); Crisp and Slote (1997); Flanagan and Rorty (1990); Hursthouse (1999)

Vitalism

Vitalism, derived from the Latin word *vita* (life), is the belief that materialism is false and that there is a non-material 'spirit' or 'life-force' within all living things that distinguishes them from non-living things. Reality cannot be captured by purely physical accounts of the world and life will never be fully explained by scientific theories. Henri Bergson, an important vitalist, called this crucial, yet elusive, element of life '*élan vital*'. A key belief shared by vitalists is that the world is dynamic and characterised by change and 'becoming', rather than being static. Living things are in a ceaseless process of creation and development, driven by this life-force. Bergson used the idea of the *élan vital* to explain evolution in a less mechanical and more creative way than the existing scientific accounts. Nietzsche's theory also shows signs of vitalism, particularly in his idea of the will. There are certain similarities between the idea of the *élan vital* and Taoism's conception of *tao*. More recently, vitalism has been associated with aspects of Deleuze's philosophy.

See also: **Deleuze; dualism; materialism; Nietzsche; physicalism; reductionism; tao; Taoism**

Further reading: Bergson (1907); Marks (1998); Mullarkey (1999)

V

Williams, Bernard (1929–2003)

One of the most important moral philosophers of the 20th century, Williams criticised traditional moral theories such as deontology and utilitarianism for attempting to create unified and systematic accounts. According to Williams, these attempts to 'codify' morality bear little resemblance to our everyday ethical lives, which are often chaotic and contradictory. Our lives do not allow for the simple application of an abstract, reductionist theory of what is good and bad. Williams was particularly critical of utilitarianism, arguing that its insistence on consequences causes it to ignore the importance of agency. Indeed, he argues that the impartiality required by utilitarianism (and also deontology) is impossible because it is incompatible with the fact that the practical deliberation of an action is always made by an agent, and no agent can make the calculation required by utilitarianism with regard to the positive and negative consequences of an action. The difference, say, between my shooting someone and someone being shot because I refuse to pull the trigger of a gun is an important one, and yet the difference is not recognised by utilitarianism.

Related to this idea of agency is Williams' analysis of 'internal' and 'external' reasons. Williams argues that all reasons for action are internal, and therefore we can have no genuine reasons for an action that are entirely disconnected from our own interests and experiences. For Williams, a moral theory must take into account such factors as history, psychology, culture and politics. In moving away from the importance of abstract moral theories, which emphasise impersonal duties, motives and consequences, Williams could be seen as heralding a return to the practical question posed by many early Greek philosophers: 'How am I to live my life?'. Critics of Williams complained that his philosophy was overly critical and offered nothing of positive substance. The response might be that his work only seems negative from the perspective of those who defend the systematic theories he wished to challenge.

See also: **consequentialism; deontology; morality; impartiality; utilitarianism**

Further reading: Callcut (2009); Jenkins (2006); Smart and Williams (1973); Williams (1972, 1973, 1985)

Wittgenstein, Ludwig (1889–1951)

A sharp distinction is drawn between two periods in Wittgenstein's work. In his early period, Wittgenstein concentrated on analytic philosophy, influenced by his acquaintance with Bertrand Russell at Cambridge. It was during this period, whilst held in a prison camp during the First World War, that he wrote his classic *Tractatus Logico-Philosophicus* (1921) in which he argues that the world consists of 'facts' which are represented by our thoughts and propositions. These thoughts and propositions are 'pictures' of reality and the logical structure of our thoughts mirrors the logical structure of reality. As suggested by the opening line of *Tractatus Logico-Philosophicus* – '[t]he world is everything that is the case' – Wittgenstein defends a realist conception of reality in which our thoughts directly correspond to how the world is. Logical analysis of our propositions is the method by which we can discover the basic propositions which are the pictures of reality. Because our thoughts are representations of reality, the limit of our thought is the limit of our world. What lies beyond thought is literally non-sense. The nature of this 'nonsense', that which cannot be pictured, has been much discussed and is far from clear.

Wittgenstein's later philosophy is encapsulated in his *Philosophical Investigations* (1953). The ideas and the style of writing are markedly different, moving from a clear, logical form to a series of often disconnected and ambiguous sentences. Wittgenstein's *Investigations* had the revolutionary aim of rejecting the belief, which had underpinned all traditional philosophy, that words passively represent objects in the world. Rather than the meaning of words being derived from the things they represent, Wittgenstein argues that the meaning of a word is its use. The context in which a word is used fixes its meaning and explains how the same word can have a multiplicity of meanings and change its meanings over time. This idea of meaning is expressed in Wittgenstein's concept of a 'language-game'.

Another aim of Wittgenstein's later work is to move meaning from the private to the public sphere. Before Wittgenstein, philosophers had generally assumed that each of us had a private realm of experience, a 'private theatre', which we call our minds. A person's mind produces or contains a reality which only they can experience and understand. Against this view Wittgenstein argues that if this were the case, then I would be able to construct a 'private language' meaningful only to me. However, such a private language cannot be formulated because language is rule-based. An individual is unable on their own to both create a rule and judge whether it has been correctly followed. Consequently, the supposedly private experiences of the mind only become meaningful within a shared, public language. Understanding other minds is achieved through examining language-use and behaviour, rather than introspection. This offers a counter-argument to the denial that we can know what other people's minds are like.

See also: **analytic philosophy; context; correspondence theory; Derrida; facts; Foucault; Gadamer; hermeneutics; introspection; knowledge; language game; linguistic relativism; other minds; postmodernism; private language argument; realism; Russell; solipsism; truth**

Further reading: Grayling (2001); Pears (1971); Sluga and Stern (1996); Wittgenstein (1921, 1953, 1958); Vesey (1974)

W

Xeno's paradoxes
See **Zeno's paradoxes**

Yin-Yang

The concepts of *yin* and *yang*, combined into the single concept *yin-yang*, are important features of many Chinese philosophies. The idea of *yin-yang* can be traced back to the 14th century BCE, when it described the natural phenomenon of day (*yang*) and night (*yin*). From this developed the idea that *yang* represents movement and *yin* represents rest. Soon *yin-yang* became the idea that the universe is governed by a process of opposing forces, *yin* and *yang*, which are themselves two parts of the one process known as *tao* (the 'way' of the world/reality). Harmony in the world is achieved by balancing *yin* and *yang*, and all change is generated and governed by the interaction of these two forces.

Yin has such characteristics as femaleness, darkness, completion, cold, night, materiality and passivity. *Yang* has such characteristics as maleness, lightness, creation, heat, day, Heaven and activity. The constant interaction between *yin* and *yang* within the all-encompassing process of *tao* reveals the common Chinese idea of reality as cyclical. All things change into their opposites over time – health turns to illness, happiness to sadness, warmth to coldness – and these changes can be understood as the temporary dominance of either *yin* or *yang*. Although the ideas of *yin* and *yang* were present in Confucianism and Taoism, there was also the *Yinyang* school (c. 800–200 BCE), which explored methods of divination using the concept of *yin-yang*. *Yin-yang* continues to be an influential concept today and is used in many forms of Chinese medicinal treatments, where the aim is to restore harmony between *yin* and *yang* in order to restore health.

See also: **Chinese philosophy; Confucianism; tao; Taoism**

Further reading: Billington (1997); Chan (1973); Yu-Lan (1948)

Zen

Zen, also referred to as Chan Buddhism, is a form of Buddhism which originated in China but was fully developed in Japan. (The term 'Zen' is Japanese, although derived from the Buddhist word *dhyana* meaning 'meditation'.) Zen represents a merging of Buddhism with Taoist philosophy. Zen teaches that all of us possess a 'Buddha-nature' and the practices of meditation and daily mindfulness help us to realise this Buddha-nature and thus achieve enlightenment. Zen advocates the Buddhist teaching that our belief in a substantial self is a mistake and that in order to become enlightened we must lose our desires and attachments, which arise from selfish thoughts of 'me' and 'mine'. According to Zen there is no correct perspective on the world; each person's viewpoint is a particular way of seeing and judging things rather than representing how things actually are. Furthermore, Zen teaches that reason, logic and language will not lead one to ultimate understanding and knowledge. Instead, practical wisdom acquired through meditation, which quietens the mind, loosens attachments and breaks down the illusion of self and ego, allows true insights into the nature of reality.

The Zen suspicion of logical reasoning as a means to attain truth is captured in its use of *koans*. *Koans* are puzzles which do not have a literal, true answer, such as the famous 'what is the sound of one hand clapping?' Through *koans*, Zen students may find they gradually suspend their reasoning altogether, reaching a state called 'no-mind', which can open up an experience of existence itself. Such an experience occurs when the mind does not impose itself upon the world, but passively reflects it (hence the common Zen imagery of the enlightened mind becoming like a mirror). Much of Zen teaching is transmitted silently, through meditation, or apparently mysteriously, such as when a Zen master instructs a student to sweep leaves, or hits them with a stick in order to induce sudden enlightenment. Achieving enlightenment (*nirvana*) is associated with seeing all things as one, although linguistic descriptions of this state cannot begin to convey what it is like.

See also: **Buddhism; enlightenment; 'I'; karma; knowledge; logic; personal identity; perspectivism; reason; self, the; tao; Taoism; transcendence**

Further reading: Heine and Wright (2006); James (2004); Masao (1989); Wright (1998)

Zeno's paradoxes

Zeno, a Greek philosopher born in the 5th century BCE, is said to have produced some 40 paradoxes which have provoked much philosophical discussion. The most famous are the paradoxes of motion, which are designed to show that change is impossible. One such paradox involves a slow runner being chased by a fast runner. In order for the fast runner to reach the slow runner he must cover half the distance between them. In order to cover half the distance between them, he must cover half this distance. Because the distance between two points can always be halved, the fast runner can never reach the slow runner. Another paradox of motion is the arrow paradox. Imagine an arrow in flight. If it is moving then it must be either moving to where it is not (into the distance) or moving to where it is (from where it just was). However, in each instant that we look at the arrow it is neither moving to where it is nor moving to where it is not – it is actually right where it is. Because at each instant the arrow is not moving anywhere, it can never be moving because there is nothing more than each instant put together. Therefore an arrow cannot move. It would appear that these paradoxes must be resolvable, because things in the world do seem to move and catch up with one another. However, just how these paradoxes can be resolved is far from settled. One line of reasoning is that these paradoxes demonstrate that the world simply cannot be analysed logically, for this only gives rise to such paradoxes.

See also: **Greek philosophy, ancient; logic; paradox**

Further reading: Clark (2002); Lee (1967); Salmon (2001)

Zoroastrianism

Zoroastrianism was a religious school of thought founded by the Persian philosopher Zarathustra in the 6th century BCE. Zarathustra taught a form of monotheism, that there is only one God, thus breaking with the established polytheistic religions of the time. This God, called Ahura Mazda, was said to be benevolent (all-good), omnipotent (all-powerful), omniscient (all-knowing), omnipresent (everywhere) and the creator of all things. Zoroastrianism was clearly a strong influence on the conceptions of God in Christianity, Judaism and Islam. The presence of good and evil in the world were explained by Ahura Mazda creating twin spirits, one of whom was good and the other evil. Zarathustra was also the name given to the central character in Nietzsche's *Thus Spake Zarathustra* (1885), although there is little connection between the beliefs of the original Zarathustra and Nietzsche's creation.

See also: **creationism; evil; God; Nietzsche**

Further reading: Boyce (2001); Clark (1998); Waterhouse (1934)

Z

References

Adams, E.W. (1975) *The Logic of Conditionals*, Oxford, Oxford University Press.

Adams, I. and Dyson, R.W. (2007) *Fifty Major Political Thinkers* (2nd edn), New York, Routledge.

Adams, M.M. and Adams, R.M. (eds) (1990) *The Problem of Evil*, Oxford, Oxford University Press.

Adler (1927) *Dialectic*, London, Paul, Trench, Trubner & Co.

Adorno, T.W. (1966], 1997) *Negative Dialectics* (trans. E.B. Ashton), New York, Continuum.

Adorno, T.W. ([1970], 1997) *Aesthetic Theory* (trans. R. Hullot-Kentor), Minneapolis, University of Minnesota Press.

Alexander, T.M. (1987) *John Dewey's Theory of Art, Experience, and Nature: The Horizons of Feeling*, Albany, State University of New York Press.

Allison, H. (1987) *Benedict Spinoza: An Introduction*, New Haven, Yale University Press.

Alston, W.P. (ed.) (2002) *Realism & Antirealism*, Ithaca, NY, Cornell University Press.

Anagnostopoulos, G. (ed.) (2009) *A Companion to Aristotle*, Oxford, Blackwell.

Annas, J. (1993) *The Morality of Happiness*, New York, Oxford University Press.

Appiah, K.A. (1992) *In My Father's House: Africa in the Philosophy of Culture*, New York, Oxford University Press.

Appiah, K.A. and Gutmann, A. (1996) *Color Conscious: The Political Morality of Race* (Princeton, Princeton University Press.

Archer, M.S. (1995) *Realist Social Theory: The Morphogenetic Approach*, Cambridge, Cambridge University Press.

Archer, M.S. (2000) *Being Human: The Problem of Agency*, Montreal and Kingston, McGill–Queen's University Press.

Archer, M.S., Bhaskar, R., Collier, A., Lawson, T. and Norrie, A. (eds) (1998) *Critical Realism: Essential Readings*, London, Routledge.

Arendt, H. (1951) *The Origins of Totalitarianism*, New York, Harcourt.

Arendt, H. (1958) *The Human Condition*, Chicago, University of Chicago Press.

Arendt, H. (1962) *On Revolution*, New York, Penguin.

Arendt, H. (1970) On Violence, New York, Harcourt.

Ariew, R. (1976) *Ockham's Razor: A Historical and Philosophical Analysis of Ockham's Principle of Parsimony*, Champaign-Urbana, University of Illinois Press.

Aristotle ([350 BCEa], 1984) 'Metaphysics', in J. Barnes (ed.) *The Complete Works of Aristotle: Volumes I and II*, Princeton, Princeton University Press.

Aristotle ([350 BCEb], 1984) 'Nicomachean Ethics', in J. Barnes (ed.) *The Complete Works of Aristotle: Volumes I and II*, Princeton, Princeton University Press.

Armour-Garb, B. and Beall, J.C. (eds) (2005) *Deflationary Truth*, Chicago, Open Court Publishing.

Armstrong, D.M. (1963) 'Is Introspective Knowledge Incorrigible?' *Philosophical Review* 72, 417–432.

Armstrong, D.M. (1968) *A Materialist Theory of Mind*, London, Routledge.

Armstrong, D.M. (1973) *Belief, Truth and Knowledge*, Cambridge, Cambridge University Press.

Armstrong, D.M. (1978) *Universals and Scientific Realism*, Cambridge, Cambridge University Press.

Armstrong, D.M. (1989) *Universals: An Opinionated Introduction*, Boulder, CO, Westview Press.

Armstrong, D.M. (1997) *A World of States of Affairs*, Cambridge, Cambridge University Press.

Armstrong, D.M. (2004) *Truth and Truthmakers*, Cambridge, Cambridge University Press.

Armstrong, J.A. and Botzler, R.G. (eds) (2003) *The Animal Ethics Reader*, London, Routledge.

Armstrong, K. (1994) *A History of God: The 4,000-Year Quest of Judaism, Christianity and Islam*, New York, Ballantine Books.

Arpaly, N. (2003) *Unprincipled Virtue: An Inquiry into Moral Agency*, New York, Oxford University Press.

Ashcraft, M.H. (2002) *Cognition*, Upper Saddle River, NJ, Prentice-Hall.

Astley, J., Brown, D. and Loades, A. (2003) *Evil: A Reader*, London, T. & T. Clark.

Audi, R. (1998) *Epistemology: A Contemporary Introduction to the Theory of Knowledge*, London, Routledge.

Augustine ([386–387], 1995) 'Against the Skeptics', in *Against the Academicians and the Teacher* (trans. P. King), Indianapolis, Hackett Publishing.

Augustine ([391–401], 1961) *Confessions*, Harmondsworth, Penguin.

Austin, J.L. (1961) *Philosophical Papers*, Oxford, Clarendon Press.

Austin, J.L. (1962a) *How To Do Things With Words*, Cambridge, MA, MIT Press.

Austin, J.L. (1962b) *Sense and Sensibilia*, Oxford, Clarendon Press.

Avramides, A. (2001) *Other Minds*, London, Routledge.

Ayer, A.J. (1935) 'The Criterion of Truth', *Analysis*, 3, 28–32.

Ayer, A.J. (1936) *Language, Truth, and Logic*, London, Gollancz.

Ayer, A.J. (1940) *The Foundations of Empirical Knowledge*, London, Macmillan.

Ayer, A.J. (ed.) (1959) *Logical Positivism*, London, Allen & Unwin.

Ayer, A.J. (1969) *Metaphysics and Common Sense*, London, Macmillan.

Ayer, A.J. (1984) *Freedom and Morality and Other Essays*, Oxford, Clarendon Press.

Badmington, N. (ed.) (2000) *Posthumanism*, Basingstoke, Palgrave.

Baggini, J. (2004) *What's It All About? Philosophy and the Meaning of Life*, Oxford, Oxford University Press.

Baggott, J. (2004) *Beyond Measure: Modern Physics, Philosophy and the Meaning of Quantum Theory*, Oxford, Oxford University Press.

Baghramian, M. (2004) *Relativism*, Abingdon, Routledge.

Baier, K. (1958) *The Moral Point of View*, Ithaca, Cornell University Press.

Baker, G. and Morris, K.J. (2002) *Descartes' Dualism*, London, Routledge.

Baldwin, T. (1990) *G.E. Moore*, London, Routledge.

Baldwin, T. (ed.) (1993) *Moore: Selected Writings*, London, Routledge.

Barnes, J. (ed.) (1984) *The Complete Works of Aristotle: Volumes I and I*, Princeton, Princeton University Press.

Barnes, J. (ed.) (1995) *The Cambridge Companion to Aristotle*, Cambridge, Cambridge University Press.

Baron, J. (2006) *Against Bioethics*, Cambridge, MA, MIT Press.

Batchelor, S. (1997) *Buddhism Without Beliefs*, London, Riverhead Books.

Baumeister, R.F. and Beck, A. (1999) *Evil: Inside Human Violence and Cruelty*, New York, Henry Holt.

Beauchamp, T.L. and Rosenberg, A. (1981) *Hume and the Problem of Causation*, New York, Oxford University Press.

Beebee, H. and Dodd, J. (eds) (2005) *Truthmakers: The Contemporary Debate*, New York, Oxford University Press.

Beiser, F.C. (2005) *Hegel*, London, Routledge.

Bekoff, A.C. and Lauder, G. (eds) (1998) *Nature's Purposes*, Cambridge, MA, MIT Press.

Bell, D. (1990) *Husserl*, London, Routledge.

Bell, L.A. and Blumenfeld, D. (eds) (1995) *Overcoming Racism and Sexism*, Lanham, Rowman & Littlefield.

Benhabib, S. (1992) *Situating the Self: Gender, Community and Postmodernism in Contemporary Ethics*, Cambridge, Polity.

Benhabib, S. (1996) *The Reluctant Modernism of Hannah Arendt*, London, Sage.

Benjamin, A. (ed.) (1989) *The Lyotard Reader*, Oxford, Blackwell.

Benn, P. (1998) *Ethics*, London, UCL Press.

Bennett, J. (1988) *Events and Their Names*, Oxford, Clarendon Press.

Bennett, J. (2003) *A Philosophical Guide to Conditionals*, Oxford, Clarendon Press.

Benson, B. (ed.) (2006) *A Companion to Plato*, Oxford, Blackwell.

Benson, P. (1994) 'Free Agency and Self-worth', *Journal of Philosophy*, 91(12), 650–658.

Bentham, J. ([1789], 2005) *An Introduction to the Principles of Morals and Legislation*, Chicago, University of Chicago Press.

Bentham, J. ([1859], 2001) *The Works of Jeremy Bentham. Published under the Superintendence of His Executor, John Bowring (Vol. I–XI)*, Boston, MA, Elibron Classics.

Bergson, H. ([1907], 1998) *Creative Evolution* (trans. A. Mitchell), New York, Dover.

Berkeley, G. ([1709], 2005) *An Essay Towards a New Theory of Vision*, Cirencester, The Echo Library.

Berkeley, G. ([1710], 1998) *A Treatise Concerning the Principles of Human Knowledge*, Oxford and New York, Oxford University Press.

Berkeley, G. ([1713], 1998) *Three Dialogues Between Hylas and Philonous*, Oxford and New York, Oxford University Press.

Bernasconi, R. (ed.) (2001) *Race*, Oxford, Blackwell.

Bernd, M. and Higgins, K.M. (eds) (1996) *The Cambridge Companion to Nietzsche*, Cambridge, Cambridge University Press.

Bhaskar, R. (1997) *A Realist Theory of Science*, London, Verso.

Billington, R. (1997) *Understanding Eastern Philosophy*, London, Routledge.

Bird, A. (1998) *Philosophy of Science*, London, UCL Press.

Bird, A. (2000) *Thomas Kuhn*, Chesham, Acumen.

Blaauw, M. (ed.) (2005) *Epistemological Contextualism*, Amsterdam, Rodopi.

Blackburn, S. (2001) *Being Good: An Introduction to Ethics*, Oxford, Oxford University Press.

Blackburn, S. (2005) *Truth: A Guide for the Perplexed*, London, Penguin.

Blackmore, S.J. (2003) *Consciousness: An Introduction*, Oxford, Oxford University Press.

Blaug, R. and Schwarzmantel, J. (eds) (2001) *Democracy: A Reader*, Edinburgh, Edinburgh University Press.

Block, N. (1980) *Readings in the Philosophy of Psychology, Volumes 1 and 2*, Cambridge, MA, Harvard University Press.

Block, N. (1981) 'Psychologism and Behaviourism', *The Philosophical Review*, 90: 5–43.

Block, N., Flanagan, O.J. and Guzeldere, G. (1997) *The Nature of Consciousness: Philosophical Debates*, Cambridge, MA, MIT Press.

Boghossian, P. and Peacocke, C. (eds) (2000) *New Essays on the A Priori*, Oxford, Clarendon Press.

Bohm, D. ([1965], 1996) *The Special Theory of Relativity*, London, Routledge.

Bonevac, D.A. (1987) *Deduction: Introductory Symbolic Logic*, Palo Alto, CA, Mayfield.

Boyce, M. (2001) *Zoroastrians: Their Religious Beliefs and Practices* (2nd edn), London, Routledge.

Boyd, R., Gasper, P. and Trout, J.D. (eds) (1991) *The Philosophy of Science*, Cambridge, MA, MIT Press.

Braddon-Mitchell, D. and Jackson, F. (1996) *Philosophy of Mind and Cognition*, Oxford, Blackwell.

Bradley, F.H. ([1893], 1959) *Appearance and Reality: A Metaphysical Essay*, Oxford, Oxford University Press.

Brady, M. and Pritchard, D. (eds) (2003) *Moral and Epistemic Virtues*, Oxford, Blackwell.

Brandom, R. (ed.) (2000) *Rorty and His Critics*, Oxford, Blackwell.

Brenkert, G.G. (1991) *Political Freedom*, London, Routledge.

Brentano, F.C. ([1874], 1973) *Psychology from an Empirical Standpoint*, London, Routledge & Kegan Paul.

Brickhouse, T.C. and Smith, N.D. (1994) *Plato's Socrates*, New York, Oxford University Press.

Broad, C.D. (1978) *Kant: An Introduction*, Cambridge, Cambridge University Press.

Brown, C.M. (2005) *Aquinas and the Ship of Theseus: Solving Puzzles about Material Objects*, London, Continuum.

Brueckner, A.L. (1986) 'Brains in a Vat', *Journal of Philosophy*, 84(3), 148–167.

Buford, T.O. (ed.) (1970) *Essays on Other Minds*, Chicago, University of Illinois Press.

Burr, V. (1995) *An Introduction to Social Constructionism*, London, Routledge.

Butchvarov, P. (1979) *Being Qua Being*, Bloomington, Indiana University Press.

Butler, C. (2002) *Postmodernism: A Very Short Introduction*, Oxford, Oxford University Press.

Butler, J. (1988) 'Performative Acts and Gender Constitution: An Essay in Phenomenology and Feminist Theory', *Theatre Journal*, 40(4), 519–531.

Butler, J. (1990) *Gender Trouble: Feminism and the Subversion of Identity*, New York, Routledge.

Butler, J. (1993) *Bodies That Matter: On the Discursive Limits of 'Sex'*, New York, Routledge.

Butler, J. (2004) *Undoing Gender*, New York, Routledge.

Cahoone, L.E. (ed.) (1996) *From Modernism to Postmodernism: An Anthology*, Oxford, Blackwell.

Callcut, D. (ed.) (2009) *Reading Bernard Williams*, Abingdon, Routledge.

Campbell, K. (1990) *Abstract Particulars*, Oxford, Blackwell.

Campbell, T. (2006) *Rights: A Critical Introduction*, Abingdon, Routledge.

Camus, A. ([1942], 2000) *The Outsider* (trans. J. Laredo), London, Penguin Classics.

Carnap, R. ([1928], 1967) *The Logical Structure of the World* (trans. R.A. George), Berkeley, University of California Press.

Carr, B. and Mahalingam, I. (1997) *Companion Encyclopedia of Asian Philosophy*, London, Routledge.

Carter, I., Kramer, M.H. and Steiner, H. (eds) (2007) *Freedom: A Philosophical Anthology*, Oxford, Blackwell.

Casati, R. and Varzi, A.C. (eds) (1996) *Events*, Aldershot, Ashgate.

Cascardi, A.J. (1992) *The Subject of Modernity*, Cambridge, Cambridge University Press.

Casullo, A. (2003) *A Priori Justification*, Oxford, Oxford University Press.

Cavanagh, M. (2002) *Against Equality of Opportunity*, Oxford, Clarendon Press.

Cedarblom, J. and Paulsen, D.W. (2006) *Critical Reasoning: Understanding and Criticizing Arguments and Theories* (6th edn), Belmont, CA, Wadsworth.

Chadwick, H. (1986) *Augustine*, Oxford, Oxford University Press.

Chalmers, D.J. (1996) *The Conscious Mind: In Search of a Fundamental Theory*, Oxford, Oxford University Press.

Chan, W. (1973) *A Source Book in Chinese Philosophy*, Princeton, Princeton University Press.

Chandler, D. (2002) *Semiotics: The Basics*, Abingdon, Routledge.

Chappell, V. (1994) *The Cambridge Guide to Locke*, Cambridge, Cambridge University Press.

Cheng, C. and Bunnin, N. (2002) *Contemporary Chinese Philosophy*, Oxford, Blackwell.

Chodrow, N. (1978) *The Reproduction of Mothering: Psychoanalysis and the Sociology of Gender*, Chicago, University of Illinois Press.

Chriss, J.J. (2007) *Social Contract: An Introduction*, Cambridge, Polity Press.

Churchland, P.M. (1981) 'Eliminative Materialism and the Propositional Attitudes', *Journal of Philosophy*, 78, 67–90.

Churchland, P.M. (1988) *Matter and Consciousness* (2nd edn), Cambridge, MA, MIT Press.

Churchland, P.S. (1986) *Neurophilosophy: Toward a Unified Science of the Mind/Brain*, Cambridge, MA, MIT Press.

Civil Liberty, available online at: http://www.civilliberty.org.uk/ (accessed 24/10/2009)

Clark, A. (1997) *Being There: Putting Brain, Body, and World Together Again*, Cambridge, MA, MIT Press.

Clark, A. and Chalmers, D.J. (1998) 'The Extended Mind', *Analysis*, 58, 7–19.

Clark, M. (2002) *Paradoxes from A to Z*, London, Routledge.

Clark, M.T. (1994) *Augustine*, London, Geoffrey Chapman.

Clark, P. (1998) *Zoroastrianism: An Introduction to an Ancient Faith*, Brighton, Sussex Academic Press.

Clark, S.R.L. (1977) *The Moral Status of Animals*, Oxford, Oxford University Press.

Cohen, M. (2005) *Wittgenstein's Beetle and Other Classic Thought Experiments*, Oxford, Blackwell.

Cohen, S.M., Curd, P. and Reeve, C.D.C. (eds) (2005) *Readings in Ancient Greek Philosophy* (3rd edn), Cambridge, MA, Hackett Publishing..

Cohen-Almagor, R. (1994) *The Boundaries of Liberty and Tolerance: The Struggle Against Kahanism in Israel*, Gainesville, University Press of Florida.

Colebrook, C. (2006) *Deleuze: A Guide for the Perplexed*, London, Continuum.

Collier, A. (1994) *Critical Realism: An Introduction to Roy Bhaskar's Philosophy*, London, Verso.

Comte, A. ([1856], 2007) *A General View of Positivism* (trans. J.H. Bridges), Whitefish, MT, Kessinger.

Connor, S. (ed.) (2004) *The Cambridge Companion to Postmodernism*, Cambridge, Cambridge University Press.

Cook, J.W. (1999) *Morality and Cultural Differences*, New York, Oxford University Press.

Cooper, D.E. (ed.) (1992) *A Companion to Aesthetics*, Oxford, Blackwell.

Cooper, D.E. (1996a) *Thinkers of our Time: Heidegger* , London, The Claridge Press.

Cooper, D.E. (1996b) *World Philosophies*, Oxford, Blackwell.

Cooper, J. (ed.) (1997) *Plato: The Complete Works*, Indianapolis, Hackett Publishing.

Cornforth, M.C. (1961) *Dialectical Materialism: An Introduction*, London, Lawrence & Wishart.

Cottingham, J. (1984) *Rationalism*, London, Paladin.

Cottingham, J. (1986) *Descartes*, Oxford, Blackwell.

Cottingham, J. (ed.) (1992) *The Cambridge Companion to Descartes*, Cambridge, Cambridge University Press.

Coutinho, S. (2004) *Zhuangzi and Early Chinese Philosophy*, Aldershot, Ashgate.

Craig, W. and Moreland, J. (eds) (2000) *Naturalism: A Critical Analysis*, London, Routledge.

Crane, T. and Patterson, S. (eds) (2000) *History of the Mind–Body Problem*, London, Routledge.

Crick, B. (2002) *Democracy: A Very Short Introduction*, Oxford, Oxford University Press.

Crisp, R. and Slote, M. (eds) (1997) *Virtue Ethics*, Oxford, Oxford University Press.

Critchley, S. and Schroeder, W. (eds) (1998) *A Companion to Continental Philosophy*, Oxford, Blackwell.

Curd, M. and Cover, J.A. (eds) (1998) *Philosophy of Science: The Central Issues*, New York, W.W. Norton & Co.

Currie, G. (1982) *Frege: An Introduction to his Philosophy*, Brighton, Harvester Press.

Curtis, M. (ed.) (1998) *Marxism: The Inner Dialogues*, Somerset, NJ., Transaction Publishers.

Cutrofello, A. (2005) *Continental Philosophy: A Contemporary Introduction*, London, Routledge.

Dahl, R.A. (2000) *On Democracy*, London, Yale University Press.

Daly, M. (1979) *Gyn/Ecology: The Metaethics of Radical Feminism*, London, Women's Press.

Dancy, J. (1985) *An Introduction to Contemporary Epistemology*, Oxford, Blackwell.

Dancy, J. (1987) *Berkeley: An Introduction*, Oxford Blackwell.

Darwall, S. (ed.) (2003a) *Consequentialism*, Oxford, Blackwell.

Darwall, S. (ed.) (2003b) *Deontology*, Oxford, Blackwell.

Darwin, C. ([1859], 1985) *The Origin of Species*, London, Penguin Classics.

Daston, L. and Galison, P. (2007) *Objectivity*, New York, Zone.

Davidson, D. (1982) 'Rational Animals', *Dialectica*, 36, 318–327.

Davidson, D. (1984) *Inquiries into Truth and Interpretation*, Oxford, Clarendon Press.

Davidson, D. (2001) *Essays on Actions and Events* (2nd edn), Oxford, Clarendon Press.

Davidson, D. (2005) *Truth, Language, and History: Philosophical Essay*, Oxford, Oxford University Press.

Davies, B. and Leftow, B. (eds) (2004) *The Cambridge Guide to Anselm*, Cambridge, Cambridge University Press.

Davies, M. and Stone, T. (eds) (1995) *Folk Psychology: The Theory of Mind Debate*, Oxford, Blackwell.

Davion, V. and Wolf, C. (eds) (1999) *The Idea of Political Liberalism: Essays on Rawls*, Lanham, MD, Rowman & Littlefield.

de Beauvoir, S. (1944) *Pyrrhus et Cinéas*, Paris, Gallimard.

de Beauvoir, S. ([1947], 1996) *The Ethics of Ambiguity* (trans. B. Frechtman), New York, Citadel Press.

de Beauvoir, S. ([1949], 1972) *The Second Sex* (trans. H.M. Parshley), Harmondsworth, Penguin.

Deleuze, G. (1953) *Empiricism and Subjectivity*, New York, Columbia University Press.

Deleuze, G. (1968) *Difference and Repetition*, New York, Columbia University Press.

Deleuze, G. and Guattari, F. (1972) *Anti-Oedipus – Capitalism and Schizophrenia*, New York, Viking Press.

Deleuze, G. and Guattari, F. (1980) *A Thousand Plateaus – Capitalism and Schizophrenia*, Minneapolis, University of Minnesota Press.

Della Rocca, M. (2008) *Spinoza*, New York, Routledge.

Dennett, D.C. (1986) *Content and Consciousness*, London, Routledge.

Dennett, D.C. (1987) *The Intentional Stance*, Cambridge, MA, MIT Press.

Dent, N.J.H. (2005) *Rousseau*, Abingdon, Routledge.

DePaul, M.R. and Zagzebski, L.T. (eds) (2003) *Intellectual Virtues: Perspectives from Ethics and Epistemology*, New York, Oxford University Press.

Derrida, J. ([1967a], 1997) *Of Grammatology* (trans. G.C. Spivak), Baltimore, Johns Hopkins University Press.

Derrida, J. ([1967b], 1978) *Writing and Difference* (trans. A. Bass), Chicago, University of Chicago Press.

Derrida, J. ([1972a], 1981) *Dissemination* (trans. B. Johnson), Chicago, University of Chicago Press.

Derrida, J. ([1972b], 1981) *Positions* (trans. A. Bass), London, Athlone.

Derrida, J. (1995) 'The Time is Out of Joint', in A. Haverkamp (ed.) *Deconstruction is/in America* (trans. P. Kamuf), New York, New York University Press.

Descartes, R. (1637) *Discours de la Méthode*, Paris, Librairie Larousse.

Descartes, R. ([1641], 1996) *Meditations on First Philosophy: With Selections from the Objections and Replies* (trans. J. Cottingham) (2nd edn), Cambridge, Cambridge University Press.

Desjardins, R. (2004) *Plato and the Good: Illuminating the Darkling Vision*, Leiden and Boston, Brill.

Devitt, M. (1991) *Realism and Truth* (2nd edn), Princeton, Princeton University Press.

Dewey, J. (1903) *Studies in Logical Theory*, Chicago, University of Chicago Press.

Dewey, J. ([1916], 1966) *Democracy and Education: An Introduction to the Philosophy of Education*, New York, Free Press.

Dewey, J. (1925) *Experience and Nature*, London and Chicago, Open Court Publishing.

Dilman, I. (1999) *Free Will: An Historical and Philosophical Introduction*, London, Routledge.

Diprose, R. and Reynolds, J. (2008) *Merleau-Ponty: The Key Concepts*, Stocksfield, Acumen.

Docherty, T. (ed.) (1993) *Postmodernism: A Reader*, London, Harvester Wheatsheaf.

Donner, W. (1993) *The Liberal Self: John Stuart Mill's Moral and Political Philosophy*, Ithaca, Cornell University Press.

Dostal, R.J. (ed.) (2002) *The Cambridge Companion to Gadamer*, Cambridge, Cambridge University Press.

Dretske, F. (1981) *Knowledge and the Flow of Information*, Cambridge, MA, MIT Press.

Dreyfus, H.L. (1991) *Being-in-the-World: A Commentary on Heidegger's Being and Time Division I*, Cambridge, MA, MIT Press.

Dreyfus, H.L. (1992) *What Computers Still Can't Do*, New York, MIT Press.

Dreyfus, H.L. and Wrathall, M.A. (eds) (2006) *A Companion to Phenomenology and Existentialism*, Oxford, Blackwell.

Due, R. (2007) *Deleuze*, Cambridge, Polity Press.

Duhem, P. (1954) *The Aim and Structure of Physical Theory*, Princeton, Princeton University Press.

Dummett, M. (1977) *Elements of Intuitionism*, Oxford, Clarendon Press.

Dummett, M. (1981) *The Interpretation of Frege's Philosophy*, Cambridge, MA, Harvard University Press.

Dupré, J. (1993) *The Disorder of Things: Metaphysical Foundations of the Disunity of Science*, London, Harvard University Press.

Dworkin, R. (1986) *Law's Empire*, Cambridge, MA, Harvard University Press.

Eagleton, T. (1991) *Ideology: An Introduction*, London, Verso.

Earman, J. (ed.) (1992) *Inference, Explanation and Other Frustrations: Essays in the Philosophy of Science*, Berkeley, University of California Press.

Ellis, B. (2002) *The Philosophy of Nature*, Chesham, Acumen.

Elshof, G.T. (2005) *Introspection Vindicated: An Essay in Defense of the Perceptual Knowledge of Self Knowledge*, Aldershot, Acumen.

Endicott, T.A.O. (2000) *Vagueness in Law*, New York, Oxford University Press.

Engel, S.M. (1994) *With Good Reason: An Introduction to Informal Fallacies* (5th edn), New York, St. Martin's Press.

Englebretsen, G. (2006) *Bare Facts and Truth: An Essay on the Correspondence Theory of Truth*, Aldershot, Ashgate.

Erikson, E.H. (1963) *Childhood and Society* (2nd edn), New York, Norton.

Erwin, E. (ed.) (2002) *The Freud Encyclopedia: Theory, Therapy and Culture*, London, Routledge.

Esfield, M. (2001) *Holism in Philosophy of Mind and Philosophy of Physics*, Dordrecht, Kluwer Academic Publishers.

Etienne, G. (2002) *God and Philosophy* (2nd edn), London, Yale University Press.

Eugenie, C.S. (2005) *Evolution vs. Creationism: An Introduction*, Berkeley, University of California Press.

Evans, G. and Altham, J.E.J. (1973) 'The Causal Theory of Names', *Proceedings of the Aristotelian Society*, Supplementary Volume 47, 187–225.

Evans, G.R. (1989) *Anselm*, Oxford, Clarendon Press.

Ewing, A.C. (1934) *Idealism: A Critical Survey*, Palo Alto, Stanford University Press.

Eysteinsson, A. (1990) *The Concept of Modernism*, Ithaca, Cornell University Press.

Fairweather, A. and Zagzebski, L.T. (eds) (2001) *Virtue Epistemology: Essays on Epistemic Virtue and Responsibility*, New York, Oxford University Press.

Farrelly, C. (2004) *An Introduction to Contemporary Political Theory*, London, Sage.

Faulconer, J.E. (2003) *Transcendence in Philosophy and Religion*, Bloomington, Indiana University Press.

Fiala, A.G. (2005) *Tolerance and the Ethical Life*, London, Continuum.

Finlayson, A. and Valentine, J. (eds) (2002) *Politics and Post-Structuralism: An Introduction*, Edinburgh, Edinburgh University Press.

Fischer, J.M. (ed.) (1993) *The Metaphysics of Death*, Palo Alto, CA, Stanford University Press.

Fischer, J.M., Kane, R., Pereboom, D. and Vargas, M. (2007) *Four Views on Free Will*, Oxford, Blackwell.

Fitzgerald, A.D. (ed.) (1999) *Augustine Through the Ages: An Encyclopedia*, Grand Rapids, MI, Eerdmans.

Flanagan, O. and Rorty, A.O. (eds) (1990) *Identity, Character and Morality*, Cambridge, MA, MIT Press.

Flood, G. (ed.) (2003) *Blackwell Companion to Hinduism*, Oxford, Blackwell.

Fodor, J.A. (1998) *Concepts: Where Cognitive Science Went Wrong*, Oxford, Clarendon Press.

Fodor, J.A. (2001) *The Mind Doesn't Work that Way: The Scope and Limitations of Computational Psychology*, Cambridge, MA, Bradford Book.

Fodor, J.A. and LePore, E. (1992) *Holism: A Shopper's Guide*, Oxford, Blackwell.

Foster, J. (1991) *The Immaterial Self*, London, Routledge.

Foucault, M. ([1961], 2006) *The History of Madness in the Classical Age* (ed. J. Khalfa and trans. J. Murphy and J. Khalfa), London, Routledge.

Foucault, M. ([1969], 1972) *The Archaeology of Knowledge* (trans. A.M. Sheridan-Smith), London, Tavistock.

Foucault, M. ([1976], 1978) *The History of Sexuality: An Introduction* (trans. R. Hurley), New York, Pantheon Books.

Foucault, M. (1980) *Power/Knowledge: Selected Interviews and Other Writings, 1972–1977* (ed. C. Gordon and trans. C. Gordon, L. Marshall, J. Mepham and K. Soper), New York, Pantheon Books.

Foucault, M. (1984) *The Foucault Reader* (ed. P. Rabinow), Harmondsworth, Penguin.

Frederickson, G. (2002) *Racism: A Short History*, Princeton, Princeton University Press.

Freeman, S. (ed.) (2003) *The Cambridge Companion to Rawls*, Cambridge, Cambridge University Press.

Freeman, S. (2007) *Rawls*, London, Routledge.

Frege, G. ([1892a], 1980) 'Concept and Object', in P. Geach and M. Black (eds) *Translations from the Philosophical Writings of Gottlob Frege* (trans. P. Geach and M. Black) (3rd edn), Oxford, Blackwell.

Frege, G. ([1892b], 1980) 'On Sense and Reference', in P. Geach and M. Black (eds) *Translations from the Philosophical Writings of Gottlob Frege* (trans. P. Geach and M. Black) (3rd edn), Oxford, Blackwell.

Frege, G. ([1918], 1980) 'The Thought. A Logical Enquiry', in P. Geach and M. Black (eds) *Translations from the Philosophical Writings of Gottlob Frege* (trans. P. Geach and M. Black) (3rd edn), Oxford, Blackwell.

French, P.A., Wettstein, H.K. and Fischer, J.M. (2005) *Free Will and Moral Responsibility*, Oxford, Blackwell.

Freud, A. ([1936], 1966) *The Ego and the Mechanisms of Defence. The Writings of Anna Freud Vol. 2*, New York, International Universities Press.

Freud, S. ([1900], 1999) *The Interpretation of Dreams* (trans. J. Crick), Oxford, Oxford University Press.

Freud, S. ([1901], 2003) *The Psychopathology of Everyday Life* (trans. A. Bell), New York, Penguin Classics.

Freud, S. ([1905], 1953) 'Three Essays on the Theory of Sexuality', in J. Strachey (ed.) *The Standard Edition of the Complete Psychological Works of Sigmund Freud, Volume VII (1901–1905): A Case of Hysteria, Three Essays on Sexuality and Other Works*, London, Hogarth Press, pp. 123–246.

Freud, S. ([1913], 1958) 'Totem and Taboo', in J. Strachey (ed.) *The Standard Edition of the Complete Psychological Works of Sigmund Freud Vol. XIII*, London: Hogarth Press, pp. 1–162.

Freud, S. ([1914], 1957) 'On Narcissism: An Introduction', In J. Strachey (ed.) *The Standard Edition of the Complete Psychological Works of Sigmund Freud, Vol. XIV* London, Hogarth Press, pp. 67–102.

Freud, S. ([1923], 1949) *The Ego And The Id*. London: Hogarth Press.

Freud, S. ([1920], 1975) *Beyond the Pleasure Principle*, New York, Norton.

Fricker, M. (1995) 'Intuition and Reason', *The Philosphical Quarterly*, 179(45), 181–189.

Frie, R. (1997) *Subjectivity and Intersubectivity in Modern Philosophy and Psychoanalysis: A study of Sartre, Binswanger, Lacan and Habermas*, Lanham, MD, Rowman & Littlefield.

Friedan, B. (1963) *The Feminist Mystique*, New York, Norton.

Friedman, M. (1999) *Reconsidering Logical Positivism*, New York, Cambridge University Press.

Fry, I. (2000) *The Emergence of Life: A Historical and Scientific Overview*, London, Free Association Books.

Gabbay, D.M., Johnson, R.H., Ohlbach, H.J. and Woods, J. (eds) (2002) *Handbook of the Logic of Argument and Inference: The Turn Towards the Practical*, Amsterdam, Elsevier Science.

Gadamer, H. ([1960], 2000) *Truth and Method* (trans. J. Weinsheimer and D.G. Marshall), New York, Continuum.

Gadamer, H. ([1976], 2008) *Philosophical Hermeneutics* (trans. D.E. Linge), Berkeley, University of California Press.

Gadamer, H. (1981) *Reason in the Age of Science* (trans. F.G. Lawrence), Cambridge, MA, MIT Press.

Gale, R.M. (1999) *The Divided Self of William James*, Cambridge, Cambridge University Press.

Gale, R.M. (2005) *The Philosophy of William James*, Cambridge, Cambridge University Press.

Gallagher, S. and Shear, J. (eds) (1999) *Models of the Self*, Exeter, Imprint Academic.

Gardiner, P.L. (2002) *Kierkegaard: A Very Short Introduction*, Oxford, Oxford University Press.

Garrett, B. (1998) *Personal Identity and Self-consciousness*, London, Routledge.

Garrett, D. (ed.) (1996) *The Cambridge Companion to Spinoza*, Cambridge, Cambridge University Press.

Gauch, H.G. (2003) *Scientific Method in Practice*, Cambridge, Cambridge University Press.

Gaus, G.F. (1990) *Value and Justification: The Foundations of Liberal Theory*, New York, Cambridge University Press.

Gauthier, D. (ed.) (1970) *Morality and Rational Self-Interest*, Englewood Cliffs, NJ, Prentice-Hall.

Gay, P. (ed.) (1995) *The Freud Reader*, London, Vintage.

Gellner, E. (2006) *Nations and Nationalism* (2nd edn), Oxford, Blackwell.

Gendler, T. and Hawthorne, J.P. (eds) (2002) *Conceivability and Possibility*, Oxford, Oxford University Press.

Gensler, H.J. (1998) *Ethics: A Contemporary Introduction*, London, Routledge.

Geoghegan, V. (1987) *Utopianism and Marxism*, London, Methuen.

Gettier, E.L. (1963) 'Is Justified True Belief Knowledge?', *Analysis*, 23, 121–123.

Gibson, R.F. (ed.) (2004) *The Cambridge Companion to Quine*, New York, Cambridge University Press.

Gilman, S.L., Birmele, J., Geller, J. and Greenberg, V.D. (eds) (1994) *Reading Freud's Reading*, New York, New York University Press.

Goble, L. (2001) *The Blackwell Guide to Philosophical Logic*, Oxford, Blackwell.

Godfrey-Smith, P. (2003) *Theory and Reality: An Introduction to the Philosophy of Science*, Chicago, University of Chicago Press.

Goldin, P.R. (2005) *After Confucius*, Honolulu, University of Hawaii Press.

Goldman, A.I. (1979) 'What is Justified Belief?', in G.S. Pappas (ed.) *Justification and Knowledge* , Dordrecht, D. Reidel, pp. 1–23.

Goldman, A.I. (1986) *Epistemology and Cognition*, Cambridge, MA, Harvard University Press.

Gonzalez, F.J. (1998) *Dialectic and Dialogue: Plato's Practice of Philosophical Inquiry*, Evanston, IL, Northwestern University Press.

Gordjin, B. and Chadwick, R.F. (eds) (2008) *Medical Enhancement and Posthumanity*, New York, Springer-Verlag.

Gould, S.J. (2002) *The Structure of Evolutionary Theory*, Cambridge, MA, Harvard University Press.

Gowans, C.W. (ed.) (2000) *Moral Disagreements: Classic and Contemporary*, London, Routledge.

Graham, A.C. (2001) *Chuang-tzŭ: The Inner Chapters*, Indianapolis, Hackett Publishing.

Gray, C.H. (2001) *Cyborg Citizen: Politics on the Posthuman Age*, New York, Routledge.

Gray, T. (1991) *Freedom*, London, Macmillan.

Grayling, A.C. (1986) *Berkeley: The Central Arguments*, La Salle, IL, Open Court.

Grayling, A.C. (1996) *Russell*, Oxford, Oxford University Press.

Grayling, A.C. (1997) *An Introduction to Philosophical Logic* (3rd edn), Oxford, Blackwell.
Grayling, A.C. (2001) *Wittgenstein: A Very Short Introduction*, Oxford, Oxford University Press.
Grayling, A.C. (2008) *Scepticism and the Possibility of Knowledge*, London, Continuum.
Greco, J. and Sosa, E. (eds) (1999) *The Blackwell Guide to Epistemology*, Oxford, Blackwell.
Grewendorf, G. and Meggle, G. (eds) (2002) *Speech Acts, Mind and Social Reality*, Dordrecht, Kluwer Academic Publishers.
Grice, H.P. and Strawson, P.F. (1956) 'In Defense of a Dogma', *Philosophical Review*, LXV, 2, 141–158.
Griffin, N. (ed.) (2003) *The Cambridge Companion to Bertrand Russell*, Cambridge, Cambridge University Press.
Grøn, A. (2008) *The Concept of Anxiety in Søren Kierkegaard*, Macon, GA, Mercer University Press.
Grondin, J. (1994) *Introduction to Philosophical Hermeneutics*, New Haven, Yale University Press.
Grondin, J. (2002) *The Philosophy of Gadamer*, Chesham, Acumen.
Grondin, J. (ed.) (2007) *The Gadamer Reader: A Bouquet of Later Writings*, Chicago, Northwestern University Press.
Guignon, C. (2004) *On Being Authentic*, London, Routledge.
Gumperz, J.J. and Levinson, S.C. (1996) *Rethinking Linguistic Relativity*, Cambridge, Cambridge University Press.
Gupta, A. (2006) *Empiricism and Experience*, Oxford, Oxford University Press.
Gupta, C. (2002) *Realism Versus Antirealism*, Lanham, MD, Rowman & Littlefield.
Guthrie, W.K.C. (1971) *The Sophists*, Cambridge, Cambridge University Press.
Guttenplan, S.D. (1997) *The Language of Logic: An Introduction to Formal Logic*, Malden, MA, Blackwell.
Gutting, G. (1980) *Paradigms and Revolutions*, Oxford, Oxford University Press.
Gutting, G. (ed.) (2005) *The Cambridge Companion to Foucault*, Cambridge, Cambridge University Press.
Guyer, P. (ed.) (1992) *The Cambridge Companion to Kant*, Cambridge, Cambridge University Press.
Haack, S. (ed.) (2006) *Pragmatism, Old and New*, New York, Prometheus.
Habermas, J. ([1967], 1988) *On the Logic of the Social Sciences* (trans. S.W. Nicholson and J.A. Stark), Cambridge, MA, MIT Press.
Habermas, J. ([1971], 1973) *Theory and Practice* (trans. J. Viertel), Boston, MA, Beacon.
Habermas, J. ([1981a], 1984) *The Theory of Communicative Action: Volume I: Reason and the Rationalization of Society* (trans. T. McCarthy), Boston, MA, Beacon.
Habermas, J. ([1981b], 1987) *The Theory of Communicative Action: Volume II: Lifeworld and System* (trans. T. McCarthy), Boston, MA, Beacon.
Habermas, J. (1986) 'A Review of Gadamer's Truth and Method', in B.R. Wachterhauser (ed.) *Hermeneutics and Modern Philosophy* (trans. T. McCarthy and F. Dallamayr), Albany, State University of New York Press, pp. 243–276.
Hahn, L.E. (ed.) (1992) *The Philosophy of A.J. Ayer*, La Salle, IL, Open Court.
Hahn, L.E. (ed.) (1999) *The Philosophy of Donald Davidson*, Chicago, Open Court.
Haldane, R.B. (1926) *Human Experience: A Study of its Structure*, London, J. Murray.
Hales, S.D. and Welshon, R. (2000) *Nietzsche's Perspectivism*, Champain, University of Illinois Press.
Hall, D.E. (2004) *Subjectivity*, New York, Routledge.
Hall, E.W. (1952) *What is Value?: An Essay in Philosophical Analysis*, London, Routledge & Kegan Paul.
Hall, J.A. (ed.) (1988) *The State of the Nation: Ernest Gellner and the Theory of Nationalism*, Cambridge, Cambridge University Press.
Hamblin, C.L. (1970) *Fallacies*, London, Methuen.
Hamilton, P. (1996) *Historicism*, London, Routledge.
Hamilton, S. (2001) *Indian Philosophy: A Very Short Introduction*, Oxford, Oxford University Press.
Hanfling, O. (1981a) *Logical Positivism*, Oxford, Basil Blackwell.
Hanfling, O. (ed.) (1981b) *Essential Reasons in Logical Positivism*, Oxford Blackwell.
Hanfling, O. (ed.) (1992) *Philosophical Aesthetics: An Introduction*, Oxford, Blackwell.

Hanfling, O. (1999) *Ayer*, London, Routledge.

Hann, C.M. (1993) *Socialism: Ideals, Ideologies, and Local Practices*, Abingdon, Routledge.

Hansen, H.V. and Pinto, R.C. (eds) (1995) *Fallacies: Classical and Contemporary Readings*, University Park, PA, Penn State Press.

Hansen, P. (1993) *Hannah Arendt: Politics, History and Citizenship*, Cambridge, Polity Press.

Haraway, D. (1991) *Simians, Cyborgs, and Women: The Reinvention of Nature*, London, Free Association Books.

Hare, R.M. (1952) *The Language of Morals*, Oxford, Clarendon Press.

Hare, R.M. (1963a) *Descriptivism*, London, British Academy.

Hare, R.M. (1963b) *Freedom and Reason*, Oxford, Clarendon Press.

Hare, R.M. (1981) *Moral Thinking: Its Level, Method, and Point*, Oxford, Clarendon Press.

Hare, R.M. (1989) *Essays on Political Morality*, New York, Oxford University Press.

Harland, R. (1987) *Superstructuralism: The Philosophy of Structuralism and Post-Structuralism*, London, Methuen.

Harman, G. and Thomson, J.J. (1996) *Moral Relativism and Moral Objectivity*, Oxford, Blackwell.

Harmless, W.S.J. (2007) *Mystics*, New York, Oxford University Press.

Harper, A.W.J. (1997) *The Philosophy of Time*, New York, Edwin Mellen Press.

Harris, J. (ed.) (2001) *Bioethics*, Oxford, Oxford University Press.

Harrison, R. (1983) *Bentham*, London, Routledge.

Harvey, P. (1990) *An Introduction to Buddhism: Teachings, History and Practices*, Cambridge, Cambridge University Press.

Hastings, A. (1997) *The Construction of Nationhood: Ethnicity, Religion and Nationalism*, Cambridge: Cambridge University Press.

Hawkes, D. (1996) *Ideology*, London, Routledge.

Hawkes, T. (2003) *Structuralism and Semiotics* (2nd edn), London, Routledge.

Hawley, K. (2001) *How Things Persist*, Oxford, Clarendon Press.

Healey, R.A. (1991) *The Philosophy of Quantum Mechanics: An Interactive Interpretation*, Cambridge, Cambridge University Press.

Hecht, J. (2004) *Doubt: A History*, New York, HarperCollins.

Hegel, G.W.F. ([1807], 1977) *Phenomenology of the Spirit*, Oxford, Oxford University Press.

Hegel, G.W.F. ([1822], 1991) *Elements of the Philosophy of Right*, Cambridge, Cambridge University Press.

Heidegger, M. ([1927], 1997) *Being and Time* (trans. J. Macquarrie and E. Robinson), Oxford, Blackwell.

Heidegger, M. ([1953], 1959) *An Introduction to Metaphysics* (trans. R. Manheim), New Haven, Yale University Press.

Heidegger, M. ([1967], 1998) *Pathmarks* (originally published in 1967 as *Wegmarken*), Cambridge, Cambridge University Press.

Heil, J. (1998) *Philosophy of Mind*, London, Routledge.

Heine, S. and Wright, D.S. (eds) (2006) *Zen Classics: Formative Texts in the History of Zen Buddhism*, New York, Oxford University Press.

Herskovits, M.J. (1972) *Cultural Relativism: Perspectives in Cultural Pluralism*, New York, Random House.

Heshusius, L. and Ballard, K. (eds) (1996) *From Positivism to Interpretivism and Beyond: Tales of Transformation in Educational and Social Research (The Mind–Body Connection)*, New York, Teachers College Press.

Heyd, D. (1982) *Supererogation*, New York, Cambridge University Press.

Higginbotham, J., Pianesi, F. and Varzi, A.C. (eds) (2000) *Speaking of Events*, Oxford, Oxford University Press.

Hill, J.L. (1996) *The Case for Vegetarianism: Philosophy for a Small Planet*, Lanham, MD, Rowman & Littlefield.

Hill, T.E. (1992) *Dignity and Practical Reason in Kant's Moral Theory*, Ithaca, Cornell University Press.

Hill, T.E. (ed.) (2009) *The Blackwell Guide to Kant's Ethics*, Oxford, Blackwell.

Hobbes, T. ([1651], 2009) *Leviathan*, Oxford, Oxford University Press.

Hobbes, T. ([1655], 1981) *De Corpore* (trans. A.P. Martinich), Indianapolis, Hackett Publishing.

Hoffman, J. and Rosenkratz, G.S. (1994) *Substance Among Other Categories*, Cambridge, Cambridge University Press.

Hoffman, J. and Rosenkratz, G.S. (1997) *Substance: Its Nature and Existence*, London, Routledge.

Hofstadter, D.R. and Dennett, D.C. (1981) *The Mind's I: Fantasies and Reflections on Self and Soul*, Brighton, Harvester Press.

Holdcroft, D. (1978) *Words and Deeds: Problems in the Theory of Speech Acts*, Oxford, Clarendon.

Holdcroft, D. (1991) *Saussure: Signs, Systems, and Arbitrariness*, New York, Cambridge University Press.

Holland, J.H., Holyoak, K.J. and Nisbett, R.E. (1986) *Induction: Processes of Inference, Learning and Discovery*, Cambridge, MA, MIT Press.

Hollingdale, R.J. (1973) *Nietzsche*, London, Routledge & Kegan Paul.

Holmes, R. (1995) *The Transcendence of the World: Phenomenological Studies*, Ontario, Wilfried Laurier University Press.

Holstein, J.A. and Miller, G. (1993) *Reconsidering Social Constructionism: Debates in Social Problems Theory*, New York, Aldine de Gruyter.

Holyoak, K.J. and Morrison, R.G. (eds) (2005) *The Cambridge Handbook of Thinking and Reasoning*, Cambridge, Cambridge University Press.

Honderich, T. (1991) *Conservatism*, Boulder, CO, Perseus Book Group.

Honneth, A. (1995) *The Struggle for Recognition: The Moral Grammar of Social Conflicts* (trans. J. Anderson), Cambridge, Polity.

Honneth, A. and Joas, H. (eds) (1991) *Communicative Action: Essays on Jürgen Habermas's Theory of Communicative Action*, Cambridge, MA, Polity Press.

Hookway, C. (1990) *Scepticism*, London, Routledge.

Horgan, T. and Timmons, M. (2006) *Metaethics after Moore*, Oxford, Clarendon Press.

Horkheimer, M. and Adorno, T.W. ([1947], 2002) *Dialectic of Enlightenment* (trans. E. Jephcott), Stanford, Stanford University Press.

Horowitz, T. and Massey, G.J. (eds) (1991) *Thought Experiments in Science and Philosophy*, Lanham, MD, Rowman & Littlefield.

Horwich, P. (1998) *Truth* (2nd edn), New York, Oxford University Press.

Hossack, K. (2007) *The Metaphysics of Knowledge*, Oxford, Oxford University Press.

Howells, C. (ed.) (1992) *The Cambridge Companion to Sartre*, Cambridge, Cambridge University Press.

Howson, C. (1997) *Logic with Trees: An Introduction to Formal Logic*, London, Routledge.

Hoyningen-Huene, P. (1993) *Reconstructing Scientific Revolutions: Thomas S. Kuhn's Philosophy of Science* (trans. A.T. Levine), Chicago, Chicago University Press.

Hudson, W.D. (ed.) (1969) *The Is-Ought Question*, London, Macmillan.

Hughes, C. (2004) *Kripke: Names, Necessity, and Identity*, Oxford, Oxford University Press.

Hume, D. ([1739–1740], 1978) *A Treatise of Human Nature*, Oxford, Clarendon Press.

Hume, D. ([1748], 1993) *An Enquiry Concerning Human Understanding*, Indianapolis, Hackett Publishing.

Hume, D. ([1751], 1983) *An Enquiry Concerning the Principles of Morals*, Indianapolis, Hackett Publishing.

Hume, D. ([1757], 1957) *The Natural History of Religion*, Stanford, CA, Stanford University Press.

Hume, D. ([1779], 2007) *Dialogues Concerning Natural Religion*, Cambridge, Cambridge University Press.

Hursthouse, R. (1999) *On Virtue Ethics*, Oxford, Oxford University Press.

Hursthouse, R. (2000) *Ethics, Humans and Other Animals*, London, Routledge.

Husserl, E. ([1900–1901], 1973) *Logical Investigations* (trans. N.J. Findlay), London, Routledge.

Husserl, E. ([1913], 1982) *Ideas Pertaining to a Pure Phenomenology and a Phenomenological Philosophy* (trans. F. Kersten), The Hague, Nijhoff.

Husserl, E. ([1931], 1988) *Cartesian Meditations*, Dordrecht, Kluwer Academic.

Hutto, D.D. and Ratcliffe, M. (eds) (2007) *Folk Psychology Re-assessed*, London, Springer.

Hyland, P., Gomez, O. and Greensides, F. (eds) (2003) *The Enlightenment: A Sourcebook and Reader*, London, Routledge.

Hylton, P. (2007) *Quine*, New York, Routledge.

Inwood, B. (ed.) (2003) *The Cambridge Companion to the Stoics*, New York, Cambridge University Press.

Ivison, D. (2008) *Rights*, Stocksfield, Acumen.

Jackson, F. (1982) 'Ephiphenomenal Qualia', *Philosophical Quarterly*, 32, 127–136.

Jackson, F. (1986) 'What Mary Didn't Know', *Journal of Philosophy*, 84(5), 291–295.

Jacquette, D. (2002) *A Companion Guide to Philosophical Logic*, Oxford, Blackwell.

Jagger, J. (2002) *Judith Butler: Sexual Politics, Social Change and the Power of the Performative*, London, Routledge.

Jagose, A. (1996) *Queer Theory: An Introduction*, New York, New York University Press.

James, S.P. (2004) *Zen Buddhism and Environmental Ethics*, Aldersthot, Ashgate.

James, W. (1879) 'Are we Automata?', *Mind*, 4, 1–22.

James, W. (1884) 'What is an Emotion?', *Mind*, 9, 188–205.

James, W. ([1890], 1981) *The Principles of Psychology*, Cambridge, MA, Harvard University Press.

James, W. ([1897], 1979) *The Will to Believe and Other Essays in Popular Philosophy*, Cambridge, MA, Harvard University Press.

James, W. ([1902], 2002) *The Varieties of Religious Experience*, London, Routledge.

James, W. ([1907], 1979) *Pragmatism*, Cambridge, MA, Cambridge University Press.

Jamieson, D. (1999) *Singer and His Critics*, Oxford Blackwell.

Janaway, C. (ed.) (1999) *The Cambridge Companion to Schopenhauer*, Cambridge, Cambridge University Press.

Jarvis, S. (1998) *Adorno: A Critical Introduction*, New York, Routledge.

Jay, M. (1984) *Adorno*, Cambridge, MA, Harvard University Press.

Jeffrey, R.C. and Burgess, J.P. (2006) *Formal Logic: Its Scope and Limits* (4th edn), Indianapolis, Hackett Publishing.

Jenkins, M.P. (2006) *Bernard Williams*, Chesham, Acumen.

Jennings, J. (2003) *Socialism: Critical Concepts in Political Science*, London, Routledge.

Johnson, E.L. (1992) *Focusing on Truth*, London, Routledge.

Johnson, M.R. (2005) *Aristotle on Teleology*, New York, Oxford University Press.

Johnson-Laird, P.N. and Byrne, R.M.J. (1991) *Deduction*, Hove, Erlbaum.

Johnstone, A.A. (1991) *Rationalized Epistemology: Taking Solipsism Seriously*, Albany, State University of New York Press.

Jolley, N. (ed.) (1995) *The Cambridge Companion to Leibniz*, Cambridge, Cambridge University Press.

Jolley, N. (2005) *Leibniz*, London, Routledge.

Jones, O.R. (ed.) (1971) *The Private Language Argument*, London, Macmillan.

Jones, R.H. (2000) *Reductionism: Analysis and the Fullness of Reality*, Cranbury, NJ, Associated University Presses.

Jordan, J. (ed.) (1994) *Gambling on God: Essays on Pascal's Wager*, Lanham, MD, Rowman & Littlefield.

Joseph, M.A. (2004) *Donald Davidson*, Montreal, McGill–Queen's University Press.

Jung, C.G. ([1933], 1955) *Modern Man in Search of a Soul*, London, Kegan Paul, Trench, Trübner.

Kane, R. (1996) *The Significance of Free Will*, New York, Oxford University Press.

Kant, I. ([1781], 1963) *Critique of Pure Reason* (trans. N.K. Smith), London, Macmillan.

Kant, I. ([1783], 1950) *Prolegomena to Any Future Metaphysics* (trans. L.W. Beck), New York, Liberal Arts Press.

Kant, I. ([1784], 1989) 'What is Enlightenment', in *Foundations of the Metaphysics of Morals and, What is Enlightenment?* (trans. L.W. Beck), London, Collier Macmillan.

Kant, I. ([1785], 1989) 'Foundations of the Metaphysics of Morals', in *Foundations of the Metaphysics of Morals and, What is Enlightenment?* (trans. L.W. Beck), London, Collier Macmillan.

Kant, I. ([1788], 1993) *Critique of Practical Reason* (trans. L.W. Beck) (3rd edn), New York, Macmillan.

Kant, I. ([1790], 1987) *Critique of Judgement* (trans. W.S. Pluhar), Indianapolis, Hackett Publishing.

Katz, S.T. (ed.) (1978) *Mysticism and Philosophical Analysis*, London, Sheldon.

Katz, S.T. (ed.) (1983) *Mysticism and Religious Traditions*, Oxford, Oxford University Press.

Kavka, G. (1986) *Hobbesian Moral and Political Theory*, Princeton, Princeton University Press.

Keefe, R. (2000) *Theories of Vagueness*, Cambridge, Cambridge University Press.

Keefe, R. and Smith, P. (eds) (1996) *Vagueness: A Reader*, Cambridge, MA, MIT Press.

Kenny, A. (ed.) (1986) *Rationalism, Empiricism, and Idealism: British Academy Lectures on the History of Philosophy*, Oxford, Clarendon Press.

Kenyon, I.R. (1990) *General Relativity, Oxford*, Oxford University Press.

Kierkegaard, S. ([1843a, 1987) *Either/Or* (trans. H.V. Hong and E.H. Hong), Princeton, Princeton University Press.

Kierkegaard, S. ([1843b], 1985) *Fear and Trembling* (trans. A. Hannay), Harmondsworth, Penguin.

Kierkegaard, S. ([1844], 1981) *The Concept of Anxiety* (trans. R. Thompste and A.B. anderson), Princeton, Princeton University Press.

Kierkegaard, S. ([1846], 1992) *Concluding Unscientific Postscript to The Philosophical Fragments* (trans. H.V. Hong and E.H. Hong), Princeton, Princeton University Press.

Kim, J. (1993) *Supervenience and Mind: Selected Philosophical Essay*, Cambridge, Cambridge University Press.

King, R. (1999) *Indian Philosophy: An Introduction to Hindu and Buddhist Thought*, Edinburgh, Edinburgh University Press.

Kirk, R. (1954) *The Conservative Mind*, London, Faber.

Kirk, R. (1999) *Relativism and Reality: A Contemporary Introduction*, London, Routledge.

Klein, M. (1952) 'The Mutual Influences in the Development of Ego and Id', *Psychoanalytic Study of the Child*, 7, 51–3.

Klein, M. ([1957], 2001) *Envy and Gratitude*, London, Routledge.

Klein, P. (1981) *Certainty: A Refutation of Scepticism*, Minneapolis, University of Minnesota Press.

Klostermaier, K. (2007) *A Survey of Hinduism* (3rd edn), Oxford, Oxford University Press.

Knott, K. (2000) *Hinduism: A Very Short Introduction*, Oxford, Oxford University Press.

Knowles, D. (2001) *Political Philosophy*, London, Routledge.

Koedt, A., Levine, E. and Rapone, A. (eds) (1973) *Radical Feminism*, New York, Quadrangle Books.

Koffka, K. (1935) *Principles of Gestalt Psychology*, New York, Harcourt, Brace & World.

Kolak, D. and Martin, R. (eds) (1991) *Self and Identity: Contemporary Philosophical Issues*, New York, Macmillan.

Kolakowski, L. (1981) *Main Currents of Marxism: Its Origins, Growth and Dissolution*, Oxford, Oxford University Press.

Kolocotroni, V., Goldman, J. and Taxidou, O. (eds) (1998) *Modernism: An Anthology of Sources and Documents*, Edinburgh, Edinburgh University Press.

Kripke, S.A. (1980) *Naming and Necessity*, Oxford, Blackwell.

Kripke, S.A. (1982) *Wittgenstein on Rules and Private Language: An Elementary Exposition*, Cambridge, MA, Harvard University Press.

Kuhn, T. (1962) *The Structure of Scientific Revolutions*, Chicago, University of Chicago Press.

Kuhn, T. (1977) *The Essential Tension*, Chicago, University of Chicago Press.

Kuhn, T.S. (2000) *The Road Since Structure; Philosophical Essays, 1970–1993, with an Autobiographical Interview*, Chicago, University of Chicago Press.

Kukla, A. (1998) *Studies in Scientific Realism*, New York, Oxford University Press.

Kukla, A. (2000) *Social Constructivism and the Philosophy of Science*, London, Routledge.

Kumar, K. (1991) *Utopianism*, Milton Keynes, Open University Press.

Kupperman, J.J. (2001) *Classic Asian Philosophy: A Guide to Essential Texts*, Oxford, Oxford University Press.

Lacan, J. (1968) *The Language of the Self, the Function of Language in Psychoanalysis* (trans. A. Wilden), Baltimore, Johns Hopkins University Press.

LaFollette, H. (ed.) (2002) *Ethics in Practice: An Anthology* (2nd edn), Oxford, Blackwell.

Lakoff, G. and Johnson, M. (1999) *Philosophy in the Flesh: The Embodied Mind and its Challenge to Western Thought*, New York, Basic Books.

Lamont, C. ([1949], 1997) *The Philosophy of Humanism* (8th edn), New York, Humanist Press.

Lane, M. (ed.) (1970) *Structuralism: A Reader*, London, Cape.

Lansford, T. (2007) *Communism*, New York, Benchmark Books.

LaPorte, J. (2004) *Natural Kinds and Conceptual Change*, Cambridge, Cambridge University Press.

Laudan, L. (1996) *Beyond Positivism and Relativism*, Boulder, CO, Westview Press.

Lawson, T. (1997) *Economics and Reality*, London, Routledge.

Layton-Henry, Z. (ed.) (1982) *Conservative Politics in Western Europe*, New York, St. Martin's Press.

Le Poidevin, R. and McBeath, M. (eds) (1993) *The Philosophy of Time*, Oxford, Oxford University Press.

Lee, D.H.P. (ed.) (1967) *Zeno of Elea*, Amsterdam, Adof Hakkert.

Lefebvre, H. (1968) *Conservative Politics in Western Europe*, London, Cape.

Leibniz, G.W. ([c.1675–1715], 1989) *Philosophical Essays* (trans. R. Ariew and D. Garber), Indianapolis, Hackett Publishing.

Leibniz, G.W. ([1704], 1996) *New Essays Concerning Human Understanding* (trans. P. Remnant and J. Bennett), Cambridge, Cambridge University Press.

Leibniz, G.W. ([1710], 1985) *Theodicy: Essays on the Goodness of God, the Freedom of Man and the Origin of Evil* (trans. E.M. Huggard), La Salle, IL, Open Court.

Leighton, S. (ed.) (2003) *Philosophy and the Emotions*, Ontario, Broadview.

Lemos, N.M. (1994) *Intrinsic Value: Concept and Warrant*, New York, Cambridge University Press.

Lemos, R.M. (1995) *The Nature of Value: Axiological Investigations*, Gainesville, University Press of Florida.

Lenneberg, E.H. and Roberts, J.M. (1953) 'The Denotata of Color Terms', paper presented at the Linguistic Society of America, Bloomington, Indiana.

Leopold, S. (1998) *Consciousness and Qualia*, Amsterdam, John Benjamins.

Levinson, P. (ed.) (1982) *In Pursuit of Truth: Essays in Honour of Karl Popper on the Occasion of his 80th Birthday*, Atlantic Highland, NJ, Humanities Press.

Levy, N. (2002) *Sartre*, Oxford, Oneworld.

Lewis, D. (1983) *Philosophical Papers (Volume I)*, Oxford, Oxford University Press.

Lewis, D. (1986a) *On the Plurality of Worlds*, Oxford, Blackwell.

Lewis, D. (1986b) *Philosophical Papers (Volume II)*, Oxford, Oxford University Press.

Lewis, D. (1998) *Papers in Philosophical Logic*, Cambridge, Cambridge University Press.

Light, A. and Rolston, H. (eds) (2003) *Environmental Ethics: An Anthology*, Oxford, Blackwell.

Lippert-Rasmussen, K. (2005) *Deontology, Responsibility, and Equality*, Copenhagen, Museum Tusculanum Press.

Lipton, P. (1991) *Inference to the Best Explanation*, London, Routledge.

Lloyd, G. (1984) *The Man of Reason: 'Male' and 'Female' in Western Philosophy*, London, Methuen.

Locke, J. ([1689a], 1960) *Two Treatises of Government*, London, Cambridge University Press.

Locke, J. ([1689b], 1983) *A Letter Concerning Toleration* (ed. J. Tulley), Indianapolis, Hackett Publishing.

Locke, J. ([1690], 1997) *An Essay Concerning Human Understanding*, New York, Penguin.

Lombard, L.B. (1986) *Events: A Metaphysical Study*, London, Routledge & Kegan Paul.

Long, A.A. (1986) *Hellenistic Philosophy: Stoics, Epicureans, Sceptics* (2nd edn), London, Duckworth.

Long, A.A. (1999) *The Cambridge Companion to Early Greek Philosophy*, Cambridge, Cambridge University Press.

Loux, M.J. (ed.) (1979) *The Possible and the Actual: Readings in the Metaphysics of Modality*, London, Cornell University Press.

Loux, M.J. (1998) *Metaphysics: A Contemporary Introduction*, London, Routledge.

Lovelock, J. ([1979], 2000) *Gaia: A New Look at Life on Earth*, Oxford, Oxford University Press.

Lowe, E.J. (2000) *An Introduction to the Philosophy of Mind*, Cambridge, Cambridge University Press.

Lowe, E.J. (2002) *A Survey of Metaphysics*, New York, Oxford University Press.

Lowe, E.J. (2005) *Locke*, London, Routledge.

Lowe, E.J. (2006) *The Four-Category Ontology: A Metaphysical Foundation for Natural Science*, Oxford, Clarendon Press.

Lowe, E.J. and Rami, A. (eds) (2009) *Truth and Truth-Making*, Stocksfield, Acumen.

Lycan, W.G. (ed.) (1989) *Mind and Cognition: A Reader*, Oxford, Blackwell.

Lycan, W.G. (1995) *Consciousness*, Cambridge, MA, MIT Press.

Lycan, W.G. (2000) *Philosophy of Language*, London, Routledge.

Lynch, M.P. (ed.) (2001) *The Nature of Truth: Classic and Contemporary Perspectives*, Cambridge, MA, MIT Press.

Lyotard, J. ([1979], 1984) *The Postmodern Condition: A Report on Knowledge* (trans. G. Bennington and B. Massumi), Manchester, Manchester University Press.

Lyotard, J. (1985) *Just Gaming* (trans. W. Godzich), Minneapolis, University of Minnesota Press.

Lyotard, J. (1988) *The Differend: Phrases in Dispute* (trans. G. Van Den Abbeele), Minneapolis, University of Minnesota Press.

Machan, T.R. (ed.) (1982) *The Libertarian Reader*, Totowa, NJ, Rowman & Littlefield.

Machan, T.R. (2004) *Objectivity: Recovering Determinate Reality in Philosophy, Science, and Everyday Life*, Aldershot, Ashgate.

Machiavelli, N. ([1513], 1998) *The Prince* (trans. P. Bondanella and M. Musa), Oxford, Oxford University Press.

Machiavelli, N. ([1531], 2003) *The Discourses*, (eds. B. Crick and L.J. Walker) (trans. L.J. Walker), London, Penguin.

Mackie, J.L. (1974) *The Cement of the Universe: A Study of Causation*, Oxford, Clarendon Press.

Mackie, J.L. (1977) *Ethics: Inventing Right and Wrong*, Harmondsworth, Penguin.

Macquarrie, J. (1972) *Existentialism*, Harmondsworth, Penguin.

Magee, B. (2002) *The Philosophy of Schopenhauer* (2nd edn), Oxford, Oxford University Press.

Malachowsky, A.R. (2002) *Richard Rorty*, Teddington, Acumen.

Malcolm, N. (1971) *Problems of Mind: Descartes to Wittgenstein*, Sydney, Allen & Unwin.

Malpas, S. (2003) *Jean-François Lyotard*, London, Routledge.

Mansfield, N. (2000) *Subjectivity: Theories of the Self from Freud to Haraway*, New York, New York University Press.

Margolis, E. and Laurence, S. (eds) (1999) *Concepts: Core Readings*, Cambridge, MA, MIT Press.

Marks, J. (1998) *Gilles Deleuze: Vitalism and Multiplicity*, London, Pluto Press.

Martin, C. (ed.) (1988) *The Philosophy of Thomas Aquinas: Introductory Readings*, New York, Routledge.

Martin, R. and Barresi, J. (eds) (2003) *Personal Identity*, Oxford, Blackwell.

Martin, R. and Barresi, J. (2006) *The Rise and Fall of Soul and Self: An Intellectual History of Personal Identity*, New York, Columbia University Press.

Martinich, A.P. (2005) *Hobbes*, New York, Routledge.

Marx, K. ([1844], 1970) *Economic and Philosophical Manuscripts of 1844* (trans. M. Milligan), London, Lawrence & Wishart.

Marx, K. (1859) *A Contribution to a Critique of Political Economy*, London, Lawrence & Wishart.

Marx, K. ([1867], 1970) *Capital*, London, Dent.

Marx, K. and Engels, F. ([1845], 1998) *The German Ideology: Includes Theses on Feuerbach and an Introduction to the Critique of Political Economy*, Amherst, NY, Prometheus Books.

Marx, K. and Engels, F. ([1848], 1967) *The Communist Manifesto*, Harmondsworth, Penguin.

Marxists Internet Archive, available online at: http://www.marxists.org/ (accessed 24/10/09.

Masao, A. (1989) *Zen and Western Thought* (ed. W. LaFleur), Honolulu, University of Hawaii Press.

McGowan, J. (1997) *Hannah Arendt: An Introduction*, Minneapolis, University of Minnesota Press.

McHoul, A.W. and Grace, W. (1995) *A Foucault Primer: Discourse, Power and the Subject*, London, UCL Press.

McInerny, R. (ed.) (1998) *Thomas Aquinas: Selected Writings*, Harmondsworth, Penguin.

McInerny, R. (2004) *Aquinas*, Cambridge, Polity Press.

McKim, R. and McMahan, J. (eds.) (1997) *The Morality of Nationalism*, Oxford, Oxford University Press.

McLaughlin, R.N. (1990) *On the Logic of Ordinary Conditionals*, Albany, State University of New York Press.

McClellan, D. (1988) *Marxism: Essential Writings*, Oxford, Oxford University Press.

McLure, R. (2005) *The Philosophy of Time: Time Before Times*, New York, Routledge.

McMahon, D.M. (2006) *Happiness: A History*, New York, Grove Press.

McTaggart, J.M.E. (1927) *The Nature of Existence*, Cambridge, Cambridge University Press.

Meinong, A. ([1904], 1933) *Investigations in the Theory of Objects and Psychology*, New York, Oxford University Press.

Melia, J. (2005) 'Truthmaking Without Truthmakers', in H. Beebee and J. Dodd (eds) *Truthmakers: The Contemporary Debate*, New York: Oxford University Press.

Mellor, D.H. and Oliver, A. (eds) (1997) *Properties*, Oxford, Oxford University Press.

Mendus, S. (2002) *Impartiality in Moral and Political Philosophy*, New York, Oxford University Press.

Mendus, S. and Edwards, D.S. (eds) (1987) *On Toleration*, New York, Oxford University Press.

Merleau-Ponty, M. ([1942], 1968) *The Structure of Behaviour* (trans. A.L. Fisher), Boston, MA, Beacon Press.

Merleau-Ponty, M. ([1945], 1969) *Phenomenology of Perception* (trans. C. Smith), New York, The Humanities Press.

Merleau-Ponty, M. ([1964], 1968) *The Visible and the Invisible* (trans. A. Lingis), Evanston, Northwestern University Press.

Messiah, A. (1999) *Quantum Mechanics*, New York, Dover Publications.

Metzinger, T. (ed.) (1999) *Conscious Experience*, Thorverton, Imprint Academic.

Midgley, M. (1991) *Can't We Make Moral Judgements?*, Bristol, Bristol Press.

Mill, J.S. ([1843], 2002) *A System of Logic*, Honolulu, University Press of the Pacific.

Mill, J.S. ([1859], 1955) *On Liberty*, Chicago, Gateway Edition.

Mill, J.S. (1861a) *Considerations on Representative Government*, Buffalo, Prometheus Books.

Mill, J.S. ([1861b], 1998) *Utilitarianism*, Oxford, Oxford University Press.

Mill, J.S. ([1865], 1963) 'An Examination of Sir William Hamilton's Philosophy', in J.M. Robson (ed.) *Collected Works of John Stuart Mill*, Toronto, University of Toronto Press.

Mill, J.S. ([1869], 1988) *The Subjection of Women*, Indianapolis, Hackett Publishing.

Miller, D. (1984) *Anarchism*, London, Dent.

Miller, D. (ed.) (2006) *The Liberty Reader*, Boulder, CO, Paradigm Publishers.

Millett, K. (1970) *Sexual Politics*, New York, Doubleday.

Mills, S. (1997) *Discourse*, London, Routledge.

Mills, S. (2003) *Michel Foucault* , London, Routledge.

Moi, T. (1990) *Feminist Theory and Simone de Beauvoir*, Hanover, NH, Wesleyan University Press.

Moore, A.W. (ed.) (1993) *Meaning and Reference*, Oxford, Oxford University Press.

Moore, G.E. ([1903], 1993) *Principia Ethica*, Cambridge, Cambridge University Press.

Moore, G.E. (1912) *Ethics*, London, Williams & Norgate.

Moran, D. (2000) *Introduction to Phenomenology*, New York, Routledge.

More, T. ([1516], 1994) *Utopia* (introduced by R. Marius), London, Everyman.

Moreland, J.P. (2001) *Universals*, Chesham, Acumen.

Morgan, M.L. (ed.) (2002) *Spinoza: The Complete Works*, Indianapolis, Hackett Publishing.

Morland, I. and Willox, A. (eds) (2005) *Queer Theory*, Basingstoke, Palgrave Macmillan.

Morris, C.W. (ed.) (1999) *The Social Contract Theorists: Critical Essays on Hobbes, Locke, and Rousseau*, Oxford, Rowman & Littlefield.

Mothersill, M. (1984) *Beauty Restored*, Oxford, Clarendon Press.

Mou, B. (ed.) (2003) *Comparative Approaches to Chinese Philosophy*, Aldershot, Ashgate.

Mulhall, S. (2005) *Routledge Philosophy Guidebook to Heidegger and Being and Time* (2nd edn), London, Routledge.

Mulhall, S. (2007) *Wittgenstein's Private Language: Grammar, Nonsense and Imagination in Philosophical Investigations*, New York, Oxford University Press.

Mullarkey, J. (ed.) (1999) *The New Bergson*, Manchester, Manchester University Press.

Næss, A. (1973) 'The Shallow and the Deep, Long-Range Ecology Movement: A Summary', *Inquiry*, 1(16).

Næss, A. (1989) *Ecology, Community and Lifestyle* (trans. D. Rothenberg), New York, Cambridge University Press.

Nagel, T. (1979) *Mortal Questions*, Cambridge, Cambridge University Press.

Nagel, T. (1991) *Equality and Partiality*, Oxford, Oxford University Press.

Narveson, J. (1988) *The Libertarian Idea*, Philadelphia, Temple University Press.

Nash, R. (1989) *The Rights of Nature: A History of Environmental Ethics*, Madison, University of Wisconsin Press.

Natoli, J.P. and Hutcheon, L. (eds) (1993) *A Postmodern Reader*, Albany, State University of New York Press.

Neale, S. (2001) *Facing Facts*, Oxford, Clarendon Press.

Neujahr, P.A. (1995) *Kant's Idealism*, Macon, GA, Mercer University Press.

Neville, R.C. (1992) *The Highroad Around Modernism*, Albany, State University of New York Press.

Newman, A. (2002) *The Correspondence Theory of Truth: An Essay on the Metaphysics of Predication*, Cambridge, Cambridge University Press.

Newman, M. (2005) *Socialism: A Very Short Introduction*, Oxford, Oxford University Press.

Newton-Smith, W.H. (ed.) (2000) *A Companion to the Philosophy of Science*, Oxford, Blackwell.

Nicholson, L.J. (ed.) (1990) *Feminism/Postmodernism*, London, Routledge.

Nietzsche, F. ([1882], 1974) *The Gay Science* (trans. W. Kaufmann), New York, Random House.

Nietzsche, F. ([1885], 1969) *Thus Spake Zarathustra* (trans. R.J. Hollingdale), London, Penguin.

Nietzsche, F. ([1886], 1966) *Beyond Good and Evil, Prelude to a Philosophy of the Future* (trans. W. Kaufmann), New York, Random House.

Nietzsche, F. (1887) *On the Genealogy of Morals* (trans. M. Clark and A.J. Swensen), Indianapolis, Hackett Publishing.

Niinjuluoto, I. (1998) *Critical Scientific Realism*, New York, Oxford University Press.

Nishtani, K. (1990) *The Self-Overcoming of Nihilism* (trans. G. Parkes and S. Aihara), Albany, State University of New York Press.

Nola, R. (ed.) (1988) *Relativism and Realism in Science*, Dordrecht, Kluwer Academic.

Nolan, D. (2005) *David Lewis*, Chesham, Acumen.

Noonan, H.W. (2003) *Personal Identity* (2nd edn), London, Routledge.

Norman, R.J. (2004) *On Humanism*, London, Routledge.

Norris, C. (1987) *Derrida*, London, Fontana.

Norton, D.F. (ed.) (1993) *The Cambridge Companion to Hume*, Cambridge, Cambridge University Press.

Nozick, R. (1974) *Anarchy, State and Utopia*, New York, Basic Books.

Nozick, R. (1981) *Philosophical Explanations*, Cambridge, MA, Harvard University Press.

Nozick, R. (1989) *The Examined Life: Philosophical Meditations*, New York, Simon & Schuster.

Nozick, R. (2001) *Invariances: The Structure of the Objective World*, Cambridge, MA, Belknap Press.

Numbers, R.L. (2006) *The Creationists: From Scientific Creationism to Intelligent Design*, London, Harvard University Press.

Nussbaum, M. (2001) *Upheavals of Thought: The Intelligence of Emotions*, Cambridge, Cambridge University Press.

O'Connor, D. (ed.) (2000) *The Adorno Reader*, Oxford, Blackwell.

Oderberg, D.S. (1993) *The Metaphysics of Identity Over Time*, Basingstoke, Macmillan.

O'Hear, A. (1984) *Experience, Explanation and Faith: An Introduction to the Philosophy of Religion*, London, Routledge & Kegan Paul.

Ollman, B. (1976) *Alienation: Marx's Conception of Man in Capitalist Society*, 2nd edn, Cambridge, Cambridge University Press.

Olson, T. (1982) *Millenialism, Utopianism, and Progress*, Toronto, University of Toronto Press.

Orend, B. (2002) *Human Rights: Concept and Context*, Ontario, Broadview Press.

Ortega y Gasset, J. ([1923], 1961) *The Modern Theme* (trans. J. Cleugh), New York, Oxford University Press.

Orwell, G. ([1945], 2003) *Animal Farm: A Fairy Story*, London, Penguin.

Otsuka, M. (2003) *Libertarianism without Inequality*, Oxford, Clarendon Press.

Owen, H.P. (1971) *Concepts of Deity*, New York, Herder & Herder.

Paine, T. ([1791], 1969) *Rights of Man* (Harmondsworth, Penguin.

Parfit, D. (1984) *Reasons and Persons*, Oxford, Oxford University Press.

Pascal, B. ([1660], 1950) *Pensées* (trans. H.F. Stewart), London, Routledge & Kegan Paul.

Paton, H.J. (1947) *The Categorical Imperative: A Study of Kant's Moral Philosophy*, London, Hutchinson's University Library.

Patton, P. (ed.) (1996) *Deleuze: A Critical Reader*, Oxford, Blackwell.

Pears, D.F. (1971) *Wittgenstein*, London, Fontana.

Perry, J. (ed.) (2008) *Personal Identity*, Berkeley, University of California Press.

Peterson, M., Hasker, W., Reichenbach, B. and Basinger, D. (2008) *Reason and Religious Belief: An Introduction to the Philosophy of Religion* (4th edn), Oxford, Oxford University Press.

Pipes, R. (2001) *Communism: A History*, New York, Modern Library.

Plantinga, A. (1974) *The Nature of Necessity*, Oxford, Oxford University Press.

Plantinga, A. (1977) *God, Freedom, and Evil*, Grand Rapids, MI, Eerdmans.

Plato ([c. 360 BCE], 2000) *The Republic* (trans. T. Griffith), New York, Cambridge University Press.

Pojman, L.P. and Westmoreland, R. (eds) (1998) *Equality: Selected Readings*, Oxford, Oxford University Press.
Pollock, J. (1986) *Contemporary Theories of Knowledge*, Totowa, NJ, Rowman & Littlefield.
Popper, K. ([1957], 2002) *The Poverty of Historicism*, New York and London, Routledge & Kegan Paul.
Popper, K. (1959) *The Logic of Scientific Discovery*, New York, Basic Books.
Popper, K. (1963) *Conjectures and Refutations: The Growth of Scientific Knowledge*, London, Routledge.
Popper, K. (1972) *Objective Knowledge: An Evolutionary Approach*, Oxford, Clarendon Press.
Popper, K. (1992) *In Search of a Better World: Lectures and Essays from Thirty Years* (trans. L.J. Bennett), London, Routledge.
Porter, R. (1990) *The Enlightenment*, London, Macmillan.
Potter, J. (1996) *Representing Reality: Discourse, Rhetoric and Social Construction*, London, Sage.
Prado, C.G. (2000) *Starting with Foucault: An Introduction to Genealogy* (2nd edn), Boulder, CO, Perseus Books.
Preyer, G. and Siebelt, F. (eds) (2001) *Reality and Humean Supervenience: Essays on the Philosophy of David Lewis*, Lanham, MD, Rowman & Littlefield.
Price, H.H. (1953) *Thinking and Experience*, London, Hutchinson's University Library.
Price, H.H. (1969) *Belief*, London, Allen & Unwin.
Priest, S. (2000) *The Subject in Question: Sartre's Critique of Husserl in the Transcendence of the Ego*, London, Routledge.
Priest, S. (2003) *Merleau-Ponty*, London, Routledge.
Pritchard, H.A. (1968) *Moral Obligation and Duty and Interest: Essays and Lectures*, London, Oxford University Press.
Psillos, S. (1999) *Scientific Realism: How Science Tracks Truth*, London, Routledge.
Pusey, M. (1987) *Jürgen Habermas*, London, Ellis Horwood & Tavistock.
Putnam, H. (1981) *Reason, Truth and History*, Cambridge, Cambridge University Press.
Putnam, H. (1983) *Realism and Reason*, Cambridge, Cambridge University Press.
Quine, W.V.O. (1953) *From a Logical Point of View*, Cambridge, MA, Harvard University Press.
Quine, W.V.O. (1960) *Word and Object*, Cambridge, MA, MIT Press.
Rahula, P. (1959) *What the Buddha Taught*, Oxford, Oneworld.
Ralph, H. and Blair, J.A. (eds) (1994) *New Essays in Informal Logic*, Windsor, Ontario, Informal Logic.
Ramsey, F.P. (1927) 'Facts and Propositions', *Proceedings of the Aristotelian Society (Supplementary)*, 7, 153–170.
Ramsey, F.P. (1931) 'Knowledge', in R.B. Braithwaite (ed.) *The Foundations of Mathematics and Other Essays*, New York, Harcourt Brace.
Rawls, J. (1971) *A Theory of Justice*, London, Oxford University Press.
Rawls, J. (1993) *Political Liberalism*, New York, Columbia University Press.
Rawls, J. (1999) *Collected Papers* (ed. S. Freeman), Cambridge, MA, Harvard University Press.
Rea, M. (ed.) (1997) *Material Constitution: A Reader*, Totowa, NJ, Rowman & Littlefield.
Reath, A. (2006) *Agency and Autonomy in Kant's Moral Theory*, Oxford, Oxford University Press.
Rée, J. and Chamberlain, J. (eds) (1998) *Kierkegaard: A Critical Reader*, Oxford, Blackwell.
Regan, T. (1983) *The Case for Animal Rights*, Berkeley, University of California Press.
Regan, T. (2001) *Defending Animal Rights*, Urbana and Chicago, University of Illinois Press.
Reiman, J. (1990) *Justice and Modern Moral Philosophy*, New Haven, Yale University Press.
Reinhardt, G. (1992) *The Existence of the World: An Introduction to Ontology*, London, Routledge.
Rescher, N. (1973) *The Coherence Theory of Truth*, Oxford, Oxford University Press.
Rescher, N. (ed.) (1985a) *The Heritage of Logical Positivism*, Lanham, MD, University Press of America.
Rescher, N. (1985b) *Pascal's Wager: A Study of Practical Reasoning in Philosophical Theology*, Indianapolis, University of Notre Dame Press.
Rescher, N. (ed.) (1986) *Current Issues in Teleology*, Lanham, MD, University Press of America.
Rescher, N. (2001) *Paradoxes: Their Roots, Range, and Resolution*, Chicago, Open Court.
Rescher, N. (2003) *On Leibniz*, Pittsburgh, University of Pittsburgh Press.
Ricoeur, P. (1974) *The Conflicts of Interpretation: Essays in Hermeneutics* (trans. W. Domingo et al.), Evanston, Northwestern University Press.

Ridley, M. (ed.) (1997) *Evolution*, Oxford, Oxford University Press.

Riley, P. (ed.) (2001) *The Cambridge Companion to Rousseau*, Cambridge, Cambridge University Press.

Robey, D. (1973) *Structuralism: An Introduction*, Oxford, Clarendon Press.

Robinson, H. (1994) *Perception*, New York, Routledge.

Robinson, W.S. (2004) *Understanding Phenomenal Consciousness*, Cambridge, Cambridge University Press.

Rockmore, T. (2004) *On Foundationalism: A Strategy for Metaphysical Realism*, Lanham, MD, Rowman & Littlefield.

Rodríguez-Fernández, J.L. (1999) 'Ockham's Razor', *Endeavour*, 23, pp. 121–125.

Roessler, J. and Eilan, N. (2003) *Agency and Self-awareness: Issues in Philosophy and Psychology*, Oxford, Clarendon Press.

Rogers, C. (1961) *On Becoming a Person: A Therapist's View of Psychotherapy*, London, Constable.

Rorty, R. (1979) *Philosophy and the Mirror of Nature*, Princeton, Princeton University Press.

Rorty, R. (1982) *Consequences of Pragmatism*, Brighton, Harvester.

Rorty, R. (1989) *Contingency, Irony and Solidarity*, Cambridge, Cambridge University Press.

Rose, S. (1997) *Lifelines: Biology, Freedom, Determinism*, London, Penguin.

Rosen, R. (1999) *Essays on Life Itself*, New York, Columbia University Press.

Rosen, S. (2000) *Nihilism: A Philosophical Essay* (2nd edn), Indiana, St. Augustine's Press.

Rosenberg, A. (2000) *Darwinism in Philosophy, Social Science and Policy*, Cambridge, Cambridge University Press.

Rosenthal, D.M. (ed.) (2000) *Materialism and the Mind-Body Problem* (2nd edn), Indianapolis, Hackett Publishing.

Rosenthal, D.M. (2005) *Consciousness and Mind*, New York, Oxford University Press.

Rousseau, J. ([1750], 1997) 'Discourse on the Arts and Sciences', in V. Gourevitch (ed.) *The Discourses and Other Early Political Writings*, Cambridge, Cambridge University Press.

Rousseau, J. ([1762a], 2000) *Emile* (trans. B. Foxley), London, Everyman.

Rousseau, J. ([1762b], 1997) 'The Social Contract' in V. Gourevitch (ed.) *The Social Contract and Other Later Political Writings*, Cambridge, Cambridge University Press.

Rowlands, M. (1999) *The Body in Mind: Understanding Cognitive Processes*, Cambridge, Cambridge University Press.

Royle, N. (ed.) (2000) *Deconstruction: A User's Guide*, Basingstoke, Palgrave Macmillan.

Royle, N. (2003) *Jacques Derrida*, London, Routledge.

Rozemond, M. (1998) *Descartes's Dualism*, Cambridge, MA, Harvard University Press.

Rubin, G. (1975) 'The Traffic in Women: Notes on the "Political Economy" of Sex', in R. Reiter (ed.) *Toward an Anthropology of Women, New York*, Month Review Press.

Ruse, M. (2006) *Darwinism and its Discontents*, Cambridge, Cambridge University Press.

Russ, S. (ed.) (2008) *Metaethics*, London, Routledge.

Russell, B. (1903) *The Principles of Mathematics*, Cambridge, At the University Press.

Russell, B. (1905) 'On Denoting', *Mind*, 14: 479–93.

Russell, B. ([1910], 1994) *Philosophical Essays*, London, Routledge.

Russell, B. ([1912], 2001) *The Problems of Philosophy*, Oxford, Oxford University Press.

Russell, B. (1918) *Proposed Road to Freedom: Socialism, Anarchism and Syndicalism*, New York, Cornwall Press.

Russell, B. (1921) *The Analysis of Mind*, London, George Allen & Unwin.

Russell, B. ([1925], 1993) *The ABC of Relativity* (4th edn), London, Routledge.

Russell, B. (1927a) *The Analysis of Matter*, London, Kegan Paul.

Russell, B. (1927b) *Why I Am Not a Christian*, London, Watts.

Russell, B. (1948) *Human Knowledge: Its Scope and Limits*, New York, Simon & Schuster.

Russell, B. and Whitehead, A.N. ([1910], 1962) *Principia Mathematica*, Cambridge, Cambridge University Press.

Russell, K. (1954) *The Conservative Mind*, London, Faber.

Russell, M. (2006) *Husserl: A Guide for the Perplexed*, London, Continuum.

Russell, S.J. and Norvig, P. (2003) *Artificial Intelligence: A Modern Approach* (2nd edn), New Jersey, Prentice Hall.

Ryle, G. (1949) *The Concept of Mind*, New York, Barnes & Noble.

Sachse, C. (2007) *Reductionism in the Philosophy of Science*, Frankfurt, Ontos.

Sainsbury, R.M. (1995) *Paradoxes* (2nd edn), Cambridge, Cambridge University Press.

Salih, S. (2002) *Judith Butler*, London Routledge.

Sallis, J. (ed.) (1987) *Deconstruction and Philosophy: The Texts of Jacques Derrida*, Chicago, University of Chicago Press.

Salmon, W.C. (ed.) (2001) *Zeno's Paradoxes* (2nd edn), Indianapolis, Hackett Publishing.

Sandel, M.J. (1982) *Liberalism and the Limits of Justice*, Cambridge, Cambridge University Press.

Sandel, M.J. (2007) *Justice: A Reader*, New York, Oxford University Press.

Sankey, H. (1994) *The Incommensurability Thesis*, Aldershot, Avebury.

Sargisson, L. (1996) *Contemporary Feminist Utopianism*, London, Routledge.

Sartre, J. ([1937], 1989) *Transcendence of the Ego: An Existential Theory of Consciousness* (trans. F. Williams and R. Kirkpatrick), New York, Hill & Wang.

Sartre, J. ([1943], 1956) *Being and Nothingness* (trans. H.E. Barnes), New York, The Philosophical Library.

Sartre, J. ([1944], 1989) 'No Exit' (*Huis Clos*), in *No Exit and Three Other Plays*, New York, Vintage Books.

Sartre, J. ([1946], 1989) 'Existentialism is a Humanism', in W. Kaufman (ed.) *Existentialism from Dostoyevsky to Sartre*, New York, Meridian.

Sartre, J. ([1958], 1968) *Search for a Method* (trans. H.E. Barnes), New York, Random House.

Sarup, M. (ed.) (1989) *An Introductory Guide to Post-Structuralism and Postmodernism*, Athens, University of Georgia Press.

Satris, S. (1986) *Ethical Emotivism*, Dordrecht, Kluwer Academic.

Saussure, F. ([1916], 1974) *Course in General Linguistics*, Glasgow, Fontana.

Savellos, E.E. and Yalçin, Ü.D. (eds) (1995) *Supervenience: New Essays*, New York, Cambridge University Press.

Savitt, S. (ed.) (1995) *Time's Arrow Today: Recent Physical and Philosophical Work on the Direction of Time*, Cambridge, Cambridge University Press.

Savulescu, J. and Bostrom, N. (eds) (2009) *Human Enhancement*, Oxford, Oxford University Press.

Sayre-McCord, G. (1988) *Essays on Moral Realis*, Ithaca, Cornell University Press.

Scarre, G. (1996) *Utilitarianism*, London, Routledge.

Scarre, G. (2007) *Death*, Stocksfield, Acumen.

Scheffler, S. (1982) *Consequentialism and its Critics*, Oxford, Oxford University Press.

Schiebinger, L. (ed.) (2000) *Feminism and the Body*, Oxford, Oxford University Press.

Schlick, M. (1979a) *Philosophical Papers: Volume 1* (ed. H.L. Mulder and B. van de Velde-Schlick), Dordrecht, Reidel.

Schlick, M. (1979b) *Philosophical Papers: Volume 2* (ed. H.L. Mulder and B. van de Velde-Schlick), Dordrecht, Reidel.

Schlipp, P.A. (ed.) (1942) *The Philosophy of G.E. Moore*, Evanston, IL, Northwestern University Press.

Schmidtz, D. (ed.) (2002) *Robert Nozick*, New York, Cambridge University Press.

Schmitt, F.F. (ed.) (2004) *Theories of Truth*, Oxford, Blackwell.

Schopenhauer, A. ([1813], 2007) *On the Fourfold Root of the Principle of Sufficient Reason* (trans. K. Hillebrand), New York, Cosimo.

Schopenhauer, A. ([1818], 1966) *The World as Will and Representation* (trans. E.F.J. Payne), New York, Dover Publications.

Schopenhauer, A. ([1840], 1995) *On the Basis of Morality* (trans. E.F.J. Payne), Providence, Berghahn Books.

Schwartz, R. (ed.) (2004) *Perception*, Oxford, Blackwell.

Schwartz, R.M. (ed.) (2004) *Transcendence: Philosophy, Literature, and Theology Approach the Beyond*, New York, Routledge.

Scriven, M. (1976) *Reasoning*, New York, McGraw-Hill.

Searle, J.R. (1969) *Speech Acts: An Essay in the Philosophy of Language*, Cambridge, Cambridge University Press.

Searle, J.R. (1980) 'Minds, Brains and Programs', *Behavioural and Brain Sciences*, 3(3): 417–457.

Searle, J.R. (1983) *Intentionality: An Essay in the Philosophy of Mind*, Cambridge, Cambridge University Press.

Searle, J.R. (1984) *Minds, Brains and Science: The 1984 Reith Lectures*, London, BBC.

Searle, J.R. (1995) *The Construction of Social Reality*, New York, Free Press.

Sedley, D.N. (ed.) (2003) *The Cambridge Companion to Greek and Roman Philosophy*, Cambridge, Cambridge University Press.

Seung, T.K. (2007) *Kant: A Guide for the Perplexed*, London, Continuum.

Shafer-Landau, R. (2003) *Moral Realism: A Defense*, Oxford, Oxford University Press.

Shaver, R. (1999) *Rational Egoism: A Selective and Critical History*, Cambridge, Cambridge University Press.

Shields, C. (2003) *The Blackwell Guide to Ancient Philosophy*, Oxford, Blackwell.

Shneidman, E.S. (ed.) (1976) *Death: Current Perspectives*, Los Angeles, Mayfield.

Shook, J.R. and Margolis, J. (eds) (2006) *A Companion to Pragmatism*, Oxford, Blackwell.

Sidelle, A. (1989) *Necessity, Essence, and Individuation: A Defense of Conventionalism*, New York, Cornell University Press.

Sider, T. (2001) *Four-Dimensionalism: An Ontology of Persistence and Time*, Oxford, Clarendon Press.

Siderits, M. (2007) *Buddhism as Philosophy: An Introduction*, New York, Oxford University Press.

Simons, M.A. (ed.) (1995) *Feminist Interpretations of Simone de Beauvoir*, University Park, Pennsylvania University Press.

Singer, P. (1973) *Democracy and Disobedience*, Oxford, Clarendon.

Singer, P. (1975) *Animal Liberation: A New Ethics for our Treatment of Animals*, New York, Random House.

Singer, P. (1979) *Practical Ethics*, Cambridge, Cambridge University Press.

Singer, P. (ed.) (1991) *A Companion to Ethics*, Oxford, Blackwell.

Singer, P. (1995) *Rethinking Life and Death: The Collapse of Our Traditional Ethics*, Oxford, Oxford University Press.

Singer, P. (1997) *How Are We to Live? Ethics in an Age of Self-Interest*, Oxford, Oxford University Press.

Singer, P. (2000) *Marx: A Very Short Introduction*, Oxford, Oxford University Press.

Singer, P.A. and Viens, A.M. (eds) (2008) *The Cambridge Textbook of Bioethics*, Cambridge, Cambridge University Press.

Sinnott-Armstrong, W. (2006) *Moral Skepticisms*, New York, Oxford University Press.

Skinner, B.F. ([1948], 2005) *Walden Two*, Indianapolis, Hackett Publishing.

Skinner, B.F. (1971) *Beyond Freedom and Dignity*, New York, Knopf.

Skinner, Q. (2000) *Machiavelli: A Very Short Introduction*, Oxford, Oxford University Press.

Skorupski, J. (1989) *John Stuart Mill*, London, Routledge.

Skorupski, J. (ed.) (1998) *The Cambridge Companion to John Stuart Mill*, Cambridge, Cambridge University Press.

Sluga, H.D. and Stern, D.G. (eds) (1996) *The Cambridge Companion to Wittgenstein*, Cambridge, Cambridge University Press.

Smart, J.J.C. and Williams, B.A.O. (1973) *Utilitarianism: For and Against*, Cambridge, Cambridge University Press.

Smith, D.L. (1999) *Freud's Philosophy of the Unconscious*, Dordrecht, Kluwer Academic.

Smith, D.W. and Thomasson, A.L. (eds) (2005) *Phenomenology and the Philosophy of Mind*, Oxford, Clarendon Press.

Smith, H. (1991) *The World's Religions: Our Great Wisdom Traditions* (2nd edn), San Francisco, HarperCollins.

Smith, N.J.J. (2008) *Vagueness and Degrees of Truth*, Oxford, Oxford University Press.

Soames, S. (1999) *Understanding Truth*, Oxford, Oxford University Press.

Solomon, R.C. (ed.) (2004) *Thinking About Feeling*, New York, Oxford University Press.

Solomon, R.C. and Sherman, D. (eds) (2003) *The Blackwell Guide to Continental Philosophy*, Oxford, Blackwell.

Sorenson, R. (1992) *Thought Experiments*, Oxford, Oxford University Press.

Sorenson, R.A. (2005) *A Brief History of the Paradox: Philosophy and the Labyrinths of the Mind*, New York, Oxford University Press.

Sosa, E. (1991) *Knowledge in Perspective: Selected Essays in Epistemology*, Cambridge, Cambridge University Press.

Sosa, E. and Bonjour, L. (2003) *Epistemic Justification: Internalism vs. Externalism, Foundations vs. Virtues*, Oxford Blackwell.

Sosa, E. and Villanueva, E. (eds) (2004) *Epistemology*, Oxford, Blackwell.

Spade, P.V. (1999) *The Cambridge Companion to Ockham*, Cambridge, Cambridge University Press.

Speight, A. (2001) *Hegel, Literature and the Problem of Agency*, New York, Cambridge University Press.

Spelman, E.V. (1988) *Inessential Woman: Problems of Exclusion in Feminist Thought*, Boston, MA, Beacon Press.

Spencer, C. (2000) *Vegetarianism: A History* (2nd edn), London, Grub Street.

Spencer, H. (1864, 1867) *The Principles of Biology*, London, Williams & Norgate.

Spinoza, B. ([1677], 2000) *Ethics* (trans. G.H.R. Parkinson), New York, Oxford University Press.

Stadler, F. (1997) *The Vienna Circle: Studies in the Origins, Development and Influence of Logical Empiricism* (trans. C.G.J. Nielson), New York, Springer.

Stadler, F. (ed.) (2003) *The Vienna Circle and Logical Empiricism: Re-evaluation and Future Perspectives*, Dordrecht, Kluwer.

Statman, D. (ed.) (1993) *Moral Luck*, Albany, State University of New York Press.

Stern, R. (2002) *Routledge Philosophy Guidebook to Hegel and the Phenomenology of Spirit*, London, Routledge.

Stevenson, C.L. (1944) *Ethics and Language*, New Haven, Yale University Press.

Steward, H. (1997) *The Ontology of Mind: Events, Processes, and States*, Oxford, Clarendon Press.

Stich, S.P. (ed.) (1975) *Innate Ideas*, Berkeley, University of California Press.

Stich, S.P. (1983) *From Folk Psychology to Cognitive Science: The Case Against Belief*, Cambridge, MA, MIT Press.

Stiglitz, J.E. (1994) *Whither Socialism*, Cambridge, MA, MIT Press.

Stokes, G. (1998) *Popper: Philosophy, Politics, and Scientific Method*, Oxford, Polity Press.

Storr, A. (2001) *Freud: A Very Short Introduction*, Oxford, Oxford University Press.

Stratton-Lake, P. (2000) *Kant, Duty and Moral Worth*, London, Routledge.

Strauss, L. and Cropsey, J. (eds) (1987) *History of Political Philosophy* (2nd edn), Chicago, University of Chicago Press.

Strawson, G. (1950) 'On Referring', *Mind*, 59: 320–344.

Strawson, G. (1989) *The Secret Connexion: Causation, Realism, and David Hume*, Oxford, Oxford University Press.

Streiffer, R. (2003) *Moral Relativism and Reasons for Acting*, New York, Routledge.

Stroud, B. (1977) *Hume*, London, Routledge & Kegan Paul.

Stump, E. (2003) *Aquinas*, London, Routledge.

Sturrock, J. (2003) *Structuralism* (2nd edn), Oxford, Blackwell.

Sullivan, N. (2003) *A Critical Introduction to Queer Theory*, Edinburgh, Edinburgh University Press.

Sunstein, C.R. and Nussbaum, M.C. (eds) (2004) *Animal Rights: Current Debates and New Directions*, New York, Oxford University Press.

Swinburne, R. (1979) *The Existence of God*, Oxford, Clarendon Press.

Swinburne, R. (2001) *Epistemic Justification*, Oxford, Clarendon Press.

Szasz, T.S. (1960) 'The Myth of Mental Illness', *American Psychologist*, 15: 113–118.

Taylor, C. (1989) *Sources of the Self: The Making of the Modern Identity*, Cambridge, Cambridge University Press.

Taylor, C. and Hansen, M.B.N. (eds) (2005) *The Cambridge Companion to Merleau-Ponty*, Cambridge, Cambridge University Press.

Taylor, C.C.W. (2000) *Socrates: A Very Short Introduction*, Oxford, Oxford University Press.

Tiles, J.E. (1988) *Dewey*, London, Routledge.

Timmons, M. (1999) *Morality Without Foundations: A Defense of Ethical Contextualism*, Oxford, Oxford University Press.

Tittle, P. (2005) *What If ... Collected Thought Experiments in Philosophy*, New York, Pearson Longman.

Tomassi, P. (1999) *Introduction to Logic*, London, Routledge.

Tong, R.P. (1998) *Feminist Thought: A More Comprehensive Introduction*, Boulder, CO, Perseus Book Group.

Tooley, M. (1997) *Time, Tense and Causation*, Oxford, Oxford University Press.

Townsend, D. (1997) *An Introduction to Aesthetics*, Oxford, Blackwell.

Tsohatzidis, S.L. (ed.) (1994) *Foundations of Speech Act Theory: Philosophical and Linguistics Perspectives*, London, Routledge.

Tuck, R. (2002) *Hobbes: A Very Short Introduction*, Oxford, Oxford University Press.

Turbayne, C.M. (1982) *Berkeley: Critical and Interpretative Essays*, Minneapolis, University of Minnesota Press.

Turing, A. (1950) 'Computing Machinery and Intelligence', *Mind*, 59(236): 433–460.

Urmson, J.O. (1958) 'Saints and Heroes' in A. Melden (ed.) *Essays in Moral Philosophy*, Seattle, University of Washington Press, pp. 198–216.

Vallentyne, P. and Steiner, H. (eds) (2000) *Left Libertarianism and its Critics: The Contemporary Debate*, New York, Palgrave.

van Fraassen, B. (1980) *The Scientific Image*, Oxford, Oxford University Press.

van Inwagen, P. (1993) *Metaphysics*, Oxford, Oxford University Press.

van Inwagen, P. (2006) *The Problem of Evil*, Oxford, Oxford University Press.

van Inwagen, P. and Zimmerman, D.W. (eds) (1998) *Metaphysics: The Big Questions*, Oxford, Blackwell.

Varela, F.J., Thompson, E. and Rosch, E. (1991) *The Embodied Mind: Cognitive Science and Human Experience*, Cambridge, MA, MIT Press.

Vesey, G. (ed.) (1974) *Understanding Wittgenstein*, Ithaca, Cornell University Press.

Villa, D. (ed.) (2000) *The Cambridge Guide to Arendt*, Cambridge, Cambridge University Press.

Viroli, M. (1998) *Machiavelli*, Oxford, Oxford University Press.

Vygotsky, L.S. (1978) *Mind in Society: The Development of Higher Mental Processes*, Cambridge, MA, Harvard University Press.

Waley, A. (1945) *The Analects of Confucius*, London, George Allen & Unwin.

Waley, A. (1987) *The Way and its Power*, London, Unwin Hyman.

Walker, R.C.S. (1989) *The Coherence Theory of Truth: Realism, Anti-realism, Idealism*, London, Routledge.

Walters, K.S. and Portmess, L. (eds) (1999) *Ethical Vegetarianism: From Pythagoras to Peter Singer*, Albany, State University of New York Press.

Walton, D.N. (1989) *Informal Logic: A Handbook for Critical Argumentation*, New York, Cambridge University Press.

Walton, D.N. (1992) *Slippery Slope Arguments*, Oxford, Clarendon.

Warnock, G.J. (1989) *J.L. Austin*, New York, Routledge.

Waterfield, R. (2000) *The First Philosophers: The Presocratics and Sophists*, Oxford, Oxford University Press.

Waterhouse, J. ([1934], 2006) *Zoroastrianism*, San Diego, The Book Tree.

Weedon, C. (1999) *Feminism, Theory, and the Politics of Difference*, Oxford, Blackwell.

Wertheimer, M. ([1924], 1938) 'Gestalt Theory', in W.D. Ellis (ed.) *Source Book of Gestalt Psychology* (trans. W.D. Ellis), New York, Harcourt, Brace.

Westcott, M.R. (1968) *Toward a Contemporary Psychology of Intuition: A Historical, Theoretical and Empirical Enquiry*, New York, Holt.

Westphal, J. (ed.) (1996) *Justice*, Cambridge, MA, Hackett Publishing.

White, S. (2006) *Equality*, Oxford, Blackwell.

Whitehead, A.N. ([1929], 1957) *Process and Reality*, New York, The Free Press.

Whorf, B.L. (1956) *Language, Thought and Reality: Selected writings of Benjamin Lee Whorf*, Cambridge, MA, MIT Press.

Wiggershaus, R. (1995) *The Frankfurt School: Its History, Theories and Political Significance* (trans. M. Robertson), Cambridge, MA, MIT Press.

Wiggins, D. (2001) *Sameness and Substance Renewed*, Cambridge, Cambridge University Press.

Williams, B. (1972) *Morality: An Introduction to Ethics*, New York, Harper & Row.

Williams, B. (1973) *Problems of the Self*, Cambridge, Cambridge University Press.

Williams, B. (1981) *Moral Luck*, Cambridge, Cambridge University Press.

Williams, B. (1985) *Ethics and the Limits of Philosophy*, London, Fontana.

Williams, C.J.F. (1981) *What is Existence?*, Oxford, Clarendon Press.

Williams, C.J.F. (1992) *Being, Identity, and Truth*, Oxford, Oxford University Press.

Williams, M. (1991) *Unnatural Doubts: Epistemological Realism and the Basis of Scepticism*, Oxford, Blackwell.

Williams, R.R. (1992) *Recognition: Fichte and Hegel on the Other*, Albany State University of New York Press.

Williams, T. (2007) *Anselm: Basic Writings*, Indianapolis, Hackett Publishing.
Williamson, T. (1994) *Vagueness*, New York, Routledge.
Wills, G. (1999) *Saint Augustine*, New York, Lipper/Viking.
Wittgenstein, L. (1921) *Tractatus Logico-Philosophicus* (trans. C.K. Ogden), London, Routledge & Kegan Paul.
Wittgenstein, L. (1953) *Philosophical Investigations* (trans. G.E.M. Anscombe), Oxford, Blackwell.
Wittgenstein, L. (1958) *The Blue and Brown Books*, Oxford, Blackwell.
Wolff, J. (1991) *Robert Nozick: Property, Justice, and the Minimal State*, Stanford Stanford University Press.
Wood, A.W. (2000) *Karl Marx* (2nd edn), London, Routledge.
Woodcock, G. (ed.) (1977) *The Anarchist Reader*, Glasgow, Fontana.
Woodfield, A. (1976) *Teleology*, Cambridge, Cambridge University Press.
Woods, M. (1997) *Conditionals*, Oxford, Clarendon Press.
Worrall, J. (ed.) (1994) *The Ontology of Science*, Dartmouth, Aldershot.
Wright, C., Smith, B. and Macdonald, C. (eds) (1998) *Knowing our Own Minds*, Oxford, Clarendon Press.
Wright, D.S. (1998) *Philosophical Reflections on Zen Buddhism*, Cambridge, Cambridge University Press.
Yandell, K. (1993) *The Epistemology of Religious Experience*, New York, Cambridge University Press.
Yao, X. (2000) *An Introduction to Confucianism*, Cambridge, Cambridge University Press.
Yolton, J.W. (ed.) (1991) *The Blackwell Companion to the Enlightenment*, Oxford, Blackwell.
Young, R. (ed.) (1981) *Untying the Text: A Post-Structuralism Reader*, Boston, Routledge & Kegan Paul.
Yu-Lan, F. (1948) *A Short History of Chinese Philosophy*, New York, Free Press.
Zagzebski, L.T. (1996) *Virtues of the Mind: An Inquiry into the Nature of Virtue and the Ethical Foundations of Knowledge*, New York, Cambridge University Press.
Zahavi, D. (2006) *Subjectivity and Selfhood: Investigating the First-Person Perspective*, Cambridge, MA, MIT Press.
Zangwill, N. (2001) *The Metaphysics of Beauty*, Ithaca, Cornell University Press.
Zuriff, G.E. (1985) *Behaviorism: A Conceptual Reconstruction*, New York, Columbia Free Press.

Index

Page numbers in **bold** indicate definitions

PROPERTY OF
SENECA COLLEGE
LIBRARIES
KING CAMPUS